IRON

TECHNOLOGY

IN

EAST

AFRICA

SYMBOLISM,

SCIENCE, AND

ARCHAEOLOGY

PETER R. SCHMIDT

IRON

TECHNOLOGY

IN

EAST

AFRICA

SYMBOLISM,

SCIENCE, AND

ARCHAEOLOGY

INDIANA UNIVERSITY PRESS   *Bloomington / Indianapolis*

JAMES CURREY   *Oxford*

Published in North America by Indiana University Press, 601 North Morton St., Bloomington, Indiana 47404 and in Great Britain by James Currey Publishers, 73 Botley Road, Oxford OX2 0BS

The paper used in this publication meets the minimum requirements of American National Standard for Information Sciences—Permanence of Paper for Printed Library Materials, ANSI Z39.48-1984.

Manufactured in the United States of America

Library of Congress Cataloging-in-Publication Data

Schmidt, Peter R. (Peter Ridgway), date
Iron technology in East Africa : symbolism, science, and
archaeology / Peter R. Schmidt
     p.   cm.
Includes bibliographical references and index.
ISBN 0–253–33255–9 (cloth : alk. paper).
— ISBN 0–253–21109–3 (pbk. : alk. paper)
1. Haya (African people)—Industries. 2. Metal-work, Haya. 3. Haya (African people)—Social life and customs. 4. Iron-works—Tanzania—History. 5. Iron—Tanzania—Metallurgy. 6. Smelting—Tanzania—History. 7.Ethnoarchaeology—Tanzania. 8. Tanzania—Antiquities. I. Title.
DT443.3.H39S24   1997
669'.141'096—dc21   96-46107

1 2 3 4 5 02 01 00 99 98 97

British Library Cataloguing in Publication Data

Schmidt, Peter R.
  Iron technology in East Africa : symbolism, science, and archaeology
  1. Iron - Africa, East - Metallurgy 2. Haya (African people) - Industries 3. Metal-work, Haya 4. Smelting - Africa, East - History
  I. Title
  669.1'41'09676

  ISBN 0–85255–744–2 (cloth)
      0–85255–743–4 (paper)

Contents

THIS BOOK IS DEDICATED TO THE MEMORY OF:

My mother, Elizabeth Ridgway Schmidt . . . SHE POINTED THE WAY AND INSPIRED

Ta Herman Kariba, Master Iron Smelter . . . HE LED THE WAY AND CAJOLED

Ta Norbert Kajuna, Master Iron Smelter . . . HE KNEW THE WAY AND SMILED

Ta Mutaihwa Lubelwa, Friend and Mentor . . . HE SHOWED THE WAY

Preface

Among the profound changes that Africa has experienced over the last century, there are few that illustrate better the erosion of African economic life and technological genius than the decline of iron smelting. The rapid disappearance of local traditions of iron production also marks the disappearance of traditions of innovation and invention. Each local technological adaptation had a distinctive history to tell—a history of scientific experimentation and creative problem solving that arose out of the need to cope with local resources and the distinctive difficulties that they posed.

Such loss cannot be reversed, and, consequently, many important lessons to be learned from the history of iron technology in Africa have been erased. This book is about one African technology that nearly succumbed to the ravages of culture change—the iron smelting technology of the Haya people of northwestern Tanzania. This is the story of how I came to learn about iron production in Buhaya. It is a story that follows a number of aged iron smelters as they attempted to re-create a way of life that was once a part of their everyday experience. It is also a remarkable tale about the resilience of several of these elders who risked social condemnation to return to traditional beliefs and rituals forbidden by their churches. And it is an account of scientific experiment and bricolage that unfolded as these men tried to recuperate their technological expertise.

No study can begin to capture the rich fabric of African technological life as it must have been in the precolonial past. Whatever we come to understand today is only an approximation of the past. However, as we gain more knowledge from various African cultures where some technological practices remain, we are gradually building an awareness that much of the genius of African iron technology lies in its variety. Each technological system had distinctive ways to solve problems. Thus, out of such variation comes unique insight into local innovation. This means that each technological history—from culture to culture—has a different and unique story to tell. Though most of those histories will remain forever silent, there is still time to capture the poignant lessons of a few remaining technologies.

The elderly men who tried to recuperate iron smelting technology in Buhaya during 1976, 1979, and 1984 are no longer living. Their deaths bring into sharper focus the magnitude of their gift to African history as well as how close we are to the loss of other technological knowledge. In spite of what younger men learned from the nine smelts conducted during that period of time, the finely nuanced understandings are now missing; a deep reservoir of experience, tempered by pragmatic applications, can never be recovered.

While the story of iron smelting in Buhaya is about an intrepid group of elderly smelters, the rendering of that story was the responsibility of a team of investigators, both Haya and foreign. I was fortunate to have the assistance of Donald H. Avery, who was then a colleague at Brown University in the Engineering Department. Avery had for many years experimented with bloomery iron production. An expert metallurgist and scholar of thermodynamics, Avery agreed to join me in the field in 1976 for part of the field study of iron smelting. He accompanied me again in 1979 when we studied Barongo iron smelting south of Victoria Nyanza (Lake Victoria) and also conducted a follow-up study on iron smelting in Buhaya. His counsel and constant good humor have contributed in many ways to the success of this project.

During the late 1970s I was joined in the field by Terry Childs, who was then a graduate student at Boston University. Childs's participation in the archaeological phase of the research was important. Under a grant from the NEH, she returned to the field with me in 1983 to sample a broad range of clay resources in Buhaya. This research focused on the chemical and firing characteristics of different clays with the goal of better understanding what kinds of clays were best suited for different tasks in iron smelting. Of particular interest were the refractory—heat resistance—characteristics of clays used for tuyeres (blow pipes). Subsequently Childs also analyzed many of the iron and slag samples that provided technological evidence for what happened inside the iron smelting furnaces. Her collaboration has been a critical part of this endeavor.

Many others have contributed to this research. Ruth Laseski, then a graduate student in geology at Brown, came to the field in 1977 to conduct a collaborative investigation into the prehistory of vegetational change in the region. Her research dovetailed with archaeological research into settlement history. The goal was to establish a better understanding of how vegetational history could be linked to the history of settlement and industrial exploitation. My friend and colleague M. M. Mulokozi, now with the Institute of Kiswahili at the University of Dar es Salaam, has also been a dedicated collaborator. His analysis of the smelting songs has opened many new and important insights into the esoteric and symbolic language associated with iron smelting. Dr. Mulokozi's extensive background in the epic poetry of the Haya provided an extraordinary backdrop against which much of the metaphorical language of the songs could be assessed.

Acknowledgments

I am deeply indebted to the many assistants who made up the research team in Buhaya, especially Cleoface Kanantuki, Gosbert Kyaruzi, Hussein Abdallah, and Alphonce Feliciani. The critical advice and commentaries of two Haya friends, N. J. Karoma and Fred Kaijage of the University of

Dar es Salaam, have been invaluable. I have been assisted since I began research in Buhaya in 1969 by scores of people in Buhaya other than the iron smelters of Nyungwe village. To all of those who have taken the time to share their knowledge of history and culture, I give my deepest appreciation and thanks. I am especially indebted to two Haya mentors in local history: Augustine Kaindoa and Mutaihwa Lubelwa. I also want to acknowledge the special assistance of Mukama Petro Nyarubamba of Kianja kingdom and Mukama E. Lukamba of Kyamutwara kingdom. They assisted in important ways in the making of *The Tree of Iron,* a film about Haya iron production.

The Tree of Iron was the first attempt to communicate these research results to a wider audience—far beyond the relatively restricted audiences that read specialized journals or even widely distributed scientific journals such as *Science,* in which our research results were first published. Judging from responses to public broadcasts of *The Tree of Iron* on National PBS, the most important effect has been an increased awareness that the history of iron technology in Africa contradicts popular and scholarly stereotypes and gives voice to alternative perspectives emphasizing local creativity and genius. The collaboration of Peter O'Neill, Frank Muhly, and Winnie Lambrecht in making *The Tree of Iron* has been one of the high points of research into iron production in Buhaya. Each of these talented filmmakers brought important human insights to this project. I am grateful for their friendship, patience, and artistic sensibilities. The staff of the Audio Visual Institute in Dar es Salaam also assisted significantly in the shooting of the film in Buhaya.

Filming and producing *The Tree of Iron* was one of several intervening events that punctuated the synthesis of research that appears here. Immediately after shooting the film, I spent a two-year stint starting a new Archaeology Unit at the University of Dar es Salaam, which in turn was followed by a seven-year term as director of African Studies at the University of Florida. An administrative leave of absence provided by the University of Florida has assisted significantly in the completion of this volume.

I am particularly grateful to Melanie Brandt, who has done a wonderful job in producing the line drawings for this book and a companion volume, *The Culture and Technology of African Iron Production.* Her attention to detail and design has contributed significantly to the final product. My heartfelt thanks also go to my family. My wife, Jane, has been a steadfast and supportive companion in the field, assisting with excavations and supervising laboratory analysis. My children have experienced the joys of field work while also learning firsthand about others' ways of life.

I want to thank Jan Vansina, David Schoenbrun, Terry Childs, Don Avery, Kathy Weedman, Nic David, and an anonymous reader for their helpful and careful readings of various parts and versions of the manuscript. On many occasions Priscilla Reining, the first American anthropologist to conduct research in Buhaya, gave helpful advice and keen insights into Haya cultural ecology. I am very grateful for the editorial assistance of Diana Lutz and Carol Bernard. I alone am responsible for any errors and omissions.

The research discussed here was sponsored by the National Science Foundation (BNS75-19611 and BNS78-07855) and the National Endowment for the Humanities (RO-10570-83). Special thanks go to the Antiquities Unit of the United Republic of Tanzania and to the former Tanzania National Scientific Research Council (now the National Council for Science and Technology) for permission to conduct archaeological, ethnographic, and historical research in northwestern Tanzania. I was blessed by very helpful local governments, with the cultural officers of both Bukoba District and Kagera Region providing many helpful services.

I gratefully acknowledge Academic Press for permission to publish chapter 10, which provided the basis for P. R. Schmidt and B. B. M. Mapunda, "Ideology and the Archaeological Record in Africa: Interpreting Symbolism in Iron Smelting Technology," *Journal of Anthropological Archaeology* 16 (1997).

IRON

TECHNOLOGY

IN

EAST

AFRICA

SYMBOLISM,

SCIENCE, AND

ARCHAEOLOGY

1.

1.

Remaking Knowledge about Iron Technology

*The function of knowledge is
to provide a guide to action,
in fact to cooperative, i.e.
social action. . . . A science
then is not just a set of rules
and formulae that describe
things and their relations,
but rather formulae that
yield rules for action. The
truth of the rules is guaran-
teed by the success of actions
guided thereby.*

Childe 1949: 805

The purpose of this book is to recuperate the history of African iron technology. In subsequent
chapters I present a critical archaeology that is
intended to deconstruct a false historical edifice
built on untested and unproved ideas about
ancient African iron technology. The historical
construct that I offer as an alternative is based on
scientific testing and observation, on physical evidence derived from technological contexts, and
on material remains recovered archaeologically. I
bring these forms of evidence together in a complex fabric into which are woven cultural beliefs
or ideologies that interpenetrate the operation and
control of the productive economy during the last
two thousand to twenty-five hundred years on the
western shores of Lake Victoria, a region today
known as Buhaya.[1] The rich symbolic metaphors
that infuse ironworking with cultural meaning are

viewed as historical phenomena that—like the material technology—can be traced out in the culture history of Buhaya. Skeptical readers may think that it is difficult if not impossible to read the history of symbolic meanings in the archaeological record. However, through a cross-cultural and comparative approach, I will show that it is possible to recognize both changes and significant continuities in the symbolism that conferred meaning to iron smelting over two millennia in East and Central Africa.

The result is a perspective on the development of iron technology in Africa that brings to life a socially constructed technology as well as one that fosters the idea that we should use knowledge in a way that will improve the quality of the world in which we live. Quality of life, in this instance, is linked directly to replacing a view that denigrates African accomplishment with one that recuperates the positive attributes of innovation and invention with richly informed cultural meanings, leading to a more stable foundation for historical identity.

The evidence I present here is a deep-time view of iron technology in one region of Africa. It helps mitigate the regrettable paucity of critical scholarship on this important aspect of the African past. And it complements other important efforts to reconfigure our understanding of iron production in Africa by integrating the cultural meanings that inform iron technology with a study of the technological processes (van der Merwe and Avery 1987; Avery, van der Merwe, and Saitowitz 1988; David et al. 1989; Killick 1990; Schmidt 1996c). Because I am concerned with the cross-cultural regularities that punctuate the ideology of iron production, this study shows similarities to other studies of the social construction of iron production in Africa (e.g., Cline 1937; Celis and E. Nzikobanyanka 1976; Echard 1983; de Maret 1985; Celis 1989; Childs 1991; Childs and Killick 1993; Collett 1993; Herbert 1993). Such studies have been valuable in emphasizing the commonalties that prevail among so many iron-producing cultures on the continent. Their emphasis on cultural meanings and symbolic forms over the last century, however, means that these studies have a synchronic quality, that ideologies are seen only in the context of the colonial and immediate postcolonial periods. Thus it is a field of study that is for the most part concerned with very recent history—the last century—which is then often used as an inferential surrogate for a deeper history of both belief systems and their related technologies. Even studies that do address historical concerns are limited in scope in that they address mostly histories that reach back only several hundred years (van der Merwe and Scully 1971; Fowler 1990; Killick 1990).

I take as my inspiration the thoughts of V. Gordon Childe, because Childe's perspective was that archaeology was to serve history, that it is one of the devices by which history is written and revised. The role that archaeology has to play in African history is perhaps more significant than in most parts of the world, given the relatively limited period of time that written history has been applied to the continent. Except for historical linguistics, the only way that a substantive history of the ancient African past can be constructed is by applying archaeology to important historical problems.

The Historical Problem

Among the more important problems in African history are ideas about African technological achievement, ideas generated over the last century by Africa's colonizers. The historiography of Africa represents technological achievement on the continent as derivative, retarded, backward, and otherwise lacking in innovation. Such representations have grave implications for African history, for they are assertions that form the foundation for a host of subsidiary ideas, such as the absence of complex sociopolitical organization in Bantu-speaking Africa before the present millennium. The idea of African technological inferiority has been applied, ironically, to iron technology, which is the most complicated of all of Africa's technologies.

Historical representations about African technology are an ideological means of masking the African past. In place of an accessible past, there is the illusion of impoverishment, of only primitive achievement. This masking process is best illustrated in the equation made between ancient European iron technology and recent African iron technology. Historians of metallurgy have until recently seen African iron technology as a survival of ancient iron technology in Europe, even referring to recent African iron technology as ancient: "The EIA [Early Iron Age] phase has persisted in Africa until the present day but is fast dying out" (Tylecote 1976: 47). As a survival, it can be used to explain how Europeans produced iron at the beginning of the Iron Age. Most investigators have been content to study the products of the early European technologies to arrive at interpretations of technological process. The model of the iron bloomery has been derived, strangely, from European material analysis and experiment. Until recently this model was applied to Africa to explain the operation of all its iron technologies, an analytical and comparative process that resulted in the historical homogenization of African iron technology (Schmidt 1996b).

Because African technologies came to be equated with those of ancient Europe, there was no apparent need to study the technologies themselves. Since they were accepted as a primitive survival, there was no reason to believe that examining them would shed new light on technological process. This historical mask has inhibited questions that otherwise might have revealed different technological developments distinctive to Africa. How else do we explain the fact that for several generations, archaeologists of the African Iron Age have excavated and described iron technology but, until the 1970s, largely ignored questions about technological process?[2]

These perceptions about African iron technology have had a profound effect on African self-perception and identity. Such perceptions, as a central canon of historical thought about Africa, have inevitably shaped the direction of recent science and technology in Africa. It is common wisdom that the present is dependent upon the past, that all cultures are shaped by their historical experiences. There is also a relationship between how a culture sees its past and how it views the future. In contemporary North America, for example, our history of technological achievement is positively emphasized. The ideology underwrites a determination to innovate, to overcome adversity with technological breakthroughs, and to look to the future with a sense of confidence that this tradition of achievement will lead to equally important technological developments in the future.

The historical constructs about technology in Africa stand in stark contrast to the Western experience. The paradigm of African inferiority in technological life is widely taught throughout the West and Africa. Thus, Africans believe that there is little of value in their technological past; that there were no technological achievements of importance; that technological innovation is alien to Africa. This has alienated Africans from their historical past. Such alienation has undoubtedly affected how the present and future are perceived. I suggest that underlying some African problems in development, particularly where technology transfer is concerned, may be an alienated history that emphasizes the absence of innovation and achievement. If an alien ideology obscures an indigenous history of innovation and accomplishment, then it is imperative that we try to reveal alternative knowledge that overturns the dominant paradigm.

I have made clear that one of my primary concerns is to deconstruct Western representations about African iron technology.[3] This requires that I identify how iron technology is characterized and what led to that characterization. Such deconstruction is a political activity, however, an implication V. Gordon Childe recognized. A challenge to established, entrenched historiography, especially one that underwrites continued Western technological domination of Africa, will elicit strong reaction. My first focus, then, is the historical literature that reflects and legitimizes this paradigm. We will see that the historical literature on African iron technology is an artifact of Western interaction with African cultures and technologies. The way that Westerners view African iron technology is partly the consequence of criteria and assumptions that do not fit African technology. The assumption that such technologies are primitive survivals is a perspective that makes the past into the present and denies change and development.

Western science until recently has failed to comprehend even the most elementary aspects of African iron technology. Why? The answer is revealing and disquieting. Western science is capable of the study of indigenous technologies, and the methods required for the study of African iron technology, for example, have been available for decades. Yet we remain ignorant about all but a few of them.[4] Western obsession with material progress and the future, a product of our historical experience, precludes serious scientific study of the history of iron technology in Africa.

This contemporary culture of science is often manifest in the belief that time and effort devoted to such historical questions are unprofitable, for such endeavors are "backward looking" and contradict a future-oriented and applied science. A common attitude is that there is nothing to be learned from a study of African iron smelting that we do not already know from a relatively low level of metallurgical knowledge. Such a perspective militates against developing an awareness of African invention and innovation in the past. It is also partially responsible for the long delay in serious scientific inquiries into African iron technology.

The myth of African technological inferiority has grown out of and has been structured by the history of Western technology vis-à-vis Africa in a colonial and imperial setting. Superiority in military power that led to conquest was and is often equated with European technological superiority. The myth of inferiority arose partly out of the apparent technological contrasts between Africa and Europe, particularly during the late nineteenth century. A question of scale enters the equation of misapprehension, for the European observer used as a frame of reference the large, highly productive blast furnaces of Europe when assessing African iron technology. The error equated the scale of the furnaces to a level of technological complexity; the large European furnaces were seen as advanced, the small African smelting furnaces as simple and primitive. Level of complexity in the European mind was also related to the size of the iron bloom produced. This period was an enormously productive and innovative time in European steel technology, and it is from this context that such judgments arose.

Europeans found the African technological traditions dissonant with theirs, and wanting. If the scale of production was inferior, so too were seasonal production, labor organization, and the final product. Add exotic ritual to this, and the primitive stereotype was assured. Along with differences in scale and organization, there was a distinct contrast in the form of furnaces, which in many cases departed so severely from the European form as to support the assumption that the African furnaces operated less efficiently with a final product of inferior grade.

The consequence of these converging and interdependent perceptions was the acceptance of the myth of technological inferiority and the absence of any systematic investigation into what actually occurs in an African iron smelting furnace. The absence of scientific inquiry has reinforced the nineteenth-century characterization of iron production as a primitive survival and has legitimized its projection back through all of Iron Age African history, a projection that erases a rich and varied technological history.

The structure of Western attitudes of superiority and the distancing of scientific investigation can be seen in our formal historical literature on

Africa. The myth of inferiority is so deeply seated, so unquestioned, that it is an integral part of the structure of historical thought on Africa. Its unconscious currency in African historiography is perhaps best illustrated by its expression in the work of even the most eminent historians and anthropologists of Africa. I now turn to several case studies that illustrate this point, focusing on the texts, not on the authors.

If the patterns of historical discourse are examined, it is possible to isolate several subjects that manifest a structure of thought in which the question of technological hierarchy looms large. The first text is taken from a pamphlet that introduces university students to African history. After first denying the validity of comparisons between Western and African cultures, Philip Curtin claims that

> Technology, however, is an aspect of culture where rational judgment is possible. If technology is broadly defined as the body of knowledge and skill about the *means* of producing goods and services, then each technique can be measured by its effectiveness in serving the desired end. . . . In the field of technology—and, one is tempted to add, in that field alone—it is possible to make rough estimates of the degree of advancement achieved by differing cultures.
>
> Limiting our judgment to technology alone, it is clear that African culture lagged behind that of Western Europe in the nineteenth century. The historian's problem, however, remains: how great was this lag, and how may it be explained historically?
>
> There is no serious problem in understanding why progress might be slow in the far south, toward the tip of the African continent. That part of the world was obviously the end of the road, and any invention or discovery made elsewhere could only be received after a long process of diffusion down the whole length of the African continent.
>
> (Curtin 1964: 24)

The above passage illustrates several of the underlying, untested assumptions about African technology, under which iron production is subsumed. It is informative that these remarks are predicated by the statement that rational judgment is possible in making comparative technological evaluations. Yet, we are not given scientific evidence that backs up the basic contention that nineteenth-century Africa lagged behind Europe. To which technological activities is this generalization to be applied? What is so critical about the nineteenth century, and why does the author ignore, for example, the vast and radical technological changes that occurred between the beginning of the century and 1900 in Europe?

These matters aside, a question of more serious concern is the absence of any scientific evidence to substantiate the structuring paradigm from which thinking about African technology is derived: Western technology is to African technology as complexity is to backwardness. Scientific evidence is not required under this paradigm, for it is a given, an accepted historical reality. Professor Curtin suggests that it is the task of the historian to determine the dimensions of the technological lag in Africa and to explain it. I suggest, however, that there is a much higher-order problem, and that is to test critically the inferiority paradigm over the entire period of a technology's history. This is precisely where archaeology can help solve problems in historical interpretation, and we have in this case a major interpretative problem in Western historiography.

The concept of backwardness, of a technological gap where Africa is the laggard, is apparently related to other, less explicit ideas that attribute the success of the European imperial experience in Africa to Africa's supposed technological backwardness. This perspective is inherent in Jack Goody's book *Technology, Tradition, and the State* (1971), in which Goody subscribes to the myth of technological inferiority when he argues why African smiths failed to produce guns: "The reasons for the failure of Africans successfully to take up the manufacture of this powerful new weapon is a simple one. They did not possess the requisite level of craft skill in iron working. As a result, Africans were at an enormous disadvantage when the scramble for their continent began" (Goody 1971: 36).

Goody then goes on to assert that African smiths were not technically able to produce guns because the forge temperatures would have been too low "for the manufacture of guns from scratch" (ibid.). It is instructive to examine this position more closely. First, Goody claims that Africans lack sufficient skill necessary for gun production. This assertion is meaningless unless it is supported by close documentation of exactly what kind of skills are required and exactly which were lacking. But no scientific evidence is presented, for the "truth" of the paradigm is so strong that evidence is not required; its power is such that it allows Goody to ignore his own observation that the nineteenth-century warrior Samory had smiths who could turn out perfect copies of French repeaters. Second, Goody claims that the forge temperatures would have been too low. How does he know this? He offers no documentation for minimum requirements, nor does he offer scientific observations to support his claim.

In the absence of any substantiating evidence, then, either the evidence is not available or it is so widely known that citation is not necessary. The latter possibility may be eliminated as incompatible with the historiography, leading to the conclusion that such evidence is not available. Why did such an eminent scholar accept a bogus position, devoid of scientific merit, in such an important argument? Because Goody's assertions, like Curtin's, reflect a structure of mind linked to a tradition of belief in African technological inferiority. Technological history has been eclipsed by myth in which the gun is a metaphor for European superiority in iron technology. In fact, forge temperatures in Africa commonly reach 1,200 to 1,300°C, more than enough to manufacture guns. African smiths had the skills, but they lacked the cultural repertoire for gun fabrication, as did Europeans before them. The repetition of the myth in this text has disturbing implications, for an exegesis of its structure shows that Western representation of

African technology is structured by the historical experience of European dominance. This hierarchical paradigm flows directly from historical experience and provides the structure for the myth of technological inferiority.

The cautious reader might protest and ask if such ideas are not now out of date, given that both Curtin and Goody were writing twenty-five to thirty years ago. Sadly, this is not the case. While the literature may have shed some of these more obvious positions in the last few years, the concepts of primitive and backward continue to infuse our historical thinking. For example, hierarchical ideas about the backwardness of certain kinds of African smelting furnaces is seen in a highly respected and popular textbook, *African History* (Curtin et al. 1990). Here, in comparing the productivity of an open bowl furnace with a shaft furnace (that supposedly produced 5 kg of iron), it is argued that the open bowl type furnace (without a superstructure) "would yield only one kilogram [of iron] at best" (Curtin et al. 1990: 21–22; also see Schmidt 1996b). Such facile conclusions convey the false impression that efficiency studies and quantification of smelting yields have been conducted. Yet scientific study *has not* informed these conclusions. Rather, what we see is the unconscious expression of deeply ingrained ideas about African technology based on myth.

Our task is to deconstruct this false historical representation by drawing on sound empirical evidence that is collected according to scientific canons. This necessarily engages me in an ideological project: I am involved in depreciating historical representation that portrays African inferiority. The project inevitably also engages me in political activity, because such an ideology has been instrumental in the economic and psychological subjugation of Africa, and any challenge to such an important buttress of domination will meet resistance. Resistance will also come from those who believe that archaeology should remain above politics and outside the domain of ideological debate. Such simplification ignores the fact that archaeology is often political because it deals with historical ideas, many of which are manipulated by those who control the political economy (Hall 1984; Leone and Kryder-Reid 1992; McGuire 1992).

Theoretical Backdrop

Three interrelated principles are recognized in this study: (1) Scientific archaeology has an important contribution to make to the history of the people related to or descended from the ancients we study; I join Bruce Trigger (1980) in deploring the trend toward a scientific archaeology in North America that creates a dichotomy between science and history at the expense of the latter (Schmidt and Patterson 1995a, 1995b). (2) There is a special responsibility to tackle questions that have importance to historical interpretations about Africa. (3) We must meet the challenge to develop new methodologies that draw on all sources of cultural information about the past.

I and others working in Africa have been actively engaged in developing interpretative methodologies, some long before the self-conscious use of "postprocessual" in archaeology to describe archaeological perspectives sensitive to history and context (cf. Posnansky 1966, 1969; Schmidt 1978).[5] I operate, then, with a set of premises that are distinct to African archaeology (Schmidt 1983a), yet also complement interpretative perspectives developed in Great Britain (e.g., Donley-Reid 1982; Hodder 1982a, 1982b, 1986, 1991; Miller and Tilley 1984; Tilley 1993), interpretative perspectives in North America (e.g., Deetz 1977, 1993; Yentsch 1994), and critical archaeologies developing in North America (e.g., Handsman 1981, 1983; Leone, Potter, and Shackel 1987; Paynter and McGuire 1991; McGuire 1992; Patterson 1995). An interpretative approach is appropriate for the task at hand, for I am drawing on many different forms of cultural information to excavate the obscured historic and symbolic meanings that inform iron production in Buhaya.

In a previous book on ancient Buhaya (Schmidt 1978), I explored ritual, oral traditions, oral histories, and the application of structural and contextual analysis to such cultural information in order to elicit periods of significant social and political transformation over the past five hundred years. This approach has led to the isolation of coeval transformations, some of which can be read in the archaeological record. Inevitably, such a methodology has also led me to explore the history of ritual, myth, politics, religion, and the productive economy. An *exclusively* materialist approach overwhelms the rich cultural information pertaining to past contexts (Schmidt 1983a). Yet a materialist approach also frames the inquiry that follows. By necessity, a history of iron technology must account for why the technology took hold, what environmental consequences it had, why and how it changed through time, how its symbolic representations figured into its longevity as well as its continuity and change, and what role it played in the economy of the region. The end product is a marriage of interpretation and science that overcomes the tired debate between scientific archaeology and humanistic—so-called postprocessual—archaeology (Schmidt and Patterson 1995b; Wylie 1995).

This research will demonstrate, I hope, that science has a central role to play in the development of a more humanistic archaeology, a position that places my perspective outside the rhetorical posturing that has so far characterized the interactions between interpretative and scientific schools of thought (Wylie 1992). The theoretical position of this book, then, is that a historically informed archaeology sensitive to context can accommodate scientific approaches. The research that follows illustrates the value of a scientific approach in the service of history and the practice of humanistic science.

There is little question, however, that the idea of science and history in archaeology does not fit within the dichotomized theoretical world that is often found in Western archaeology (Schmidt and Patterson 1995b).[6] Archaeology as practiced in much of the non-Western world is more concerned with constructing interpretations that are better in tune with local historical sensibilities and that complement local archaeologies. While much of the Western world is mired in debate over whether a particular archaeology meets orthodox criteria, archaeologists of Africa, Latin America, and Asia struggle to negotiate the tension between their scientific training and the need for histories that can be read and understood by people in their immediate communities (Schmidt 1983a, 1995; Andah 1995; Handsman and Lamb-Richmond 1995; Vargas Arenas 1995).[7] These concerns are peripheral if not inimical to most Western thinking about the role of archaeology in today's world. Marginalization of local historical voices and needs creates tensions between archaeologists who are struggling to overthrow the hegemonic paradigms of the colonial and neocolonial experience and those of their colleagues who are insulated from these intellectual trends and unaware of the concerns that prevail in non-Western settings.

We face another dilemma when we attempt to make an African past compatible with local history making: such a project arises out of a *Western* belief that a scientific approach is an appropriate tool, in this instance, to recuperate a history of African iron technology that accounts for African cultural views. Such a methodology demands a critical posture that continually examines the assumptions of Western scientific practice as the project unfolds.

Some theoretical perspectives that deal with this dilemma have been opened by Alison Wylie's (1994, 1995) explanation of standpoint theory (using Harding 1986, 1991). Wylie draws on feminist theorists who advocate that a continuous reflexive analysis of the conditions of knowledge production be *joined* with detailed empirical inquiry, a process that also appears to be appropriate in producing historical and archaeological knowledge within African settings. The power of insight afforded by science projects is one of the most important lessons to be drawn from this feminist perspective (Wylie 1987, 1992, 1995): "We are forced *by the evidence* to consider interpretive possibilities completely different from those which we had entertained in the past, and even to rethink deep-seated orienting presuppositions about the nature of cultural phenomena" (Wylie 1994: 25). This critical approach provides us with a means by which interpretative claims, both external and internal to the science project, can be evaluated and used to critique and replace historical claims that bolster Western ideological hegemony in Africa. Also attractive in this feminist perspective is its rejection of relativism, one of the main faultlines of interpretative approaches in archaeology (Wylie 1994). Wylie suggests that the "master's [scientific] tools" *can* be appropriated and that the methods of systematic empirical inquiry—along lines developed by postpositivist philosophers—can be used to construct alternative histories, along with a reflexive understanding of the limits of such accounts (Wylie 1995).

The application of empirical science in non-Western contexts, believes Wylie, is not inimical to non-Western cultures or views of history. But it demands constant vigilance, rather like "rebuilding the ship in which you float continuously, as you travel." The problem is how to build alternative histories that challenge the political, economic, and cultural circumstances (standpoints) that have influenced history making, while simultaneously challenging the assumptions that the investigator holds (Wylie 1995). This critical process, then, regards the products of scientific inquiry as theory-laden yet useful, and in this respect it resembles ideas held by African thinkers. For example, the Nigerian philosopher and literary theorist Irele Abiola sees that any refutation of a colonial thesis is conducted within the frame of colonial concepts (the master's tools), but that a positive quality results when the counterdiscourse "creates a collective introspection that fulfills the conditions of historical reflection" (Irele 1991: 62; Schmidt 1995).

Negotiating the tensions in the use of systematic empirical inquiry while reflexively questioning the sources and presuppositions of that inquiry also allows us to listen and learn from the intellectual contests about history outside of the West, where there is often much greater clarity and consciousness about the political consequences of history making. By this marriage of critical approaches with scientific methodology and interpretative stances, I hope to open sufficient space for the emergence of local historical and cultural interpretations as well as the recognition of indigenous scientific practice.

An Experimental Approach

The investigations that I report here are organized around an experimental approach in archaeology. A reflexive analysis of these field studies quickly reveals that there were two types of experimental processes that occurred during these studies: (1) those conducted by anthropologists and metallurgists (me and my collaborators) concerned with unwrapping the technical "mysteries" of iron production and their material correlates, and (2) those conducted by the iron smelters who as technical and ritual bricoleurs successively pieced together various combinations of material and ideological ingredients to arrive at different material results. Thus, experimentation was conducted simultaneously in three domains: (1) a formal scientific, anthropological inquiry, (2) a local system of material bricolage based on experience, insight, inspiration, negotiation, and repetitive experimentation, and (3) a local system of ritual bricolage in which the Haya smelters experimented with various ritual solutions.[8]

The anthropological inquiry itself—with its specific scientific goals and need for the construction and operation of smelting furnaces—precipitated an urgent and unusual quest by Haya elders and their assistants that departed from their daily and seasonal work routines and their contemporary values. Fifty years after the activity was abandoned, the very idea of smelting was out of the ordinary—a condition that compels reflection upon the impact of such a study. The former smelters openly declared that they did not have much interest in engaging again in such dirty and unattractive activities. Their initial resistance to the idea, however, was quickly replaced by a shrewd labor negotiation in which they showed that they clearly understood the value of the difficult work they were about to perform. Once the smelters agreed to smelt, they then engaged in a process of bricolage leading to the performance of scientific protocols both remembered and spontaneously fabricated. Thus we became involved in the study of an indigenous science as well as an anthropology of the technology, as a technical system and as a social response to our own science. The interaction of our scientific inquiry with Haya scientific and technological performance has created something quite different from what someone would have observed in 1880 if peeking from behind a bush. Therefore what I report here should in no way be taken to represent the fabric of Haya iron production as it would have appeared in 1880 or 1900 or even 1920. It is important to keep in mind that the iron smelting episodes were interactive performances conducted in an environment far removed from experience, routine, and memory. In spite of these limitations, there is much to learn from these extraordinary old men who revitalized a social and technological system in a setting far removed from traditional realities.

When I returned to Buhaya in 1976 to begin this series of ethnoarchaeological inquiries of Haya iron smelting, I did not anticipate or imagine such a complex interaction of different sciences (Western and local) and the interlinking qualities of local scientific practices with ritual processes. Yet it soon became obvious that perhaps one of the most important observations arising from this study would be the ways in which the Haya smelters developed scientific protocols to solve a variety of technological and social challenges that they confronted over the eight-year period during which these studies were conducted.

Formal inquiry focused on both social and technical activities that surrounded iron smelting and forging; the technical activities were conducted under experimental conditions in which specific hypotheses were tested about the operation of various technological processes. Thus, mine is an explicitly experimental approach within the context of ethnoarchaeology (cf. Tringham 1978). It could be called experimental ethnoarchaeology, but that rubric would obscure the fact that all ethnoarchaeology is to some degree experimental. In this ethnoarchaeology I observed the social contexts in which material culture was created, used, and discarded—being particularly observant of physical "fingerprints" left behind by the *technological processes.* This model, which unites social with material dynamics, is then used to search for similarities *and* differences in the archaeological record, an exercise that is fundamentally comparative and that leads to strong inference (cf. Stahl 1993).

Previous Research and the History of Buhaya

The perspectives on which this book is based do not arise solely out of the ethnoarchaeological observations conducted between 1976 and 1984. My introduction to Haya culture and history goes back to 1966, when I first visited the region during a field trip while I was studying African prehistory at Makerere University in Kampala, Uganda. Little studied by the late 1960s, Haya history was organized in long genealogical records of patrilineages, clans, and royal dynasties. Most exciting, perhaps, was the deep history of contests between clan and dynastic histories, a tension between periphery and center that promised to provide important insight into the way history was made and negotiated in an important region in the Great Lakes Region. Beyond this there was also the promise that oral traditions were closely linked with physical places, suggesting that archaeological inquiry into the Haya past could engage in a dialectical discourse with local histories to arrive at a view that not only created a richer historical fabric, but allowed us to understand the structure of the warp and weft of that fabric.

This book emerges naturally from an earlier treatment of oral traditions, history, and archaeology among the Haya, published as *Historical Archaeology: A Structural Approach in an African Culture* (Schmidt 1978). The result of two years of research conducted during 1969 and 1970, this earlier work discusses the regional setting of the Haya, the cultural ecology of the region, and the oral texts that so richly characterize the archaeology. Some of the arguments developed in this book draw on the oral traditions that are documented in *Historical Archaeology.* Between 1974 and 1984 I continued research into the ecological history of the region as well as carried out extensive archaeological surveys and excavations that now make the early history of the region one of the best understood in East Africa. Simultaneously, I continued ethnographic inquiries into the way that history has been constructed during the ancient and recent past in the region. I mention this to explain that it was not only iron technology in its contemporary and ancient settings that concerned me in this period. This was only one—albeit very important—dimension of the project to make an ancient past that was comprehensible from both archaeology and history.

Out of this long-term research has come a basic framework for the ancient history of the region. A short review of this mostly archaeologically informed background will help set the scene for the chapters that follow. As a summary it focuses only on the major cultural developments and the underlying continuities that form the backdrop to the more particular discussions of iron technology and its systems of meaning. A fuller consideration of the cultural history and ecological changes is presented in chapter 11.

FIG. 1.1 Map of Tanzania showing the location of Kagera Region. Archaeo-logical and historical research occurred in the Bukoba Rural and Muleba districts, mostly along a 30-km-wide zone west of Victoria Nyanza (Lake Victoria) that is also known as Buhaya—where the Haya live.

The earliest evidence for the practice of iron technology in Buhaya is linked to the Kaiija shrine at the Rugomora Mahe site, which dates to the middle of the first millennium B.C. A number of radiocarbon dates, once but no longer thought by some to be too early for this period, are directly associated with an ancient forge (see chapter 7) and other features linked to iron production. These dates no longer stand alone. There is a series of mid-first-millennium B.C. dates as well as second-millennium B.C. dates—distinctive to this area alone—from Burundi and Rwanda for an iron tech-nology that bears many affinities to that of ancient Buhaya (Van Grunderbeek, Roche, and Doutrelepont 1983a; Clist 1987; Van Grunderbeek 1992). I have cautioned against too eager an acceptance of the second-millennium B.C. dates in Buhaya (Schmidt 1978; Schmidt and Childs 1985), pointing out that they are clearly tied to the charcoals of ancient forest fires that are intersected and incorporated into the features of later ironworkers. Nonetheless, the dates that cluster in the mid-first millennium B.C. are unquestionably tied to cultural features that mark what appears to be the first occurrence, the pioneering practice of iron smelting and forging in the region. It is all the more unusual that the Kaiija shrine has been commemorated in myth, ritual, and political history in such a way that its prominence as a sacred ironworking site in East and Central Africa is now apparent.

Who were the first iron smelters in Buhaya? Was it Bantu-speaking peoples who built and operated the ancient forge at the Kaiija tree shrine? Abundant ceramic evidence associated with these early ironmaking structures unequivocally points to a cultural association with the Urewe pottery tradition (also once known as Dimple-based pottery). This ceramic tradition is widely tied to Bantu-speaking peoples in other regions of East and Central Africa, so it is probable that such an affiliation also prevailed in this case and that the descendants of the proto–Eastern Bantu (or, Ehret's Mashariki), called Great Lakes Bantu, settled in eastern Buhaya in the mid-first millennium B.C. (Schoenbrun 1994). There they practiced root-crop cultivation along with hunting, fishing, gathering, and some cereal cultivation and livestock keeping, most likely goats, also picked up from earlier contact with Central Sudanic speakers (Schoenbrun 1993a: 13). However, one puzzle remains. Linguistic analysis of loan words in Bantu shows that the early Bantu populations borrowed ironworking from Central Sudanic speakers (Schoenbrun 1990: 268; Ehret 1991, n.d.) who were in the region before the arrival of the proto–Eastern Bantu speakers. Sudanic-speaking populations, with their mixed economy of pastoralism and cereal agriculture, were known to have been resident in the western part of the Great Lakes Region in the first millennium B.C. (Schoenbrun 1993a, 1993b; Ehret n.d.). Were these populations responsible for the introduction of ironworking among the first proto–Eastern Bantu speakers in the region?

If ironworking is to be linked to Sudanic-speaking peoples, as linguists suggest, then we might expect that such evidence would be forthcoming from the archaeology of the region. However, to date we have not observed any evidence that suggests that the earliest ironworking thus far documented can be tied directly to Sudanic-speaking peoples. It may well be that the initial Bantu infiltration into the western fringes of the region found a Sudanic-speaking population that had a repertoire of ironworking and that such skilled persons and their potentially enormously valuable knowledge were quickly assimilated into Bantu-speaking groups, thus obscuring any distinctive material culture associated with either their ceramics or their ironmaking. The answer to this linguistic riddle is not likely to be found any time soon.

Little is known of iron production or settlement in the Buhaya area between 600 B.C. and 200 B.C. The population densities of the initial pioneer ironworkers may have been so insignificant that traces of their presence on the landscape are difficult to find. Or, it is possible that initial settlement was short-lived and that these earliest populations, which by this time would have incorporated some grain agriculture—mostly finger millet—from Sudanic speakers, relocated to more open environments. If the agricultural repertoire of these earlier settlers had come to depend on some cereals, then the wet, heavily forested ridges of eastern Buhaya would not have been as hospitable as the more easily cleared patches of savanna woodlands of uplands Burundi and Rwanda, forest not so tropical and dense and where several communities dating to the mid-first millennium, and earlier, have been documented (Van Grunderbeek, Roche, and Doutrelepont 1983a). By 200 B.C., however, we see the first strong evidence for the settlement of Early Iron Age peoples along the shore of Victoria Nyanza.

Between 200 B.C. and A.D. 0 there was a significant expansion of groups engaged in iron production along the lakeshore. This is also a period during which these Bantu-speaking peoples would have been in regular contact with Cushitic speakers living in the Karagwe Depression immediately to the west of the ridges of central Buhaya (Schoenbrun 1993a).[9] Such interaction would have considerably diversified the subsistence economy. Other cereal crops such as sorghum gained in popularity, and along with the increased importance of cattle would have helped to meet the needs of a growing population (Schoenbrun 1993a). Evidence for population growth and the proliferation of communities as well as technological locales is particularly strong in the area surrounding Kemondo Bay and its environs (Schmidt 1980, 1981). These were not isolated communities.

Archaeological surveys and excavations in the region present us with a picture of Early Iron Age life that is surprisingly rich in its technological complexity but frustratingly sparse in direct evidence for subsistence and other economic activities. This mixed blessing means that certain domains of economic activity continue to elude us, but we can now speak with considerable confidence about the mainstay of the early productive economy, iron production. We live with this bias in the archaeological record, making do as best we can with the excellent supplementary evidence from historical linguistics. Because the early economy seems to have been significantly engaged in the production of iron, such evidence is found scattered in many of the sites that date to the period of A.D. 0 to 600. These sites with industrial debris usually contain Early Iron Age ceramics, with their distinctive scrolled, incised, and channeled motifs and beveled rims. The variation in the types of pots, which also include what appear to be large jars used for storage (Schmidt 1980), suggests that the diverse and unspecialized distribution of pottery types marks domestic settings where a wide variety of domestic uses were employed. Certainly the pottery assemblages do not suggest a specialization linked to iron production alone.

The presence of Urewe ceramics on sites with evidence for iron production has led to the suggestion that the Urewe ceramics may be associated with ironworking and thus mark non-habitation sites (Stewart 1993). This interpretation overlooks the fact that some industrial sites also incorporate habitation.[10] Settlement sites and industrial sites *cannot* be considered separate entities. In ancient Buhaya, settlement and industry are often found within the same space, and any attempt to separate them must be recognized as an attempt to obscure the past in favor of speculative alternatives. Many of the Early Iron Age settlements along the ridge between the Mulelezi River and the Karagwe Depression (in which Lake Ikimba is situated), for example, are very large settlements—sometimes more than fifty hectares in size—showing little or no sign of industrial activity (Schmidt 1980). While some of these sites appear predominantly domestic, I want to be cautious that a false dichotomy is not drawn between settled life and iron production. Such a dichotomy appears to be based partly on the hidden inference that iron smelting would have been conducted outside village precincts, an idea that is drawn from inappropriate and incomplete ethnographic analogy: that iron smelting is always conducted in secret outside of villages. In fact, iron smelting was sometimes conducted within village precincts (cf. Killick 1990) and, in the case of the recent Haya smelting, in a zone immediately contiguous to village precincts. If Early Iron Age smelters conducted their smelts on the periphery of their villages or even in more remote areas, those sites would have been quickly occupied by growing settlements. Such probable admixture through time diminishes any claim that the presence of ironworking ipso facto denies the presence of settlement. Simple logic also informs us that people must have lived nearby their places of work, as house floors contiguous to iron smelting furnaces at both the Rugomora Mahe and KM2 sites attest (Schmidt 1978; Schmidt and Childs 1985). The presence of domestic ceramics, ironworking, and house structures at these sites suggests that similar conditions prevailed elsewhere in the region during antiquity.

The margin of Victoria Nyanza appears by A.D. 0 to have been settled from about 10 kilometers north of today's regional headquarters, Bukoba, to about 30 kilometers south of Kemondo Bay by communities practicing iron production and a form of subsistence that likely drew significantly from the cereal diet and pastoralism borrowed from the earlier Southern Cushitic speakers in the region (Ehret 1991, n.d.; Schoenbrun 1993a). Along with hunting, gathering, root crops, and a growing use of beans (Schoenbrun 1993a), these early communities likely continued to draw extensively from the rich fish resources of Victoria Nyanza to supplement their diets. As forest clearance occurred along the valleys and ridges near the lake, the conditions for cereal agriculture would have grown more attractive. Clearance of the gallery forests would have been a demanding task, but certainly one mitigated by the ready supply of iron tools.

These early communities were likely lineage- and clan-based groups, some of which monopolized control of iron production. This interpretation, inferred from the organization of many Bantu-speaking societies in the Great Lakes, suggests some social differentiation based on wealth. Even among the iron-producing groups there appear to have been differences, with some groups following parallel but distinct lines of technological development. While each ironworking group shared a common idea about how to build iron smelting furnaces, there were clearly differences among them about how to go about smelting iron. Some of these differences were expressed in the types of clay resources that were exploited in this early period for the purpose of making tuyeres (blow pipes used to conduct the air blast).

Between A.D. 0 and 200, some groups working at the KM2 site just 200 meters from Kemondo Bay appear to have been more privileged in the quality of clay they used in making heat-resistant tuyeres. Their use of better clays would have led to more effective smelting of iron that, in turn, would have meant an economic advantage over their close neighbors smelting only about 1 kilometer away at the KM3 site (Schmidt and Childs 1985; Childs 1988, 1989a). It is difficult to tease out other differences between these early groups that point to differences in power, but this certainly is one domain in which control over technologically advantageous resources would have led to different levels of technological achievement, productive capacity, and wealth. Thus, even among iron-producing groups there appears to have been social and economic differentiation based on control of resources, perhaps the beginnings of social ranking and possible social stratification among the Early Iron Age peoples of Buhaya.

Both ironworking and non-ironworking social groups voraciously consumed the forested environment for both agricultural and industrial purposes. This had two immediate consequences: Smaller groups hived off, some possibly before A.D. 0, to settle more interior areas, such as the Kamachumu Plateau, where competition for resources and productive agricultural land was not as intense. Those groups that continued to reside on the margins of the lakeshore turned to more marginal forest resources as the wet gallery forest dwindled. By A.D. 200 to 300, communities were established along the northern edge of the plateau, along its southern end as well as at its base.[11] Iron working on the plateau seems to have differed in scale and style, with smaller furnaces and a level of production lower than that observed along the lake.

By A.D. 200, some social groups involved in ironworking along Victoria Nyanza appear to have lost some of the distinctive adaptations that distinguished them in the first two centuries. The technology appears more standardized, with more universal access to critical resources such as heat-resistant clays (Schmidt and Childs 1985; Childs 1986, 1988). The archaeological record at the KM2 site indicates that these ironworkers apparently lost some of their technical advantage over their neighbors at KM3 (Schmidt and Childs 1985). This overall decline in economic differences may be linked to population growth, a larger labor force, and the failure of particular social groups to monopolize critical resources. Standardization of production may also point to the growth of centralization, where a central authority grew to control resources and the standards of production.

With the passage of time and increased agricultural and industrial production, ecological stresses increased along the lake margins. By A.D. 300 to 500, iron-producing groups were forced to exploit more difficult-to-reach forests, while others continued to seek new opportunities in the hinterland. By A.D. 300 to 400, and possibly earlier, the area around Lake Ikimba had been settled. Its more open woodland environment and woody grasslands had likely already been utilized by southern Cushitic speakers for cereal agriculture and cattle pastoralism, uses that may have made it more susceptible to environmental degradation once it was occupied by Bantu-speaking agriculturists. The 400-500 era in Buhaya, as well as in Rwanda, was a turning point for Early Iron Age populations (Van Grunderbeek, Roche, and Doutrelepont 1983a, 1983b; Schmidt 1994). Faced with erosion difficulties, diminished forests, and hundreds of communities of significant size—some up to 50 hectares or more in size—these peoples witnesssed a failure of technology to keep pace with a degraded resource base.

After A.D. 600 the production of iron finally sputtered to a stop in the once-prosperous factory sites around Kemondo Bay and in the interior. The prosperity of the first half of the millennium had passed. The most poignant testimony to this decline was the rapid diminution of communities in the interior, away from the lake margins. At this time we cannot say what happened to these populations, although there is suggestive linguistic evidence that many of these "Rutaran-speaking" peoples left the region and moved into the area that we know today in the north as Ankole, western Buganda, and Bunyoro (Schoenbrun 1993b). We do not have any direct evidence for disease or widespread epidemics, though such events, exacerbated by malnutrition brought on by a diminished agricultural capacity, may well have contributed to movements out of the region. The increasing popularity of pastoralism—perhaps linked to more grasslands resulting from deforestation—undoubtedly contributed to the movement north into open grasslands, where pastoral peoples seem to have established either ritual centers or centralized polities by the eleventh century A.D. at sites such as Ntusi (Reid 1990, 1991; Robertshaw 1994).

By the end of the millennium, the only permanent communities were located on the shores of Victoria Nyanza, where there would have been still-reliable rains for cereal agriculture and root crops as well as the ever-reliable fish resources of the lake. Otherwise, the landscape appears to have been mostly empty of human occupation. Over time the land healed and forests again partly took hold until the end of the first quarter of the second millennium, when once more the interior of Buhaya was occupied, at least as far as the eastern margin of the Lake Ikimba basin. These people were also iron producers and agriculturists, but they brought with them an agricultural repertoire much more varied than before—many varieties of banana as well as a plethora of new cattle breeds (Schoenbrun 1993a, 1993b).

These new crops and the manure provided by the cattle undoubtedly helped the inhabitants to make a living on soils that had only partly recovered from the abuse of the previous millennium. Ironworking also flourished, but archaeology has yet to develop fully an understanding of its attributes during the era A.D. 1300 to 1800. However, there were a number of distinct differences between the material culture of these later peoples and those who occupied the region in the first millennium A.D. First, the ceramics were completely different, with a new form of decoration based on a carved roulette. While it is not necessary to tie such ceramics to any groups from the outside, it is nonetheless informative that similar types of pottery have been documented to the area around Lake Albert in northwest Uganda (Soper 1971; Connah 1991, 1996), a zone where there was considerable influence from cattle-keeping Sudanic speakers—Madi in origin—on the Nyoro language between A.D. 1000 and 1250 (Ehret n.d.). Moreover, recent research in Uganda at sites such as Ntusi, Mubende Hill, and Munsa indicates that carved roulette pottery started to become popular during the first quarter of this millennium (Robertshaw 1994).

Others have noted that a similar carved roulette is associated with Ubangian speakers who came in contact with East African peoples near northwestern Uganda during the early part of the second millennium (David 1982: 90). The firm dating of this ceramic complex in western Bunyoro, eastern Buganda, and Buhaya to the first quarter of this millennium suggests strongly that the carved roulette ware is antecedent in Buhaya to pottery decorated with a twisted grass roulette.[12] It is possible that such ceramics may be related to cattle-keeping groups, possibly Nilotic speakers (Schoenbrun 1990; Sutton 1993), who came from these contact points in the north and made their way south with new cattle breeds and new varieties of bananas. An equally attractive alternative idea is that the distinctive carved roulette ware is an internal development that is associated with new communities and new identities that arose from a new economy based on cattle keeping and breeding and a rich array of bananas (Schoenbrun 1993b). Haya oral traditions point to a similar kind of historical picture, namely, the coming of large numbers of cattle tended by their owners in the pasturelands of the Karagwe Depression just west of coastal Buhaya.

Iron production during the second quarter of the second millennium A.D. differs from the preceding technology. Furnaces were no longer built of mud brick laid in circular courses and fitted to the furnace equipment where necessary. The furnace superstructure appears to have been more ephemeral, built much the same way that the recent Haya smelters built theirs: in a conical shape with mud and pieces of slag obtained from previous smelts, a form of chimney construction that does not preserve well in the archaeological record. The change in furnace form, however, does not seem related to changes in the internal dynamics. It may indicate, however, a growing concern with reduced labor investment, less specialized production, and an expanded production system that may reflect a more widespread practice of the technology incorporating more social groups. These newer furnace forms could not have accommodated the distinctive decorations applied to some early first-millennium furnaces. This plainer technology may also be related to a growing lack of concern by ironworking groups to mark out special social and political identities. Among other changes during this era is a shift from wood charcoal used in the below-ground pit (where slag collects) to swamp grasses, a change that may mark an increased concern for conservation of forest resources.

Oral histories indicate that social groups controlling large cattle herds on the western periphery of Buhaya interacted economically and politically with the older indigenous groups to their east over several hundred years (Schmidt 1978). Despite such intimate contact, the western groups did not succeed in establishing effective political hegemony over their eastern neighbors—those along the ridges bordering Victoria Nyanza—during this long period. When political tensions erupted between indigenous social groups (including ironworking clans) and cattle-keeping peoples during the latter seventeenth century, iron production was very likely in decline again. By this time, the ridges along the lake would have been completely reoccupied and denuded of large stands of forest. The vegetational history of the region explains some of the stresses over land management and contests over the best agricultural land that arose during the previous several hundred years. Cattle-keeping peoples also had an important commodity, manure, which they appear to have used as leverage to control land held by indigenous groups.

By the end of the seventeenth century in Buhaya there had been successful attempts by the cattle-keeping dynasties, most notably the Babito and the Bahinda, to gain political control over the peoples of the coastal zone. This was partly accomplished by seizing and then identifying with the most important sacred sites, especially those associated with iron production. For the Bahinda dynasty in Kyamutwara kingdom, power over sacred symbolic space marked a major change in the political economy. It also led to the use of ancient history and the sacred symbols associated with iron production to make new histories that directly linked the new dynasty with the past, conferred legitimacy on the new rulers, and opened a new path for central taxation and direct management of iron production.

This milestone in Haya history takes us directly into the manipulation of history as an ideological tool that is used to the political and economic advantage of the new dynasties. The political history of Buhaya is closely linked to a history of manipulation of rituals, symbols, and beliefs that are associated with iron smelting. The establishment of new political authorities based on traditional idioms of myth, history, and ritual in Kyamutwara kingdom is also seen in the purposeful development of new cults of affliction in Kiziba kingdom (Schmidt 1978), which threatened and undermined the authority of the traditional religious and political leaders.

By the time the first Europeans traversed Buhaya at the end of the nineteenth century, they found a region still economically prosperous but also partly dependent upon iron goods imported from neighboring regions. Forests, except for small pockets protected by sacred authorities, were scarce. Iron production had become a luxury that the Haya could no longer afford at the level that had prevailed centuries earlier. Dependency on imports had replaced self-sufficiency. Thus, the availability of cheap scrap steel of European manufacture found ready acceptance among ironworkers, who often had to travel long distances to produce iron under difficult conditions during the first three decades of this century.

The important role that iron production played in the distant past is no longer seen in Buhaya. A few forges are found in some villages, but production is restricted to repair of mass-produced utensils or to making specialized agricultural tools, such as the small hoe used to plant beans or the heavy chopper (now fashioned from a spring) used to cut out the roots of banana plants. Even these tools are being replaced as the machete is increasingly used as a digging and planting tool and is also used to cut and trim banana plants. And so the forging trade steadily diminishes. Well-meaning but naive European development "experts" have interceded and tried to revitalize ironsmithing by supplying several smiths with large bellows meant to conserve labor. Such efforts have also supplied the smiths with foreign iron anvils and with blank hoes rejected by factories. In these cases, indigenous tools and raw materials have been replaced by artificial devices that demand constant supply or maintenance. Not only are such efforts destined to fail, they also betray a serious lack of understanding of the economic forces that have led to the diminishment of ironworking in the region over the last two thousand years.

Today the Haya continue to live in large villages with dispersed homesteads in which plantain cultivation remains as the dominant form of subsistence. Manuring continues to be an important part of the agroecological system, and the more productive farms are invariably those that apply significant cow manure. Green manuring also remains an important part of the intercropping scheme used by the Haya, who plant beans among their bananas and coffee trees. Maize and cassava are increasingly important to many, especially on the peripheries of the villages, where more open land is available for crop diversification. Hoe agriculture remains the dominant form of cultivation, with deep (1 m) cultivation not unusual in areas where farmers try to rid their plots of tenacious nuisance grasses. Planting and harvesting of food crops remain predominantly female activities, although the traditional division of labor is gradually eroding.

As the Haya cultivate their land with iron hoes, they often come upon industrial materials that date to two thousand years ago. Ancient furnaces filled with bricks, slag, and charcoal are commonly encountered. A shrewd farmer will immediately recognize the value of the charcoal and ash and will often dig deeper into an ancient refuse pit or furnace, churning it up and scattering its contents. Through this means the past is being diminished by the very processes that created it in the first place: the quest for agricultural production through the use of iron tools.

2.

Historical

and Cultural

Contexts

Excavating

History,

Myth, and

Ritual

The archaeology for the last two thousand years or more in Buhaya presents a more visible record of the material remains of iron production than of any other aspect of ancient life. This is partly the consequence of a soil chemistry hostile to preservation, high levels of rainfall combined with severe leaching of the soil, and patterns of land utilization. Land use has been most significant, for deep hoe cultivation in villages situated in the same places as Early Iron settlements has meant the steady and nearly complete obliteration of structures such as house floors, hearths, ancient garbage pits, and perhaps even burials. As already observed, farmers seek out prehistoric features rich in ash and organic soil to enrich their fields. The impact of agriculture on ancient technological structures also has been severe in some areas, depending on the depth of the Early Iron Age smelting furnaces. Structures such as furnace pits filled with slag and bricks tend to resist the attacks of hoe farming more than do other structures, but those that lie close to the surface, such as those found only 10 to 15 centimeters below the surface of a banana and coffee planting at the KM3 site, suffer constant attrition.

The transformations introduced into the archaeological record, then, are of two varieties: (1) chemical and physical alterations, and (2) cultural modifications, mostly through agriculture. Thus, the record reflects only specific domains of prehistoric behavior, and these domains themselves have been altered significantly by the pattern of later settlement and agriculture. This fragmentary, transformed record is not unique to Buhaya or to archaeology (e.g., Schiffer 1987). But it limits the kinds of questions that reasonably can be asked about prehistoric times; it also tends to create biases and directs our focus toward the productive economy of iron production.

If we operate within such limitations, then it is particularly important to develop as complete an understanding as possible of the contextual meanings of iron production during the recent past and in the present in the same region. The critical use of a direct historical approach is one way to illuminate important characteristics of iron technology and to tack between the present and the past. Because a direct historical approach favors continuities and tends to erase change, it is all the more important to address discontinuities as critically as the continuities on which the method depends—leading to greater confidence that change will not be overlooked. I am presenting here, therefore, an ethnoarchaeology that brings together observational evidence with pertinent ethnography, oral histories, and other documentary accounts to construct a historical context for iron production in Buhaya and in related Bantu-speaking cultures. The understandings that result from this historically informed synthesis then enrich the behavioral-material models derived from conventional ethnoarchaeology using observations alone.

As these understandings or models are informed historically, they can provide insight into processes of economic change, the possible function and meaning of material remains, the role of innovation in technological development and change, and the role of iron in the political history of Buhaya. Though much of this story about iron production emphasizes and depends on a single culture, it extends far beyond the particularities of the Haya world. Haya ways of socially constructing meaning for iron production bear strong similarities to those of many neighboring Bantu-speaking peoples. Regardless of the differences that exist in various technologies, iron smelting and its associated behaviors display strong cross-cultural similarities in ideology (Childs and Killick 1993; Herbert 1993).

If we attach cultural meanings to the history of iron production, then we must work with information that dates mostly to this century. This is not without problems, for immense changes have taken place in most African cultures over the last hundred years. The same is also true in Buhaya.

Nonetheless, it is apparent from field studies, archival materials, ethnography, and an increasing amount of archaeological information that powerful cross-cultural similarities in ritual and symbolic meanings associated with ironworking can be observed despite culture change.

History, Myth, Ritual, and Iron

I first look at what iron technology means in various cultural contexts within Buhaya. Our observations of the smelters at work between 1976 and 1984 contribute to the most detailed and reliable information on the productive sphere. These observations are invaluable in elucidating behavior and belief that are linked—though distantly and through the lens of much culture change—to a precolonial tradition. As we move from industrial production to other domains, such as the social and the ritual, an important source of information for views on the political value of iron symbolism is the testimony of informants who at one time were connected with royal authority in some way. Such connections were both direct and reactive. Those who participated in the political process or performed in sacred royal rituals provide direct information, whereas observers of sacred ritual, or keepers of alternative political traditions that challenge the royal history, are indirect and counteractive sources. Such a diversity of sources in Buhaya, especially the alternative clan histories that challenge royal histories (Schmidt 1978), offer a rich understanding of the meaning of iron production from different social points of view. As rich as they may be, however, we must always remember that they are only fragments of the realities that prevailed more than a century ago.

In the face of such significant religious change in Buhaya, comparative ethnology is a final way to understand the ritual past. Because there are such similar ritual practices associated with iron production in Africa (Cline 1937; Herbert 1993; Schmidt 1996b), further elucidation of symbolic meanings of ritual practices associated with Haya iron production can be found elsewhere, particularly in Bantu-speaking cultures. I draw on comparative evidence for two purposes: to illustrate the widespread distribution of such belief systems, and to better elucidate phenomena in Buhaya when comparison to other, related cultures helps flesh out understandings of relationships and meanings that have eroded over the last hundred years in Buhaya. Even then I limit the evidence to several cultures in which the themes I isolate are particularly well developed and well preserved.

Peeling Back the Onion Skin of History: What Oral History Says in Buhaya

Buhaya provides an important and unique laboratory to develop a more humanistic and scientific archaeology of Africa. One of the challenges in this effort is to decode the messages in oral histories that are linked to the archaeological record. On a theoretical level, this should be possible when change observed in the material record is coeval in time with change seen in either emic historical commentary or etic analysis of oral texts. The analysis of oral texts for structural transformations is a process that parallels and is analogous to the analysis of the archaeological record for change. Thus I am engaged in an archaeology of historical and symbolic texts, a process that naturally leads to a hermeneutic style (David 1992a). Such an approach necessarily means that I must also excavate historical and ritual texts, discern their stratigraphy, decode their messages about time, and correlate these with the material record. This hermeneutic process, this excavation of meaning, is what I call peeling back the onion skin of history—a metaphor first employed by Eva Hunt (1977). Peeling back onion skins resembles archaeological excavation as it deals with a stratified layers, each of which holds part of the history of the whole; once the last layer is reached, the excavation is complete, the soil sterile.

One of the most effective tools in this enterprise is the careful and limited application of structural analysis (e.g., Feierman 1974; Hunt 1977; Schmidt 1978), which is particularly useful in revealing paradigmatic shifts—the relationship of major elements—such as the reconfiguration of textual elements from clearly different domains, a process that often signals rearrangements in political and social relations. The mixing of different and once-separate elements to form a new text is of particular interest here. Mixing historical texts, for example, with mythological texts that are part of the Kitara epic occurs in the history of King Rugomora Mahe of Kyamutwara kingdom (Schmidt 1978).

The mixing of textual fragments from different cultural domains signifies major change—in this case a major shift in power relations between indigenous social groups and those, like the Bahinda and Babito dynasties, who trace their origins to areas outside of Buhaya. It is common in human history that histories and symbolic motifs identified with those in power are manipulated or destroyed during periods of dynastic change— the alteration of Hatshepsut's public symbols, such as her obelisk at the Temple of Amun in Karnak, comes immediately to mind—to create new historical and cultural illusions as groups vie for power. The struggle for legitimacy is tied closely to how indigenous groups identify with the new order; familiar historical and mythological paradigms wrapped around a new group's history create familiar ground and commonality. The manipulation of history and symbol in oral texts is accessible to us, as it would be for any historian or other person practicing a comparative approach. It is within this context that I carefully have applied structural analysis.

As we peel back the onion skins of history, symbol, and myth in Haya culture, we come closer to exposing the core transformational tropes of Haya culture. The most profoundly transforming tropes in the Haya world are those that are metonymic—signaling a semantic shift—and it is these metonymic processes from which symbolic life springs. As Terrance Turner (1991) has shown, the movement from metonymy, including synecdoche, to metaphor leads to different levels of symbolic expression. The occurrence of metonymic representations and processes also signals important historic moments; these pulses in symbolic meanings *punctuate* the flow of history. Eva Hunt's (1977) study of Central American myth and history again helps here, for she recognizes not only that myth and ritual symbolism reflect contemporary society, but that they "also include symbols where meanings come from crucial states of its history." In a society such as that of the Haya with linear, genealogically organized histories, it is possible to use a critical comparative approach to assess the chronological contemporaneity of the genealogies of different social groups as well as to discern periods of regularity and change from content of texts. Once a comparative approach draws out the contradictions and commonalities of alternative histories from different social groups, then we can begin to understand what transformations, at various shared moments of history, have occurred in social organization and simultaneously in symbol systems. This is what my book *Historical Archaeology* addressed in 1978. A summary of those findings touches directly on the results of the approach and method discussed above.

Using such methods, we should be able to isolate periods of radical change in the social relations of production and political power as well as to identify different processes of change by the structural configurations that are residual in myth, history, and ritual. An archaeology of symbols requires that we be able to recognize the archaeological signatures that identify sociohistoric changes.

An archaeology of symbols also depends on decoding meaning found in myth, history, and ritual, all of which arise out of a "society's collective history, and the cultural processes that gave birth to the meanings" (Hunt 1977: 32). Hunt's vision of an archaeology of symbols incorporates the idea that symbolic meanings can be decoded first by defining the stratigraphic layers of culture that are embedded in ephemeral media such as myth and ritual, and then by unraveling the historical threads of the symbols (ibid.). That perspective is one that is now widely recognized in structural analysis of historical information (e.g., Schmidt 1978; de Heusch 1982; Willis 1981), but also one that has created healthy and deserved skepticism in some quarters (Vansina 1983, 1994).

The first assumption I make is that significant changes in the patterning of history or the abrupt rise of altered symbol systems mark periods of rapid historical change. Symbolic and ritual systems often are transformed to accommodate new political orders or significant shifts in the relations of production. As different social groups gain access to power through control over critical resources, symbolic and ritual systems associated previously with maintaining power and masking social and economic distinctions are manipulated and altered to the advantage of the ascendant social group(s). Recent thinking by some British and American archaeologists has elegantly laid the theoretical groundwork for our inquiry into the processes of mystification that the social groups in control of the economy use to make their relations with others to appear to be natural, without contradiction (see Kus 1979, 1983; Hodder 1982a; Handsman 1981, 1983; Leone 1984; Miller and Tilley 1984; McGuire 1992).

Eva Hunt provides an important perspective on the identification of transformations in these domains of the cultural system when she recognizes that periods of radical change in history often introduce an arbitrariness into symbol systems. When radical change occurs, ritual specialists, priests, and philosopher-historians entrusted with specialized symbolic knowledge experience severe change, to the point where whole cults are eliminated, temples occupied and destroyed, and belief systems systematically destroyed and altered. If such processes occurred—as we will see, there is strong evidence that such changes have indeed happened—then we are left with bits and pieces, fragments of the past—a situation parallel to any other archaeological record. This process of erosion (what Schiffer might call a cultural transform) is similar, Hunt believes, to what Lévi-Strauss means by history erasing structure, "that historical losses in symbolic structure hide, over time, the structure's total meaning" (Hunt 1977: 35). Our task is to devise a methodology that reveals that meaning from the current residuum, the fragments that we can make sense of.

If movement toward less elaboration in symbolic systems or toward the interplay of the most fundamental tropes—as an index of increased manipulation—is characteristic of times of radical change, when institutions charged with maintaining symbolic systems are altered significantly, then we should expect to see diagnostic archaeological signatures for these transformations. To do this, I turn to a number of oral texts. These previously published texts testify to significant change and manipulation, the most important moment of which occurred in Buhaya during the late seventeenth century. The purpose of these analyses is practical and straightforward. One of my goals is to find symbolic meanings that make cultural differences seem natural; the other is to isolate ways in which symbolic armatures within iron production have been appropriated as a means of masking new forms of political and economic control. Both forms of analysis can help isolate mystifications that symbolically obscure social and historical relationships.

Why Tropes Are Important ———

One of the first steps is to isolate major symbolic readjustments and any other semantic shifts—including but not limited to movements toward arbitrariness—found in Haya oral texts. One of the most helpful and illuminating approaches is the distinction that Roman Jakobson drew between metaphor and metonymy (Jakobson 1956). In his study of aphasic speech disorders, Jakobson isolates and clearly defines two tropes, metaphor and metonymy, and observes that a competition between them is manifest in any symbolic process—interpersonal or social (1956: 80). In its most general sense, metaphor is the relationship that exists between entities of separate domains by virtue of the relationship each has with entities within its domain (Seitel 1972; Fernandez 1977). The principle of similarity underlies metaphor and analogy (Aristotle's 4th class of metaphor), with *substitution* of one set of relations for the other being at the center of this symbolic process, and with the metaphoric tension arising out of the known differences that exist between the two entities.

Metonymy, a symboling process much overlooked because of our preoccupation with metaphor, is any relationship that exists between entities by virtue of their mutual inclusion in the same domain (Durham and Fernandez 1991). This is often a relationship of contiguity (cf. Seitel 1972; Fernandez 1977; Durham and Fernandez 1991; Tilley 1993). Metonymy is profoundly transformational, for it involves a reduction to sameness or identity as a consequence of contiguous relationships. It also may involve naming (or, renaming), a process that results from the projection of habitual contiguity so that, for example, a whole is represented by a part or a part by a whole—a commonly recognized class of metonymy called synecdoche; the examples "fighting city hall" and "setting a fine table" are immediately recognizable. In the city hall example, it is the habitual relationship of contiguity—the bureaucrats inside the structure—that causes their being named as the structure. They share the same domain, and the same identity; this also points to the idea of *combination* that develops out of this contiguity (Ricoeur 1977), and it shows the powerful role that synecdoche plays in metonymy (Turner 1991). In both cases, one object is designated by the name of the other.

Naming, then, is central to this symboling process. Ricoeur notes that despite the simplicity of Jakobson's analysis of the bipolarity of metaphor and metonymy, its strength lies in that it extends beyond "the sentence into the realm of style, beyond intentional use of linguistic signs into dreaming and magic" (Ricoeur 1977: 178). This is precisely why the analysis of metonymy is so central to my analysis of ritual, myth, and magic associated with iron production and its social control: It is shifting contextual relationships, often traced to new synecdoches, that lead to new metonymies and metaphors in ritual and magic. Naming and mystifications that result from contiguity are two of my primary interests. At points in oral histories where such processes occur—what Turner (1991) would call a "play of tropes"—we must be on the lookout for other changes.

I look at metonymic processes closely in all pertinent fields, for they hint at periods of major cultural change, when semantic shifts are more likely to occur. Congruent with this analysis, I examine the changes in the relationship among elements of the religious, social, and political systems. Analysis at this level can help to show when certain common mythological structures are combined with oral history and legend. Mixing conventional oral legend with sacred myth (especially myth associated with the ancient Bacwezi gods, best known from the Kitara epic) points to the purposeful manipulation of historiography for reasons of political hegemony. Such mixing or combination reveals the creation of new contextual linkages, new linkages that result from the syntactical mixing of concepts and motifs from two wholly different domains. This would appear to be a masking process that obscures the differences between the two separate traditions by including them in the same domain. It makes the transformed situation appear natural, and it confers legitimacy on the transformed text by linking it to the ancients, the progenitors of the cultural system.

This introduces more clearly questions of legitimacy and hegemony that will underlie much of the subsequent discussion, as well as that found in chapter 9. The manipulation of symbols of power, for example, can occur in such a way as to confer legitimacy on those who are identified with the symbols. Shift in contiguous association with legitimizing symbols, then, may be a definitive marker for changes in power relationships as one group extends its hegemony over others. It is only a short step to the concomitant realization that control over the productive economy is not possible in some Bantu-speaking cultures until the symbol systems that confer legitimacy and power are first controlled.

Analysis of oral traditions also has an important role to play in determining the development and dissolution of political alliances among different social groups, the development of new religious configurations, and the growth of certain ritual practices. Political alliance, especially between outsiders and those indigenous social groups traditionally associated with control of magic, religion, and the productive economy, often may lead to new structural arrangements; the content of the oral traditions gives clues to periods of restructured social and political relations.

Application of the Method

One of the best-known but least understood aspects of power and economics in Bantu-speaking Africa is the important status, high rank, wealth, and significant symbolic power of ironworkers in African chiefdoms and kingdoms (Sasoon 1983; Schmidt 1983b; de Maret 1980, 1985; Herbert 1993). The earliest social and political leaders in Buhaya are represented in oral traditions as the first ironworkers. In Kyamutwara kingdom (fig. 2.1), the progenitor of the indigenous Bayango clan is Kayango, who "came from Buzinza (to the southeast), smelting iron and shaking his shoulders. They called him *Kayango kitengya mabega* (Kayango the shoulder shaker)" (Schmidt 1978: 97). His shoulders shake because the pumping of bellows causes a smith's or smelter's shoulders to rise and fall very rapidly.

Kayango is also associated in Bayango clan traditions—one of the most prominent and oldest of indigenous clans—with rainmaking and is linked in the genealogies with descent from the Bacwezi, the ancients whose spirits also possessed certain *embandwa* or spirit mediums and diviners. In the kingdom of Kyamutwara under the Bahinda dynasty, the Bayango

FIG. 2.1 Map of the traditional kingdoms of Buhaya. These entities have been replaced with regional and district boundaries that now form the basis of new geopolitical identities.

are later referred to as the Bayango-Bahinda, a metonymic naming device that incorporates the alien Bahinda clan into the domain of more legitimate Bayango. Such naming creates an identity between the two social groups and marks an alliance that retains for the Bayango certain royal privileges, such as burial of the clan head as a king. It also associates the much later Bahinda with the origins of ironworking. In order to follow this discussion about the major actors in Haya social and political history, I have provided a king list that shows two variants: the first is a royal perspective and the second is an indigenous Bayango perspective:

Table 2.1

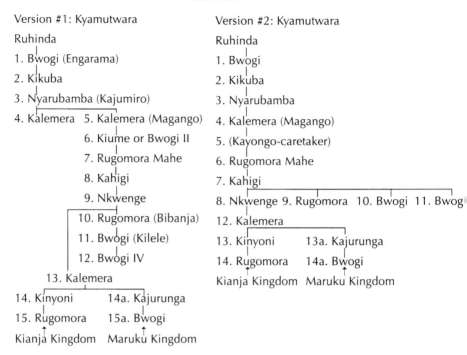

Version #1: Kyamutwara

Ruhinda
1. Bwogi (Engarama)
2. Kikuba
3. Nyarubamba (Kajumiro)
4. Kalemera   5. Kalemera (Magango)
6. Kiume or Bwogi II
7. Rugomora Mahe
8. Kahigi
9. Nkwenge
10. Rugomora (Bibanja)
11. Bwogi (Kilele)
12. Bwogi IV
13. Kalemera
14. Kinyoni   14a. Kajurunga
15. Rugomora   15a. Bwogi
Kianja Kingdom   Maruku Kingdom

Version #2: Kyamutwara

Ruhinda
1. Bwogi
2. Kikuba
3. Nyarubamba
4. Kalemera (Magango)
5. (Kayongo-caretaker)
6. Rugomora Mahe
7. Kahigi
8. Nkwenge 9. Rugomora 10. Bwogi 11. Bwogi
12. Kalemera
13. Kinyoni   13a. Kajurunga
14. Rugomora   14a. Bwogi
Kianja Kingdom   Maruku Kingdom

The Bayango, then, are identified with the origins of ironworking in Kyamutwara kingdom. They are also unambiguously identified as descendants of the Bacwezi. To the north of Kyamutwara in Kiziba kingdom, the earliest ironworkers are said to be Bike's clan, the Bagina. It is important to note that the Bagina also claim Bacwezi descent. Eventually, the Bagina are replaced by the Bayango-Bahinda, a parallel condition of identity. This clan later became known as the Bakuma (Schmidt 1978).[1] Of particular significance is that the Bakuma clan occupied the land that belonged to Bike and continued to do so throughout this century. This example gives the first hints of how legitimacy is tied to the appropriation of symbolic space (the ironworker/leader's palace site).

This process of spatial appropriation is also metonymic, for it rests principally upon relationships of contiguity. We read about such processes historically when later, usurping social groups—the Babito in Kiziba kingdom and the Bahinda in Kyamutwara kingdom—incorporate themselves into (live within) the spatial domain identified, ritually and symbolically, with the earliest ironworkers. This initiates a relationship of contiguity by which the legitimizing symbols of iron production mask an alien identity. As in Kyamutwara, the Bayango-Bahinda in Kiziba initially appear to be displaced politically by the Babito "royal" clan, related to the Bahinda.[2] Parallel to the Kyamutwara case, history reveals certain metonymic processes that retain for the indigenous clans a royal name and critical functions in the central court, including the installation of a new Mukama and the demarcation of his palace boundaries.

The relationship between iron production and leadership is common to other parts of Bantu-speaking Africa, particularly in Zaire, Rwanda, and Burundi. In most areas where there is an association between leadership and ironworking, it is on the side of smithing, not iron smelting. This separation does not lack significance, for the process of smelting involves much more restricted and esoteric practices that are profoundly transformational. Smithing is more accessible and more public, and its symbols are more easily appropriated by social-political groups who are not tied directly to ironworking. However, if ironworking is tied consistently to leadership, then it is apparent that the symbolic association of "outsider" groups with ironworking may be central to legitimacy. Because iron smelting is more deeply transformational, we might expect to see the incorporation of smelting symbolism as an index to more profound change in the social relations of production. I will return to this theme in chapter 9.

Immediately to the southwest of Buhaya in Burundi, the first Mwami (king) of the Burundi dynasty is linked to the introduction of ironworking (Celis and Nzikobanyanka 1976), as are the chiefs or quasi-kings (Bayango) of Kyamutwara. The same is true of Buganda. The association of kingship with smithing is particularly strong among the Kuba in oral tradition and among the Luba during coronation ceremonies (Vansina 1978; de Maret 1985). Pierre de Maret's exegesis on this subject shows that the critical symbols of power derived from ironworking are the anvil and the hammer (de Maret 1985). If not directly linked to political power, blacksmiths are often involved by virtue of their forging the royal emblems of power or special ritual roles during royal coronations (Dewey and Childs 1996).

The rituals of royal installation symbolically transform Haya kings into blacksmiths. Oral traditions show that the Babito and Bahinda clans had no predynastic association with ironworking. Moreover, ritual practices that transform the king into a blacksmith appear to have developed subsequent to the foundation of these later dynasties. The older ruling clans and their leaders are identified explicitly with ironworking; therefore, for those social groups such ritual transformations would have been pointless. Installation rituals that cast the king-to-be in the role of blacksmith were performed in both Kiziba and Kianja kingdoms (Kianja was once a part of greater Kyamutwara kingdom). The most direct and helpful history of this ritual comes from Petro Nyarubamba, the king of Kianja, who comments on his own coronation held during the late fifties:

> On the 4th day of my coronation, very early at six A.M. the smiths had started to forge iron. I entered their forge to join them as ritual requires. I beat the bellows and hammered the iron. The people outside cheered. I had become king of Kianja kingdom. I was iron. (P. Nyarubamba, June 29, 1984)

The king's testimony poignantly illustrates the transformation that occurs under these ritual circumstances. As a Muhinda royal, he lacks any knowledge of ironworking and is a quintessential outsider. During the ritual he is conducted to the hut of the smiths, admitted inside, and given the bellows to pump. This ritual procedure accepts him *within* the domain of the smiths; he is contained within the *luiija* or forge—a ritually imposed contiguity. This is a metonymic transformation, whereby he assumes the attributes and identity of an ironworker. Within the indigenous domain of the ironworkers, the Mukama plays a subordinate role vis-à-vis the iron-workers and demonstrates his dependency on them. This theme is also articulated by the Bakuma clan head of Kiziba:

> In the old days when a new king was installed on the throne, one of the important rituals during the installation ceremonies was a visit by the new king to the newly built hut of the blacksmiths in the palace compound. Once the hut was completed, he would enter it, ritually take the sticks of the bellows in hand and pump the bellows for the forging fire. This indicated that smithing was something all men could do, even the king. The ritual also symbolized the special relationship that existed between the king and the iron workers. It is like a smith who brings his youngest male child to the forge and makes him oper-ate the bellows. (Mutaihwa Lubelwa, Bakuma clan head; August 3, 1976, in Kigarama, Kiziba)

The installation ritual, to use the image of Mutaihwa Lubelwa, places the Mukama in a role that is analogous to that of a child, for bellows pumpers at forges are often children and apprentices. This acknowledges clearly the power and influence of ironworkers in their relationship to the throne. If the ritual brings the king into a subordinate relationship within the domain of the ironworkers, it also asserts symbolically that outsid-ers—those from non-ironworking clans—could also participate in this as-pect of the productive economy, a critical part of the royal ideology under the Bahinda of an open economy where one social group did not have exclusive control over iron production (Schmidt 1983b). However, the subordinate relationship is acted out ritually in a larger context—within the palace grounds of the Mukama. This larger context signifies the actual relationship between the royals and the ironworkers—the subordination of the ironworkers to the Bahinda and Babito dynasties, who came to have the control over the resources used by ironworkers, the power to levy special taxes on iron production, and the power to require smiths to per-form annual service in the royal court. The ritual *containment* of the iron-workers within the domain of the king is a metonymic inversion of the natural order of things, which can be represented as royal space : king (royal domain) :: hinterland : ironworkers (indigenous domain). Thus, un-der transforming conditions of the ritual, the metonymic mixing of do-mains under the new relationships of contiguity leads to

royal space : ironworkers :: hinterland : king
Mixed Domains — royal/indigenous   indigenous/royal

The royal ritual is a double metonymy (king inside ironworkers' space, ironworkers inside king's space), and as such it is a powerful ideological

FIG. 2.2 Emblems of royal authority, as well as chiefly and clan-head authority: a *Muhoro* (used in war and for agricultural purposes) and a spear. The implements pictured here were passed on to the current Mukama or king of Kianja kingdom from his father. Photo by Winnie Lambrecht.

device that masks the unequal relationship between the royals and the ironworkers. It makes the ironworkers appear to be equals of the king, a mystification that creates the illusion of parity. Thus, the double metonymy with its inverted containers and parallel mixed domains (royal space : ironworkers :: luiija : king) not only confers symbolic values of great antiquity on the king, but also necessarily obscures social and political differences between the two groups.

The double metonymy also gives birth to the metaphor whereby the king assumes the role of the "Iron King." The king's sovereignty over his kingdom is symbolized by the ritual distribution to all parts of his kingdom of iron goods that he and his fellow craftsmen make: iron : territory :: king : sovereignty.

Thus, the power, sovereignty, and legitimacy of the king are symbolized in these two ritual procedures that transform a Muhinda royal into the Iron King. The ritual also makes clear that royal sovereignty is impossible without direct power over ironworking and the legitimacy of its symbolism. We will see later in this discussion that it is highly improbable, given the history of both dynasties, that these ritual procedures came into play in the Bahinda or Babito dynasties before the sixth and eighth kings, respectively. The development of this ritual procedure appears to parallel other changes in the relationship between these two dynasties and their indigenous populations at that time in their histories.

In Buhaya, centralized authority has long been signified by an iron spear and a *muhoro,* or chopping knife. These two iron objects figure prominently in rituals of investment at the royal level as well as at the level of clan headship (fig. 2.2). The Mukama is closely identified with the iron symbols of authority. The royal spear and knife, passed on to the king from his predecessor during the installation rituals, were displayed contiguous to the throne for all visitors to gaze upon. The relationship of contiguity that prevailed between the king and the iron symbols of his power reinforced the ideology of the iron king. The "iron king" is an emic identity that the king himself expressed as a consequence of certain transformations in his identity effected during his installation rituals (Mukama P. Nyarubamba of Kianja, June 1984).

Reprise of Oral History Analyses

In this section I review some of the primary observations that resulted from earlier analysis of oral traditions in Kiziba and Kyamutwara kingdoms (Schmidt 1978). This will illustrate what kinds of social, religious, and political changes occurred in the two kingdoms and will demonstrate how interlocking transformations in one kingdom parallel similar changes in the other.

The starting point is Kiziba kingdom, where analysis reveals that the Babito royal house had a very difficult time establishing its legitimacy during the reigns of the first eight Bakama.[3] Oral traditions from Kiziba kingdom show that approximately twenty-one generations ago (from today), the Babito clan attempted to wrest power from the Bayango-Bahinda (later the Bakuma) clan by a magical ruse. This immediately set up an opposition between the indigenous rulers of putative Bacwezi descent and the foreign cattle-keeping Babito clan from Kitara in Uganda. Though it was once popular to cast Bahinda and Babito rule as the imposition of centralized power by outsiders, there is now good reason to discard this interpretation for one that recognizes that these foreign groups struggled for up to eight generations before consolidating their power in either kingdom. As a way of illustrating these long-term contests, I will draw on oral histories by royal as well as nonroyal informants. For example, table 2.2 is a Kiziba king list running beyond the turn of this century (until 1916) given by a nonroyal informant. He related a history that identifies Ikanga, following Nyarwangu, as an interregnum ruler—an interpretation missing from the royal histories.

Table 2.2

1. Kibi
2. Ishamura
3. Wanumi
4. Matwi
5. Magembe
6. Muzinga
7. Mwigara
8. Burungu I
9. Magembe II
10. Mboneko I
11. Nyarwangu
12. [Ikanga]
13. Ruhangarazi
14. Rutajwa
15. Burungu II
16. Ruhangarazi II
17. Mutatembwa
18. Mutahangarwa (early 20th century, d. 1916) (Schmidt 1978)

The content of the Kiziba royal and alternative clan histories tells us that the first two Babito leaders experienced severe opposition from the displaced ruling indigenous clan of Bacwezi descent. Indigenous opposition included religious leaders such as the embandwa priests who plagued the Babito with possession by the spirits of Bacwezi leaders. This opposition reached crisis proportions during the reign of Wanumi, the third Babito king (see table 2.2). Oral traditions about Wanumi reveal that he was transformed by the possession of Wamara's spirit, and that burial customs were restructured to accommodate his altered state to a Mucwezi spirit. This appears to have weakened Babito rule, for it meant that Wanumi became illegitimate and was forced to abdicate. The indigenous clans appear to have thrown the royal house into chaos, with severe succession problems as one result.[4]

The next clear, unsuppressed piece of evidence for weakness in Babito rule occurs during the reign of Magembe, the fifth Mukama. Again the royal family was harassed by spirit possession, and Magembe found it necessary to enter into an alliance with Mugasha in order to prevail in a conflict with Karagwe kingdom to the west near Rwanda. Mugasha, the god of the storms, is a mythological figure associated with rainmaking cults. The most powerful rainmaker, leader of an influential indigenous clan (usually the Batundu), was seen as the living personification of Mugasha. Any union with Mugasha represents a political alliance with one of the most powerful local social groups that was politically, ritually, and symbolically opposed to the Bacwezi (Schmidt 1978). This is a significant alliance, one that exploits the rivalry between the followers of Mugasha and Wamara. It also acknowledges that the Babito house could not rule without the assistance of indigenous rainmakers, who ensured that the kingdom would remain prosperous and fertile. The absence of rain threatened to diminish any legitimacy that may have developed.

The tenuous hold of the Babito continues into the next reign, that of Muzinga, who along with his father is possessed by the spirit of Mwigara, an outsider from Karagwe kingdom. Appeasement of the opposition leads to outside marriage for Muzinga, who then names his son after the possessing spirit, Mwigara. We see in these oral histories a consistent pattern of illegitimacy in the Babito house. The pattern changes abruptly at the death of Mwigara, whose body disappears under an anthill while being transported to the traditional burial place in Kitara (Uganda). Mwigara's successor, Burungu I, orders that sand be brought from all the previous kings' graves and be distributed to various parts of Kiziba. Comparative analysis of royal and nonroyal oral traditions shows that there is a major transformation of religious institutions during this period. These changes merit closer review, for they signal fundamental political realignments, the creation of new institutions, and the final consolidation of Babito power and authority at the expense of the indigenous clans associated with iron-working.

The distribution of sand from the kings' graves precipitated the creation of a new possession cult, one that successfully rivaled the Bacwezi cult. The kings' spirits possessed a person in each location where the sand was distributed, and the king built all necessary cult houses, staffed each *gashani* (royal burial estate) with a symbolic queen mother, a virgin, and eighteen cows. This process has clear implications for a more extensive Babito hegemony throughout Kiziba. Land was appropriated, a new redistributive system to supply the needs of the cult leaders was put into effect, and representatives of the kings were placed throughout the kingdom. The symbolic structure of the new cult was opposed to the Bacwezi in all domains of activity, successfully neutralizing Bacwezi opposition to the Babito. Royal legitimacy was ensured by a new religious institution that not only neutralized the Bacwezi-identified clans—particularly those that were iron-workers—but also helped to establish a new geopolitical presence on the landscape.

This short explanation of change in social institutions seen in Kiziba history takes on more meaning against the backdrop of Kyamutwara history. In Kyamutwara, royal consolidation is coeval with Kiziba but focuses much more on royal attempts to wrest power from the Bayango, the first ironworkers. The Bahinda of Kyamutwara appear to have avoided the kind of confrontation with the Bacwezi that characterizes the Babito experience in Kiziba. However, it is also noteworthy that the first six or seven kings (depending on which genealogy is being consulted) located their capitals in the interior, away from the heavily populated coastal zone, where indigenous clans such as the Bayango and Batundu were entrenched. The Bahinda incorporated the Bayango into their plan of leadership, for the clan head of the Bayango served as Katikiro or prime minister. The oral traditions of the first kings tell us nothing of difficulties between the Bahinda and indigenous groups until the reign of Kalemera Magango, the sixth king. His history is colored with bloody legend. Known for his vicious response to wives who killed his favorite son, Kalemera killed all but one of his children and most of the mature men in his dominion (Schmidt 1978).

The repressive rule of Kalemera can be seen as a period when force was used by the Bahinda to overcome internal opposition to the royal line. Ultimately this strategy proved misguided, for subsequent to Kalemera the kingdom slipped back into the hands of the Bayango (see table 2.1). Although the royal histories acknowledge no interregnum, it is abundantly clear that Kalemera's one living son, whom he blinded, was illegitimate. Kayango—the Katikiro or prime minister—assumed the throne in the absence of a Hinda successor after Kalemera's death. Structural analysis of the oral traditions about Kalemera, his blind son Kiume, and Kiume's illegitimate son Mahe shows that the oral traditions are structured according to formulas derived from ancient Bacwezi epic myth (Schmidt 1978). The mixing of Bacwezi mythological paradigms with Bahinda royal history creates a new contiguity, a new syntagmatic relationship between elements of Bacwezi and Bahinda history. This textual contiguity leads to a historical concatenation that combines and unifies two domains of history that are from "absolutely separate wholes" (Ricoeur 1977: 56).

The new combination of historical attributes, the mixing of historical domains, is clearly metonymic and marks a state of profound transformation during the reign of Rugomora Mahe. It is a mystification that creates the illusion of Bahinda continuity with the past. It makes the alien Bahinda history appear to be indigenous and natural, a process that leads to a legitimacy for the Bahinda. Metonymic transformations may also be seen in the naming of Bacwezi actors with Bahinda names, so that the Bahinda take on Bacwezi attributes. Structural comparison between the Kitara epic and Bahinda oral history helps us understand why the traditions associated with Rugomora Mahe are so much more elaborate than those of any other king and how the derived traditions function within the context of royal history.

The reestablishment of Bayango rule in Kyamutwara was a political crisis for the Bahinda. It meant that the indigenous clan associated with symbols and myths of ironworking remained in control of the political system and the productive economy. It was essential that Bahinda find a way to neutralize Bayango power and to obtain an equivalent kind of legitimacy. This fell to Rugomora Mahe, who returned eventually from exile in Uganda and found his kingdom ravaged by famine—with no crops and rain because of the king's absence. Rugomora Mahe ("he who satisfies," as he came to be known) first entered into an alliance with Mugasha, the rain-making cult of Kyamutwara dominated by the Batundu clan.[5] This alliance took advantage of a local political competition between the Bayango (with Bacwezi identity) and the Mugasha cult of rainmakers—a theme also played out in sacred Bacwezi myth.

When Rugomora Mahe returned to Buhaya, he came with magical trees and an iron hammer given to him by Mugasha. On his trek to his new palace site, the Bahinda king planted the iron hammer on land belonging to the Bayango (north of today's Bukoba town),[6] and, he planted the magical trees on farms belonging to other important clans. This process is parallel to that in Kiziba, where soil from graves is planted, symbolically displacing the local owners and establishing the direct authority of the king over those places. In this instance the symbol of power is an iron hammer. It neutralized the ironworking symbolism already associated with the Bayango. The planting of the iron hammer of Rugomora Mahe on land belonging to the Bayango may also be seen as a metonymic transformation, one that introduces a new contiguity in which the iron symbolism of the Bayango is juxtaposed to and spatially identified with that of the Bahinda.

I have previously introduced the idea that the isolation of metonymic transformations also points to periods of profound change, when symbol systems often undergo significant manipulation. The history of King Rugomora Mahe provides several important insights into this process. Among the symbolic manipulations of Rugomora Mahe is his altered relationship with ironworkers. As Rugomora Mahe made his way to his new capital site in Katuruka, he encountered ironworkers known as the Bamani.[7] When he passed by, the craftsmen continued to work without greeting him. He took affront at their refusal to acknowledge him and, determined that they be punished, he called them the Bahuge, "the forgetful ones." By renaming them, Rugomora Mahe established his domination and authority over this group, for they have thereafter been known by this derogatory name. Their status was changed from independent to subordinate ironworkers. This metonymic naming process is a powerful symbolic act that sets the scene for a change in the social relations of production—where the Bahinda come to directly control the once-independent ironworking groups.

We have seen, then, that the Bayango and other indigenous clans are among the primary targets in Bahinda attempts to co-opt powerful iron symbolism. The selection of a capital site by Rugomora Mahe is consistent with that pattern, for he returned to the village of his peasant mother and wife, where his diviners determined that he should build his new palace. He placed his palace on the site occupied by the *kaiija* shrine tree (fig. 2.3). It is highly probable that this sacred shrine—like its counterpart shrine at Kya Rugomora tree—belonged to the Bayango clan, identified with the origins of ironworking. One of Rugomora Mahe's first moves in consolidating his position was to reaffirm his political alliance with the Mugasha

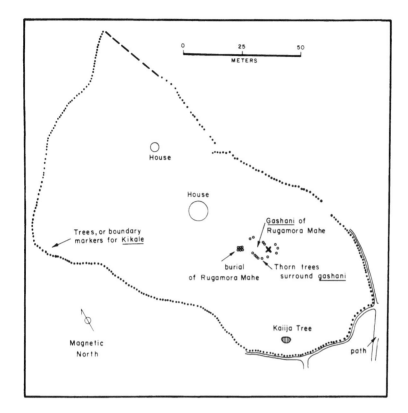

Fig. 2.3 A map of the *kikale* or palace of Rugomora Mahe in Katuruka village. This is an abbreviated version of the former kikale; it is a section dedicated to the *gashani* or burial estate. The most important features are the gashani of the king—with the Mulinzi (*Erythrina abyssinica*) or thorn trees that surround it—and Kaiija tree, which marks the place where the smiths forged iron to build the legendary iron tower to the heavens.

rainmakers (the Batundu) by calling Mugasha to the site and by building a special palace for him. The oral traditions, especially in the presence of mnemonic devices such as the Kaiija shrine, say that this Bahinda king then built an iron tower to the heavens:

> Rugomora Mahe told his smiths that he wanted to build an iron tower high enough to see where the clouds ended. Rugomora Mahe built the tower both in Katuruka and Nkimbo, Kanyangereko. At Nkimbo there is a tree called Kya Rugomora which marks the place where the tower was built. The ironworkers and smiths made the tower so high that the top could not be seen, and then it collapsed, killing many people. Parts of the tower fell as far as Katerero-Omunyoma.[8]

The corporate ownership of the Kaiija shrine by the Bayango ironworkers is affirmed by the fact that the Kya Rugomora shrine tree several kilometers to the southeast (fig. 2.4), where one of the legs of the iron tower was located—is sacred Bayango territory where until recently rituals were carried out during the new moon. However, the origins of Kaiija shrine have been submerged by the long Bahinda identification with the ancient mythology attached to the place. We have seen that two other important Bayango locales (one tied explicitly to the tower, the other north of Bukoba) were seized by the Bahinda. And as the Bayango are directly associated with the origins of ironworking, it is reasonable to conclude that the etiological myth of the iron tower is also linked to the Bayango.

The iron tower myth, sometimes referred to as the Tower of Babel myth, is widespread in Bantu-speaking Africa, especially among the Lunda and Luba of Central Africa.[9] In some of the Haya versions, it is often related as

FIG. 2.4 The *Ficus* shrine tree, Kaiija, is located at the western boundary of the palace of Rugomora Mahe.

a quest on the part of Rugomora Mahe to reach Kazoba, the sun god. Luc de Heusch sees the myth as an attempt by man to gain immortality, an attempt to annihilate time (1982: 58). As a metaphor this fits closely with Bahinda ideology, that is, to annihilate discontinuity between themselves and ancient time and create continuity between their history and the past. De Heusch's (1982) exegesis of solar symbolism in divine kingship in Central Africa and its application to a similar Lunda myth mixed into historical text also helps us to further insights. He sees the quest for the sun as an attempt to unite the terrestrial fire of ironworking and the celestial fire of royalty. The key element here is that Kazoba, the sun god, is a Bacwezi god.[10] Though there is no evidence for solar symbolism in Haya kingship, it is significant that Rugomora Mahe is identified as the active agent who controls the activities of the ironworkers and is on a quest to connect with Kazoba.

If we turn to the mythology of Bunyoro, there is further insight into what the myth may have been like before its appropriation and modification by the Bahinda. There the myth is etiological, as it explains the origins of iron: "In those days Heaven was quite close to earth, it was propped up with a fig tree, a Kirikiti (Erythrina) pole, and a bar of iron. When it had been made quite secure Ruhanga commanded Nkya to remain on earth, while he would go to heaven to see how things were going on there" (Fisher 1970: 70).

The bar of iron in this case is an *axis mundi,* a pillar that links heaven and earth. Ruhanga departed earth in order to escape the corruptions that this creation had caused: "So Ruhanga and Nkya left the earth, and in order to prevent any intercourse between themselves and mankind, they loosened the props that held heaven to earth, so that it departed upward, and the iron bar fell; breaking into pieces, it was scattered all over the world, and provided man with tools and bracelets" (Fisher 1970: 75).

While the cosmic iron tower myth of Kaiija and Kya Rugomora has been stripped of any etiological qualities, its insertion into Bahinda history provides a direct cosmogonic linkage among the Bahinda, the Bacwezi, and the myth associated with ancient iron-producing groups. The myth's association with the Kaiija tree creates a symbolic space, which is then physically occupied by the Bahinda. The Bahinda relationship with the symbolic places is one of contiguity: The Bahinda contained these places within the boundaries of their palace, yet they are literally contained within these ritual and symbolic places—as their history is contained within the associated Bacwezi myth. Thus unfolds a metonymic concatenation—through the agency of synecdoche—of mythological paradigms and symbolic space, whereby Bahinda identity and history are transformed, so as to appear ancient. This ideological mystification draws on the ritual and symbolism associated with iron production, profoundly mystifying in its effect.

The primary source of wealth and power in the industrial sector was iron production. Without the legitimate right to tax production and con-

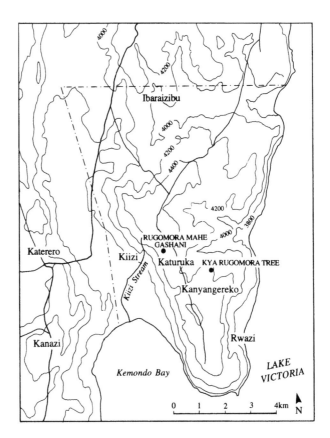

FIG 2.5 Map of the Kanyangereko area showing the relationship of Kaiija shrine to Kya Rugomora shrine tree, another first-
millennium a.d. site. A Urewe-type pot was excavated beneath
the Kya Rugomora tree (Schmidt 1978).

trol the resources used to produce iron, Bahinda hegemony over industrial production was incomplete. Those clans that were associated with
the symbolism of iron production had exclusive power over that mode of
production. As power and political leadership are tied to symbols of iron
production, several questions arise from this exegesis. When did the
Bahinda occupy the Kaiija shrine? How can we be certain that the Kaiija
shrine is associated with ironworking and ancient times? And what in the
symbolism of the site makes it so important?

I will return to these questions when I explore the archaeology of iron
symbolism in chapters 9 and 10. In the meantime, this discussion helps to
explain the role that iron and its attendant symbolic meanings had in the
political and religious history of the Haya over the last four centuries. It
also lays the foundation for more complete understanding of related symbolic meanings that arise during the practice of iron smelting.

3.

Ethnoarchaeology

and

Experiment

in Iron

Technology

African archaeology has long recognized the value of local histories as an essential part of archaeological methodology (Posnansky 1966, 1969; Vansina 1965; Willet 1970; Shaw 1977; Schmidt 1978, 1983b, 1990; Stahl 1994), especially in contexts where local histories are preserved in a genealogical form (Posnansky 1968; Schmidt 1978). Previous research among the Haya illustrates that a comprehensive ethnoarchaeology that incorporates local history is a sensitive and sensible methodology to elicit a diachronic understanding of how and why certain modes of production such as iron production have changed through time and how they have come to gain their contemporary meaning. One danger inherent to ethnoarchaeology is that it focuses almost exclusively on contemporary processes of exploitation of resources, production, consumption, discard, recycling, and other behaviors associated with material culture in a contemporary productive system. An ethnoarchaeology that incorporates both indigenous histories and the ethnohistory recorded by outside observers can overcome some of the shortcomings of a synchronic ethnoarchaeology that looks only to present behavior.

An important source of information in such a holistic ethnoarchaeology is the indigenous history of Buhaya and other Bantu-speaking culture areas with similar technological and political histories. Indigenous history, often falling under the misleading rubric of ethnohistory—a term in common usage for European accounts of non-European societies—is derived from oral traditions and direct historical testimonies.[1] Such histories often provide important facts and interpretations about processes of development and change that are not accessible in written and published histories (Vansina 1965; Schmidt 1978, 1983c). Archaeological investigations offer only a skeletal outline for the past context of a productive system such as ironworking. So it is imperative that we draw upon indigenous histories, assess critically their utility and historical veracity, and apply them as part of a developmental picture that incorporates not just aspects of the technological process, but the social, ideological, economic, and political matrix in which that technology was embedded.

The importance of ethnohistory has been demonstrated for the archaeological interpretation of settlement patterns and political organization in African Iron Age archaeology (e.g., Huffman 1984, 1986), and in the interpretation of rock art in areas where only ethnohistoric accounts of meaning are available (e.g., Lewis-Williams 1981, 1982; Lewis-Williams and Dawson 1994). Ethnohistoric data often elucidate aspects of the African past as diverse as the meaning of rock art to processes of succession responsible for change in the location of royal capital sites, but that positive perspective appears not to apply to complicated technologies such as iron smelting. The histories of iron smelting fall mostly into two categories: indigenous accounts and foreign observations. Each type of evidence has its own distinctive problems.

Foreign observers of iron technology rarely had the expertise to understand the technical aspects of iron production; thus almost all reports on iron technology in Africa have been devoid of scientific value. This arises mainly from the lack of formal scientific training; observers did not know what to look for, and they did not know what data were germane for assessing how a particular iron smelting system operated as it did. There are exceptions, such as Bellamy's now widely cited report of iron smelting in Yoruba, Nigeria, in 1904 and Stanley's study of replication of Shona iron smelting during the 1930s (Bellamy and Harbord 1904; Stanley 1931). These two studies are exceptional in their scientific value, but their obscurity until the last two decades has seriously blunted the impact that they should have had long ago on historical literature.

European accounts, moreover, are often biased according to the beliefs and worldview and historical experience of the observers, an important consideration when we realize that most early descriptions were made by singularly opinionated and strong-minded individuals—explorers, colonial administrators, and missionaries. All, to varying degrees, were preoccupied with the exotic rituals, especially blood sacrifice, that often accompanied iron smelting. The resulting description either dismissed the process as "heathen ritual" or focused almost exclusively on the ritual behavior (Schmidt 1996b).

African accounts are a very different phenomenon. I find that if an informant was not involved directly in the production of iron in a smelting furnace, then his testimony is suspect and often without value. Blacksmiths, for example, often extrapolate their particular knowledge to iron smelting. The two domains of iron production are linked in a productive chain and share symbolic meanings, but technical principles of forging have no applicability to smelting. Similarly, the offspring of iron smelters may have fond memories of watching the process as children, but such recollections are virtually devoid of important technological data. Such accounts may assist us in locating production areas, but people who give secondhand verbal accounts—those who have not participated in the technology themselves—rarely give information of value about exploitative or productive practices.

Caution must also be applied to the most reliable informants—those who were master smelters at a mature age. In most African cultures, many decades have passed since aged informants habitually practiced this complicated technology. Our observations of Haya and Barongo iron smelting indicate the multitude of tasks, each with its proper sequence and its distinctive ideological or technological justification, that make up one smelt. The precise routine of production in which these tasks were performed has been dulled by the passage of a half-century (the Haya) or a quarter-century (the Barongo). Memories have grown dim. Age often has abbreviated recollections into idealized composite pictures. Comparing oral descriptions of iron smelting with the actual behavior of the same iron smelters/informants reveals that most details of technological importance are omitted or glossed over. Verbal description of technical procedures is not part of the tradition. Explanation occurs through performance. These assessments are applied to both written and oral accounts to judge their relative reliability as documents pertinent to technological characterizations. Regardless of such cautionary remarks, it is important to realize that oral histories provided by old smelters can provide valuable evidence, particularly when such accounts affirm the general pattern of work, when they provide an unusual piece of information such as the location of specific resources hitherto unknown, or when they provide a technical observation that departs from other, generalized accounts.

When I first inquired into the history of Haya iron smelting during my investigations, I consulted the oldest ethnography on the Buhaya culture area, Rehse's *Kiziba: Land und Leute* (1910), a work particularly sensitive to material culture and profusely illustrated. Among Rehse's interests was ironworking. He published a photograph of Kiziba iron smelters, some fourteen men posed with bellows mostly on one side of a furnace 70 to 80 centimeters high made with what appears to be blocks of slag (fig. 3.1). The blocks of slag are held in place with numerous short sticks. The photograph was taken at a time that is known to have been an active period of iron smelting in Kiziba.

Close examination of the photo leads one to questions about the authenticity of the furnace depicted. First, there are many more smelters present than could fit around this size furnace. Moreover, sticks would not suffice to keep the furnace wall in place during smelting, and there is a mass of iron ore on the top of the furnace. These problems about the veracity of the photograph were stimulated by contrary information given by the direct historical testimony of men who once smelted iron. Oral histories collected from former smelters revealed that a furnace much larger than the one depicted could accommodate no more than twelve men,

Fig. 3.1 A photograph published by Rehse (1910) purporting to show iron smelters in Kiziba around a smelting furnace. The photograph is staged and not representative of what occurred in this area during iron smelting. The furnace is not constructed of mud and slags, but has been hastily erected with only slag blocks, which are held in place with props. And the putative smelters—14 in number—are too large a number for this size furnace; moreover, they are all gathered on one side of the furnace posing for the photo. However, the smelters are all wearing the traditional *kishenshe* raffia skirt worn by smelters.

that most furnaces were twice as high and built of slag and mud, and that the iron ore was placed both in the bottom of the furnace and mixed with charcoal in the chimney stack.

Local oral histories led us to reject the Rehse photograph and see it for what it was—a staged event with a jerry-built furnace. Yet, had Kiziba resembled most African cultures with their lost knowledge of iron smelting, we might have accepted the photo as an authentic document. This local case study impresses on us that outside perspectives on African iron technology must be approached with strong skepticism and examined most critically. Local oral histories from former smelters may provide important evidence, as they did in this instance. But the contradictory information provided by informants was not technical; it was germane to a general description of the process, not technical procedures. In this case the idealized, summary descriptions were significant.

This realization that life histories of iron smelters and interviews about their technological knowledge can often uncover important information (particularly about technologies on which there is little recorded evidence) developed during 1969 and 1970, a time when there were many more living smelters in a once-active iron smelting area between Kemondo Bay and the Kerebe bridge over the Ngono River. Interviews with former iron smelters revealed certain information that was eventually critical to our idea that the Haya iron smelters may have used a technique that resulted in a hot air blast, or preheated air blast, inside the furnace. The oral histories covered apparently mundane descriptions such as the variable sizes of furnaces, the placement of the tuyeres (blow pipes) inside the furnace, and an outline of furnace construction (Schmidt 1974, 1978). These interviews took on great importance, for they suggested that scientific observation of Haya iron smelting techniques, particularly the placement of the tuyeres inside the furnace (documented in these early interviews), could help to explain an apparent technological anomaly—high temperatures for slag formation—confronted during our analysis of slags from Early Iron Age smelting furnaces at the Rugomora Mahe site.

Genesis of the Preheating Hypothesis

One of the steps that I took during our analysis of technological materials of the Rugomora Mahe site was heat analysis of slags that were excavated from EIA smelting furnaces (Schmidt 1978, 1981). Our goal was to observe the temperatures at which the slag began to slump and show liquid characteristics, working on the rough assumption that we could approximately replicate the temperatures at which the slag was formed.[2] At that time, twenty-four years ago, this was an unusual test to apply to African prehistoric slags, though today it is a lesser test among more powerful chemical tests and microscopic examinations that more accurately determine temperatures at which slags are formed. Nonetheless, the tests results were significant, for they suggested that these prehistoric slags had been formed at temperatures between 1,350 and 1,400°C (Schmidt 1978, 1981, 1983a).

These results contradicted the European bloomery model that said that slag was formed at approximately 1,150 to 1,250°C—upper limit 1,300°C. Why and how did the ancient furnaces operate at temperatures sufficient to produce such slag? With the assistance of Donald H. Avery, a metallurgist at Brown University, the preheating hypothesis was formulated to explain how higher than expected temperatures had been obtained in the past. Avery and I (Schmidt and Avery 1978) reasoned that if the clay pipe or tuyere had been placed inside the smelting furnace, then the clay would have been heated to high temperatures and air expressed through the pipe would have picked up heat from the pipe, preheating the air. Preheated air introduced into an African iron smelting furnace would have significantly altered the thermodynamics of iron smelting. It would have increased the flame temperature by an amount theoretically equal to the preheat, assuming no significant heat losses (Schmidt and Avery 1978; Avery and Schmidt 1979).

The viability of this hypothesis was further affirmed by our observations of broken tuyere fragments, some 39 percent of which displayed physical properties such as slag deposition, vitrification, and reduction (black coloring of the clay)—all characteristics that supported the idea that the tuyeres had been inside the prehistoric furnaces. We proposed then, but could not confirm, that preheating by this technique had led to high furnace temperatures when used by early ironworking peoples in this coastal lake environment.

The technological and historical implications of this hypothesis were immense. Because it conserves fuel and leads to more efficient reduction of iron at elevated temperatures, preheating is a more efficient way to smelt iron. If it was employed during the ancient past in Africa, then its different thermodynamic effects would have led to a formation process in the iron distinct—in its own genius and inventiveness—from that of the bloomery of prehistoric Europe or that practiced elsewhere in Africa. History tells us that once the principle of preheating caught hold in Europe, productivity increased by as much as threefold in the steel industry. Such increases have a transforming effect on any economy.

If our hypothesis, generated from our observations of archaeological analysis and the historical testimonies of elderly iron smelters, was valid, testable, and ultimately confirmed, then its importance to the technological history of Africa would be manifest. Confirmation would mean that a revolutionary technological innovation had been discovered and perfected in Africa almost two thousand years ago. This would suggest that the evolutionary trajectory in iron technology had taken a very different direction from that of Eurasia. If such a technology existed, it begged to be explained.

When I felt confident that we had isolated a scientific problem which we could use to question popular and scholarly historical interpretations of African technology, my commitment to a scientific and humanistic inquiry deepened. I decided to use replicable scientific tests that would obtain data both relevant and adequate to the tests. To avoid a tautology, that is, a circular and logically invalid argument, I needed data that were independent of the archaeological information responsible for the hypothesis. As I began to plan a scientific strategy, I again turned to a group of texts from oral interviews with former smelters in Buhaya collected by my brother, M. T. Schmidt, during his 1969 sojourn with iron smelters in Kianja. Though imprecise on technical questions, these interviews were invaluable in establishing that the tuyeres were inserted inside recent historical furnaces (Schmidt 1978).

The 1969 interviews instilled confidence that an independent context existed for the testing of the preheating hypothesis. If I could find former iron smelters able and willing to smelt again for us, then I would, ideally, have a nonarchaeological setting in which I could test the hypothesis as well as conduct an ethnoarchaeological study of ironworking in Buhaya. Immediately after I finished writing up the initial research in 1974, I returned to Buhaya to survey smiths and former smelters who lived in Kikukwe village, about 10 kilometers south of the Uganda border. This initial reconnaissance turned up two former smelters who said that they remembered how to smelt, knew other smelters in a village across the swamp, and felt confident that they could organize such a project.

After these assurances, I proposed research among the smelters of Kikukwe-Nyungwe that would (1) test the hypothesis for preheating in a context where the clay blow pipes are placed inside the furnace, and (2) build material-behavioral models based on this recent, recuperated technology that could be used to interpret more accurately the residues of technological processes found in the archaeological record. The first aspect of the research is what I call experimental ethnoarchaeology, in which specific scientific hypotheses are tested in an "ethnographic" setting. There were two dimensions to the experiment. I intended to conduct explicit tests of an experimental hypothesis with as little disruption as possible to the technological process. I also keenly recognized that our request to the iron smelters of Kiziba not only was a transformation of contemporary reality (by the artificial resurrection of a long-nonfunctional part of the past) but also would be a series of experiments for them as they struggled to regain the skills that were once an unconscious part of their lives.

The second goal was to build material-behavioral models from this research that could be applied to the archaeological record to interpret prehistoric similarities and differences in technology. This aspect of the research, essential for assessing change and continuity between the past and present, is more in the mainstream of ethnoarchaeology, wherein, by using a comparative method (Gould and Watson 1982), I try to establish the material consequences of specific kinds of technological and exploitative behaviors. Yet, any ethnoarchaeology that intrudes upon the consciousness of those being observed transforms the behavior of the subject population, as they adapt to and accommodate the peculiar behavior of the investigator. I want to make explicit my recognition of the effect of these investigations on daily life, as well as the significant amount of change that has occurred in the productive economy over the last sixty years.

In this experimental procedure, I realized that I first had to determine that the preheating hypothesis was testable: that is, if blowpipes are placed inside an iron smelting furnace, then is it possible to devise an adequate test and gather data that are germane to the hypothesis? This led us to construct an experimental furnace, an eclectic design based on Haya descriptions and observations of structurally similar furnaces build by the Dime in southwestern Ethiopia (Childs and Schmidt 1985; Todd 1985). Although there were problems in the experimental design and we did not succeed in smelting iron, we did show that it was possible to demonstrate some preheating in a clay tube inserted inside the furnace. These results, though ambiguous, lent support to the idea that the research could proceed in an experimental ethnographic context.

The Experiential Setting: Northwestern Tanzania

The next step occurred during July 1976, when we returned to Buhaya with the express purpose of conducting our experimental ethnoarchaeology among the Haya smiths and smelters. Our introduction to Nyungwe village, a subsection of Kikukwe in the former Kiziba kingdom, took place in early July. Our initial interviews revealed that there were four active forges in this village of approximately fifty households. None of the active smiths had direct knowledge of smelting, but they were able to introduce us to three elders who had once smelted iron.

I found our first negotiations with these experts very difficult, as these former smelters were reluctant to interrupt their daily activities to engage in an activity that they had abandoned five decades before. They saw no reason to resurrect this almost forgotten technology. The most senior of the smelters at first refused to participate, while a second was too aged to be involved actively. The senior smith, along with one of the smelters, eventually prevailed upon the head smelter to participate. Until he committed himself several days later, two smiths called together all the younger men in the village who had any experience with ironworking to discuss the issue and to learn if it was possible to recruit necessary labor for the endeavor. This palaver led to the conclusion that they would be giving up other productive enterprises and would be engaged in daily labor, so they should be financially recompensed.[3]

This seemed a fair request, though I was concerned that interviews and collection of other relevant background and contextual data not be in-

cluded in this agreement. With the assistance of a local government official, we concluded a satisfactory contract for the remuneration of labor. It
was apparent from the start that recruitment of labor posed a problem for
the study. In the past, iron smelting required eight smelters and a head or
supervising smelter as well as young apprentices who participated as relief for the primary bellows operators. The availability of only two smelters
from Nyungwe and two from neighboring Ishozi village posed real problems about expertise. It also meant that labor recruitment would in no
way resemble the intralineage and intraclan recruitment that likely prevailed when ironworking groups were still independent in Buhaya—before the late seventeenth century—and that still occurred in some locales
as late as the early twentieth century.

The two organizing elders were compelled to go to the ranks of local
smiths, who at least understood the arduous task of bellows operations.
For tasks other than the smelting itself, the elders recruited young men to
perform the manual labor required for many of the subsidiary tasks such
as grass cutting, charcoal making, and ore mining. The smiths, busy with
their profitable trade, refused to engage in these smelting enterprises without assistance from younger men. Thus, the organization of work bore no
resemblance to past circumstances, when each individual smelter used to
be responsible for gathering, in a communal work group, the iron ore and
charcoal that he would need for a given number of smelts. These resources
would then be used to conduct smelts on a rotational basis, with each
smelter contributing the resources for one smelt. All iron from the smelt
then went to the one individual, except a share for the head smelter and a
portion for the king.

The former system of resource procurement was clearly much more
efficient than the labor-intensive system devised by the elders, who themselves were unable to do manual labor. Hence, it became apparent that
any attempt to study labor input in this context and to measure efficiency
would be a futile exercise. The young laborers had no familiarity with the
work, nor did they have a strong motive to work efficiently. This contrast
with past practices made it clear that our observations of the preparatory
and procurement processes were more valuable for understanding resource
location, standards of acceptability, and processing of raw materials than
any understanding of labor requirements.

After several days of organization, the smelters and their helpers traveled south to Bwanjai-Karuyenje, a mine approximately 12 kilometers
away.[4] They chose this mining site after long discussion about another site
that they had also once worked near the swamp north of Mugana Catholic
mission at Kantale (fig. 3.2). Karuyenje was the last site that they had worked
during the 1920s. A much more prominent mining site is located closer to
the north in Kikukwe, but by 1976 the mining pits on this site had been
filled in because of the danger they posed to cattle. The smelters also
remembered Kikukwe as a dangerous mine that had claimed several lives
through cave-ins during the early part of this century. At Karuyenje we

found six clear mining pits ranging in depth from 1 to 2.5 meters deep and 1 to 2 meters in diameter. There were several other outlines of pits that had apparently been filled by erosion. Karuyenje was located near the base of a hill about 10 meters above the swamp that separates Bwanjai from Gera.

The head smelter directed the workmen to begin excavations in the largest open mining shaft. Detritus filled the bottom, but when it was removed, it was apparent that there was no ore on the floor of the shaft. The following day, mining resumed in the same pit and an adjacent pit with the use of an *enshumo,* a long curved pick, round in cross-section (fig. 3.3). This tool was used to scour the edges of the pits in order to locate peripheral deposits and dislodge iron ore. Loose fill around the margins of the pits indicated that the contiguous areas had already been mined and the shafts refilled with mining debris returned by erosion. The smelters remarked that they had previously found deposits in an already known

FIG. 3.2 Map showing the location of Nyungwe village and the mining location of Karuyenje. Other mines are marked with a triangle symbol.

Fɪɢ. 3.3 An *enshumo* mining pick in use at the Karuyenje mines, as the smelters and their laborers dig into an old working.

Fɪɢ. 3.4 Laborers removing iron ore from a new mining pit at Karuyenje. An old mine is under the tree located behind the young man in the white shirt next to the bucket. The iron ore processing area is located to the right rear.

and proven area by simply putting down random pits until hitting an undisturbed deposit. They finally decided to do this the third day, coming on a satisfactory ore deposit at −1.8 meters during the fourth day (fig. 3.4).

Once the ore was removed from the 1 × 2 meter pit, it was laid out to dry on one side of the shaft. At this point it was remembered that a special cylindrical basket with a loose weave called an *ensharo* (see fig. 3.17 for one in use during charcoal processing) was required to remove dirt from the ore so that it could be inspected and the fines could be sifted out. These specialized baskets are found only in one village to the northwest, Ruzinga, so a special messenger was dispatched to purchase as many as possible. The next day mining resumed, with the head smelter agitating the iron ore in the one ensharo basket obtained. Clouds of dust surrounded him while he removed the dirt by abrasion. After the ore was processed this way, the dark gray and heavier chunks were removed to natural anvils, flat sandstone boulders where the workmen and smiths began to beat them with hammers and hammer stones.

A circular section of twisted grass, *engata*, was used to contain the 1- to-2-centimeter pieces when they shattered (fig. 3.5). Only the two elder smelters understood the process at this point, and they had to instruct all the other participants in the selection process. The head smelter quickly lost patience with those who did not immediately catch on to ore process- ing, as he constantly threatened to fire or beat those who erred. Accept- able ore was judged by sight and apparent density. A dark gray color, even black, is preferred, and the ore should be heavy; this type is called *kasina*. The second variety, *musa*, is red or orange and often mottled with gray and black spots; musa is not considered as good as kasina, but it is ac- cepted and used. The remainder, especially if it displays any sign of ka- olin, is waste referred to as *bibale*, or "no ore." This is a term derived from

Fɪɢ. 3.5 One of the two head smelters, Ta Norbert Kajuna, (*on right*), is assisted by a smith while breaking up iron ore in an *engata*. It is then sorted by color and weight.

the word for iron ore, *embale.* A sample of processed ore showed that 52 percent of the material processed was accepted for smelting.

During the ensuing days we observed variable rates of processing, but at their best the workmen prepared approximately 4 kilograms per hour of high-grade ore. Once the ore was processed, it was then wrapped in a long banana bast and grass package, *mushenga* (fig. 3.6), suspended on a stick (or made rigid with the stick if one man was carrying the bundle) for transportation to the smelting site (fig. 3.7). At this juncture the head smelter called together the group to discuss several of the primary taboos associated with iron smelting. He emphasized that women should not touch the iron ore and that menstruating women in particular must not touch it or the smelt would certainly fail to produce iron. With great solemnity he announced to all the men who would be participating as smelters that they must stop all sexual intercourse at least three days before smelting or the smelt would not be successful.

Once the ore arrived at the smelting site, it was laid out to dry in the sun for several days before the smelting (fig. 3.8). At the drying site the head smelter delivered a spontaneous public warning about how menstruating women must be kept away during this vulnerable time when the ore is exposed. This explanation by the head smelter was the first *public* acknowledgment of ritual taboos that had not been discussed previously with us.

FIG. 3.6 Packing the iron ore in grass and banana bast, making a *mushenga* for transportation of the ore.

FIG. 3.7 Ta Norbert carrying a mushenga filled with iron ore from the Karuyenje mines.

FIG. 3.8 Iron ore set out to sun-dry before the smelting begins.

Prior to the commencement of any activities associated with iron-working, I had interviewed each of the former smelters. All had vehemently denied that there were any rituals associated with smelting, though they mentioned the taboo on intercourse. The assertion that no rituals were associated with smelting struck us as exceedingly unlikely, for observation of most related cultures in the Great Lakes region suggested that ritual was a vital part of the process at one time. I initially attributed this reluctance to admit to and discuss ritual to contemporary religious beliefs. Most of the elders were converted Christians and clearly feared retribution from the church. Later events confirmed this as the reason for their denial of ritual. The prohibition on menstruating women, however, was a most important revelation. It was the first acknowledgment that material that went inside the furnace must not be associated with a state of menstruation. A menstruating woman is at the height of her fertile powers, whereas the male smelters are also in a state of heightened fertility: the sexual "hotness" (as the Haya say) of the abstaining smelter. I will return to the importance of these beliefs in chapters 9 and 10, particularly with a deeper consideration of menstruation taboos and their deeper symbolic importance in the metaphoric reproductive cycle of iron smelting.

I observed that with the close proximity of ore processing to the mining pits, the detritus and overburden are situated very close to the pits and quickly wash back into them during the rains. This, and the fact that some of the previous pits were already half-filled, would suggest that all signs of mines could be obscured within one or two centuries. In this instance the iron ore deposit was concentrated between −180 and −240 centimeters as a shale in which the iron had been hydrodeposited from leached laterite. Decomposed sandstone from an outcrop higher on the hill was found mixed with lateritic soil in the overlying deposits.

After five days of earnest but often interrupted mining, the head smelter concluded that there was sufficient iron ore processed for six smelts. Attention was then turned to the collection of large blocks of slag used to build the furnace superstructure. These large blocks of slag were obtained from farms within the village where the elders had themselves once smelted. Called *empiga,* the slag skulls were circular in shape, sometimes donutlike, about 70 to 90 centimeters in diameter and about 10 to 15 centimeters thick. They had been formed by slag dripping and draining around swamp grasses (*Miscanthidium violaceum*) to the bottom of the furnace (fig. 3.9). Many slag blocks had been incorporated into fences that demarcated farms, and some were still in a circular form. The collection of these slags was essential to the construction of the furnace foundation.

Ironically, the initiation of the experiment was now leading to the removal of archaeological evidence. I noted each site's characteristics as the process continued with the trimming and shaping of larger blocks. Slag was also broken up into smaller pieces, *bigaliro,* to be used with mud to construct the upper portion of the furnace. The slag was very porous and filled with air spaces caused by the penetration of grasses.

FIG. 3.9 A large slag skull, discarded after smelting in the 1920s, is pried from a Nyungwe hillside for use as an *empiga,* one of the foundation blocks of the smelting furnace. This large donut-shaped piece would subsequently be broken in half. This activity created certain tensions for the investigators, for the material evidence that marked former smelting sites was carried off to build furnaces, thus lessening the visibility of these sites on the landscape.

It was clear that this material would make an excellent refractory construction material, since air pockets retard the conduction of heat through the slag wall. As more sites were exploited for empiga, the head smelter began to reject some earlier choices as too fluid looking and replaced them with those that contained more air spaces. I should note that the technology itself would have altered older smelting sites because of the recycling of slag for furnace construction. Further transformation takes place when slag is recycled for other uses. It is often moved to new locales for fencing and is used to build homes, common occurrences anywhere smelting was plentiful during the last several centuries. These practices caution us that any attempt to estimate productivity based on extant slag heaps may be naive and potentially meaningless. Moreover, for hundreds of years slag has been used as tempering material in domestic pottery in Buhaya. These various recycling activities have significantly altered the industrial landscape. No archaeologist should assume that slag heaps are pristine, untouched waste heaps. Slag is a resource often widely utilized by cultures in subsistence, domestic, ritual, and technological activities. The Barongo recycling of slag as an integral part of the smelting process is an unambiguous lesson that slag is not a static phenomenon or a waste product (Schmidt 1996c).

The procurement of clay to make the tuyeres was of special interest, for if the smelters placed the tuyeres inside their furnace, then a high-quality refractory clay would be necessary to withstand the high furnace temperatures. Much discussion preceded the trek to obtain clay. The elders refused to go 1.5 kilometers south to Buchwero, located at the edge of the large swamp that borders Nyungwe on its east. Heavy rains had flooded the site where they used to obtain tuyere clay for smelting. This problem necessitated a compromise choice, a clay from Kikukwe-Ibanga, some 8 kilometers to the north. The Ibanga clay source was not a swamp like Buchwero, but a small stream originating in a seepage some 100 meters from the swamp and about 4 meters higher. A blue-gray clay was mined from a depth of 45 centimeters. The local landowner, a smith, said that he knew that this clay had been used for at least four generations to make tuyeres for the forge. The use of a clay adequate for forging tuyeres was a decision that would have serious and negative implications for iron smelting.

Once the clay was brought back to the smelting site, there was another discussion about whether pulverized slag or sherds from old tuyeres and pottery should be used as tempering material in the tuyere clay. Both views were argued strongly until it was decided to proceed with slag, a material commonly used to temper clay used for pottery and in forging tuyeres, not smelting tuyeres. This was a case where the specialized technological knowledge of the smiths was accepted, as we will see, at the expense of the advice of the head smelter. Small pieces of slag were brought near the smelting site, where they were pulverized on nearby boulders. The very fine slag powder was then mixed into the clay by kneading and pounding the clay with feet.

During clay-tempering activities on the second day, a dispute erupted between the head smelter and his smith assistants over the slag-tempering material and the size of the slag inclusions. The head smelter insisted that he had never before used slag as tempering; rather, he had crushed used tuyeres (grog). Moreover, he objected strenuously to the size of the crushed slag, saying that it was much too fine. Initially the smiths prevailed on this point, but less than an hour later the head smith had divided the clay into several batches, some of which were set aside to await advice on grog tempering by the head smelter's maternal uncle from Ishozi village. Once well mixed, the tempered clay was taken to a shady banana grove, where the *enkero* or tuyere manufacture began. A 20 × 20 × 25 centimeter block of clay is slipped over the end of a specially carved shaft (*mubumbiro*) which is coated with ash to keep the clay free of the wood. The clay is then molded around the mandrel until it reaches a length of 50 to 60 centimeters (fig. 3.10). This results in a tube with walls approximately 12 to 15 millimeters thick and an internal diameter of approximately 3.7 to 4.0 centimeters, depending on the size of the mandrel. A 15-centimeter-wide flare is then added to one end. Once completed, the tuyere is slipped from the stick and set upright in the sun to dry. The supervising elders had to instruct the smiths in the proper dimensions. A running dialogue ensued

FIG. 3.10 Ta Norbert, one of the two head smelters, forming a tuyere around a *mubumbiro,* using ash to lubricate the mandrel.

FIG. 3.11 The furnace pit is excavated after being marked out by small stakes.

between two smiths and the head smelter, who constantly instructed, objected, and occasionally interjected his own hand to correct mistakes.

During the first day of tuyere manufacture, the head smelter also organized the excavation of the furnace pit. The site was situated on the edge of Nyungwe's southwesternmost farmstead and approximately 9 meters from an active forge, or luiija, that belonged to one of the older smiths. A primary reason for the site selection was the availability of unused land that belonged to a participating smith. Oral testimony indicates that in the past, smelting was sometimes located inside the village, but usually in a peripheral zone outside the observation of other villagers. This removed the smelt from public view and helped maintain technological secrets and the aura of mystery and magic that surrounds the process. Shade from the afternoon sun was also a consideration in siting the furnace. A circular area was marked out with a stick and a string and then excavated to a depth of approximately 60 to 70 centimeters (fig. 3.11). However, the first time the pit was excavated, it was taken down to a depth of 1.05 meters and made 1.85 meters in diameter. The elders, uncomfortable with its size, mocked up part of a furnace wall on the edge of a pit to check its dimensions, but came to no clear decision on the issue. A small trench 30 centimeters wide and 15 centimeters deep was then excavated around the circumference of the pit 18 centimeters from its edge.

During the excavation of the furnace pit, workmen traveled a short distance from the site to a termite hill at the same altitude. Earth was re-

Fɪɢ. 3.12 In a reversal of the smiths' influence over decision making, the assistants break up pottery sherds and pieces of tuyere to make grog tempering for tuyeres.

moved from the mound and carried back to the site, where it was pulverized and later mixed with water several meters from the pit. The following day the head smelter voiced his clear discontent with the large size of the pit. He had also concluded that the tuyeres would henceforth be tempered with small (2 to 4 mm) pieces of broken pot and tuyere (fig. 3.12). These changes in procedure resulted from the serious questions that the head smelter had raised about both these steps in the process. When his own memory was vague on particulars, he was initially ignored by the younger smiths, who self-confidently proceeded, using knowledge based only on their experience with iron forging. One consequence of these contradictions was a dialogue often raised to an acrimonious and feverish pitch as the head smelter attempted to badger and threaten the smiths to do it his way. Our later observations confirmed that the head smelter was correct in his assessments of tuyere tempering and size of the furnace pit.

As a consequence of the altered plan of work, the workmen and smiths were instructed to fill in the bottom of the pit with approximately 30 centimeters of fill; no other modifications were made to lessen the diameter of the pit. Work continued with the wetting of the earthen wall and the application of the termite mud to the wall and the pit bottom. As the mud walling rose some 30 centimeters above the floor, chopped straw was added to the mud as reinforcement (fig. 3.13). This material covered the upper wall, the partition between the pit and the trench, and the trench itself. Mud was thrown and then packed by being paddled with feet, with

Fɪɢ. 3.13 The earth from a termite mound is mixed with water and straw to make a construction paste. While such earth seems not to confer any technological advantage (Childs 1986), it seems possible that wetting of the cementing substance secreted by termites may provide a firmer mud less inclined to crack and spall.

the final finish applied using a slurry. The final internal diameter at the top of the bowl was 137 centimeters; it was 85 centimeters wide at the bottom and 63 centimeters deep.

In the meantime tuyeres were being made by three of the smiths; they produced about two tuyeres per hour, while workmen descended to the eastern swamp to cut and bundle Ishanga grass (*Miscanthidium violaceum*). A tall reedlike grass that grows in tufts in the peat swamp, this is one of the important components in the smelting process. Large bundles 80 centimeters in diameter and 3 meters long were transported from the swamp and stored to the south of the furnace site for drying (fig. 3.14). Cutting of Ishanga grass continued for several days, as between twelve and fourteen bundles, each weighing 15 to 20 kilograms dry, are needed for each smelt.

As the furnace liner and the Ishanga grass dried, the smiths and several workmen traveled across the western swamp to Bugwe forest, some 2 kilometers from dry ground. Most of the journey to the swamp forest is through Ishanga grass and then *Syzygium cordatum* swamp trees that fringe the forest. Inside the forest they constructed two charcoal-burning platforms, 3 to 4 meters in diameter, from peat in the surrounding deposits. They selected the Mucwezi tree, *Syzygium guineense,* as the preferred wood for making charcoal. The stand appeared to be predominantly this species, and trees varying in size from 8 centimeters to 50 centimeters were felled nearby (fig. 3.15). The trunks were cut into 60-centimeter sections and then split into rails 10 to 15 centimeters thick. The wood was

FIG. 3.14 Bundles of *Miscanthidium violaceum* or Ishanga grass being carried from the swamp—where it was harvested—to the smelting site for drying prior to smelting.

FIG. 3.15 Assistants to the smelters felling and cutting *Syzygium guineense* (Mucwezi, sing.) trees in Bugwe forest for charcoal burning.

carried to the platforms and stacked in 2-meter hexagons until several meters high. Once the stack was solid with wood, tinder was ignited and the wood began to burn wet. The burning went on for about two hours as the smiths stirred the wood to ensure combustion. As the pile collapsed into a heap of charcoal and embers, the smiths who were gathered around the platform removed the few remaining burning rails and doused the fire with water from the surrounding ditch. This marks one of the final steps in what is a long and messy process, a time when a song about the importance of what they have done begins. They sing of producing in the domain of women, of making charcoal for the hearth that cooks well, that gives birth to living matter. (See chapter 9 for more details.)

While the song was being sung, the pile of charcoal was soaked thoroughly and then stirred before the smiths and their helpers began to refine and sort the charcoal (fig. 3.16). This was done by placing the charcoal in small baskets (ensharo) with an open weave and agitating them to remove the fines. The amount of fines removed varied according to the size of the openings in the baskets, but monitoring showed that about 19 percent of the charcoal by weight was discarded in this way. The wet wood was weighed prior to burning and the charcoal after burning; we found that the charcoal weighed 10 percent of the wet wood weight.[5] This distillation process is not as efficient as an enclosed burn under reducing conditions.

FIG. 3.16 A smith, accomplished in charcoal burning and acting as an assistant to the head smelters, uses a basket to sift charcoal—removing fines—from a recently doused charcoal fire in Bugwe forest. The small pile of wood burning in the background was rebuilt from partially burned and unburned rails in the main burn.

FIG. 3.17 Pouring charcoal into a *gunia* (gunny sack) for transport across Bugwe swamp to the smelting site.

A significant amount of energy value is lost under the oxidizing conditions that prevail during much of the burn. The residue of fines on the burning platforms is distinctive in its discrete and restricted location. One should be able to recognize similar phenomena should they appear in the archaeological record, especially in sections of swamp cores taken for vegetational histories.

Carrying 30 kilometers of charcoal on one's head through the swamp is demanding work (fig. 3.17). It is also an exquisite dance from tuft to tuft, featuring balance, strength, and grace. Without those skills (and without loads) I struggled, constantly falling into the swamp. Once removed from the swamp, the charcoal was stored in a protected environment—the nearby forge. Even then its storage caused concern that it might be polluted by the presence of menstruating women. Close watch was kept, but the forge's vulnerability during the night left open the possibility that hostile forces might gain access to the charcoal. The elders had estimated about six gunia (gunny sacks) of charcoal for each smelt, or between 130 kilograms (dry) and 180 kilograms of charcoal. This was the difference between dry and wet weights. During subsequent years (1979, 1984) the charcoal had more time to dry, so that an average bag of dried charcoal weighed approximately 22 kilograms. In 1976, after many years' absence from smelting and during the rush to get a successful experiment going, this important detail was overlooked. Bags of charcoal used during some of our first smelts came from the swamp for immediate use and weighed as much as 33 kilograms. This 50 percent additional weight was caused by water saturation during the dousing phase. The use of water-saturated charcoal caused the failure of one smelt and adversely affected at least two others.

At this juncture in the experiment, I began to gain insight into how the experiment could be manipulated by certain participants to their advantage, particularly in matters of status and remuneration. Suffice it to say that the eldest smith thought that his participation in the process stopped at pumping the bellows. He considered this activity the business of younger folk, especially children and young apprentices in the forge. But participation in the project had been determined by the smelters on the basis of one's possession of a bellows and some knowledge of ironworking. The elders handled the crisis by forfeiting part of their supervisory powers to this smith if he agreed to pump his bellows. This difficult compromise, overseen by the elders, allowed the smelting to proceed. Following these difficult negotiations, the head smelter announced that the taboo against sexual intercourse commenced at this point, prior to the roasting of the ore. He later explained that this taboo normally would have continued throughout the three months of dry season smelting.

Six days before the first smelt and three days after lining the furnace pit, the smiths had completed sixty-six tuyeres, slightly more than thirteen per day, with two smiths working for a total of three and a half hours per day. After an initial batch of eight short tuyeres that the head smelter rejected, the head smelter used a 60-centimeter-long template mandrel to encourage standard length. After thirty-six hours of drying, most of the shrinkage had occurred, with up to 5 percent loss in length and some fine cracking. Repairs were also made to the furnace liner by paddling wet termite earth with a flat stone into the many cracks, some up to 2 centimeters, that had developed.

Before presmelting or roasting the iron ore, I talked with the smelters in greater detail about some of the scientific tests that we wanted to conduct during the smelting. Our concerns were both cultural and scientific. I did not want to do anything that would be upsetting to the smelters, that would violate sacred beliefs surrounding the smelt, that might be seen as contaminating to the process, or that would in some way interfere with the technological process. I recognized that at best the process I would observe would represent a series of experiments, as the iron smelters, the *Bajumba,* struggled to master the nuances of a technology long ago practiced.

I wanted to document the process of innovation and response to adversity that the smelters were almost certain to face, but I did not want our team or team members to become problems ourselves. One of the scientific tests, for example, involved the insertion of thermocouples down into the tuyeres, and I knew from other iron-producing cultures that the tuyeres were associated with sexual meaning. If our scientific apparatus entered the furnace via receptacles with potent symbolic meaning and the smelt failed, then the failure might easily be attributed to us, and the study might be terminated. I simply did not know what to expect when I asked the elders if we could embed chrome-alumel thermocouples in the walls of two tuyeres, two diameters from the tip and 5 millimeters from the inside wall. We hoped this test would show how much heat transfer occurs from the outside to the inside of the hot tuyere. The elders had no objection to this procedure, at least at this stage.

In the several days before the first smelt, scheduled for a Friday, the smiths and their helpers continued to produce charcoal in Bugwe forest. By the time that four days of burning had occurred, a patch some 40 meters across had been cleared in the swamp. Much of this growth was secondary, as many trees ranged from 8 to 20 centimeters in diameter. This species, *Syzygium guineense,* is continually used by other charcoal makers. The smiths do not use Syzygium for forging charcoal, since they prefer a different species called Mishasha (*Saprium ellipticum*), a few of which are found on the margins of the thicker swamp forests and at the edge of swamps.

Smelting proper, from both a technological and an ideological point of view, starts the day before the construction of the furnace. The taboo on sexual intercourse begins with the roasting of the iron ore, which involves the first alteration of the ore. On the day scheduled for roasting the iron ore in the smelting pit, we found the liner in the furnace pit remarkably dry on its surface, though with its considerable thickness it was certain that the interior was still wet. Our Western scientific knowledge almost became an impediment here, as one of our party insisted that the wet clay was bound to blow up and that the smelt was destined to fail as a consequence. But the smelters expressed little concern, and their better sense prevailed over this quickly muted voice.

Roasting the Ore: The First Step in Iron Smelting

The roasting process itself took us by surprise. Our preliminary interviews had not revealed this important step in the smelting process. This underscores how general interviews and even pointed questions often fail to reveal critical aspects of a technological process. Secondary procedures are often not considered to be directly associated with smelting, or the linguistic reference is so esoteric and specialized that without prior knowledge one may fail to elicit responses about specific technological steps.

Roasting began by stacking freshly cut Mucwezi wood in 60-centimeter lengths inside the smelting pit on top of some previously laid tinder. Once the fire had taken hold, the first batch of iron ore, some 26.8 kilograms, was poured over the burning wood and then covered with a heap of wood reaching more than 30 centimeters above the pit's rim (fig. 3.18). With the ignition of the new wood, further ore was added to the fire, and we began to monitor the fire with a chrome-alumel thermocouple inserted inside the fire near the center top. After twenty minutes the temperature rose to 266°C, then rapidly increased to 600°C over the subsequent fifteen minutes. Ore again was added around the circumference of the pit when the elders saw that most of the wood was deeply charred and the embers were consolidated. The remainder of the wood and ore (to the center) was added to the pit, with a total of 84.5 kilograms of ore used, and what we estimated as approximately 250 kilograms of wet wood.[6]

The thermocouple had been moved to the bottom of the pit and buried under the ore changes. It recorded low temperatures after the last major ore charge, and we could see that the ore in the bottom of the pit was being roasted under strongly reducing conditions. After two to two and a half hours there was a rapid temperature rise from 300 to 800°C as the pile of embers collapsed. During this period, the internal fire in the bottom of the pit was observed to be burning quite well, with visible flames. A gas reading showed the CO to be at 7.5 percent, lower than what might be expected at the bottom of the pit. This can be accounted for, however, by the oxygen from the iron ore.

An exothermic reduction of the ore explains the rapid increase in temperature and would provide an O_2 source for burning. The CO reacts with the ore to partially reduce it to a porous iron sponge. When the oxygen from the ore is used up, the flames die back down, and the CO_2 atmosphere reoxidizes the spongy ore to iron oxide and codeposited carbon (Avery and Schmidt 1979). As the thermocouple was placed in the center of one of the last ore pockets to be added, it seemed reasonable to believe that we were monitoring that specific microenvironment within the furnace. As we observed the roast, we could see pieces of ore that remained unbonded. It became clear, then, that this was more than a simple roast in which the water would be driven off, but more on the order of a presmelt.

After this process the head smelter told one of our assistants that he was going to consult an embandwa (spirit medium/diviner) to see if any menstruating women had touched the ore. He was in a state of anxiety about whether the smelt would work the next day.

A similar state of mind prevailed with our consulting metallurgist; he was convinced that only a miracle would suffice to prevent an utter failure. The use of the still-wet furnace pit to roast iron ore defied conven-

FIG. 3.18 Dry wood burning in the partially dried smelting pit that is used to roast the ore. The iron ore is poured onto the wood as it catches fire, leading to a partial reduction of the ore, a presmelting process.

tional wisdom of ceramic engineering, but the termite clay experienced only slight spalling, and the pit remained remarkably solid and intact. Western scientific assumptions vis-à-vis the behavior of the Nyungwe smelters highlighted the dichotomy between Western assumptions of material performance and indigenous scientific knowledge based on long experience and experimentation. These initial contradictions between the two scientific traditions were manifest several times, until the successful experimentation of the smelters eventually impressed upon our team that many of our conventional assumptions about material performance and technological behavior could not stand up against local technological experience and knowledge.

4.

Ethno-

archaeology

and

Bricolage

Engaging

Iron

Smelting

The prelude to actual smelting provided a variety of important insights into crisis management and technological behavior under stress. The Nyungwe smelters as well as their cohorts from Ishozi village to the east had at last admitted the importance of a ritual process that is central to the technology in so many iron smelting cultures in East and Central Africa. Such a compromise of contemporary values unquestionably was threatening to the social legitimacy of the smelters in their home communities. Their decision to continue under traditional ritual values was so sensitive that I have masked their identities in their discussions of these affairs, even though they have asked that their identities be revealed in other publications that have featured their activities.

One theme emerged quite clearly during the operation of the iron smelting furnaces: the smelters understood processes of experimentation and observation. As they experienced failures in materials, the reasons for such failures were often attributed to cultural factors, such as violation of the sexual abstinence taboo. Yet, parallel with such attributions, they continued to search for physical solutions to problems, such as melting clay used in tuyeres. The way that they went about solving such problems is structurally parallel to Western scientific procedures of proposing hypotheses of material performance and submitting selected materials to systematic, repetitive tests until acceptable results indicate that one material is superior to another. However, the ways that they approached such testing more closely resemble the concept of bricolage, or fabrication using whatever materials and knowledge are at hand (Schmidt 1996c). The way in which various pieces of material and ritual knowledge are combined cannot always be predicted and depends on the background and ritual knowledge of the master smelters.

Observations about Haya technological experimentation or bricolage are particularly important for opening understanding of other African science and innovation. I believe that these studies reveal that experimental processes, both technological and ritual, are operative in African scientific traditions. The following discussion of Haya iron smelting will show that the exercise of experimental principles is instrumental in problem solving and also central to the achievement of technological complexity in Africa.

Smelting Begins

The morning after the roasting of the iron ore marked the beginning of smelting, with the elders determined to get off to an early start at 5 A.M. The head smelter, off consulting a diviner, did not arrive until nearly two hours later. First the iron ore and charcoal were removed from the pit and spread out over a 2-meter area to the west of the furnace, and the larger pieces of charcoal were removed. The ore from the bottom of the pit was a metallic gray and had numerous fissures. At this point I was faced with a problem in methods, for when I asked if we could separate the iron ore and charcoal for separate weighing, I was told clearly that we were not to touch the iron ore. We had not been asked to follow the taboos, though in fact we were practicing continence. This made no difference to the head smelter, who insisted that only he and the other elders could handle the iron ore at this stage. This effectively illustrated to us the considerable contrast that a field situation presents to a controlled laboratory setting. There was no alternative but to consent to the elders' directions. This remains a methodological problem (from a scientific point of view only) that has not been solved in subsequent smelts.

After the arrival of the head smelter, the smiths began to burn Ishanga grass in the furnace pit (fig. 4.1). The grass bundles were burned one by one in the pit while the smiths stirred the grass to keep it burning. A mixture of ash and charred stalks, the burning mass was compacted into the

FIG. 4.1 Ishanga grass—*Miscanthidium violaceum*—being burned in the furnace pit early on the morning of a smelt. Bundles of dried grass lie to the left of the furnace. The ash and charred grass are packed into the pit by being shoved down with a hoe.

bottom of the pit with hoes to prevent complete combustion and to compress it. Another bundle was added immediately and the procedure was repeated. Over a three-hour period, nineteen bundles of grass were burned. This was approximately 50 percent more than in subsequent smelts, because the pit for the first smelt was much larger than that used in later smelts. While the Ishanga grass was being burned, several of the smiths and other men designated to smelt began to work the goatskins used for bellows covers, and two workmen began to mix water with termite earth to make mud for construction of the furnace chimney. The newer skins were rubbed with sandstone blocks to work out the tough creases and to make the skin more supple. After an hour, beef fat was rubbed into the skin to render it even more pliable. This was a compromise from the butterfat that is used normally but was not available. Once the fat was applied to the skins, the workmen kneaded them by balling them up and treading on them with their feet (fig. 4.2).

At midmorning, just prior to completion of the grass burning, the head smelter placed a cone of unburned Ishanga grass in the pit. Earlier in the morning I had observed him carrying what was whispered to be a special medicine from the diviner he had consulted. He remained silent about its contents; I suspected, but failed to witness, that the medicine was secreted in this special bunch of grass placed in the pit. During subsequent smelts no such device was added to the furnace. This probable but secret ritual alerted us to the fact that the explicit denial about rituals was a mask meant to mislead the community as well as us. Once the char and ash from the Ishanga grass had been heaped into a cone some 40 centimeters higher than the rim (fig. 4.3), the head smelter spread 40 kilograms of charcoal over the grass char. Work then turned toward erecting the furnace superstructure.

Fig. 4.2 Three smiths prepare their goat- and sheepskins for the smelt by kneading them and softening them with butter applied to their surfaces.

Fig. 4.3 The heap of charred grass and ash in the furnace pit immediately before construction of the chimney begins.

The empiga blocks for the foundation were brought forward and set on end at the lip of the pit. These 50-to 70-centimeter-high slag blocks were balanced with small pieces of slag at their bases and gaps left between them for tuyere openings. Eleven empiga were set up, three more than the eight initially discussed by the elders and the eight used in all subsequent smelts (fig. 4.4). Another 20 kilograms of charcoal was added, mostly against the empiga. However, there were not enough bellows available, so one tuyere hole between the foundation blocks was plugged with mud and slag. Mudding of the empiga bases was followed by the insertion of the tuyeres, which were placed well inside the furnace and pointed up at a 30 degree angle with only the flared end outside (fig. 4.5). The space between the tuyeres in the furnace center was 80 centimeters, a greater than normal amount (40 to 55 cm) and a condition caused by the unusually large pit diameter. As the tuyeres were laid in place, several types of grass were used to seal the area around the tuyeres, which were then enclosed by mud. With the foundation blocks mudded up, the head smelter then turned to charging the furnace with unroasted iron ore.

FIG. 4.4 The head smelter, Ta Herman Kariba (*left, without shirt*), directs his helpers in constructing the first furnace of 1976, when 11 empiga blocks were used on the large base.

FIG. 4.5 Positioning the tuyeres within the furnace (a later smelt), showing the degree of internal penetration and angle at the early stage before smelting begins.

81

ETHNOARCHAEOLOGY AND BRICOLAGE

Fig. 4.6 The head smelter sits dejectedly at right, while the second master smelter (*left*) and assistants cope with the collapse of the first furnace.

The addition of unroasted ore was also an unexpected event, another part of the process that had not come out during the earlier interviews. Eighty-four and one-half kilograms of ore was placed in separate, layered pockets directly against all the empiga. This is a lower temperature zone along the periphery of the furnace, so that roasting of ore for the next smelt would occur during the regular smelt. We also noted, however, that the ore appeared to lend some stability to the teetering blocks.

One hour after the last charcoal charge, another 28 kilograms of charcoal was added, for a total of 88 kilograms before the furnace had even been constructed.[1] A second course of slag was then set into place, forming a shelf above the row of empiga. At noon, with several additional courses in place and the height at 1 meter, the western wall of the furnace collapsed completely to the base (fig. 4.6), and some of the slag blocks fell on the foot and leg of one elder. The slag and mud were cleared away immediately, but then everyone sat in stunned silence. Finally, an hour later the elders visited the landowner's home to give him 40 cents so he could make an offering to the only spirit on this hill, Mugorora. The smith explained that when men went mad, they came to make an offering at a special rock with a hole in it located about 50 meters south of the furnace. He assured the elders that this spirit would help to prevent another misfortune such as the furnace collapse.

The reason for the collapse was attributed to the most infirm of the elders injured by the incident. It was alleged that he did not use enough small slag blocks as filler and then placed a slag block that was much too large on an upper course, causing the wall to fall. Three tuyeres were broken in the collapse, and only seven empiga were left standing. The smiths seized the initiative from the elders and began to build the furnace by stacking the slag blocks as one would a wall of field stone. The smiths were allowed to dominate the construction at this point, with periodic advice from the head smelter, who seemed despondent. The smiths took advantage of the situation by claiming, again, that they were not bound by the original contract and that as experts they should not be pumping the bellows. This last minute holdout deeply angered the head smelter, who let everyone within earshot know about his displeasure. Some four hours after the furnace collapsed, the head smelter began to prepare the roasted iron ore for charging as well as added the remainder of a 33-kilogram gunny sack of charcoal to the furnace.

The actual bellows pumping started almost twelve hours after the beginning of the day, two hours before nightfall (fig. 4.7). Eight drum bellows were aligned around the furnace, each resting with its double-nozzled tip about 3 to 5 centimeters away from the flare of the tuyere. These wooden bellows, *mujuba* (sing.; *mijuba*, pl.), are carved from one piece of wood and have two independent chambers of $15 \times 25 \times 10$ centimeters, each of which connects to a 60-to-70-centimeter tube carved inside the long nose. *Mujuba* means "to fish for," so the bellows are "fishing for iron." A sheepskin (in this case goatskin, because sheepskins were not available) is tied hair side down over each chamber, which lacks a valve; the skin is also tied to a stick that is used to pick it up and push it down.

Because the bellows are valveless, the air going into the bellows chambers must pass through the same tube used to express air into the furnace. While air is passing into one chamber, it is passing out the other. The exchange occurred with great rapidity, as the smelters began at 480 strokes per minute, only later to drop to 320 strokes. The operation of the bellows is of great interest, for the sucking in of air obviously has an effect on the airflow inside the tuyere. This reverse flow draws hot air from the furnace partway up the tuyere, thus creating a push-pause effect that holds the air inside the clay pipe for a fraction of a second—a key technological characteristic further discussed in chapter 5.

Shortly before the bellows pumping started, the head smelter dumped out another 31-kilogram bag of charcoal contiguous to the area west of the furnace where the roasted ore was spread. More charcoal was mixed with the iron ore, which was then used to charge the furnace in irregular amounts. Almost as soon as the smelt began, the head smelter began to voice strong doubts followed by loud complaints about the tuyeres. He constantly patrolled the circumference of the furnace, stooping to check each tuyere, getting down on his knees to ream out the melting ends with the central stem of a banana leaf. As the smelt progressed, the distal ends of the tuyeres began to drop down into the ashy zone of the pit; after an hour they were nearly horizontal to the pit floor. The rounded rim of the furnace pit allowed the tuyeres to pivot downward on the rim.

FIG. 4.7 The head smelter charges the first furnace after it is constructed for the second time.

We began our monitoring program an hour into the smelt. The elders did not oppose or object to our placing thermocouples inside the tuyeres and through the tuyeres into the blast zone. They insisted that we start data collection immediately, for in their eyes that was the purpose of the smelting. Thus, we embarked on our experimental observations immediately. The quality of the first furnace was such that we had strong reservations about it, but it promised to provide interesting comparative evidence to subsequent smelts: it resembled a small water tank rather than a cone; the wall was improperly constructed; the internal diameter was much too large for an eight-man smelt.

Methods

In order to test for preheating of air within the clay tuyere, we inserted a ceramic-coated thermocouple inside a tuyere at 2.5-centimeter intervals starting at the tuyere mouth and passing to the tuyere tip and sometimes into the blast zone. For scans within the tuyeres and several centimeters near the tip of the tuyere, we used the chrome-alumel thermocouple. For other tuyere scans that continued well beyond the tuyere and beyond the blast zone, we used a platinum-rhodium thermocouple. We also employed an optical pyrometer to measure temperatures of charcoal and ore near the tuyere tip and the slag boil below the tuyere mouth. We began with the bear bead of the thermocouple exposed, but eventually experimented with a number of different techniques, including bending the bead backward and devising a shield to protect it from direct radiant heat from the furnace interior. None of these techniques significantly changed any of the results.

As the thermocouple was moved from one station to the next, it was allowed to soak at each for 30 seconds, then read. We also measured all iron ore that was roasted, though it was then impossible to obtain the post-roasted weight because of local refusal to allow us to measure the ore at this stage. All charcoal was weighed before it was used to charge the furnace. Yet we found that the amount of charcoal used does not characterize the amount actually consumed during a smelt; fairly significant amounts burn as the furnace is being destroyed, and some of the remainder is scattered and trampled after the blooms are removed.

I will not specifically address particular results about the first smelt, for they tell us relatively little about smelting in a Haya furnace. Suffice it to say that the slag-tempered tuyeres and the high iron oxide content of the clay (see chapter 7) ensured that the tuyeres virtually flowed away, what with the fluxing action of the incorporated FeO (as slag and as mineral content of the clay) in the reducing zone away from the tip as well as the hot, acid slag wash over their tips. The fluxing action of the incorporated slag weakened the tuyeres, negating any natural refractory qualities, and made them more vulnerable to the slag wash. It was abundantly obvious that the Bajumba (smelters) had met severe problems with the materials used to make the tuyeres.

Several hours into the smelt, the tuyeres were mostly eroded away, and the charcoal allocated for this smelt had been entirely consumed. The last charcoal charge came only two and a quarter hours after starting, when another 61 kilograms of charcoal was added; no subsequent additions were made beyond this total of 182 kilograms. Much of the charcoal had burned during furnace construction and during the long interval when repairs were made to the furnace. Only three and a quarter hours after starting, the head smelter gave the order to dismantle the furnace. The courses of slag and mud were pulled down by a hooked tool called a *rwokezo.* The hot slag blocks and baked mud were removed to the north side of the work area. After the loss of the rwokezo inside the furnace, the smiths impatiently took charge and pushed down the walls with sticks. This shattered most of the tuyeres and created the troublesome task of extracting the hot slag and earth from the furnace. The furnace pit was then cleared of the tuyeres, and a long stick with a banana root attached, a *kikonya,* was used to pry out slags and putative iron nodules by using it as a lever against the pit rim.

As the head smelter nervously looked on, several large white-hot lumps were removed to exclamations and cheers (fig. 4.8). Though the smelters

Fig. 4.8 After the furnace is dismantled at the end of the first smelt, white-hot objects, later proving to be mostly slag, are removed from the furnace and buried at the periphery of the work area.

were very pleased with their efforts, it was impossible to tell if iron or slag was being pulled from the furnace. A denser mass was pulled from beneath one tuyere belonging to the strongest of the young assistants recruited to help. This denser lump and the other pieces were then buried in 30-centimeter-deep pits about 2 to 3 meters northwest of the furnace, presumably to keep them from oxidizing.

The total elapsed time of this smelt was much less than the estimated six to eight hours discussed by the elders before actual smelting began. This entire smelt was a series of serious compromises and experiments: slag-tempered tuyeres; forging clay used for smelting tuyeres; a large-diameter pit; a furnace chimney without the ideal cone shape and without a proper foundation; the use of much charcoal before the smelting began; and a significantly abbreviated smelting period. It was not a model smelt that generated acceptable data for understanding the technological process or any significant material-behavioral correlates. Yet the smelt did provide invaluable insight into how the smelters coped with problems of deficient materials, structural faults, and work organization. Skills were rusty, memories were uncertain on some technical details, disputes over leadership interfered, and confidence was shaken by the failure to build a proper furnace.

The euphoria that had prevailed at the end of the previous evening had completely dissipated by the next day. The head smelter insisted that the furnace pit was much too large, and that this had accounted for their failure to build an adequate chimney over the pit. There were immediate discussions of plans for alternatives to the first pit; some favored the idea of rebuilding, and others supported the construction of a new pit—a time-consuming project. The tight schedule of my consulting metallurgist began to loom as another problem; I reluctantly shared this with the elders, who then decided that rather than wait for a new furnace pit to dry, they would simply make over the first one. We noted that very little slag had penetrated the grass char in the furnace pit, so that most of the grass could be removed and stockpiled for future use. This was another clear indication that the smelt had not been conducted properly.

Thereafter, there was extensive debate over how the pit should be reconstructed. A casual passerby, a smith unfamiliar with smelting, exercised the most influence over the head smelter, who was in a quandary over the issue. Eventually the termite earth was stripped from the sides and top of the pit (fig. 4.9), crushed in its bottom, and mixed with fresh termite earth and water. This mixture was then added to the wall in two layers about 30 centimeters thick. Halfway up the wall 7-to-8-centimeter pieces of slag were added as filler and temper to this thick walling, along with the straw temper. At this point the experiment was nearly jeopar-

FIG. 4.9 An assistant removes part of the inside liner of the first furnace in preparation for its reconstruction: the goal was to remove the smooth liner, add to the roughened section, and reduce the diameter significantly to accommodate only eight bellows and tuyeres.

dized by the physical scientist on my team, who became so agitated by what he saw as an "unscientific" procedure (the thick, wet clays would "blow up") that he wanted it stopped and done differently. So, as the elders negotiated with the smiths, we were involved in a major dispute among ourselves over procedure and methods. We finally reached an understanding that the elders would proceed in any way they wished, regardless of so-called scientific insights. The final pit size was 1 meter wide at the lip, 75 centimeters wide at a 30-centimeter depth, and 60 centimeters deep.

The following day, eight men were occupied making more charcoal. Toward the end of the day, the elders moved the Ishanga grass back into the pit, burned three fresh bundles, added 15 kilograms of charcoal plus the iron ore and the charcoal recovered from the pit, and finally another 8 kilograms of charcoal. The concern here was to keep the iron ore in a reducing atmosphere and to push along the drying of the pit under low temperature conditions.

By the next day the smelters' concern for the failure of the first smelt had shifted. The head smelter greeted us with the assertion that the failure was due to violation of the taboo against sexual intercourse. It was widely known that some of the younger assistants, but none of the Bajumba, had participated in a widely talked-about party where behavior was certainly contrary to such taboos. We had also observed (though feared to report) a young couple having sexual intercourse in the forge only a few meters away during the first smelt. So the head smelter had reason for concern that the younger members of the party were not taking his warnings to heart.

Because of the multitude of problems the head smelter had experienced, he called in advisers from Ishozi village, across the swamp to the east, to help with the furnace construction. One man was a Munana by clan and age seventy-nine, while the other was a Mugabo and was approximately ninety years old. The latter elder was the head smelter's maternal uncle and was extremely fragile in physique. All the smelters agreed to remove the materials from the pit, as the remaining charred Ishanga grass had burned to ash. The charcoal and iron ore were again sorted to the west of the furnace. We still did not have access to it, but it appeared to be about two-thirds the amount that they had started with the first time. New Ishanga grass was then burned in the smaller pit, though this time the amount was considerably less, twelve bundles weighing 192 kilograms. When the tuyeres were set in place, there was a 52-centimeter-diameter space in the center. This time the tuyeres were tempered with grog made from old tuyeres and pottery, and they averaged only 51.6 centimeters in length.

The chief concern of the newly recruited elders was the quality of the iron ore. The eldest adviser claimed that all the ore should be the top grade, which he referred to as *kakara,* rather than *kasina.* The Nyungwe smelters explained that they had carefully discarded the low-grade pieces and that they were certain that the ore resembled that which they used to smelt from the same site. The elder of the two advisers pointed out certain white (kaolin) spots, *lukuuku*. However, such spots did not appear until the ore had dried, explained the head smelter, adding that he had carefully mixed the black ore with brownish-red ore (*keyaju*).[2] The second elder from Ishozi defended the choice. He said that he recognized the quality of the Karuyenje ore.

After this exchange, the head smelter lurked in the background without comment. The elder adviser then issued instructions to remove the empiga blocks and to trim them on their bottoms before they were enclosed with mud. The head smelter's recruitment of a kinsman, and a very elderly, feeble one at that, had an immediate negative impact on the head smelter's authority. First, his uncle's great age had an adverse effect on the old man's physical abilities and on his memory about the technology. It soon became apparent that the situation was perilous under the leadership of this aged adviser. However, his kin relationship with the head smelter prevented the head smelter from directly contradicting the old man's orders and questionable advice. Haya sociolinguistics are such that one must not openly confront and challenge a kinsman, so the head smelter was compelled to step back and give way. This immediately threatened his legitimacy within the group and sapped further what little authority he had salvaged after the first failure. If he did not agree with his uncle, then he had to find indirect means to have his say and to recoup the authority that he had relinquished upon the arrival of his kinsman. Further, no one had paid any attention to his suggestion that violation of the intercourse taboo was the cause of things going wrong with the smelt. Tension was high. The atmosphere was charged.

Once the aged adviser took control of the furnace construction, he also began to alter the shape of the furnace. However, this was not done until three separate pockets of iron ore were interlayered with charcoal behind each empiga. Then the adviser pushed the foundation blocks inward, changing the internal diameter from 110 centimeters to 97 centimeters. Another large charge of charcoal (for a 62 kg total thus far) brought the charcoal even with the tops of the foundation blocks. The interlocking slag pieces, placed with their long axes crossing the wall, rested on top of the charcoal rather than fitting tightly between the empiga. As mudding of the furnace continued in earnest, we noted an important use of tuyeres. Those tuyeres that had been scavenged from the last smelt were broken up and stuffed in the openings next to the tuyere to help plug the air space between it and the furnace wall.

Disaster Strikes Again

The new furnace went up rapidly under the supervision of the two advisers from Ishozi and the second elder from Nyungwe. The head smelter kept clear of the work. An hour and a half after the foundation blocks had been moved, the furnace was finished to a height of 1.45 meters. Seven minutes later the furnace collapsed (fig. 4.10). The immediate cause appeared to be structural. The locking blocks fitted between the empiga act like keystones in an arch. Unless they fit tightly, the empiga blocks will not stand. We had already observed that the locking blocks had been supported by the charcoal without being fitted tightly. This and the use of large quantities of mud in the joints, rather than small pieces of slag, meant that once the charcoal burned out from behind the empiga, the chimney was destined to fall.

Fig. 4.10 After the addition of two experts from Ishozi village (*center and right*), the furnace collapses again and the smelters grow despondent.

The almost casual mood was very different from the despondency after the first furnace collapse. The rebuilding continued exclusively at the direction of the Ishozi advisers, while the Nyungwe elders and smiths stood nearby. The head smelter started a harangue in which he blamed the collapse on violation of the intercourse taboo and witchcraft. The despair and tension among close friends were clearly manifest during this crisis. The dialogue of the smelters best captures the conflict:

> SECOND SMELTER: The cause of the failure may well be among us.
> ANOTHER: If it is not the doings of Irungu.

HEAD SMELTER: It is the vagina.

SECOND SMELTER: Which vagina? The problem may be the soil.

HEAD SMELTER: Are you older than I?

SECOND SMELTER: No, you are older.

HEAD SMELTER: Older by how many dry seasons?

SECOND SMELTER: I am not referring to the business of the vagina!

HEAD SMELTER: Then why are you arguing with me? I am asking you: I am older by how many dry seasons?

SECOND SMELTER: "Now, my lords, have I disputed the fact?"

HEAD SMELTER: Is it not true that they are fucking? Smelting abhors the vagina! Do not argue with me!

SECOND SMELTER: Now, son of my father, have I pushed the matter that far?

HEAD SMELTER: I tell you there is something afoot. . . . Even the witches are there. You cannot deceive me! These things [furnaces] abhor the vagina!

ANOTHER: Even menstruating women are coming here.

ANOTHER: They are coming and touching the furnace.

SECOND SMELTER: Which woman has touched the furnace?

When no one responded to the head smelter's strident claims that sexual intercourse was the source of difficulty, he announced that he was going to consult a diviner to discover the reason for the furnace collapses. The Ishozi advisers finally were joined by the second Nyungwe elder and several Bajumba, who completed the day's second furnace after an hour and a half. This furnace stood for a half-hour before collapsing.

This time the Ishozi advisers immediately attributed the trouble to the fact that the furnaces had been spoiled by this particular pit. They insisted on digging a new pit and starting anew, but the Nyungwe elders and smiths would not hear of it. Muttering in the ranks began, with many of the participants offering their opinions on the failures. Among the smiths, the blame was laid directly on the head smelter, who was said to have been negligent on two counts. First, he had failed to make an offering to the local spirit, Mugorora, whose abode was in a rock to the south of the furnace. It was felt to be the head smelter's responsibility, not the landowner's. Second, some felt that the head smelter had been negligent in his duty to Irungu, the Bacwezi god who governs the resources of iron smelting, such as iron ore and charcoal, found in the hinterland.

The mood was now acutely despondent. The head smelter sat by himself, off in the bordering banana plants, moaning over their failure with tears running down his proud face. His shame, he said, was that he had disappointed his guests. He could not go on without the guidance of the embandwa, the diviners who could diagnose the problems and point the way to a solution. Although opinion was divergent as to the possible reasons for the failure, with almost every participant offering a separate idea, the head smelter's idea of consultation with two different diviners was now unanimously taken up. Plans were made about which diviners in the village should be consulted. The head smelter continued to hold tenaciously to the view that violation of the taboo on sexual activity was the cause of the failures, but this notion was not openly endorsed by any of the participants. I learned that the head smelter's concern indeed lay squarely in the widespread reports in the village about the same debauch in which several younger associates were known to have participated the night before the first smelt.

The smelters and their assistants were still quite uneasy over the absence of the required rituals for Irungu. Problems with the furnace brought into the open much discussion about the necessity to perform certain rituals, including a sacrifice, to propitiate the spirit of Irungu. This question became the central focus of a large and sometimes acrimonious palaver held by all the major participants that afternoon. Now openly admitting that rituals were required prior to the smelt, the smelters and smiths were faced with a significant dilemma. Could they risk the possible condemnations by the community and religious authorities to perform the necessary ritual? The foremost issue was fear of recriminations from the church authorities and Christian neighbors. The resolution of the debate is best depicted in the words of the participants themselves:

> OLDEST ADVISER: In those days when we built the first furnace, we also built the house of Irungu behind it. When you first asked for my advice, my first question was, Where does Irungu stay? In days past we dug a small hole that symbolized the presence of Irungu. The next thing we did was to burn a hen and put its ashes in those small huts of Irungu. That was the sacrifice to Irungu. Then we could start making iron.
>
> SECOND SMELTER: The thing we did not do was that we did not build Irungu's hut. In fact, we did not build two small huts behind the furnace. And we absolutely did not roast the chicken. We have come here to stop telling lies, so that we may not be judged as deceivers.
>
> HEAD SMELTER: We have heard everything. As far as I know, we are speaking the truth. Did we really build the huts for Irungu? Do you say no? We must build those huts for Irungu and buy a hen for sacrifice. Then we must have peace. We are very lucky, since we were fetching charcoal in the forest and Irungu could have made one of us vanish. Am I speaking lies?
>
> ELDER ADVISER: If there is any Christian whom the church will prevent from taking Holy Communion because of this, let him depart the church.
>
> THIRD SMELTER: Will they be informed?
>
> HEAD SMELTER: I hope they won't meet you here.
>
> SECOND SMELTER: What will they find in those huts?
>
> HEAD SMELTER: If they find nothing in those huts, will they destroy them?
>
> ELDER ADVISER: No!

HEAD SMELTER: If they ask whether they have been here since yester-
day, we should agree.

SECOND SMELTER: Let them do whatever they like.

HEAD SMELTER: If they want to prevent me from receiving communion, let them do so. Didn't my father live without Holy Communion?

Fear of the church authorities was very real, and sufficiently strong that
it caused information to be withheld from me during my initial interviews
with the smelters. The decision reached was clearly a grave one, with the
potential for negative ramifications in the lives of these older and respected
members of the community. My research had precipitated events that affected the lives of the Haya smelters that could not have been predicted at
the outset. By now the issue had taken on a momentum of its own that was
increasingly volatile. The smelters became determined to act out their roles
with traditional integrity, whatever the consequences.

This meeting in which the smelters and smiths decided to cast their lot
with traditional beliefs also focused on an extensive discussion of a dream
experienced by one of the smiths. The second in seniority among the smiths,
this man opened the meeting with a long narrative on his dream about
Irungu, the Bacwezi god of the wilderness—the patron of hunting and
iron smelting. Irungu had come to him during the dream, said the smith,
to express his displeasure with the smelters of Nyungwe for their failure to
sacrifice a goat to him. However, the substance of the dream—the need
for a goat—was ignored by the smelters. It was this dream distortion that
stimulated the open discussion of the chicken sacrifice that was formerly
performed for Irungu, and the two spirit huts for Irungu that were normally
built behind the smelting furnace. The head smelter, in an attempt to rec-
oncile the many varied interests and points of view, related a personal
anecdote about how he normally sacrificed a chicken to Irungu when he
was unsuccessful in the hunt. He suggested, then, that they go on with the
ritual in the way that they remembered that it had been done.

The next morning, work was suspended on the furnace while the head
smelter and the second elder each consulted a separate diviner. When
asked the results of the divinations, the head smelter explained that he
had consulted an Islamic practitioner, who had given him a stick to talk to
about the problem. He then threw the stick into the air, where it remained
until the diviner had written out his prognosis on paper. In this case the
divination pointed to the cause of the furnace failures as pollution or witchcraft performed by a man who had come at night and pointed his anus at
the furnace. The embandwa consulted by the second elder was a spirit
medium for Muleguza (a historical figure that I cannot identify).

This embandwa used three different stalks of grass: one representing
Irungu and the rituals for him, the second representing the possible violation of the sexual taboo, and the third signifying possible witchcraft activity. The second elder had spoken to these grass stalks and indicated their
symbolic values to no one. These were placed on a barkcloth, whereupon

three cowrie shells were thrown until two touched together. The embandwa selected a stalk. In this case it was the grass stem representing witchcraft, and she explained that the furnaces had collapsed because someone had been sacked from the project. This person had bewitched the furnace by displaying his anus at it.

While the divinations had not directly attributed the smelters' difficulties to the absence of rituals for Irungu, the diviners did advise the smelters about what plants should be used in the construction of a spirit hut for Irungu. Certainly the sentiment of the other participants strongly favored, whatever the consequences, that the rituals for Irungu be performed. So as twilight drew close on the day of consultations, the two Nyungwe smelters began to build a spirit hut about 6 meters southeast of the furnace pit. They built a beehive-shaped hut some 18 centimeters high in the same style as their traditional houses and similar to the traditional spirit huts once commonly found next to most Haya houses (fig. 4.11). Once it was constructed, they lined the entrance with special mugaba leaves. A small

FIG. 4.11 The head smelter and his chief assistant building a hut for Irungu, the Bacwezi god of the bush, where forests, ore, and other resources are obtained.

bonfire was lit 1 meter to the west of the west-facing entrance (toward Irungu's domain), and then a chicken was brought to the hut entrance, where its neck was cut and the blood allowed to flow over the entrance.

As the chicken was sacrificed, the smelters began to chant one of several esoteric prayers, two of which I reproduce here because they provide insight into the symbolism surrounding Irungu and iron smelting. As the chicken was offered in sacrifice, the head smelter intoned:

> We have offered the chicken, here it is.
> The savory one, the flea-infested one,
> May you appear.

His reference here was to Irungu, who not only controls iron smelting and its resources, but also is a hunter and patron god of all hunters. As a hunter working with dogs, Irungu is flea-infested. The most poignant prayer was that offered by the second smelter after the chicken had been placed *in the fire* —to be burned until it was totally consumed:

> Child that is tough within,
> Child that is tough within,
> Let the things [iron lumps] be seen,
> Let them be seen, let them be seen,
> So that we may laugh,
> So that we may be happy,
> May you appear!

In this prayer, the iron smelting furnace is the subject of concern. The "child" who "is tough within" refers to a child in birth who has trouble passing through the birth canal. When it can be seen passing out, there is reason to rejoice. The symbolic rendering here is the furnace as a woman who is in the throes of a difficult birth. The "child" of the furnace is the iron bloom that is so difficult to produce. This ritual incantation was the first insight into the phenomenon of iron smelting as a transformational process, a process that is symbolically represented as human reproduction, with the furnace as woman, the furnace pit as womb, and the iron bloom as fetus (for a full exegesis in other African cultures, see Herbert 1993).

Immediately after this ritual and under cover of darkness, the second Nyungwe elder carried the three different kinds of grasses used in the divination ritual, provided earlier by the embandwa, to the furnace, touched them on the cardinal points of the furnace rim—starting on the west (Irungu's "wild" side, the direction of the swamp) and ending on the east—and then threw them away to the south near the abode of the local spirit (fig. 4.12). One of the Nyungwe smiths then appeared with coffee beans. The head smelter placed these in the blood at the entrance to Irungu's hut (fig. 4.13). The purification ritual and the sacrifice to Irungu were conducted in the utmost secrecy, with all neighbors warned not to venture close to the site, and with considerable reluctance to admit a foreigner to the proceedings.

FIG. 4.12 The sticks, grasses, and herbs used in the divination ceremony in which the reasons for the failures of the furnaces were determined. The coin was included as an offering to a nearby shrine for a local spirit.

FIG. 4.13 Irungu's hut, with the sacrificial blood of a chicken spilled on the leaves and coffee beans in the entranceway. Similar spirit huts used to grace the household compounds of Haya homesteads in traditional times.

One smelter stayed on into the night to make certain that the chicken was transformed to ash and to prevent those with possible evil intent from meddling with the sacred items and the residue of the fire.

Morale was much improved the next morning, yet everyone was on edge as a consequence of the traumatic events of the previous days. Tension was particularly high between the Nyungwe and Ishozi smelters as the Nyungwe experts maneuvered to recoup their position of leadership. Attention first passed to the burning of Ishanga grass in the furnace, but disputes soon erupted over whether the old grass char, now turned to ash, would suffice. The head smelter exercised his authority by removing the charcoal and iron ore that had been left over from the previous smelt. The Ishozi elder immediately stepped in to order the removal of the grass ash.

This was soon followed by an assessment by the aged Ishozi elder that the iron ore from the previously attempted smelt was inadequately roasted. He summarily ordered that it not be sorted—a task that the Nyungwe smelters were then conscientiously pursuing—but added to the furnace ore "pockets" to be roasted for the next smelt. The head smelter ignored this directive and began, instead, discussing his assessment of the error in removing the charred grass, which he felt was still adequate. Seizing the advantage, the head smelter then began to supervise the burning of the Ishanga grass, most of which was lying around in untied bundles that had been used previously to protect the furnace pit from rain. The head smelter used this opportunity to return much of the partially burned grass to the furnace. While he did this, he complained loudly, only in the direction of his compatriots, about their foolishness in removing the charred grass from the pit. This incident marked the reestablishment of Nyungwe authority over the process.

By midmorning the construction of the furnace began. It was apparent within minutes that several of the smiths and one of the Ishozi advisers still did not understand the principle that the lintel blocks had to interlock firmly with the upright empiga for the structure to remain upright. As work progressed on the first course, the elder Ishozi adviser tired and began to lean against the precarious structure, finally causing it to collapse. The head smelter held his usually active tongue. But at this point, after much previous discussion about the integrity of the process and the pursuit of scientific goals, I finally decided to intercede with an indirect suggestion about the structural cause of the trouble (which we could readily see). We were faced with the very real probability that one more furnace collapse would end the experiment. Later observations of attitudes under *successful* conditions confirmed the accuracy of this assessment. I suggested to one of my assistants that he unobtrusively show the head smelter how to fit the lintel blocks snugly against the empiga. The head smelter immediately shouted to his colleagues that he had been trying, unsuccessfully, to make this very point over the last several days. After this bit of verbal circumlocution, the construction continued, with the head smelter closely monitoring the correct wedging of the lintel blocks (fig. 4.14).

Fɪɢ. 4.14 Construction of a furnace proceeds after the purification rituals and sacrifice to Irungu. The key structural element is firmly in place—the piece of locking slag, which acts as a keystone, between the upright and vertical empiga or slag blocks.

FIG. 4.15 The successful construction of the furnace, with progressively smaller slag blocks being sealed with termite mud in the zone immediately over the keystones.

Fig. 4.16 The furnace construction nears completion with the placement of the last small slag blocks at the top of the furnace stack.

The head smelter, not content that the earlier construction was solid, ordered parts of the furnace rebuilt. Within an hour and a half, the furnace was completed (figs. 4.15 and 4.16). When it did not collapse, the head smelter announced that the work was completed and that they need not continue! After a stunned silence and no reaction from the other participants, I asked if he meant that he had fulfilled his obligation. He said that he had, as he had finally completed a successful furnace! He clearly was hesitant to risk his reputation any further by submitting the structure to the actual test of smelting iron. At he turned to head home, I pleaded with him to continue. With a frown and a grunt, he reluctantly agreed, once his indispensability had been acknowledged publicly by his foreign guests. He had been reestablished firmly as head smelter.

By the time smelting began at 17:15, 100 kilograms of charcoal had been placed into the furnace. Much of the charcoal had been consumed during the long construction period since midmorning, so the totals are in no way indicative of use under normal conditions. There is no way that such field conditions can be approximated to controlled laboratory situations. In retrospect and with more comparative data obtained from subsequent smelts, the total charcoal weights were biased significantly by water-saturated charcoal. For example, one bag weighed 40 kilograms, whereas the normal dry weight varies between 20 and 24 kilograms per bag. We have based our calculations of charcoal consumption on the total volume consumed times an average dry weight, less an estimated volume consumed during furnace construction, and less the volume that remained after completion of the smelt.

Our monitoring of the first authentically constructed furnace began shortly before bellows pumping commenced. We found that the temperature in the blast zone with the slight natural draft was 1,100 to 1,200°C. After pumping of the bellows began, there were immediate problems with the condition of the tuyeres; melting and slag plugs especially affected three of the tuyeres. The temperatures measured in the blast zone during the first several hours did not exceed 1,200 to 1,300°C, but we did not push the thermocouple into the zone where we could observe a white-hot slag boil below the tuyeres. We had brought an optical pyrometer with us to measure the slag temperatures by sighting into the blast zone and on the slag through the tuyere. Another 62.7 kilograms of wet charcoal was added immediately after the smelt started. This and subsequent charges of the same charcoal choked and suppressed furnace temperatures for several hours. Not until three hours into the smelt did we begin to document higher furnace temperatures—once the wet charcoal had lost its water and began to contribute actively to combustion, and the furnace gases began to flow freely out of the top of the furnace.

After the smelt was under way, the head smelter sat to the side and allowed the elder Ishozi adviser to charge the furnace with the charcoal and roasted iron ore mixture, successive charges of 8 to 12 liters of mixture every two minutes for ten-minute runs (fig. 4.17). We could only esti-

Fig. 4.17 Charging the furnace stack during the fourth smelt of 1976; note the pieces of iron ore mixed with the charcoal.

mate the weight of the iron ore charge, based on what we had weighed from prior roasting; between 72 and 86 kilograms of roasted ore was available for use. Another 29 kilograms of charcoal charge was added after an hour and a half.

At this juncture the head smelter inspected the tuyeres and exclaimed, "*Kieto!*" or "There is slag in the tuyere!" He then scrambled to unplug the flaps of clay and slag that were obstructing the tuyere mouths. The wet charcoal had caused a tremendous amount of back pressure in the furnace, and this, in turn, led to the furnace fire shooting out of cracks around tuyeres and in the furnace wall, as well as out of tuyeres when bellows pumping had been suspended. The Nyungwe smelters plugged the cracks with wet clay and seemed content, during the third hour, that the smelt was progressing satisfactorily. Our tuyere scans throughout the smelt showed preheating in the midsection of the tuyere—back more than three diameters from the tuyere tip. The preheating appeared to be in the range of 300 to 500°C, but the choked furnace conditions did not allow this advantage to be translated to a higher flame temperature.

When the smelt went into its fourth hour, the smelters asked for relief from their children and the young men who had been included in the work group. They partook freely in the large calabashes of beer near the furnace and began to sing the bawdy nuptial songs that characterize this happier, more relaxed period of the smelt. The songs address the furnace as a ripe, nubile bride ready to conceive. I will discuss this sexual symbolism in greater depth in chapter 9. At this point, with the flame well above the furnace rim, the spirits of the smelters high, and the bellows pumping vigorously under way, the efficiency of the furnace was at its peak. However, because of the earlier back pressure and melting of tuyeres (now grog-tempered), the tuyeres had lost 12 to 20 centimeters of their length, and their preheating capacity was lessened. Nonetheless, the open stack conditions meant that a more normal environment prevailed inside the furnace. Temperature scans of the tuyeres and the zone immediately in front of the tuyeres showed that preheating was still operative, though at reduced levels, and that the upper blast zone temperatures were in the 1,600°C range, with charcoal near the molten slag at even higher temperatures. Had the furnace not been choked initially, we are certain that the temperatures would have been even higher. We felt confident that the test results confirmed our hypothesis for preheating, yet we were keenly aware that formidable problems remained with materials, charcoal charging, and scheduling. Not until all these were solved would we have a smelt that we could use definitively to characterize the Haya process.

In the fifth hour of the smelt, several of the previously plugged tuyeres were opened and were more easily kept open; the free flow of gases out of the furnace and the absence of back pressure meant less stress on the tuyeres. The rate of bellows pumping had gradually diminished to about 350 to 400 strokes per minute. Suddenly a special tattoo was started by several Bajumba, who then broke into a song with the same rhythm, "Lwa-Kaliga." This song marks the beginning of the end of a smelt and signals that only an hour or less work is left. After much joking, drinking, and song, at the end of the fifth hour the smelters began to tear down the furnace (fig. 4.18). There was still a fair volume of charcoal unburned— nearly two gunny sacks, indicating that approximately 70 to 80 kilograms of (dry) charcoal had been used during the actual smelting over a five-hour period (fig. 4.19).

When the furnace structure was cleared away and the tuyeres were carefully removed for our later inspection, the molten masses were pried out of the furnace. Six of the tuyeres were fused with large blocks of slag at the mouths and bottoms of the tuyeres. Another had a large mass of consolidated iron ore (from the pocket behind) attached. Spirits plummeted when everyone thought that the smelt had produced only slag—until the second Ishozi adviser beat one mass and found that it contained iron.

The next day the iron blooms were retrieved from their pits and inspected. The head smelter processed the slagged pieces by beating away the glassy slag with a hammer, looking for malleability and sometimes discarding small, poorly consolidated pieces of iron (fig. 4.20). We collected these with the larger pieces, to find that the entire production came to .842 kilogram. One .35-kilogram piece was massive and well consolidated. The presence of much larger iron blooms produced early in the

Fig. 4.18 The disassembly of a furnace begins with removal of the furnace pieces by pulling them into a basket (a bucket was substituted here because the hot blocks burned the basket).

Fig. 4.19 At the end of the smelt (#5), after the chimney has been removed, the tuyeres can be seen in situ prior to the removal of blooms in front of each tuyere.

Fig. 4.20 The head smelter breaks away glassy slag from a bloom before it goes to the forge. This process pulverizes the glassy slag (seen below the hammer). The bloom is embedded in the lower portion of this particular mass.

century and hoarded until now tells us that each smelter once produced an individual bloom weighing between 2 and 7 kilograms, a productive capacity far in excess of the experimental one we had witnessed. Part of the explanation rested in the ravaged tuyeres and the choked furnace.

The smelters were so encouraged by these results, however meager when compared to the past, that they had already burned Ishanga grass in preparation for another smelt. This time the construction of the furnace proceeded with great rapidity, after an initial delay for an hour's argument over the elder Ishozi adviser's proclivity to place the lintel blocks on top of the charcoal. This time the head smelter made certain that at least two courses of slag in direct contact were laid and *then* covered in mud. This time 206 kilograms of fresh iron ore was placed behind the empiga for roasting. Furnace construction took less than three hours to reach a height of 136 centimeters. Before smelting even began, three bags of charcoal, apparently wet (93 kg vs. about 66 kg dry), went into the furnace. After a delay for a meal, smelting began at 16:45 as the head smelter and his helpers continued to separate unslagged pieces of iron ore from the slag of the previous smelt. This was difficult, for the erosion of the tuyeres by the slag wash and their reduced size had moved the blast zone toward the furnace wall, thus exposing the ore pockets to higher than normal temperatures and fusing the ore into a slagged mass. Pieces of ore without a slag coating were present but relatively rare, causing the smelters to use a mixture of ore from a previously failed smelt and some raw ore.

Fifteen minutes into the smelt, another 30.5-kilogram bag of charcoal went into the furnace, and the head smelter immediately gave the order for a slower bellowing pace called *kunyaika*—two hits with the left chamber and then both chambers expressed together. With all bellows operating simultaneously, the double blast acted to bring the flame quickly through the charcoal to the top of the furnace. His concern was to avoid the smothered conditions of the previous furnace, for he feared the use of this last charge and the next; both bags had been drenched by rain for two days in the forest. Shortly thereafter, the second wet bag of 29.5 kilograms was added, but kunyaika was not employed again, with rather disastrous consequences.

The furnace again suffered from extreme back pressure, with corresponding attrition to the tuyeres. After three hours and the addition of another 24.5-kilogram bag of charcoal, the head smelter ventured the opinion that the furnace fire would not break through because of the two supersaturated bags of charcoal, and that the two men who had filled in for one smith at the bellows had not followed the sexual abstinence taboo. The tuyeres had eroded badly, a fact that he attributed to poor clay rather than to the intense back pressure in the furnace. Toward the end of the fourth hour, a mostly gas flame came from the stack, and another 32-kilogram bag of charcoal was added, again temporarily smothering the furnace. This smelt lasted for close to six and a half hours and was again marked by almost constant singing of songs during the final hour. There was also a shower of sparks from the tuyere of the most vigorous *mujumba*, indicating a high carbon content in the iron in front of his tuyere.

As materials were pried from the furnace just before midnight, the smelters were eager to see if there was *kyoma* or iron in front of the western-facing tuyere, which was Irungu's tuyere. There was not, and this was taken to be a bad omen. Two pieces of definite kyoma were retrieved, the largest in front of the longest tuyere, the most effective in preheating. The tuyere scans show that preheating was most effective during the initial period when the tuyeres were longest; under these conditions, the temperature within the central reducing zone was maintained at 1,300 to 1,500°C for the first two hours of the smelt. The temperature of the incandescent charcoal at the interface with the molten slag was even higher—1,700 to 1,800°C. During this smelt we placed our platinum-rhodium thermocouple (melting point 1,820° C) on the top of the slag boil for several seconds, only to have the tip melt off. The longest tuyeres were also the only ones to produce iron, a total of 1.764 kilograms.

Concluding Reflections

Each smelt is distinctive when such an experiment is performed under field conditions and the control of local experts. The bricolage that draws on procedures partly remembered and from the experiences of others in the group varies from smelt to smelt. Experimentation with materials and ritual procedures contribute equally to the discovery of protocols that work. These are remembered and drawn upon by these bricoleurs in the next sequence, when a new bricolage occurs—as the search for a successful procedure continues. I want to focus on this initial series of smelts because I feel that they offer important and unique insight into the process of recuperating a traditional technology after years of inactivity. All of the incidents and processes that I have described portray attempts to grapple with and solve formidable problems in ritual matters, materials failure, and work organization. Problem solving in these domains gives us a glimpse into what kind of experimental procedures may have been operative in the past as iron producers moved into new environments and had to cope with new and different resources.

During 1976 we conducted another smelt under instrumented conditions, after which my collaborating metallurgist departed from the field. The smelters, prepared with charcoal and iron ore for another two smelts, were enthusiastic to continue. So we observed another two smelts during August and September. As time passed and the smelters grew more confident in their skills, fewer problems were encountered and productivity increased. Problems continued with the tuyeres, however, regardless of continued experimentation.

There are several summary observations that should be made regarding the subsequent smelts. The fourth furnace was constructed according to the form that the smelters held as ideal—a well-tapered wall with a upper rim diameter of about 40 centimeters. In an attempt to solve the clay problem with the tuyeres, the smelters had gone to the traditional forging clay site to obtain more clay. However, they took a dark gray clay from a higher stratum. This clay was less refractory than the other clay used thus far, with 16 percent of the tuyere lengths eroding away within the first two hours. The amount of roasted iron ore in the fourth smelt was weighed with its charcoal by a smelter, and the equivalent volume and weight of charcoal subtracted to find that 27.2 kilograms of roasted ore went into the furnace, considerably below the standard amount. The furnace was loaded full with large charcoal charges sufficiently wet to include many fines (very small pieces of charcoal), again leading to periodic and intense back pressure. Yet, after six and one-quarter hours, the smelters produced 2.3 kilograms of iron.

Such bricolage, essentially a search for an experimental protocol that could be consistently applied from smelt to smelt, continued into another smelt conducted five days later: two tuyeres were made from clay obtained from the traditional clay source at Buchwero. These two tuyeres held up notably better to the slag wash, and both produced distinctive and consolidated iron blooms, all of which totaled 3.21 kilograms in this smelt. Very clearly, an experimental solution was at hand for the materials problem with tuyeres.

The final smelt of 1976 was held in mid-September with tuyeres made of clay from Buchwero. This smelt started at 4 A.M.—the ideal time—and bellows pumping began shortly after 11 A.M. The entire operation ran without a hitch, with joyous singing and dancing during the final two hours, for a total smelt of seven and a half hours, again the ideal length of time. The tuyeres held up much better (see chapter 7), and the total yield was the best yet, 4.31 kilograms. There was no question that with the better tuyere performance, dry charcoal, further practice, and enhanced self-confidence, the Nyungwe smelters would soon reach the productive capacity that they had once achieved many decades before.

There is a very important cautionary tale that arises out of the 1976 field investigations. In any experimental context, and particularly with a complex technology such as iron smelting that has not been practiced for long periods, it is necessary to conduct multiple experiments. It would be a grave error to assume that one or even several observations (e.g., van Noten 1985) are an adequate characterization of a technology. Those who have conducted such observations have nonetheless contributed significantly to our knowledge of the variation seen in African iron production.

Observations of Haya iron smelting have continued over an eight-year period—with another smelt in 1979 and two in 1984. Each smelt has been distinctive and has taught us that the unexpected will always happen. The 1979 smelt was unquestionably the most successful of the nine smelts conducted over this period. The reasons for this are exactly as I have suggested above. First, the clay was obtained from the proper source—Buchwero—and at the proper depth. It was tempered with a large 3- to 6-millimeter grog and allowed to dry for several weeks. The furnace was an ideal cone shape and the charcoal was absolutely dry, averaging 22 kilograms per bag. Consequently, the furnace operated throughout with a vigorous stack fire, and the tuyeres did not experience any abnormal attrition from plugged furnace conditions. During that smelt we used an optical pyrometer to measure the temperatures of the slag boil in the molten slag mass in which the iron bloom was forming. Measurements consistently showed temperatures in the reduction zone within the high 1,500s, with oxidizing temperatures above the slag mass reaching into the mid-1,700s Celsius a half-hour after a new charcoal charge. These observations and subsequent observations during 1984 show that the slag boil occurs at high temperatures. Because the tuyeres held up so well under the 1979 smelt, the smelt was the most successful to date, yielding 10.81 kilograms of well-consolidated iron, with five blooms showing only incidental evidence for interstitial slag.

The success of the 1979 smelt can be attributed directly to the efficient preheating of the furnace by tuyeres that retained their integrity under high temperature conditions, to dry charcoal, to a full component of freshly roasted iron ore, and to a more measured schedule of furnace charging that avoided smothering the furnace. Another key variable in the process is the vigor of the bellows pumpers. Those who approach the job with a desultory attitude and who attack it at a tempo common to the forge inevitably fail to produce a bloom. Those who maintain a steady and vigorous tempo produce the larger pieces of iron. According to the smelters, in the past those who did not do their fair share and produce acceptable blooms were soon eliminated from the work group.

The 1984 smelts, however, offered a completely different perspective. One of my goals was to document all activities on 16-millimeter film. The participants differed from those of 1976 and 1979, as several of the smiths who had assisted previously were not available to assist. The two now very elderly head smelters wearied easily and were inclined to allow one dominant smith, a newcomer, to run the affair. The upshot was one smelt that produced approximately a kilogram of bloom, and a second that produced none of consequence. I discuss one of the primary structural reasons for the failures in chapter 7. But the main ingredient in the previous successful smelts was missing—the determination to prove that they could smelt again.

There were also special problems this time with conducting a ritual that included blood sacrifice. The head smelter admitted that the church authorities had been severe in their condemnation, once they had learned of the earlier rituals in 1976. He did not want to risk their ire again. The second head smelter felt no such reluctance, and he and a Muslim colleague (also feeling no compunction) conducted the necessary sacrifice to Irungu. Finally, the novelty of smelting had worn thin with the head smelter, who refused to be interviewed several times on issues that he, legitimately, felt that he had covered in previous years. Disparaging the work, he constantly pointed out that there were very good reasons why this work had been given up other than attractions such as the cash crop coffee and the availability of cheap European steel: the work was just plain hard and intolerably dirty.

The results of these experiments have major and significant implications for the history of technology in Africa. I have detailed the problems as well as the successes in this experimental procedure. These observations have shown how important it is to document African technology, yet how dangerous it is to portray the behavior as anything other than experimental. The intrusion of the ethnoarchaeologist into any situation in which he or she provides the raison d'être for the behavior or as a participant-observer is transformational in its effect. The only reason that the iron smelters of Nyungwe smelted iron again was that I asked them to do so. They initially thought that the idea was absurd. At the end of the first series of smelts in 1976, they admitted how pleased they were that they had agreed to the idea, for they realized how close they had been to losing a way of life that was once so important to them. Their participation in the project had resulted in younger men learning to smelt, ensuring that knowledge of it would pass into the next generation.

One of the more common questions that I encounter is, Why did this remarkable and complex technology nearly pass into extinction? What were the internal and external forces that led to its rapid decline and abandonment by the people of Buhaya? The reasons are varied and complex.

The prelude for decline of production goes back hundreds if not thousands of years and has to do with the capacity of forests and soils to sustain productive economies of this kind. In chapter 11, I conclude by tying in some of the ecological consequences of iron production in the region. The trends toward a stressed forest environment were seen some sixteen hundred years ago, and while some recovery occurred in the intervening millennium, they were well in train again by 1600. The twentieth century saw a much diminished capacity to produce iron in the region, with only a few forests (difficult to access) left to sustain the industry.

The overall consequence was that iron smelting was a tougher life than in the distant past. Significant labor was required to obtain charcoal and iron ore. Iron goods were also readily available from neighboring regions such as Biharamulo (Richter 1900), where vast forests supported hundreds of active workshops in the nineteenth century—many of them Barongo iron smelters. There is also little doubt that these economic stresses were exacerbated by the ready availability of cheap European iron tools and scrap steel. The Kiziba smelters tell a story, for example, about the impact of a bridge-building project conducted by the Germans. Piles of steel were left behind by the engineers, and local smiths used these to meet their needs for years. The junking of car springs and other automobile parts has also contributed significantly to cheap alternatives.

However, the coming of cash crops and the rush to capitalize farms for coffee production was one of the major contributions to the fall of smelting so early among the Haya. Male labor went to the coffee plantings, and the profits easily funded purchase of whatever tools the local community desired, or they provided the cash to purchase steel to make the specialized tools unique to Haya agriculture. While the Haya smelters and smiths genuinely enjoyed this recent revitalization of their craft and came to admit that they hadn't realized that they had lost something so precious to their culture, they were perfectly satisfied that their present circumstances, despite the difficulties, were more economically attractive than a past dependent on iron smelting.

5.

A

Technological

Model

of the Haya

Process

In some ways the conventional European understanding of African iron technology resembles the technological myths elaborated by the Babito and Bahinda clans when they sought to gain legitimacy by assuming the mantle of technological "knowledge." In this understanding, African ironworking technology is a European borrowing rather than an indigenous invention, and one in which African peoples lacked the skills to advance much beyond the primitive state in which they received it (Schmidt 1996b).

Given this context, observations of problem-solving bricolage among the modern Haya are among the more important to come out of these studies. The modern Haya had to engage in intensive bricolage to recover a half-remembered art, one they had not practiced for fifty years. But bricolage must have been an important element in the ancient tradition as well: successful management of a complex pyrotechnology such as smelting demands continual innovation to cope with the inevitable variations in raw materials.

In Africa—as in the West—the problem-solving repertoire consisted of both ritual and technological responses. When their smelts were unsuccessful, the Haya smelters stressed the importance of practicing continence and built a spirit hut for Irungu, but they also decreased the size of the furnace bowl and made tuyeres from different clay. The ritual responses will be discussed at greater length in chapters 9 and 10; in this chapter I focus on the technological responses, giving a summation of the technology processes.

The solutions to two related technological problems demonstrate clearly the existence of an independent tradition of experiment and innovation in Buhaya. The first problem is the comparative difficulty of smelting iron. The solution in Buhaya included preheating the supply air for the furnace, a technique that wasn't known in Europe until J. B. Nielson's patent in 1828. The second problem is the high phosphorus content of the smelted iron (Schmidt and Childs 1995; Childs 1996). The phosphorus problem was not so much solved as mitigated by a repertoire of techniques for working the embrittled metal. This was sometimes a problem faced by ancient European metalworkers when they had to contend with ores and fuels with a high phosphorus content.

The Bloomery Iron Smelting Process

The originality of Haya bloomery emerges clearly only against the backdrop of European bloomery and other bloomery processes in Africa. The bloomery process is an ancient technique for producing metallic iron from iron ore. In the bloomery process the iron ore is heated with charcoal in a furnace. As the ore descends slowly through the furnace stack, it encounters temperatures and levels of carbon monoxide that allow a series of chemical reactions to occur that reduce (remove the oxygen from) the iron oxides. Eventually some of the iron oxides combine with other minerals in the ore to form a viscous, glassy material called slag. The iron oxides are reduced in the presence of carbon to make metallic iron that settles out of the slag, forming spongy masses of iron interlarded with slag, called blooms (fig. 5.1).

The bloomery process differed from ancient techniques for smelting copper and other metals in one important respect: the iron rarely melted. Iron was smelted in the solid state because of its difficult chemistry and because of the limitations of ancient furnace designs. Iron has a comparatively high melting point (pure iron melts at 1,534°C, whereas pure copper melts at 1,083°C). Iron is also active chemically and will give up bound oxygen only in an atmosphere containing significant amounts of carbon monoxide, one of the few agents capable of removing oxygen from it. This chemistry is important because it is difficult to design a furnace that reaches high temperatures *and* retains a reducing atmosphere. Although a furnace

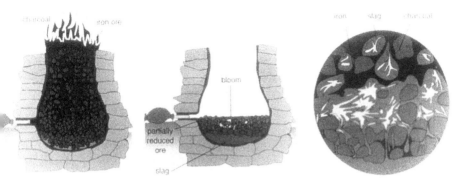

FIG. 5.1 A schematic drawing of the bloomery process as known from Europe. The panel on the left shows a furnace during operation; the middle panel shows the relative positions of the bloom to the slag mass; the panel on the right shows slag draining over charcoal, moving toward the bottom of the furnace. Courtesy of the *American Scientist.*

may reach high temperatures, such conditions often create large areas where the atmosphere is oxidizing rather than reducing.

In the absence of a technological solution to this dilemma, the best compromise is to minimize the air supply to the furnace to ensure that the atmosphere will remain reducing and to settle for adequate temperatures. The upper limit of reducing temperatures in European and other bloomery furnaces was about 1,300°C, substantially below the melting point of iron; at higher temperatures—1,600°C, for example—the iron would have been oxidized rather than reduced.

The bloomery process also had a low temperature limit, which was set by slag viscosity. Slag was not just a waste product of the smelting process but rather an active participant in it. If the slag became too viscous, the slag and metal remained mixed rather than separating, and little metal was recovered. In general, a bloomery furnace had to be operated at temperatures above 1,200°C to keep the slag fluid enough to permit the formation of an iron bloom—often called a sponge bloom because of its many interstitial spaces.

Because passage through the furnace was usually insufficient to recover all of the iron in the ore, bloomery slags often included large amounts of iron oxides. A typical bloomery slag contained silica (SiO_2) and wustite (FeO), together with small amounts of hematite (Fe_2O_3) or magnetite (Fe_3O_4). Although iron in this form was lost to the slag, it did have the beneficial effect of lowering the slag's melting temperature. Indeed, in antiquity iron ore was sometimes deliberately used as a flux (or substance that promoted the formation of slag) in the smelting of other metals such as copper. Depending on their iron content, bloomery slags are called either fayalitic (Fe_2SiO_4) or fayalite-wustite slags.

The bloomery process produced iron that had a heterogeneous carbon content. The carbon content is of interest because, in the absence of other contaminants, it determined the iron's mechanical properties. In the order of increasing carbon content, the alloys of iron and carbon are wrought iron; mild, medium, and hard steel; and pig or cast iron. Uncarburized iron is too soft and cast iron is too brittle to be satisfactory utilitarian metals—such as the axes or hoes commonly used throughout Africa. Bloomery iron was typically wrought iron or low-grade steel.

Before it was fashioned into objects, the iron bloom was reheated in the forge and hammered to expel slag. This treatment compressed the bloom and often decarburized the iron as conditions in the forge tended to be strongly oxidizing. The final bloom iron might still contain some slag stringers—characteristics that would identify it as a wrought iron.

A blast furnace operates at higher temperatures than a bloomery furnace and produces liquid rather than solid metal. At the higher temperatures, particles of iron absorb enough carbon as they pass through the furnace to depress their melting point below the ambient temperature. (The addition of carbon depresses the melting point of iron. Pure iron melts at 1,534°C, but iron with a carbon content of 4.3 percent melts at 1,147°C.) Whereas the bloomery furnace produced a heterogeneous iron with a comparatively low carbon content and considerable amounts of slag, the blast furnace produces cast iron with a high carbon content and little slag. Bloomery iron—if decarburized at the forge—sometimes had to be recarburized to gain hardness, but blast-furnace iron must be decarburized to reduce brittleness and regain malleability.

Iron smelting in Buhaya, in both ancient and modern times, was intermediate between the bloomery and the blast-furnace processes. This is a characterization that has also been used in a discussion of the Mafa smelting process in northern Cameroon (David et al. 1989), where some cast iron also results from smelting. The Haya furnaces reached higher temperatures than the typical bloomery furnace. Although the reduction of the iron was still largely a solid-state process, liquid metal was also formed. Compared to the typical bloomery product, the Haya blooms were relatively free of slag and well consolidated, had a minimal spongelike quality, and had a high but heterogeneous carbon content.

The Haya Iron Smelting Process

There are three significant features in the Haya smelts described in the last two chapters: the iron ore was roasted or presmelted before it was smelted; the tuyeres extended deep into the furnace bowl; and the bowl was filled with charred swamp reeds. These might seem like minor details, but as we came to realize, they are all aspects of a distinctive technological solution to the challenges posed by local resources. Their significance becomes clearer when the experimental smelts are described from a metallurgical rather than a social or ideological point of view.

Through chemical and petrographic analysis, we identified the ore the Haya harvested as predominantly limonite ($FeO(OH).H_2O$), or amorphous hydrated iron oxide. The hydrated oxides were probably formed when water leached the iron oxides from iron-bearing minerals, eventually depositing them in a shale matrix. The leaching would have occurred when lake levels in Victoria Nyanza were 6 to 10 meters higher. The Haya ores, then, are similar to bog ores, ubiquitous iron ores formed in bogs, lakes, or waterlogged soils.

Limonite is considered a lean ore, that is, one whose iron oxide content is comparatively low. For the Haya process, however, it had several compensating characteristics. The iron oxides in the ore form visible bands (fig. 5.2), and therefore the iron content of a furnace charge could be increased by sorting the ore before smelting. Because limonite is porous, it could be broken into small pieces before smelting and was easily penetrated by reducing gases during smelting. The hydrated limonite also shrank

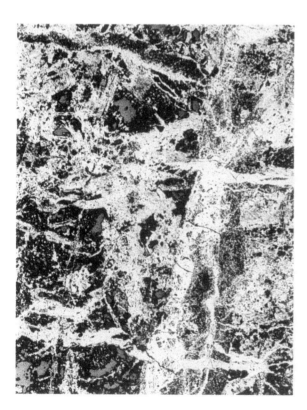

FIG. 5.2 A photomicrograph of limonite ore with goethite from the Karuyenje mine in Kiziba. Magnification 40×. Photo by Terry Childs.

and cracked when it was roasted, which created a larger surface area ideal for smelting. Finally, because limonite contains enough nonmetallic material to be self-fluxing, other materials such as calcium did not have to be added to the furnace charge to stimulate slag production.

The first point of interest in the Haya process was the presmelting or roasting of the iron ore. Roasting was more than a preparatory process intended to drive off water, although that was certainly an important result of the procedure. As described in chapter 3, once the ore had been broken into pieces 1 or 2 centimeters long (about the size of medium-grade landscaping gravel) and air-dried, it was roasted in a carbon monoxide atmosphere at temperatures between 600 and 900°C. These temperatures were well below the melting point of the metal, yet high enough to allow its partial reduction.

To document more fully the transformations the ore undergoes during roasting, we made a thin section of a piece from the roasting pit. The development of gases and their escape from the ore caused many fissures to form across the iron oxide bands (fig. 5.3) (Childs 1996). In the piece examined, the iron oxides had been transformed by reduction to Fe_3O_4 and to FeO_3. The surfaces of the ore were blackened by the reduced iron oxides and deposited carbon, which eventually became incorporated in the slag and contributed further to reduction (Avery and Schmidt 1979).

FIG. 5.3 A photomicrograph of cracks in limonite ore from the Karuyenje mine. The cracks, through which CO gases pass, are induced by presmelting. Magnification 40×. Photo by Terry Childs.

Roasting, then, began the process of reduction that was finished in the smelting furnace. Although some of the metal may have been reoxidized when it passed though the blast zone in the furnace (Avery and Schmidt 1979), roasting promoted more complete recovery of the iron in the ore. Moreover, in the case of the Haya process, roasting ore on the periphery of the furnace during a smelt very likely also conserved fuel. Indeed, this practice may have been an adaptive response to dwindling wood resources; the Barongo smelters, who live in a wood-rich environment to the southwest of Victoria Nyanza, do not roast their ore.

The Furnace Environment

The chemistry of the slag is as important to the smelting process as the chemistry of the iron ore. Most of the slag derives from minerals in the ore, but some also derive from the clay tuyeres and the fuels. Even though the tuyeres were made of heat-resistant clay, they began to melt as temperatures in the furnace rose above 1,500°C. The melting tuyeres contributed silica to the slag, helping to maintain fluid conditions in the furnace. On the other hand, the tuyeres also contributed significant amounts of alumina (Al_2O_3) to the slag—the alumina content of the clay being as high as 35 percent (Childs 1986). The refractory alumina increased the melting temperature and increased the viscosity of the slag.

We know from other research that the fuels were potentially a source of fluxes, such as calcium and potassium, that might counterbalance the alumina. Some African smelters sought out species of trees with a high calcium content for use in iron smelting. Trees such as Zizyphus contain as much as 5 percent calcium and seem to have been selected as fuels specifically because of their fluxing action. Judith Todd (1979: 69) found that the Dimi of southwest Ethiopia used a fuel with a calcium content of 3.7 percent for the same reason. We were therefore curious to learn the chemical makeup of the Haya fuels.

The Mucwezi tree (*Syzygium guineenses*), which the Haya used to make charcoal, is a hot-burning fuel that leaves little ash. Its chemical makeup held few surprises, but the calcium and potassium levels were sufficiently high that, considering that more than 100 kilograms of charcoal was burned in each smelt, they likely acted as a minor flux. The swamp grass (*Miscanthidium violaceum*) burned to ash and charred, fibrous stalks in the furnace pit. Chemical analysis showed that these residues also did not contain large amounts of calcium and potassium.

The grass nevertheless acted as a local flux. The tightly packed reeds created a maze of fine carbonaceous tubes coated by calcium- and potassium-containing ash. As pools of slag formed below the tuyeres and infiltrated the char, some of the fluid fayalitic slag drained through these tubes—assisted by a coating of calcium and potassium—toward the bottom of the furnace pit. Based on the amount of char consumed in the course of a typical smelt, we calculated that roughly 80 grams of calcium and 50 grams of potassium would enter the slag by this route.

This local fluxing action is an important feature of the Haya technology. Because the slag readily infiltrated the fluxed char, carbonaceous filaments were incorporated into it. The microenvironment created by the engulfment of carbonaceous material was instrumental to the production of a carbon steel, with metal forming along the carbon interface (Schmidt and Avery 1978; Avery and Schmidt 1979; Childs 1996) (fig. 5.4).

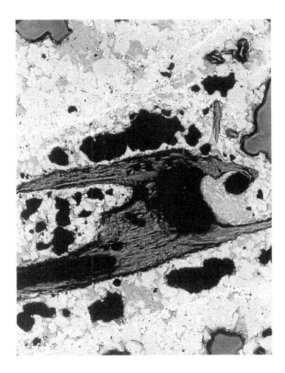

Fig. 5.4 The reduction of metal—strings of white dots—along the interface with a charred reed. Magnification 40x. Photo by Terry Childs.

The Tuyeres and Bellows

In the furnaces made by the Nyungwe smelters, a good 40 centimeters of the tuyeres typically lay within the furnace. When smelting started, the tuyeres were directed upward at an angle of between 15 and 20 degrees to the horizontal, lying against the mound of grass char and charcoal. The bellows tips were positioned close to the trumpet-shaped end of the tuyere, a carefully adjusted gap between the two. The bellows were operated by the rhythmic vertical motion of two sticks attached to the goatskins that covered twin bowls. Pumping started at a remarkable 480 strokes per minute and gradually dropped to between 350 and 400 strokes. On each stroke, half a liter of air was expressed from the bellows.

The pumped air wasn't the only air that entered the furnace, however. The jet of forced air created a low-pressure zone around it—the famous Bernoulli effect, which is also responsible for the lift generated by air moving past aircraft wings—and the low-pressure zone caused air to be aspirated into the furnace. The total air consumption, calculated from the charcoal burning rate of about 20 kilograms per hour, suggests that as much as half the air entering the furnace was aspirated rather than pumped.

As mentioned in earlier chapters, some of the bellows operators who participated in our experimental smelts were unable to maintain the ideal pumping rate, and at least two and sometimes three tuyeres were at some time blocked by slag during a smelt. Intermittent or desultory bellows operation was largely responsible for plugged tuyeres. Archaeological evidence of plugged tuyeres is not significant, however, and it seems unlikely that ancient smelters had similar failures in maintaining discipline on the bellows.

Preheating and Furnace Performance

The tuyeres were central to the success of the Haya smelting furnace because they heated the air blast as it traversed them. In most "preindustrial" furnaces the combustion air entered the furnace cold and exited hot. This was inefficient, because significant energy was expended heating the nitrogen in the air, which did not participate in the reduction reaction (Rostoker and Bronson 1990). Moreover, as suggested earlier, the use of unheated air limited the temperature that could be reached while maintaining a reducing atmosphere.

Preheating offered a solution to both problems. In preheating, hot exhaust gases are used to heat incoming air, recovering energy much as does an air-to-air heat exchanger (see Avery and Schmidt 1979, 1996). This decreased the fuel consumption needed to maintain a given furnace temperature. And, preheating allowed higher temperatures to be achieved without shifting to oxidizing conditions. The flame temperature that can be achieved while maintaining a given furnace atmosphere depends on the temperature of the incoming air. The upper limit for reducing conditions with a cold blast is about 1,300°C. With air preheated to 600°C, it becomes 1,870°C (Schmidt and Avery 1978).

One of the primary goals of our experimental smelts was to measure the temperature of the air in the tuyeres in authentic Haya furnaces. We monitored tuyere temperatures during the first four smelts in 1976 and during the 1979 and 1984 smelts. Our measurement technique has been questioned (Rehder 1986; Killick 1996), yet we have recognized that radiant heat from the blast zone and tuyere walls could interfere with accurate measurement of the temperature of the air in the tuyeres. This led us to experiment with various heat shields for our thermocouples. We found that we obtained the most accurate results when the thermocouple was placed in a protecting ceramic tube and the sensing element was bent at a right angle to the tube wall, so that it projected into the air flow.[1]

The air blast was heated primarily by the hot inner wall of the tuyere. For the last 10 or 15 centimeters, the exterior of the tuyere was coated with fluid slag at a temperature of between 1,150 and 1,300°C. Because this slag penetrated at least halfway through the tuyere wall, one might have expected the inside wall to be incandescent. The tuyeres did not appear to glow, however, and direct contact with thermocouples picked up temperatures well below the expected 1,000°C. The missing heat had been transferred from the wall to the air passing through the tuyere.

Because the Haya bellows are valveless, the air blast had a push-pause pattern, which turned out to be crucial to effective preheating. On the upstroke, the airflow in the tuyere slowed down and reversed direction, and hot gases were pulled from the furnace into the tuyere end. (The reversals of flow could be monitored by watching flaps of melting clay at the tuyere mouth—particularly during slower, hard bellows pulses.) The upstroke thus increased the dwell time of the air inside the tuyere, allowing it to reach higher temperatures than it otherwise would (Avery and Schmidt 1986, 1996) (fig. 5.5).

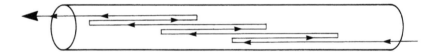

FIG. 5.5 A schematic view of a tuyere showing the increased dwell time caused by the push-pause effect of the bellows. After Avery and Schmidt (1996).

There was a subtler effect at work as well. Under conditions of continuous flow, a thin stagnant layer would have formed next to the tuyere wall. This layer, called a boundary layer, would have acted much as does the air between the panes of a double-hung window, reducing heat transfer from the wall to the airstream. But when the flow in the Haya tuyere reversed, it created turbulence that mixed the heated boundary-layer air—like strips of skin being peeled back—into the main airstream. Because there is no adequate mathematical model for reverse turbulence, we calculated the heat transfer that would occur if the turbulence were continuous (Avery and Schmidt 1986, 1996). *The heat transfer occurring under conditions of intermittent reverse turbulence is even greater.*

Other characteristics of the tuyeres may also have increased air turbulence in them. Tylecote (1965) suggests that the degree of preheat in a Nigerian (Matakam and Tchede) furnace may have increased appreciably when pebbles were placed inside the tuyere, probably because the pebbles increased turbulence and thus heat transfer. In the Haya case, the rough interiors of the tuyeres and the hanging flaps of melting clay at their mouths may have served the same purpose.

Taking into account dwell time and assuming continuous turbulence, we conservatively calculate that the air should have been heated by about 300°C during its passage through the tuyere, a result in agreement with our measurements (Schmidt and Avery 1978; Avery and Schmidt 1979, 1986, 1996). The effect was reducing temperatures in the furnace up to 150 to 200°C above the 1,300° limit of the typical bloomery (fig. 5.6).

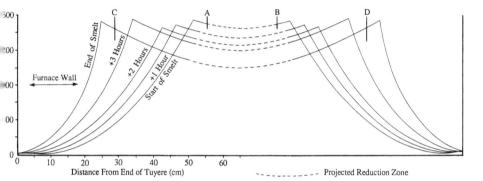

FIG. 5.6 A schematic drawing of Haya furnace temperatures over time. This is the extension of one-half of a furnace profile taken through one tuyere that was published in Schmidt and Avery 1978 (fig. 5). The mirror imaging of the profile, when combined with precise measurements of the furnace dimensions, allows us to show the isotherms with the oxidizing and reducing zones. The most important observation is that the temperatures that prevail in the interior of the furnace are reducing and do not fall below 1,200°C until the end of the smelt. This is one of the most important features of the Haya process, a critical innovation that results from preheating. After Avery and Schmidt (1996).

Smelting

The hot, reducing conditions achieved by preheating meant that the chemistry of the Haya smelts was quite different from that of most bloomery smelts. Together with the height of the furnace stack, these conditions ensured that the initial reduction process—before the formation of the slag—was exceptionally efficient. Together with the bed of charred reeds in the furnace pit, such conditions ensured that iron continued to be recovered even after the slag formed. For both reasons the hot, reducing conditions led to more efficient recovery of iron from the slag and to the formation of solid pieces of iron that often lacked the spongelike structure common to ancient European and other African processes.

The smelt typically started with the furnace stack charged two-thirds full, because a full charge tended to choke off exhaust gases, creating disadvantageous back pressure. After bellows pumping began, the furnace was periodically charged with charcoal and roasted ore in a 10 to 1 mixture. This high fuel-to-ore ratio made abundant carbon available for reduction and for carburizing the iron once it had been reduced from the ore.

Combustion of the charcoal produced carbon dioxide, which in the presence of the excess carbon reacted to form carbon monoxide. As carbon monoxide was produced and temperatures in the stack rose above 700°, metal production began again in the roasted ore as a solid-state process. The carbon monoxide reacted with the iron oxides, removing oxygen to produce wustite (FeO). As the iron ore, now partially converted to wustite, traveled down the stack, more oxygen was lost, and uncarburized iron metal, or ferrite, began to form as spheres (solid, not liquid) and platelets of iron.

For a variety of reasons, the ore had a comparatively long time to react with the reducing gases before slagging started. One was that the moderately tall stack and excavated pit created a fairly long reaction zone. Another was that the bed of larger charcoal chunks initially kept the ore suspended high in the stack (fig. 5.7). A third was that the ore pieces were also comparatively large (Childs 1996). Tholander (1987) has done laboratory experiments showing that larger ore pieces tended to stay up in a stack longer, and that these suspended pieces developed a structure with concentric layers. Analysis of the ore from the Haya smelts showed that some of it did indeed have this layered structure: an inner core of wustite

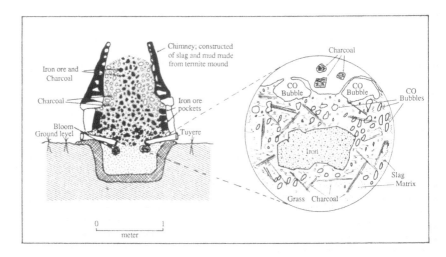

FIG. 5.7 A schematic view showing the suspension of iron ore in the furnace stack. Also shown is the function of the charred reeds and ash in creating a high carbon contact area in the furnace pit, leading to a carbon boil.

and other components lay within a layer of iron and wustite, which in turn lay within a layer of metal—where the first reduction occurred (Childs 1996). The presence of ore pieces with this structure indicates comparatively efficient reduction of the iron in the ore before it approaches the blast zone.

As the iron descended toward the tuyeres, the temperature rose. When the ore reached a temperature of about 1,175°C, the wustite and silicates (SiO_2) began to react to create a fayalitic slag (Fe_2SiO_4) that coated the iron. This coating had the beneficial effect of protecting the iron from reoxidizing as it passed through the highly oxidizing blast zone immediately in front of the tuyeres, but it also stopped the reduction of wustite to metal.

The reduction and recovery of metallic iron nonetheless continued by other means. Instead of being reduced by the carbon-rich furnace gases, the iron oxides were reduced by the carbon-rich grass char. Below the tuyeres, the iron slag dripped onto and was drawn into the bed of grass char. In the process, carbonaceous char and filaments were incorporated into the slag mass, lacing the slag with carbon. Droplets (solid particles) of iron formed when iron oxides in the slag were exposed to carbon in this way. These droplets sometimes collected into long, thin, ribbonlike sheets of iron on the outer surfaces of the grass char and charcoal (fig. 5.8) (Childs 1996). The bed of grass char promoted the formation of the bloom by a mechanical effect as well as by chemical ones. As the liquid slag flowed

FIG. 5.8 Thin lines of metal (white) reducing at the slag/charred grass interface, and then moving away from the interface because of the movement of the slag through the grass. Magnification 40×. Photo by Terry Childs.

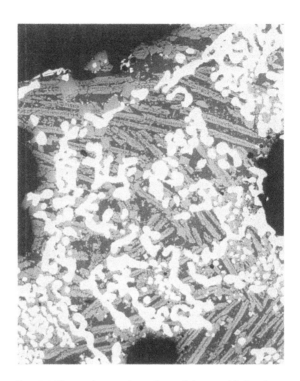

FIG. 5.9 The agglomeration of metal dots and flakes into iron sheets within fayalitic slag. Magnification 80×. Photo by Terry Childs.

through the confined spaces in the tightly packed bed of grasses, iron droplets and flakes tended to segregate from the slag and aggregate into progressively larger sheets and flakes (fig. 5.9).

Once a molten slag mass had developed below each tuyere, another, rather spectacular mechanism for the recovery of iron took over—a carbon boil. The abundant carbon from the charcoal reacted violently with oxygen in the combustion air and from the iron oxides dissolved in the slag, producing bubbles of carbon monoxide that rose through the slag and exploded on its surface (Schmidt and Avery 1978; Avery and Schmidt 1979). Iron oxides in the slag were reduced when carbon monoxide escaped from the slag in this way (see fig. 5.7).

The carbon boil also set up conditions that accelerated the formation of an iron mass. Droplets and sheets of iron that descended into the molten slag were redissolved in it. As more iron entered the slag and its oxygen content was reduced by the carbon boil, it became supersaturated with metallic iron. Iron then precipitated out in large, perfect crystals (fig. 5.10) (Schmidt and Avery 1978), much as rock candy precipitates out of a super-

Fig. 5.10 An SEM view of the large perfect iron crystals that form in the iron bloom. Photo by D. H. Avery.

Fig. 5.11 A photomicrograph showing fingery—dendritic—iron projections (white) from an iron mass into a glassy slag; 1979 smelt. Magnification 70×. Photo by Terry Childs.

saturated sugar solution. As this process continued, smaller deposits of iron joined the growing metallic mass by attaching to fingerlike (dendritic) projections that extended from the mass into the slag (fig. 5.11).

Ironically, one of the reasons this process of incremental precipitation worked was that furnace temperatures fluctuated widely during the course of a smelt. As the smelters grew tired, paid more attention to their beer gourds than to their bellows, or traded off with fresh bellows operators, the temperature varied by as much as several hundred degrees Celsius. Temperature increases caused small droplets and flakes of iron to dissolve in the slag; temperature decreases then caused the iron to precipitate out in iron "plates" (Avery, van der Merwe, and Saitowitz 1988). The cyclic temperature cycles thus encouraged the formation of large, solid pieces of iron.

As the oxygen in the slag mass was reduced by the carbon boil, the slag also became more refractory, particularly toward the end of the smelt when it was no longer "diluted" by new slag dripping down from the stack (Avery and Schmidt 1979; Childs 1996). Preheating conferred a last advantage at this stage of the process. Because the furnace was hotter, the increasingly refractory slag remained fluid longer, giving the iron more time to form in the slag mass and allowing more complete extraction of the iron. At the end of the smelt, however, temperatures sank below the solidification temperature of the slag, and slag envelopes froze near and around the tuyeres.

Carburization of the Iron

The ferritic iron reduced in the solid state high in the furnace stack or later in the slag was eventually converted to carbon steel and, sometimes, to cast iron. Two quite different mechanisms contributed to the carburization of the iron.

As the ferritic iron mass gradually grew within its slag envelope, carbon introduced by contact with the charcoal or grasses slowly diffused into the ferrite. For the most part such solid-state diffusion yielded low- to medium-carbon steel with a carbon content of between 0.2 and 0.8 percent (Schmidt and Avery 1978; Avery and Schmidt 1979; Childs 1996) (fig. 5.12).

In two furnace locations, however, enough carbon is absorbed into the iron to create liquid cast iron. First, portions of the combustion zone above and behind the tuyeres became hot enough and reducing enough to produce cast iron (Rostoker and Bronson 1990). In these zones solid grains of ferrite absorbed large amounts of carbon from the carbon monoxide gas evolved by the carbon boil. Enough carbon could be absorbed to depress the melting point of the iron below the ambient temperature. Drops of cast iron then fell on the iron bloom forming below, where they helped to carburize the ferritic iron. The dripping cast iron helps explain the high carbon concentrations on the exterior of consolidated Haya blooms (ibid.; Schmidt and Childs 1995; Childs 1996). The second location was the bed of charred fuel in the furnace pit. As the solid metal began to coalesce in this bed, very small pockets of liquid cast iron sometimes formed at the metal-fuel interface (fig. 5.13). As solid iron accumulated near the cast iron—derived mostly from the shower of cast iron from above the tuyeres—it absorbed carbon from the cast-iron layer (Schmidt and Childs 1995). One of the more successful smelts produced a layered bloom like those produced by the highly efficient Japanese *tatara* process of smelting. The bloom consisted of a top layer of cast iron, a middle layer of carbon steel, and a bottom layer of ferrite (Schmidt and Childs 1995; Childs 1996).

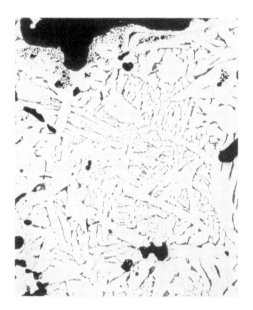

Fig. 5.12 Low-carbon steel in a 1976 smelt. The dots along the edge are phosphides. Magnification 65×; 2% nital etch. Photo by Terry Childs.

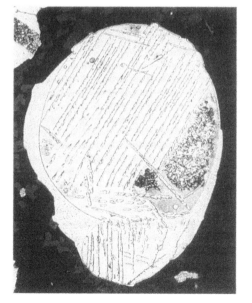

Fig. 5.13 A prill of cast iron with carbide laths and possible phosphide from the 1979 smelt. Magnification 330×; 2% nital etch. Photo by Terry Childs.

The hot, reducing conditions that lead to the carburization of the iron, however, also led to the absorption of available phosphorus. Carburization was largely desirable, since it contributed to the formation of dense blooms with little entrained slag during smelting and since a steel-like material could be shaped into tools quickly and efficiently. In any event, carburization was reversible in the forge, where oxidizing conditions could be used to remove excess carbon. Phosphorization, on the other hand, was a more difficult problem. On one hand, phosphorus—because it lowered the melting point of iron even further—also contributed to the formation of dense blooms during smelting. On the other hand, phosphorization, which was irreversible, gave the metal undesirable mechanical properties that complicated forging, particular during the cold-working phase.

We stumbled onto the role of phosphorus in Haya ironmaking technology when analysis showed that it was present in all of the blooms produced in the Haya smelts, in heirloom Haya blooms, and in slag and iron samples from Early Iron Age sites (Schmidt and Childs 1995; Childs 1996). The introduction of phosphorus into iron and its effects on fabrication have not been well investigated in Africa. Phosphorus often derives from the ore, as is the case among the Dimi of southwest Ethiopia (Todd 1979). It may also be a constituent of the fuel, ceramic refractories, or fluxing materials. Since limonite ores can have a high phosphorus content, our first conjecture was that in the Haya case the phosphorus was coming from the ores.

We were wrong. Although small amounts of phosphorus pentoxide—P_2O_5 (0.1 to 0.2%)—occur in the Tanzanian ores, the more significant source is the furnace fuels. The ash of the Mucwezi tree used to make charcoal has a phosphorus content of about 0.15 percent, and the charred swamp reeds packed into the furnace pit averaged 0.34 percent phosphorus—particularly important because of the high-contact areas that this fuel had with the molten slag.

In the conditions of the smelting furnace, phosphorus-containing compounds are reduced to phosphorus vapor, which is readily absorbed by metallic iron under reducing conditions. The amount of phosphorus entering the iron depends on the temperature. At typical bloomery temperatures, about 30 percent of the available phosphorus is absorbed by the iron, but a blast furnace extracts nearly all of the phosphorus present (Rostoker and Bronson 1990).

Like carbon, phosphorus benefited the smelting process. When iron absorbs phosphorus, it forms alloys whose melting temperatures are significantly lower than those of pure iron or iron alloyed with carbon. Analysis of slag samples and blooms from the replicated smelts demonstrated the presence of two eutectics (alloys with melting temperatures lower than those of their constituent elements). One was the iron-iron phosphide eutectic called steadite, which contains 10.5 percent phosphorus and melts at 1,050°C (Stead 1915, 1918; Hansen 1958). The second was an iron-carbon-iron phosphide eutectic, which contains 2 percent carbon and 6.9 percent phosphorus and has a melting temperature of only 953°C (Tholander 1987). By extending the range of temperatures over which liquid cast iron was formed, the phosphorus assisted the formation of dense and relatively slag-free blooms with a high carbon content (Schmidt and Childs 1995; Childs 1996).

Although it might assist the smelter, phosphorus challenged the smith (Todd and Charles 1978; Gordon 1984; Rostoker and Dvorak 1986; Tylecote and Gilmore 1986; Goodway 1987; Rostoker and Bronson 1990). In the absence of carbon, phosphorus hardens iron; indeed, it is about twice as effective at hardening iron as is carbon (Hopkins and Tipler 1958; Tylecote and Gilmore 1986). But ferritic iron that contains more than 0.5 percent phosphorus is brittle, or "cold short" (Gordon 1984). The metal tends to fracture if it is cold forged and may shatter on impact at room temperature.

The archeological evidence suggests that Haya smiths became adept at coping with the foibles of phosphorus-rich iron (Schmidt and Childs 1995; Childs 1996). Apparently they were able to recognize variations in the phosphorus content of different areas of a bloom and to select parts of the bloom likely to have mechanical properties equal to the task at hand—such as selecting pieces of bloom high in phosphorus for the manufacture of ritual objects (Schmidt and Childs 1995; Childs 1996; see chapter 6). In addition, they probably varied the technique used to work the iron according to their assessment of its characteristics. Although phosphorus-rich iron tends to crack when it is cold worked, it can often be successfully hot forged. The mechanical properties of a high-carbon, high-phosphorus metal can also be improved by reducing its carbon content in the forge.

The Uniqueness of Haya Iron Technology

The more we learned about the technology of iron smelting in northwest Tanzania, the more difficult it was to believe that borrowing had played any significant role in its development. The Haya smelt had many distinctive features, including the preheating of the blast air, the efficient recovery of iron, the carbon boil, the formation of cast iron, and the formation of phosphorus-rich cast iron. It is simply easier to believe that these many interlocking features arose from an incremental process of experimentation than to believe that they were learned as an ensemble by imitation. Moreover, reflecting on these innovations, one comes to realize that they are all, in one way or another, adaptations to the chemistry peculiar to local materials: the limonite ores, the Mucwezi charcoal, the swamp reeds, and the refractory tuyere clay. In the end, the only coherent interpretation of the Haya technology is that it is as distinctive and as indigenous as the materials it exploited.

6.

Comparative

Models

Forging a

History of

Haya Iron

Smelting

In chapter 5 I described the experimental smelts conducted by the Haya from a metallurgical point of view. The ultimate goal is not just to understand the modern technology, but rather to trace the evolution of the technology back through history and prehistory to its earliest beginnings in the region. But what can we legitimately deduce about prehistoric technology from the modern experiments? Although ancient and modern processes seem to have been broadly similar, there were clearly also differences between them. Moreover, comparison is complicated by the fragmentary physical evidence left by early smelts. At a typical Early Iron Age site only the furnace pit remains as evidence, together with some of the bottom slags, charcoal, partially reduced iron ore, fragments of tuyeres, and pieces of the furnace superstructure. The shaft has been dismantled, any iron blooms have been harvested, and most of the slag has been processed or scattered. Finished iron artifacts are also scarce, both because they too were recycled and because iron rusts easily, quickly returning to the earth in this warm and moist climate.

The experimental smelts are a reasonable point of departure for reconstructing the history of iron technology in the Kagera region for a simple but telling reason: the productivity of these smelts was roughly comparable to that of smelts conducted when smelting was routine. A study of old iron blooms kept as heirlooms showed that one man on an eight-man furnace could produce 2 to 7 kilograms of carbon steel; in exceptional cases a single bloom might weigh 9 kilograms. If the other smelters were similarly productive, a smelt might have produced between 16 and 56 kilograms of steel. Although the modern Haya smelters did not achieve this level of productivity—their highest yield was slightly more than 10 kilograms of iron—they sometimes reached the lower end of the range of yields common at the turn of the century and would probably have matched the higher yields had they continued to smelt.

But productivity is only a crude measure of the degree of similarity between smelting practices. To proceed further, we needed a method of investigation that exploited the evidence of modern smelts but did not assume that ancient practices were identical to modern ones. The method we devised was to determine the material fingerprints that technological behaviors such as preheating leave behind and then to look for these and other fingerprints in the physical remains of historic or prehistoric smelts. Like human fingerprints or other clues found at the scene of a crime, the microscopic structure of the furnace products is definitive evidence, not easily dismissed or eluded. In this way, our technological detective work holds our archaeological interpretations to a high standard of proof.

As we pursued our investigations, we tried to remain as alert to discrepancies as to similarities in the evidence from different periods in the history of smelting. Archaeologists have been concerned, for example, that the use of analogy tends to level differences between the past and the present (e.g., Gould 1980; Wylie 1985). We naturally seek similarities when we compare past cultures with present circumstances. But good critical comparison often roots out variations or differences that alert us to technological change and open fruitful ground for inquiry into the reasons for the change. It is particularly important to be alert to differences in the case of Buhaya because there is a high degree of continuity between prehistoric and modern communities in this area.

In this chapter I describe some of the material fingerprints we identified as we sought to understand the evolution of iron smelting technology in northwest Tanzania. Recognizing that most readers will be unfamiliar with metallurgy, I have chosen examples that are representative of the evidence available to us and of the problems of interpretation that arose in considering this evidence. Although this discussion is not exhaustive, I hope it will give the reader a grasp of the comparative method.

Evidence in the Slags ⸺

The physical evidence left in the greatest abundance by ancient smelting operations is slag. As we sought to build a technological model that would allow us to accurately interpret our archaeological finds, we therefore began by seeking to understand slag. We analyzed slag samples from the experimental smelts, particularly the sixth smelt in 1976 (Appendix A.2 and A.3), which was the most successful one in that year, and the 1979 smelt (Appendix A.3 and A.4), which was the most successful smelt of all. We also examined the forging slags created when a smith fashioned a sickle from one of the experimental blooms.

These investigations identified the following material fingerprints: crystals of the mineral hercynite containing solidified drops of iron are a fingerprint of a high-temperature smelting process; a low wustite content is an index of an efficient process and one likely to form iron with a high carbon content; bubbly or frothy slags are markers of a carbon boil; and a relatively high wustite content together with a relatively low hercynite content is characteristic of a forging rather than a smelting slag (S. T. Childs, personal communication).

The study of iron technology in Africa (and elsewhere) has been plagued by attempts to characterize smelting technology by surface finds of slag or slag taken from slag heaps (Bachmann 1982; Morton and Wingrove 1969, 1972), a method that implicitly assumes that all of the slags produced by a smelt are essentially identical. In fact, a furnace contains many different microenvironments, each of which has distinctive material fingerprints. As a result, an inadequate sample or samples taken out of context can easily lead to significant errors and misrepresentations.

The relative iron content of a slag, for example, depends in part on where it formed. It is therefore potentially misleading to calculate the productivity of a smelting process by comparing the iron content of the ore to that of one or even several out-of-context slag samples. Similarly, the volume of a slag heap cannot be used to estimate productivity without knowledge of the slag types, documented ratios of productivity for different slag types, and knowledge of the degree of slag recycling typical of a particular community (see Schmidt 1996c).

Because the experimental smelting furnaces were excavated as carefully as if they had been Early Iron Age furnaces, we knew the locations and the context of the slag samples later subjected to metallographic analysis. We were therefore in a unique position to comment on the significance of their microstructures. Slags were selected for analysis that were similar in appearance, or morphology, to Early Iron Age slags. Morphological types common among Early Iron Age slags include, for example, glassy slags with distinct charcoal impressions and fluid-looking slags with the ropy texture. Some researchers (Fells 1983) have not been able to correlate chemical composition and specific minerals with morphology, but they were mostly working with surface finds. We felt we were more likely to be successful because we had contextual information that would help define these associations.

Some slags selected for analysis, however, had no archaeological counterparts. These included slags whose surfaces bore the impressions of grasses (samples 2, 3, 4, and E—see fig. 6.1) and those with a light, metallic surface color and a frothy structure (samples A and D fig. 6.1). The absence of matching slags did not necessarily mean that the smelting process had changed. Instead it may simply mean that some types of slag were more likely to be recycled or beaten into tiny fragments and thus less likely to be preserved. Indeed, we know that at least one type of slag is consistently missing from the archaeological record: the slag envelope of the iron bloom that was beaten off the bloom before forging.

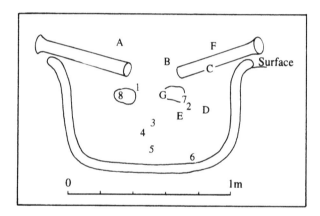

Fig. 6.1 A schematic drawing of a furnace pit showing the location of slag samples taken in 1976 and 1979, discussed in this analysis.

The locations of all the slag samples we examined are presented in fig. 6.1, a schematic cross-section of the iron smelting furnace. Density and degree of magnetism proved to be a good initial means of assessing the variability of the slags (Appendix A.1). Both characteristics reflect the amount of iron trapped in the slag as either iron oxide or magnetite. We found that the most metallic and densest slags accumulated near the top of the furnace pit and that the nonmetallic, fluid slags fell toward the furnace bottom.

We then undertook the laboratory analyses needed to determine the predominant phases and chemistry of the slag samples (Appendix A.2, A.3, and A.4). The concept of a phase may require some explanation. A phase is a homogeneous constituent (gas, liquid, or solid) that is physically distinct—in a solid it is an area distinguishable by its composition, properties, or structure from other areas of the solid. A molten material segregates into different phases as it solidifies if the elements of which it is composed have limited solubility in one another. Zinc, for example, has only limited solubility in copper. If a large amount of liquid zinc is added to liquid copper and the mixture is allowed to solidify, two phases with different proportions of the metals form. In general, by identifying the phases in a solid, one can determine their chemical environment and the temperature at which they formed.

I have mentioned that hercynite crystals proved to be a high-temperature marker. Hercynite (FeO.Al$_2$O$_3$) appears in slag samples as octahedral crystals. These crystals are particularly abundant in the slags that formed at the periphery of the blast zone and near the tuyeres. During the smelt, the temperature in these zones rose above the 1,500° melting temperature of the tuyere clay (Childs 1986, 1989b). Because the clay had a high alumina content (between 25 and 35 percent), its melting introduced considerable amounts of aluminum oxides into the slag. The oxides reacted with iron oxides from the ore to form hercynite. When the temperature then fell below the solidification temperature of hercynite (1,470°C), this mineral began to crystallize around metal droplets, which acted as nucleation centers (fig. 6.2). Hercynite grains containing solidified drops of iron, then, are a clear fingerprint of high temperatures in this furnace zone.

But the situation is actually a bit more complicated than this. The reason is that these high-temperature markers appear against a background of hercynite crystals formed by a different, lower-temperature process. Other researchers have shown that slags from lean ores, such as that used by the Haya, are characterized by the presence of spinels as well as of fayalite (Fe$_2$SiO$_4$) and wustite (FeO) (Morton and Wingrove 1972).[1] Hercynite is one of the minerals in the spinel series.

The hercynite in most of the slags from lower in the Haya furnaces (Appendix A.4) probably derives from the alumina in the ores rather than in the tuyere clays. The alumina might have formed a spinel during ore roasting by a solid-state process. The hercynite crystals, which were the final form of these spinels, were then dispersed as the fayalitic slag descended into the furnace pit. Thus, this lower slag represents earlier phases of the smelting process.

The hercynite content of the slags formed in this way is a marker of their viscosity rather than of a high-temperature process. The fluid slags surrounding the grass fuel tend to contain less hercynite and alumina than the more refractory, hercynite-rich slags near the iron bloom. In other words, proper interpretation of the hercynite fingerprint must take into account the type of slag and requires knowledge of the context in which the slag formed.

A second material fingerprint, the wustite (FeO) content of the slag, is generally considered an indicator of the efficiency of the smelting process (Morton and Wingrove 1972). If the wustite content of the slag is high, much of the iron in the ore has escaped complete reduction; if the wustite

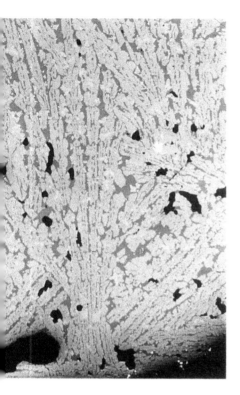 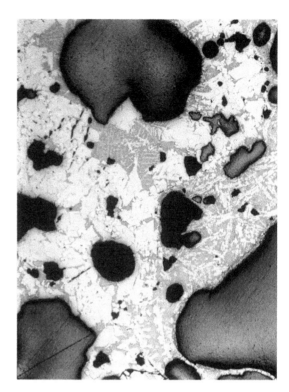

Fɪɢ. 6.2 (*left*) A dot of metal (white) surrounded by a hercynite crystal in a fayalitic slag. Magnification 80×; 2% nital etch. Photo by Terry Childs.

Fɪɢ. 6.3 (*right*) A typical bottom flow slag from a 1976 smelt. It is predominantly fayalite (medium gray) with hercynite (cubes appeared to be in relief) and occasional metal droplets (white). Magnification 40×; 2% nital etch. Photo by Terry Childs.

content is low, the iron was efficiently reduced. Bloomery slags normally contain large amounts of wustite, but the slags from the bottom of the Haya furnaces contain relatively little (fig. 6.3). Indeed, the Haya were probably able to recover useful amounts of iron from the lean ores in their environment only because they possessed a particularly efficient technology.

In the case of the Haya furnaces, the low wustite content of the slags may have an additional meaning. Some of the factors that contributed to the efficiency of these furnaces were discussed in chapter 5. The reader will remember that wustite was reduced to iron both in the furnace stack, where it reacted with the carbon-rich furnace gases, and in the bed of grass char, where it reacted with carbon-rich iron and the carbon-rich fuel bed. Although the Haya furnaces were characterized by a long primary reduction zone—when the ore slowly descended through the tall furnace stack—the later reactions in the slag below the tuyeres contributed significantly to metal formation. In the Haya context, then, a low wustite content suggests that the slag mass contained abundant carbon that allowed reduction to continue even after slagging had occurred. Moreover, the shower of cast iron onto the bloom and slag mass contributed yet more carbon, leading to yet further reduction as the wustite came into intimate contact with the iron. Low wustite is therefore an important fingerprint for a process that efficiently extracts iron.

The 1979 smelt allowed us to examine the fingerprints of a carbon boil. Because a more refractory clay was used for the tuyeres on that occasion, preheating occurred throughout the smelt, and the furnace attained higher temperatures. The carbon boil left obvious fingerprints in the form of bubbles in viscous iron-rich slags (fig. 6.4) and frothy iron-poor slags (see A and D in fig. 6.1). The fossil bubbles contain varying proportions of fayalite, hercynite, glass, and metal, but the frothy slags are very glassy and contain few iron oxides. The frothy slags were probably formed later in the carbon boil than the bubbled slags. In the interim the iron oxides were removed by the cyclic precipitation of iron in the boiling slag mass (see chapter 5).

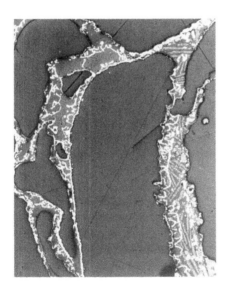

Fig. 6.4 This dramatic photomicrograph shows, in frozen form, the bubbles of CO gas that percolated through the slag in the carbon boil. The gray laths are shells of fayalitic slag. Iron has reduced (white) out along the edges of the slag from contact with CO gas. Some hercynite cubes are also present. Magnification 30×. Photo by Terry Childs.

Forging

After the most successful smelt in 1976, we asked a Haya smith to forge one of the blooms into a sickle blade. Although our primary goal was to see how the smith coped with the iron the smelt produced, this exercise also provided us with an opportunity to examine the differences between smelting and smithing slags. The smith had difficulty consolidating the

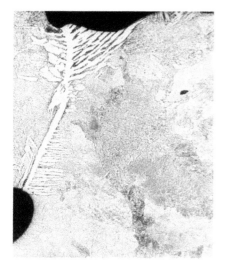

FIG. 6.5 A carbon steel structure incorporated into forging slag illustrates how metal is lost in the forging process. Magnification 120×; 2% nital etch. Photo by Terry Childs.

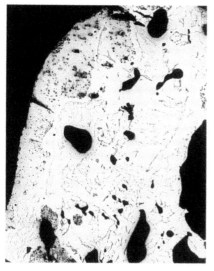

FIG. 6.6 Low-carbon steel in a forging slag, after smithing of one of the 1976 blooms. The dotted area of high phosphorus content along the metal edge may have inhibited further absorption of carbon during the smelt. Magnification 60×; 2% nital etch. Photo by Terry Childs.

bloom, which was small and tended to break apart on hammering. Comparison of two slags that broke off the bloom at different stages of forging nonetheless proved informative. The first slag retained most of the characteristics of the bloom. It consisted of areas of carbon steel surrounded by a silica-rich glass poor in iron oxide (fig. 6.5). It is likely that this piece broke off early in the forging process and dropped deep into the fuel bed. The carbon steel was preserved because the atmosphere in the fuel bed was reducing and because the temperature was too low to melt the protecting, refractory glass.

The picture is complicated by the low carbon content of some peripheral areas of the metal incorporated into the slag (fig. 6.6). These areas may have been decarburized in the forge by the oxygen-rich blast from the forging tuyere. The low carbon content may have a different explanation, however. Darkened dots of phosphorus are evident in the sample. Since the absorption of phosphorus and carbon is competitive, it is possible that the low carbon content is due to the presence of phosphorus as well as to decarburization.

In contrast to the first slag, the second slag sample showed strong evidence of having been worked and decarburized in the forge. Etching demonstrated that the metal in the slag had been heavily worked and totally decarburized (fig. 6.7). Its microstructure is a carbon-free ferrite with a distinctive patterning called veining that results from the deformation of the metal at temperatures of about 750 or 800°C. Samuels (1980) notes that veining occurs when an area of metal has been affected by carbon. For this reason, it is more likely that the metal had been decarburized in the forge than that it had always been carbon-free.

Fig. 6.7 A ferrite grain structure of a piece of iron incorporated into forging slag. It has been completely decarburized in the forge and also shows extensive veining from hot working on the forge. Magnification 60×; 2% nital etch. Photo by Terry Childs.

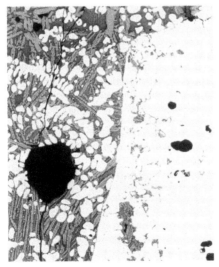

Fig. 6.8 The interrelationship of iron metal (large white mass), wustite (light gray dendrites), and fayalite (gray laths) in a forging slag. The wustite results from the reoxidation of metal in the forge. Magnification 60×. Photo by Terry Childs.

Analysis of this sample suggested that the presence of wustite and the absence of hercynite is a possible fingerprint of a forging slag. Most of the slag surrounding the metallic areas is wustite, which in this context is probably the product of the reoxidation of metallic iron in the forge (fig. 6.8). The slag is also distinguished by its lack of hercynite. As noted earlier, the more viscous slags near the iron bloom tend to be alumina- and hercynite-rich, but smiths carefully hammered away these slags before placing a bloom in the forge. Hercynite rarely survived this processing. On balance, the combination of these distinctive fingerprints probably points to forging slags.

Evidence from the Blooms ———

We analyzed three blooms from the 1976 smelts and one bloom from the 1979 smelt. Because these blooms differed significantly from one another, we felt they might represent the learning curve of the Haya as they slowly remastered the smelting process. To account for this possibility, we also analyzed several heirloom blooms dating from the colonial period, which are perhaps more representative of a routinized technology.

Despite their variability, the three blooms from the 1976 smelts provided consistent evidence of several characteristics of the Haya smelting process. Once again the mineral hercynite showed up as a high-temperature marker. Formed near the tuyeres, hercynite was sometimes trapped in the blooms as the metal grew (fig. 6.9). Because hercynite crystals are angular and hard, they tended to remain in the bloom even when it was beaten in the forge to expel the slag. The presence of hercynite in slag

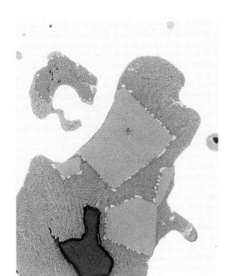

Fig. 6.9 Hercynite cubes in a fayalitic slag matrix, entrapped in iron (white). Magnification 120x; 2% nital etch. Photo by Terry Childs.

stringers within an iron or steel object is therefore another fingerprint of a high-temperature smelt. This fingerprint must be interpreted with caution, however, because abundant entrained slag also points to the production of blooms or portions of blooms that are spongelike rather than massive and consolidated.

The blooms also provided evidence of the cyclic precipitation of iron in the iron slag. All three samples showed evidence that large iron grains precipitating out of the melt had become attached to fingery, dendritic projections growing out of the iron mass into the glassy slag envelope (see fig. 5.11, chapter 5). The dissolved iron either precipitated onto these growths directly or precipitated as independent bodies in the slag that then became attached to the bloom, a process that continued as slag containing metal droplets and flakes descended through the furnace and fell into the molten slag pool below the tuyeres (Avery and Schmidt 1979; Avery et al. 1988).

The carbon content of the blooms varies considerably, ranging from ferritic iron to medium-grade carbon steel (0.3 to 0.8% C). This variability reflects the variety of microenvironments within the furnace. Near the tuyeres, local infusions of oxygen sometimes prevented the carburization of the iron. In the furnace pit, however, intimate contact between the iron and charred fuels or hot carbon monoxide gas favored the heavy carburization of the iron.

Finally, all three blooms show phosphorus contamination in the form of dark dots. When the dots were analyzed by a technique called energy-dispersive spectroscopy, they were found to contain between 0.7 and 0.9 percent phosphorus by weight. At levels above 0.3 or 0.5 percent, the phosphorus would have acted as a flux on the surrounding carbon steel, promoting the formation of liquid cast iron. The dots are typically found in dendritic formations (fig. 6.10) near the surface of the blooms, which suggests that the phosphorus infusion occurred late in bloom formation.

The bloom from the 1979 smelt, which was contained in a slag mass near the mouth of one of the tuyeres, was different from the other blooms. It consisted of two distinct layers: an upper layer of metal 1 or 2 centimeters thick and a lower layer of slag roughly a centimeter thick (fig. 6.11). For the most part, the slag layer contained the phases typically found near blooms. The metal layer, however, consisted of white cast iron containing significant amounts of phosphorus. (White cast iron is a hard, shiny material that contains abundant carbon in the form of iron carbide; gray cast iron, by contrast, is a softer dull material that contains carbon in the form of flakes of graphite.) Because cast iron has a melting temperature significantly lower than that of pure iron, this composition suggests that much of the bloom was once liquid. Indeed, further analysis identified two different eutectics, or alloys with melting points lower than those of their constituent elements. These were the iron–iron phosphide eutectic, which melts at 1,050°C (fig. 6.12), and the iron–carbon–iron phosphide eutectic, which

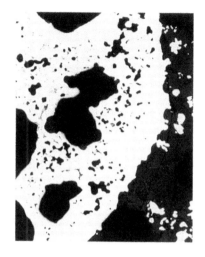

FIG. 6.10 From a section of a bloom from smelt #6: the dark dots along the edge of the bloom contain approximately 0.7 to 0.9% phosphorus by weight, sufficient to significantly affect bloom formation. Magnification 26×. Photo by Terry Childs.

FIG. 6.11 A cross-section of bloom #4 from the 1979 smelt showing the layering of metal (*top*) and slag. Photo by Terry Childs.

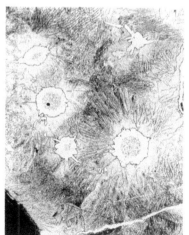

FIG. 6.12 Eutectic of iron–iron phosphide is seen as round splotches in bloom #4 from the 1979 smelt. Magnification 100×; Oberhoffer's etch. Photo by Terry Childs.

melts at 953°C (fig. 6.13). Once these eutectics had formed, they too would have acted as solvents, dissolving the surrounding bloom by converting it from carbon steel to cast iron.

Taken together, the evidence suggests that the 1979 bloom represents an intermediate stage between a solid-state bloomery process and a cast-iron process that produced liquid metal (see David et al. 1989 for a related process). Analysis of several heirloom blooms suggested, however, that the 1979 bloom was not typical of the routinized technology. The large and heavy heirloom blooms (figs. 6.14 and 6.15) contained very little slag. Their microstructure suggests, however, that they were formed under conditions that did not yield cast iron.

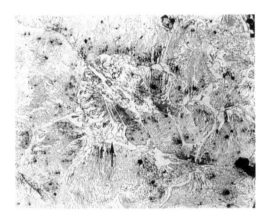

FIG. 6.13 Eutectic of iron–carbon–iron phosphide in bloom #4 from the 1979 smelt. Magnification 110×; 2% nital etch. Photo by Terry Childs.

Fig. 6.14 A traditional heirloom bloom from Nyungwe village. Photo by Terry Childs.

Fig. 6.15 A cross-section view of the traditional bloom. Photo by Terry Childs.

The carbon content of the iron was greatest at the periphery of the bloom and decreased gradually toward the center (fig. 6.16). This gradient signals that the bloom was carburized by intimate contact with ashy grass char in the furnace pit and by the rain of cast-iron droplets from the zone above the tuyeres. Most of the carburization probably occurred toward the end of the smelt, when the agglomerating metal sat in the charred fuel bed. Indeed, because carbon diffuses into iron only slowly, the mass and density of the bloom may provide a crude measure of the duration of the smelt.

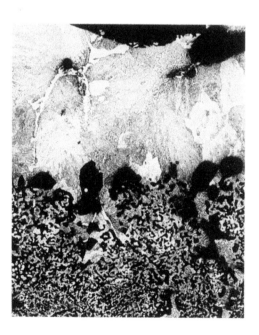

Fig. 6.16 A zone of high carbon along the edge of a bloom from smelt #5 in 1976. The darker area below is the central part of the bloom, more spongy and not carburized. Magnification 67×; 2% nital etch. Photo by Terry Childs.

Dendritic concentrations of darkened dots are present in both heirloom blooms (fig. 6.17), and in some regions of one bloom, the iron–iron phosphide eutectic is present at the grain boundaries (fig. 6.18). This evidence suggests that although the traditional process introduced phosphorus into the iron, in this instance the amount of phosphorus and the furnace conditions were not sufficient to produce cast iron.

FIG. 6.17 Dendritic concentrations of dark dots in the traditional bloom indicate an initial infusion of phosphorus. Magnification 125×; Oberhoffer's etch. Photo by Terry Childs.

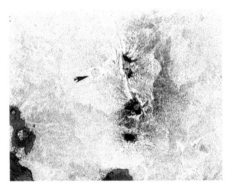

FIG. 6.18 Steadite, an iron–iron phosphide eutectic, seen as "splotches" and at the grain boundaries in a traditional bloom. Magnification 250×; 2% nital etch. Photo by Terry Childs.

The Archaeological Evidence

With these technological observations from the field and the laboratory in hand, we were now ready to examine the evolution of iron technology in northwest Tanzania. Our next step was to analyze the archaeological objects much as we have analyzed modern ones. As I have indicated, the most plentiful and helpful indicator of ancient iron technology is slag, which is found in an abundance of sizes, shapes, and types. An archaeology of slag, however, is complicated by the practice of dismantling the furnace after a smelt and the removal of the glassy slag envelope around the bloom before forging. Early furnaces were also scavenged for building materials and later disturbed by deep-hoe agriculture.

At some sites, however, we found undisturbed slags, typically small prills (solidified droplets) and flow slags on the furnace bottom. Our analyses have given us a good idea of the range of slag types and of the correlation between type and morphology. All of these factors allow us to interpret comparisons between prehistoric and modern slags with greater confidence.

Unfortunately, the archaeological record is not replete with blooms. Very occasionally we found a small, lumpy mass with a slaglike appearance that X rays revealed to have a bloomlike core. Iron objects are also relatively rare; the quickly leaching and acidic soils of the region do not favor their survival. In addition, iron had enough economic value that it was rarely discarded. Nonetheless, we did recover several (usually unrecognizable) objects from Early Iron Age sites. Finally, incidental finds, such as pieces of raw, roasted, and partially smelted ore, have also entered into our interpretation of past technologies.

Selection and Roasting of Ore

Ancient furnaces provide plentiful examples of ore cubes (see fig. 6.19 for the distribution of early ironworking sites). We now know that the ancient and the modern smelters used similar ores, mostly limonite ($FeO-OH.H_2O$). The use of these lean, hydrated ores marks a strong continuity in resource selection. The ancient ore cubes, like the modern ones, are also comparatively large, a characteristic that increased the dwell time of the ore in the furnace stack (Childs 1996).

A metallographic section of an Early Iron Age ore piece (fig. 6.20) displays many of the features noted in modern samples of roasted ores (see chapter 5). The piece contained fossilized organics that had been replaced by iron oxide minerals during ore formation (Childs 1996). The cracked ore was partially reduced to wustite during roasting, and tiny dots of iron had also formed along the cracks.

In chapter 5 we noted that a layered structure is characteristic of large ore pieces that had been smelted in a furnace with a long reaction zone. We occasionally found partially smelted ore at ancient sites that was not incorporated into a slag mass or was incorporated as a discrete body. Some of these pieces do indeed have a layered structure, consisting of an inner core of wustite and other components, an intermediate layer of iron and wustite, and an outer layer of iron. Other layered pieces are hollow; the outer layer ruptured when the iron fell into the hotter furnace zones, releasing the fluid inner core.

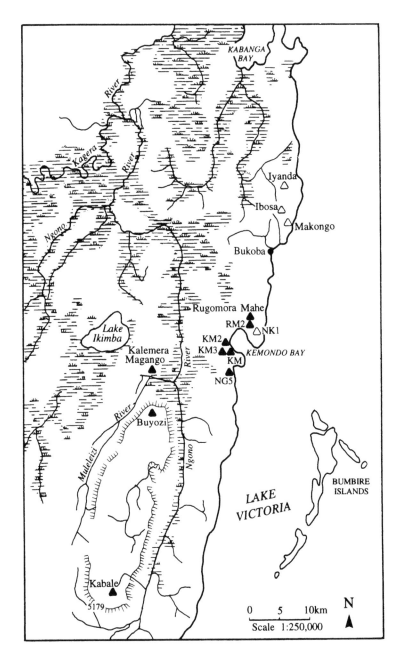

FIG. 6.19 Map of Buhaya with excavated early industrial sites—marked with a filled triangle. Other excavated Early Iron Age sites are indicated by an open triangle.

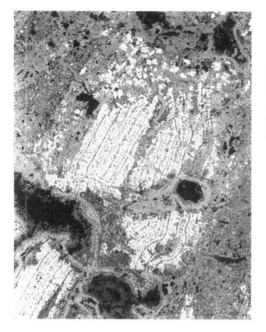

Fɪɢ. 6.20 Reduction to wustite of fossilized organics in a piece of ore from the KM2 site, furnace pit no. 34. Magnification 140×. Photo by Terry Childs.

A variety of evidence suggests that ore was exposed to reducing gases for a comparatively long time in both the ancient and the modern furnaces. Although the modern Haya may have built taller shafts (see chapter 7), both the prehistoric and the modern furnaces had long reaction zones. The Early Iron Age furnace pits were filled with charcoal logs and cubes and the stacks with charcoal cubes, whereas the modern furnace pits were filled with charred grass and the stacks with charcoal cubes. Both fuel beds probably acted to keep the ore and charcoal charge situated high in the stack, where reduction began (Schmidt and Avery 1978). Finally, both Early Iron Age and modern smelters used comparatively large ore pieces that tended to settle through the stack slowly (Tholander 1987).

What do the Early Iron Age bottom slags tell us? Some of these slags contain very little wustite, but a typical Early Iron Age bottom slag, such as a slag from furnace 34 at the KM2 site, contains somewhat more. Its wustite content, however, is still lower than that of the typical bloomery slag (Childs 1996). The low wustite content suggests that the bloomery process in this area of Africa was more efficient than the bloomery processes elsewhere in the ancient world (e.g. Morton and Wingrove 1969; Bachmann 1982; Rostoker and Bronson 1990). Given that the African smelters also used difficult-to-smelt lean ores, it also suggests that the smelters used a high fuel-to-ore ratio that favored the carburization of the iron as well as its efficient extraction.

How hot were the prehistoric furnaces? Early Iron Age slags from the Rugomora Mahe site provide some critical evidence. A lump of slag interspersed with metal from the Early Iron Age horizon shows dots of metal within hercynite cubes (fig. 6.21). Another slag sample from the same site also clearly shows metal encased in hercynite grains (fig. 6.22) (Childs 1996). As we have noted, the formation of hercynite around metal droplets is a fingerprint of high-temperature conditions and of the use of tuyeres made of refractory clay with a high alumina oxide content.

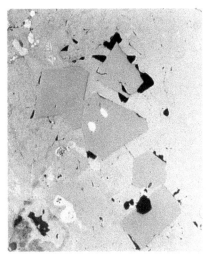

FIG. 6.21 A sample from a lump of amorphous EIA slag from the Rugomora Mahe site at Katuruka: there is abundant hercynite (gray cubes) plus metal (now oxidized and whitish), wustite (whitish and dendritic in shape), fayalite (gray background), and glass (dark gray). Magnification 60×; 2% nital etch. Photo by Terry Childs.

FIG. 6.22 A sample of another EIA slag at the RM2 site: there are prills of metal (white dots) encased in hercynite grains. Magnification 55×; 2% nital etch. Photo by Terry Childs.

Because the slag surrounding a bloom was hammered away before forging, the material fingerprints of a carbon boil are difficult to find. Traces of this process may be visible, however, in a lump of slag recovered from the Kabale site on the southern rim of the central plateau (fig. 6.23). This highly corroded specimen, which was found in association with Early Iron Age ceramics, consists of a layer of corroded metal within an envelope of glassy slag with a hint of a frozen bubble (fig. 6.24) (Childs 1996).

One of the questions we most wanted to answer was whether ancient iron had a phosphorus content similar to that of the iron produced by the Haya smelters. Many of the prehistoric blooms we have recovered contain the iron–carbon–iron phosphide eutectic in proximity to cast iron. This is the microstructure (fig. 6.25), for example, of a piece of ancient bloom recovered from a ritual pit in the bottom of furnace 8 at the KM3

FIG. 6.23 A small lump of corroded "slag" from a furnace at the Kabale site on the southern part of the central plateau. Photo by Terry Childs.

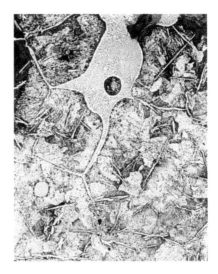

FIG. 6.24 Abundant metal was once present in the Kabale sample, but is now corroded (white), contiguous to slag that is all glass, with fayalite and scattered hercynite. At the top of the photo is a structure that looks like a frozen bubble, perhaps indicating a carbon boil. Magnification 28×; 2% nital etch. Photo by Terry Childs.

FIG. 6.25 An iron–carbon–iron phosphide eutectic in the piece of EIA bloom found in the ritual pit located in the furnace floor, furnace no. 8, KM3 site. Magnification 56×; Oberhoffer's etch. Photo by Terry Childs.

site (Schmidt 1981; Schmidt 1983a; Schmidt and Childs 1985; Schmidt and Childs 1995; Childs 1996) (see figs. 10.13 and 10.14, chapter 10).

The important effects of phosphorus on bloom formation can also be seen in other pieces of Early Iron Age bloom. A piece of bloom recovered from a furnace at the Early Iron Age site NG5, an extensive but partially excavated site located several hundred meters from Kashokero Bay on Victoria Nyanza, shows dotted structures that indicate areas of initial phosphorus concentration (Fig. 6.26).

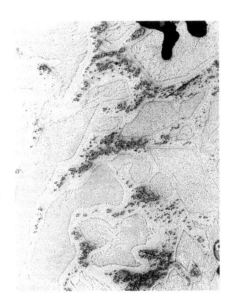

FIG. 6.26 A prehistoric bloom from furnace no. 5 at NG5, a third-century A.D. industrial site: this photomicrograph shows areas of elevated phosphorus content—dotted zones—in the NG5 bloom. Magnification 120×; Oberhoffer's etch—showing phosphorus areas in white and in relief. Photo by Terry Childs.

The occasional metal artifacts found during excavations add their own chapter to the story by providing clues about how iron was treated in the past. Most of these artifacts date to the Early Iron Age, when there was a booming smelting industry on the western shore of Victoria Nyanza. These objects have a curious characteristic, however: they often contain a fair amount of slag. Indeed, their slag content is high enough to suggest that they were made from blooms more similar to the products of traditional bloomery than the dense, relatively slag-free blooms we have been discussing. Certainly slag-free cast iron and steels containing phosphorus-rich phases were not the only products of prehistoric furnaces. And the inferior slag-infused phosphoric iron may have been more likely to survive simply because it was less likely to be reused.

Do the artifacts contain slag because smiths failed to spend sufficient time on blooms that contained large amounts of slag or because they failed to bring blooms up to the temperatures required to soften and express the slag? The removal of the slag may have been complicated by its makeup.

Several iron objects contain hercynite grains, which were apparently trapped in the metal when the slag was expressed. Because of their angularity and high melting temperature, these crystals could not be easily removed from the bloom.

Some iron objects, however, contain little slag. Does this mean they were fashioned from dense blooms or that they were fashioned by a skillful smith? An object recovered from a large refuse pit at the KM2 site (Schmidt 1983a) supports the second hypothesis. It consists of two pieces welded together by hammering, which could have been accomplished only if the smith was able to hold the forge at temperatures between 1,150 and 1,370°C. On the other hand, the tenacity of the hercynite-laden slags tends to favor the first hypothesis. Given the difficulty of expressing these slags, it seems likely that clean objects were made from clean blooms.

The carbon content of the iron artifacts was also of interest. The carbon content of the typical object is much lower than that of the blooms we examined. Whereas the blooms typically consist of cast iron and high-carbon steels, the ancient objects typically consist of low-carbon steel, wrought iron, or ferrite. The analytical evidence suggests that the smiths from the Early Iron Age and thereafter decarburized the iron before working it. Among other things, decarburization made the phosphorus-rich steels and cast irons their furnaces produced much more workable.

Either phosphorus or carbon by itself will strengthen iron and increase its work hardenability. Too much of either element, however, makes the metal brittle and difficult to work. Once phosphorus was in the bloom it was there to stay, because no efficient method for removing phosphorus from iron existed, at least in the West, until the late 1870s. Carbon, fortunately, was less recalcitrant. It could be removed simply by heating the iron in the strongly oxidizing conditions of the forge. This produced a wrought iron or low-carbon steel but one that because of its phosphorus content was as hard and strong as a medium-carbon steel—although subject to breakage when worked cold.

This history announces itself in two ways. First, the artifacts often contain veined ferrite grains, an internal structure that is sometimes associated with the presence of carbon, as we mentioned earlier, and sometimes associated with the presence of phosphorus. Second, treatment with Oberhoffer's etchant—an etchant sensitive to phosphorus—picks out alternating bands of small and large ferrite grains, a pattern characteristic of an iron with a heterogeneous phosphorus content that has been hammered into a tool (Todd and Charles 1978; Schmidt and Childs 1995; Childs 1996). The banding pattern can be seen, for example, in the object recovered from a large refuse pit at the KM2 site (fig. 6.27).

As we turn to the early first millennium A.D., evidence for forging techniques is limited to one rusted object from the Rulama site, a possible forge dated to the early fourteenth century A.D. It consists of several layers of welded metal whose ferritic grains exhibit veining from phosphorus alloying and clear phosphorus banding. These characteristics again sug-

FIG. 6.27 Phosphorus banding in an EIA object from the KM2 site, feature no. 8, a large industrial refuse dump dated to A.D. 180. Magnification 120×; Oberhoffer's etch. Photo by Terry Childs.

gest that a high-carbon, high-phosphorus bloom had been rendered malleable by decarburization in the forge.

Analysis of other objects from the latter part of the second millennium suggests that the smiths of this region had developed greater skill in dealing with the difficult phosphoric iron alloys. Among the objects is a large iron socket—probably the base or butt end of a spear that was part of the king's ceremonial regalia (fig. 6.28). This object, which was found in a known ritual area at the Rugomora Mahe site, is likely associated with the reign of that king and thus dates to the seventeenth century (Schmidt and Childs 1995; Childs 1996).

Two sections from the socket show microstructures that vary from those characteristic of high-carbon steel to those characteristic of ferrite. Distributed through the transitional areas between the higher- and lower-carbon steel are numerous spheroids that contain 7 percent phosphorus by weight, a phosphorus concentration close to that of the iron–carbon–iron phosphide eutectic (fig. 6.29). The spheroids are relic bits of this eutectic created when the metal was partially decarburized and hammered on the forge (Schmidt and Childs 1995; Childs 1996).

The microstructure shows that the smith understood how to forge phosphoric steels and cast irons without fully decarburizing them and without cracking the embrittled metal (Schmidt and Childs 1995). But we were also led to wonder whether his skill wasn't reflected as well in his choice of metal. Once it had cooled, this metal would have been brittle and subject to fracture had it received hard use. It is possible that the smith who fabricated the spear butt was aware of the attributes of the metal and deliberately selected it for this undemanding ritual application.

FIG. 6.28 A socket for the butt of a spear excavated at the royal palace of Rugomora Mahe and dating to the era of his reign, the seventeenth century. Photo by Terry Childs.

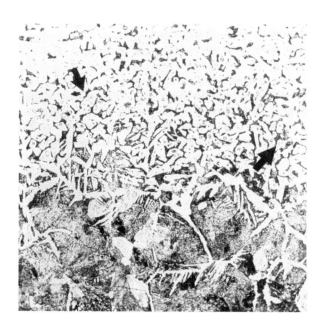

FIG. 6.29 Tiny spheroids of a high-phosphorus phase (*see arrow*) in an intermediate zone between medium- and low-carbon steels in the spear butt socket. Magnification 140×; 2% nital etch. Photo by Terry Childs.

This seems all the more likely when one considers the difficulties encountered by the smith who forged the sickle from an experimental bloom. The smith, whose expertise had been developed on scrap steel, was not familiar with the characteristics of phosphorus-rich iron. Although he coped remarkably well, he cold-worked the edge of the sickle blade, which developed several cracks (Schmidt and Childs 1995; Childs 1996). This was probably a technique he would have avoided had he been better acquainted with the foibles of his metal.

Comparative Reprise

This extended comparison of the material fingerprints of prehistoric and modern smelts supports the conclusion that the two technologies are closely related, although they differ in detail. The similarities include placement of refractory tuyeres well inside the furnace; packing the furnace pit and stack with fuel; the use of large iron ore pieces of similar chemical makeup; the attainment of high furnace temperatures; the production of hercynite-rich slags near the tuyeres; and the contribution of carbon and phosphorus to bloom formation both in the form of droplets of cast iron and through the mechanism of the carbon boil. The techniques for forging cast iron, phosphoric irons, and steels are also similar, although the smiths seem to have become more skilled at dealing with contaminants over time.

But as suggested at the beginning of this chapter, the differences between these smelting technologies are as interesting as the similarities. Indeed, the archaeology of iron technology in Buhaya includes an unsolved mystery that calls into question the continuity of this tradition: thus far there is no evidence of iron production from A.D. 700 to 1200. What are we to make of this extraordinary hiatus? If the technology remained alive, what accounts for its lack of archaeological visibility? And if it died, what accounts for the apparent technological continuities?

Some of the differences between Early Iron Age and modern artifacts, such as the prevalence of slag-infused iron, may derive from changes in the scale rather than changes in technique. The Early Iron Age furnaces may have been smaller and had shorter stacks. Since a tall-shaft furnace is particularly suitable for smelting the lean ores of the region, if the furnaces were shorter, the quality of the blooms they produced might have been more variable. Alternatively, the coexistence of slag-infused and slag-free artifacts might reflect differential access to critical resources (Childs 1989b), such as the special refractory clays needed for successful smelting, which was likely controlled by kin-based groups. In chapter 7 we will see that the use of clay in tuyeres was not consistent from site to site—suggesting that variation in iron production is linked to differential access to critical resources.

Indeed, I suspect that in the face of powerful continuities, it is the social and political transformations that will be found to explain the variability in the archaeological record. Certainly the extension of Bahinda and Babito hegemony over iron production in the seventeenth century was accompanied by technological changes. Did a larger, more inclusive workforce—not based exclusively on kin-group membership—translate into a more uniform product? Was the more entrepreneurial organization of labor related to greater productivity and to the more consistent production of dense, consolidated blooms? For these intriguing social and historical questions, there are no immediate answers.

7.

Dynamic Models for an Archaeology of Iron Technology

We have seen in earlier chapters that the ancient technology practiced along the western shores of Victoria Nyanza was not an isolated phenomenon. The ancient furnaces of Rwanda and Burundi, for example, bear close affinities to those of Buhaya. Moreover, there are other indications that related technologies—based on appearances of furnace materials—also were practiced in eastern Zaire (Hiernaux and Maquet 1960; Hiernaux 1968), in northwestern Uganda (Soper 1971), in the Teita Hills of southwestern Kenya (Collett 1985), and in the Usambara Mountains of northeastern Tanzania (Schmidt 1988). One of my goals in this chapter is to explore whether the material remains associated with these technologies are related to those found in ancient Buhaya.

The following discussion sets out the observations that show the variability of tuyere performance as well as the key characteristics that mark the practice of preheating. The material fingerprints for preheating are compared to evidence from several archaeological sites to assess degrees of affinity (or the tightness of fit)[1] and to isolate exceptions that require explanation. In the case of archaeological tuyeres, there are comparative limitations because most archaeologists have overlooked the importance of tuyeres in their analysis (for exceptions see Tylecote 1981; Childs 1986, 1990). There is considerable evidence for tuyeres at different sites in Buhaya, but for reasons of economy, comparative analysis here is limited to the large prehistoric industrial sites of KM2, KM3, and KM (Schmidt and Childs 1985; Childs 1986) in Buhaya and the Nkese iron smelting site in the western Usambara Mountains (Schmidt 1988) and the Saghasa smelting site in the Teita Hills of Kenya (Collett 1985), sites where relevant analyses have occurred.

The second part of this chapter and chapter 8 focus on other material fingerprints left by the practice of the Haya technology. Iron smelting and forging leave a myriad of physical tracks, some more ephemeral and yet others recognized in the archaeological record but often passed over without comment because their significance is not understood. I also examine several other physical indices of the smelting process, namely, the presence of partially reduced iron ore mixed with logs on the furnace floor and furnace liner.[2]

Why Tuyeres Are Important

A primary goal of ethnoarchaeology in Buhaya is to build an empirically based record of tuyere performance that can be used as a comparative model and thus assess its tightness of fit to the archaeological record. For decades tuyeres have been an artifact category that has yielded little information of importance for understanding the variability of iron technology in Africa. With the exception of research in Buhaya and the Teita Hills (Collett 1985), archaeologists dutifully have recorded mean widths of the distal ends of tuyeres and little else before moving on to other technological data. I want to rectify this analytical deficiency, while at the same time show the physical characteristics of tuyere performance under high-temperature reducing conditions. This requires a description of precisely what happens to different types of tuyeres when they are inserted in the furnace for purposes of preheating the air blast.

The Buhaya research provided an unusual living laboratory because the chemical makeup of tuyeres varied from smelt to smelt—allowing important insights to be gained about the performance of different kinds of clay and their different tempering agents. The result is several generalizations from the ethnoarchaeological observations about the characteristics of successful and failed tuyere performance under conditions of preheating in the Haya technology. I refer to these general characteristics as material fingerprints, and to their archaeological corollaries as signatures (Gould 1980; Gould and Watson 1982). This method has cross-cultural applications, for the observations on tuyere performance can be used comparatively to assess similarities and differences (and the possible application of preheating principles) with other cultures that also insert tuyeres and use a forced air blast in iron smelting furnaces. Its greatest utility, however, will be a set of empirical observations that can be compared to the archaeological record.

The struggle to find a tuyere clay that was sufficiently refractory *as well as* to find the proper kind of temper was a major problem during the smelts in 1976. The type of clay, the tempering material, and temper size are instrumental to the success of this technology (Childs 1986, 1988). As we saw in chapter 3, during the first two smelts the clay used to make tuyeres was normally used for forging. Moreover, it was tempered with fine particles of slag with FeO content; these fine pieces of slag—acceptable when used in a forging tuyere—had a fluxing action on the clay, weakening it in the reducing atmosphere and making it much more susceptible to the acidic slag wash. As table 7.1 shows, the Kikukwe (forging) clay differs markedly from the traditional smelting clay of Buchwero in its higher FeO content, 10.7 percent vs. 4.3 percent (Childs 1986). The FeO under reducing conditions has a significant fluxing action inside the tuyere walls, hence the requirement for a clay with low FeO content (Childs 1989a).

Table 7.1. Composition of Tuyere Clay Used by Nyungwe Smelters

Location	Mineral	SiO_2	Al_2O	FeO	MgO	CaO	K_2O	Na_2O	Ti_2O
Kikukwe	Kaolin	57.1	29.1	10.7	0.9	0.2	0.7	.08	1.2
Buchwero	Kaolin	61.6	30.3	4.3	0.5	0.1	0.8	.05	2.4

If we look closely at the behavior of the various clays and their tempering material, there are some obvious trends and differences over the 1976 to 1984 period. It is important to consider furnace conditions, for several times a choked stack and wet charcoal with fines caused severe back pressure that stressed the tuyeres. Table 7.2 shows the amount of melting (henceforth called tuyere loss) that the tuyeres suffered from smelt to smelt. Back pressure was a negative factor in smelts 2, 3, and 4, all of which were monitored by instruments. Each of these smelts started satisfactorily, for the many kilograms of charcoal used to precharge the furnace had dried out by the beginning of the smelt. This was also the time when the tuyeres were longest and most capable of preheating. The second smelt, on Au-

Table 7.2. Tuyere Attrition

Date	Smelt #	Period of time	Tuyere length (cm)	Length after	% loss	Clay source	Temper type
8/6/76	1	4:00	51.6	[a]	[a]	Kik.	slag
8/11/76	2	5:15	54	39	27.4	Kik.	slag & grog
8/12/76	3	6:20	53.6	25.3	52.8	Kik.	slag & grog
8/16/76	4	6:10	47.4	30	32.5	Kik. #2	grog
8/21/76	5	8:00	54.6	41	25[b]	Kik. #2 from Buch.[b]	grog
9/18/76	6	7:30	55.8	41.5	25.7	Buch.	grog
7/10/79	7	5:40	54.4 (5)	45.1	17.1	Buch.	grog
7/3/84	8	6:00	55.7	50.5	9.3	Buch.	grog
7/4/84	9	5:10	52.5	[c]		Buch.	grog

[a]Crushed in destruction of furnace, estimated to average approx. 25 cm.
[b]Two tuyeres were made from Buchwero clay and lost 17.1%. The six from Kikukwe lost 28.7%.
[c]Removed and destroyed by workers before measurements.

gust 11, was also the shortest (5 hrs., 15 min.), and therefore the 27.2 percent rate of tuyere loss is less than what would be expected over the average 6 hour and 15 minute smelt. Tuyere loss reached as high as 52.8 percent during smelt 3. The melting of the tuyeres in this case can be attributed to the clay type (high in FeO), the use of some (4) slag-tempered tuyeres, and back pressure caused by wet charcoal in the furnace stack that was choked for most of the smelt.

When experimentation to solve the tuyere problem began in earnest during smelt 4, the smelters substituted another known (forging) clay from the Kikukwe area, a dark gray clay (fine grog tempering <1 mm). The 32.5 percent loss shows the improvement achieved by this experiment, but also indicates other less than desirable conditions. Again, the furnace conditions were choked for at least 40 percent of the smelting time. A more significant experimental success is seen in smelt 5. Before this smelt, the smelters sent an emergency mission to the traditional Buchwero clay site to dive under the high swamp waters for clay. They were able to fabricate two tuyeres for this smelt. The lower incidence of tuyere failure (25%) was influenced by the performance of these two tuyeres, tempered with 4-to-6-millimeter grog (fig. 7.1). These two tuyeres experienced only a 17.1 percent loss, a success given the high temperature exposures over an eight-hour period. The results of this successful tuyere experiment are the same as during the July 1979 smelt, the most successful smelt conducted.

FIG. 7.1 Nyungwe tuyeres after smelt #3. The two tuyeres on the top were made of Buchwero clay, while the bottom tuyere was made of forging clay—high in FeO and also tempered with slag.

The two final smelts of 1976 also suffered from the use of wet charcoal, a fact that tends to obscure an otherwise successful performance of the tuyeres—particularly in the last smelt (#6) of 1976. By 1979 the smelters of Nyungwe had solved the problem of tuyere loss by using the Buchwero clay with a grog temper that helps to deal with thermal shock (Childs 1986). The 1979 tuyeres were the most refractory under the highest sustained furnace temperatures documented, but they were also the most fragile. Four tuyeres broke during the course of the smelt, and in three instances they were replaced. The substitution of full-length tuyeres during the smelt meant enhanced preheating capacity and higher productivity. The two largest iron blooms were found beneath tuyeres that had been replaced halfway through the smelt. Ironically, it appears that the fracture of tuyeres in this instance marks success rather than any systemic failure: if a refractory clay is used when bellows pumpers operate effectively and the tuyeres fracture under these conditions, then we will want to keep in mind the possibility that fractured tuyeres in smelting may in fact be an index to *successful* tuyere performance.

The least melting of tuyeres occurred during the first smelt of 1984. The grog-tempered tuyeres lost only 9.3 percent of their length. The yield of iron was 3.26 kilograms in this smelt, suggesting that there were several other problems. First, the tuyeres rested on a furnace rim that was a flat platform rather than a curved pivot. This meant that they could not and did not pass a horizontal position. Consequently, they did not fall into the ashy zone of the furnace, a condition that significantly altered the dynamics of the furnace. Moreover, bellows pumping was not up to standard because old age and death had taken away half of the original group of Bajumba by this time. If the tuyeres had been placed correctly and more vigorous bellows pumping had been employed, then the tuyeres would have experienced greater loss. The lower than normal rate of tuyere failure in this instance points to *less* than favorable furnace conditions.

Tuyere Performance: Building Analytical Models

An important objective of the research on tuyeres was to document the physical attributes of tuyeres employed in preheating. If physical evidence for tuyeres that operate under preheating conditions can be determined, then the next step is to identify similar or related processes in the archaeological record and begin to solve the problem of when and why this unusual innovation arose. Also, it is important to understand under what conditions indigenous experimentation occurs both during the recent smelting and in the past.

Tuyeres undergo a number of physical changes other than melting when they are inserted into a high-temperature iron smelting furnace. The most important fingerprints for preheating are (1) the presence of slagging, either as a slag wash or as spots or lumps of attached slag on the surface of the tuyere; (2) vitrification (glassiness); and (3) presence of black clay, which indicates a reducing atmosphere. On some of the tuyeres used to preheat Haya furnaces, the section of the tuyere next to the inside of the furnace wall sometimes displays a mixed pattern of orange, oxidized clay and black clay. This mixing of colors indicates some leakage of air through cracks in the dried mud around the tuyeres. This color mixing on the tuyere surface does not indicate reducing conditions, and therefore this zone is not included in calculations for reducing atmosphere.

There are other indicators of tuyere insertion inside a furnace. In some instances where the slag flow and vitrification around the tuyere mouth are limited, an oxidizing blast zone washes back onto the end of the tuyere behind the slag—something more likely to occur at the end of the smelt.

Under these conditions there are sometimes several centimeters of a light gray color on the tuyere rather than a distinct black color.

Of all the indicators for preheating, the presence of slag and vitrification are the most definitive. In order for these diagnostics to be used, their relative proportions vis-à-vis oxidized and reduced portions of tuyeres must be determined from tuyeres used in all the experimental smelts under different furnace conditions. I now want to examine several different smelts, both successful and problematic, to illustrate the material evidence, the fingerprints each provides.

Smelt 4 of August 16 provides several key insights into the fingerprints left on tuyeres when the tuyeres were made of the wrong materials—forging tuyere clay from Kikukwe village, just 5 kilometers north—and a furnace stack that was choked for much of the smelt by wet charcoal and fines. The back pressure in the furnace created enormous stress on the tuyeres, which, because they were made of inadequate clay with a natural flux (11% FeO) under reducing conditions, meant that 51 percent of the tuyere melted away (table 7.3). Under these hostile conditions, the amount of vitrification and slag flow on the remnant tuyeres is relatively low, only 20 percent. Even more significant, however, is that of those two characteristics, vitrification or glassiness was the predominant attribute. Vitrification, then, with limited evidence of slag signals a smelt in which there has been significant tuyere melting. As the tuyeres erode away, they retreat behind the zone in which the liquid slag descends through the furnace stack. Once only 10 to 15 centimeters of a tuyere is left inside a furnace, a slag wash no longer hits it. Melting of the clay around the mouth of these tuyeres would have begun at about 1,500°C,[3] conditions that easily prevailed, even in a migrating oxidizing blast zone. In this case the amount of physical change on the remnant tuyeres amounts to only 37 percent.

Table 7.3. Transformations of Tuyeres, Smelt 4

Length at start	Length after	Slag + vitrification	% slag/vit.	Reduced (cm)	% reduced	% total
57[a]	broken	8	42.1	0	0	42.1
54	25	5	20.0	3	12	32
57	19	7	36.8	0	0	36.8
57	17	3	17.6	5	29.4	47
49	29	4	13.8	5	17.2	31
53	40	5	12.5	10	25	37.5
52	28	6	21.4	4	14.3	35.7
Mean values						
53.6	26.3	5.0	20.4	4.5	16.3	36.7

[a] This tuyere is not included in the analysis.

When these results are compared to those of smelt 2, there are some significant differences. This August 11 smelt did not suffer from back-pressure problems. Most interesting in this example, perhaps, is what happens when there are long interruptions of individual bellowing. During this smelt, the head smelter had to remove bellows repeatedly to unstop blocked tuyeres. Only 27.4 percent of the tuyeres melted off in this smelt, but then its atypical interruptions (because the clay was melting and plugging the tuyeres) show it to be a more idiosyncratic example. The modest amount of slag and glassiness (27.6%), I believe, shows that the tuyeres periodically contributed high temperatures and operated in the drip zone for a significant portion of the abbreviated smelt.

One of the most informative smelts—#6—occurred September 18. By this time the relationship between the vigor of bellows pumping and the reactions of the tuyeres was obvious. Others also have observed that the rate of bellows operation affects the temperature in the blast zone (Friede et al. 1984). Variations in bellows pumping can be read in the record of tuyere changes. Those who maintain a high rate of vigorous stroking are invariably the most successful in producing iron—if their tuyeres hold up or can be successfully replaced. Changes in tuyeres 1 and 8 of this smelt are instructive (table 7.4). During this smelt the smelters were experimenting with the more refractory clay of Buchwero (only 4.3% FeO) while they were also using a grog temper. Tuyeres 1 and 8, as well as 7, belonged to

Table 7.4. Transformations of Tuyeres, Smelt 6

Length at start	Length after	Slag + vitrification	% slag/vit.	Reduced (cm)	% reduced	% total
1: 56	29	6	20.7	9	31	51.7
1b: 52	36	10	27.8	4	11.1	38.9
2: 58	53	7	13.2	29	54.7	67.9[a]
3: 57	49	4	8.2	18	36.7	44.9[a]
4: 53	47	6	12.8	18	38.3	51.1[a]
5: 56	52	11	21.2	15	28.8	50.0[a]
6: 55	47	4	8.5	24	51	59.5
7b: 59	29	7 vit.	24.1	3	10.3	34.4
8: 54	36	4 vit.	11.1	10	27.8	38.9
8b: 58	37	9 vit.	24.3	8	21.6	45.9
Mean values						
55.7 cm	41.5 cm	6.8 cm	17.2%	13.8 cm	31.1%	48.3%

[a]Poor bellows pumping
Note: 1b, 7b, and 8b are replacement tuyeres

the strongest bellows pumpers. These three tuyeres were replaced about three hours into the smelt; #1 and #8 were replaced because of melting, and the front of #7 broke off. The replacement tuyeres performed similarly, suggesting that good bellows operators use up even the best clay during a smelt. The best index to such success is the almost exclusive presence of vitrification on the tips of the tuyeres—a characteristic that we also see in smelt 4, when all the tuyeres melted back under different clay and furnace conditions. How do we tell the two apart? Only a chemical study of the differences in refractory properties could discriminate between these two results: a good refractory clay with such attributes would mark success, while a clay with relatively poor refractory attributes in the productive context would mark technological problems.

During this smelt, three of the bellows were operated at very desultory rates for a variety of reasons. Tuyeres 2, 3, 4, and 5 fed one-half of the furnace, where, because of poor bellows operation, there was a low-temperature blast zone and reducing zone. On this side of the furnace, the tuyeres show vitrification and slag flow well below 20 percent, though reduction is present over more than 30 percent of the tuyere surface. Inefficient bellows operation is captured in this profile. Under much-reduced temperature conditions, less fluid slag would have been moving through the low-temperature side of the furnace. The highest yields of metal from this smelt came from tuyeres 1b, 7b, 8b, the same ones that were replaced and, consequently, made the most significant high-temperature contribution to the furnace.

On July 10, 1979, after an interlude of almost three years, the most successful smelt occurred. High reducing temperatures were sustained, low tuyere loss (by slag wash) occurred, and dry charcoal was used. I already have mentioned that the tuyeres tended to fracture, but aside from this problem their refractory performance was excellent. Because the tuyeres performed well and other conditions were more ideal than three years earlier—including behavior on the bellows—this is an important case study. Five tuyeres came out of the furnace whole. These showed a mean of 32.7 percent of the tuyeres slag-coated or glassy (table 7.5): the tuyeres were preheating and maintaining their integrity and were therefore exposed to an increased volume of dripping slag. Under these conditions there was a correspondingly lower amount of reduction (22.2%). These attributes, then, are the fingerprints of a more successful preheated furnace approaching normal working conditions.

Smelters confronted a variety of new and different problems, mentioned earlier, when they again smelted in 1984 after a five-year break. Tuyere loss was not a problem during this smelt. Had the other problems been overcome, however, tuyere loss would have been approximately twice as high as the 9.3 percent documented. A fingerprint for smelting difficulty is seen in the wide variation of slagging/vitrification on the tuyeres from this smelt—between 6 percent and 40.4 percent, a much wider variation than seen in the 1979 effects (table 7.6).

Table 7.5. Transformations of Tuyeres, Smelt 7

Length at start	Length after	Slag + vitrification	% Slag/vit.	Reduced (cm)	% reduced	% total
1. 55	46.5	18	38.7	8	17.2	55.9
2. 54	45	16	35.5	11	24.4	59.9
3. 52	(29.5) BROKEN[a]					
4. 54	44.5	13	29.2	12	27	56.2
5. 53.5	41.5	12	28.9	9	21.7	50.6
6. 56	BROKEN[b]					
7. 56	38	END BROKEN[c]				
8. 55.5	48	15	31.3	10	20.8	52.1[d]
Mean values						
54.4	45.1	14.8	32.7	10	22.2	54.9

[a]Replaced after 1 hr., tip broken again
[b]Not replaced
[c]Replaced after 1.5 hrs., tip broken again
[d]Replaced after 1 hr., 25 minutes

Table 7.6. Tuyere Transformations, Smelt 8

Length at start	Length after	Slag + vitrification	% Slag/vit.	Reduced (cm)	% reduced	% total
1. 56	52	16	30.7	12	23.1	53.8
2. 54	49.5	20	40.4	16	32.3	72.7
3. 56.5	50	3	6	20	40	46
4. 56	50	13	26	13	26	52
5. 57	52	17.5	33.7	9	17.3	51
6. 55.5	49	18	36.7	11	22.4	59.1
7. 54	BROKEN					
8. 55	51	19	37.3	0	0	37.3
Mean values						
55.7 cm	50.5 cm	15.3 cm	30.1%	11.6 cm	23%	53.1%

Where do these tables and figures lead us? First, they show that when tuyeres made of tempered Buchwero-quality clay experience stress and erode away in a Haya iron smelting furnace, approximately one-third of the tuyere surfaces will be glassy and slag-coated; this will be accompanied by reduced surfaces of slightly greater than 20 percent. However, when bellows performance is inefficient with otherwise refractory tuyeres, the fingerprint will be an insignificant amount (20%) of slagging and vitrification and a larger extent (>30%) of reduction. When both tuyeres and bellows perform well, a fingerprint of a good preheating tuyere is a slagging/vitrification-to-reduction ratio of 3 to 2.

These observations of behavioral and material correlates contribute significantly to the development of several models that can be used to interpret the practice of preheating and the variable performance of tuyeres in iron smelting furnaces. The material fingerprints I have isolated by this experimental ethnoarchaeology are an initial attempt to bring a set of objective criteria to the study of this aspect of ancient African iron technology.

One of the advantages of ethnoarchaeology is that it richly informs an otherwise inanimate material culture with cultural significance and with finely nuanced technological values. This review of tuyere evidence shows that there were a number of key variables that influenced tuyere performance, some of which might have remained hidden without such observations. Archaeological evidence alone is mute about the significance of physical attributes of tuyeres. Only someone familiar with ceramic technology would have anticipated, for example, that the chemical composition of tempering material could determine whether a particular tuyere led to successful preheating applications. The archaeological consequences of such past decision making about tempering materials, however, are not likely to be read in the ancient evidence: ancient experiments are difficult but not impossible to read in the archaeological record. It is mostly repetitive success that we recover.

The applicability of some ethnoarchaeological observations to understanding the archaeological record became apparent only once the smelters' experiment on materials had been completed. For example, we now understand that iron slag is a poor tempering material for smelting tuyeres in a Haya furnace, but it is a perfectly good tempering material in a tuyere used for forging. In a forge the tuyere tip is not exposed to temperatures above 1,250°C when it sits high on the edge of the forging pit. This eliminates any need for a refractory clay. The differences between forging and smelting tuyeres highlighted in this study point to important differences in expectations for material performance in two distinct domains of the technology. These contrasts alert us to possible differences between prehistoric tuyeres that may have varied according to their use in smelting vs. forging. This example illustrates further that it is difficult to anticipate which observations in ethnoarchaeology may have useful applications for the archaeological record.

Archaeological Evidence for Tuyere Performance ————

I now turn to archaeological evidence from Buhaya, particularly tuyeres excavated at the KM, KM2, and KM3 sites—all industrial sites dating to the first half of the first millennium A.D. My purpose here is to test the applicability of the observational model to the archaeological evidence, a comparative exercise that looks for similarity and difference. As seen earlier, the most useful index for an effective preheating tuyere is the 1.5 to 1 ratio of slagging/vitrification to reduction. The best-performing tuyeres show all these physical changes on 55 percent of the surface in 1979, with the slagging and vitrification attributes (33%) being the most reliable indices. Use of this observational model is limited to whole tuyeres, however, where the proportions of attributes can be measured. Broken, highly fragmented tuyeres often display multiple attributes—both reduction and vitrification appearing on the same sherds. This makes the calculation of proportions difficult. Thus, for tuyere fragments the focus is on the amount of slagging and vitrification that occurs in the samples.

In the period before A.D. 200 at the KM2 site, there was a significant amount of slagging and vitrification on tuyeres, approximately 34 percent (fig. 7.2). Given what we know about the sizes of ancient tuyeres and furnaces, we might expect that the tuyeres would show approximately 30 percent to 35 percent of these two attributes (slagging, vitrification) had the tuyeres been preheating. Although ancient tuyeres were inserted into

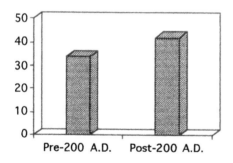

FIG. 7.2 Histograms of the frequency of slag and vitrification, as one index to preheating, at the KM2 site in the pre–A.D. 200 and post–A.D. 200 periods.

furnaces at KM2 in the early period (Schmidt and Childs 1985), after A.D. 200 at KM2, tuyeres covered with vitrification and slag increased from 34 percent to 42 percent, 4 percent more than the range of variation for the 1979 smelt. This shows that local smelters continued to experiment with tuyeres through time. Analysis of the clays also shows that these ancient smelters were using a high-quality refractory clay (Childs 1986, 1988, 1989b), very similar to that of the neighboring smelters at the KM3 site. They were not obtaining their clay from the hillsides on which they were smelting, but rather were investing labor in exploiting excellent clays high in kaolin at the edge of the large swamps (Childs 1990).

The tuyere evidence from the KM3 site, located on a hill overlooking Kemondo Bay, as well as from the KM2 site about 1.5 kilometers to the north, presents a dramatically different story. During the period before A.D. 200 there was a modest amount of vitrification and slagging observed on the tuyeres, only 23 percent, suggesting that the smelters were experiencing some problems mastering the technological principle (fig. 7.3).[4] We have seen that the insertion of tuyeres inside furnaces is a technological challenge, regardless of the use of refractory clays. Given the proximity of the KM3 work groups to those at KM2, what explains the differences between the two sites during this earlier period? The principle of tuyere insertion was known—witness the tuyere characteristics—but the KM3 smelters evidently had not fully mastered the technique, assuming that the clays were similar to those used at KM2 (Schmidt and Childs 1985; Childs 1988, 1989b).

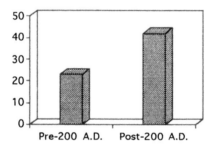

FIG. 7.3 Histograms of the frequency of slag and vitrification, as one index to preheating, at the KM3 site in the pre–A.D. 200 and post–A.D. 200 periods. There are clear differences between the two sites in the early period, but similarity in the later period.

In any event, there was a technological breakthrough during the period after A.D. 200 by smelters using the KM3 site. The performance of tuyeres at KM3 increased dramatically, reaching 42 percent of these attributes, a level identical with that of the tuyere fragments at KM2 in the same period. It seems that the smelters at the KM3 site finally had mastered the principles of preheating. Just .5 kilometer to the east at the KM site nearer the lake, an altogether different circumstance prevailed. There the smelters did not use clay that was as refractory as those used at KM2 or KM3. Instead, the KM smelters seem to have employed a potting clay (Childs 1988, 1989b), suffering a much inferior level of tuyere performance throughout industrial history in the Kemondo Bay area. The contrasts among these sites in such close proximity suggest that the differences express social and political life rather than knowledge of technological principles. Access to good-quality clay would have conferred significant technological and economic advantage to whatever group controlled that resource

(Childs 1988). If wealth and power resulted from control over good clays, then the restriction of those resources to other competing groups would have been one way for early iron producers to achieve economic superiority and build political power at the expense of other groups. Embedded within these prehistoric differences are the development of social ranking and economic stratification associated with hierarchical control over productive resources.

The most definitive evidence for preheating comes from whole or long sections of tuyeres, rather than tuyere fragments, which provide a less complete view. Moreover, the fingerprint (ratio of 3:2 slag wetting/vitrification to reduction) can be checked only when long sections are available. A long section of tuyere at KM3 provided critical evidence on behalf of ancient preheating (Schmidt 1983a; Schmidt and Childs 1985, 1996). The 36-centimeter tuyere recovered from furnace 9 (fig. 7.4) was 40 percent (14.5 cm) slag-wetted and vitrified; part of this slag-wetted section—sandwiched between the reduced portion of the heavily wetted and vitrified zone—is a gray color, suggesting some exposure to oxidation. The reduced portion constitutes another 28 percent of the remaining tuyere, a 2.86 to 2 ratio—very close to what we have observed on the experimental tuyeres, and comfortably within the expected range of variability for preheating tuyeres. The attributes displayed by this tuyere are a strong and positive commentary on the successful application of preheating principles to iron smelting at the turn of the fourth to the fifth century A.D.

Fig. 7.4 A 36-cm-long tuyere in furnace no. 9 at KM3 that shows definitive proof of preheating by the end of the third century A.D.: a vitrified tip, a slag-wetted intermediate zone (also somewhat oxidized—light gray), a black reduced zone, and a zone of mixed oxidation and reduction.

During observations of Haya smelting, I noted failed tuyeres in each smelt; the broken tuyeres are logged for each smelt on the tables that accompany this chapter. However, at that time I was not aware that observations of the broken tuyeres also might provide information that could help to clarify decision making in the past as well as clarify other indices to successful experimentation. It was not until tuyere data were analyzed during the 1980s (Schmidt and Childs 1985; Childs 1986) that characteristics of the ancient tuyere fragments were recognized as holding clues about the failure rates and success rates of ancient tuyeres. This example illustrates how archaeological evidence can help to refine methods used in observational studies. In this case, the presence of slag and vitrification on the broken edges of prehistoric tuyere fragments are testimony to the failure rates of tuyeres in ancient furnaces, yet another possible index in assessing preheating and the quality of tuyeres. These physical attributes on the edges of tuyere fragments could have developed only during smelting. In future observational studies, the fractured edges of tuyeres broken in the furnaces of replicated smelts need to be examined to see if the observational data confirm or deny the validity of the tuyere failure rates that we observe in the past. Nonetheless, these archaeological observations shed important light on technological experimentation by prehistoric smelters.

The archaeological evidence from the KM2 and KM3 sites shows that there was a relatively low proportion of altered tuyere fragments at both sites during the pre–A.D. 200 period, not exceeding 17 percent at either site (fig. 7.5). As we might expect, the rate of failure was higher at KM3 than at KM2 (Schmidt and Childs 1985; Childs 1986). There was a distinct shift in the rate of failure, however, during the post–A.D. 200 period, when it doubled at KM2 and was almost halved at KM3. What does this indicate? Preheating had become standardized at both sites by the post–A.D.

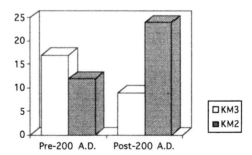

FIG. 7.5 Histograms of tuyere failure rates—based on slagging and vitrification of broken edges—at the KM2 and KM3 sites in the pre–A.D. 200 and post–A.D. 200 periods. The higher breakage rate at KM2 may suggest a local use of more tuyeres—a technique found to be effective among the recent Haya smelters.

200 period, yet there was a much higher rate of failure at KM2, where preheating expertise had grown prior to its successful application at KM3 (Schmidt and Childs 1985). It is interesting and likely informative that the KM2 tradition is older. The incidence of broken tuyeres, however, should not be seen as indicative of failure, but as in smelts 6 and 7 among the Haya, a high rate of breakage may accompany some preheating success when broken tuyeres are replaced. Differences between KM2 and KM3 could result from local preference or belief about tuyere use, or they may result from economic restrictions imposed on critical resources by more powerful social groups. Certainly the KM smelters could not gain access to better tuyere clay. So perhaps the KM3 smelters, while having access to clay of good quality, had to obtain their clay from the smelters who controlled the KM2 area. The differences may well be linked to economic reasons whereby the KM3 smelters economized and settled for using fewer tuyeres per smelt; such conservation may not have been necessary among the KM2 smelters.

If differential access to good refractory clays was linked to political control over key resources, then this also suggests some ability to organize labor to exploit the distant resources that met minimum standards. While smelters may have once exploited clays in the swamps west of the Kanyinya saddle—southwest of Kemondo Bay—they would have had to transport the clay back to Kemondo. It is also possible that they had to travel considerable distances to obtain superior clays—perhaps as far as the swamps nearby the Ngono River 8 kilometers to the west—where later iron smelters found excellent clays. These more advantaged smelters may have been able, then, to extend their hegemony over critical resources some distance away or to enter into economically attractive alliances with groups that directly controlled good clays.

Applying the Model to Other Prehistoric Technologies

Our capacity to compare similar technologies to the evidence in Buhaya is limited by the kinds of analyses that have been performed on furnace remains. For example, the numerous excavations in Rwanda and Burundi have resulted in virtually no information that can be used to assess the treatment and performance of tuyeres. One of the few considerations of tuyere characteristics is David Collett's study of the Saghasa site in the Teita Hills of southeastern Kenya (Collett 1985). Sensitive to the need to take tuyere attributes into account, Collett calculated the amount of slag and slag wash that occurred on the tuyere fragments at Saghasa. In this case the sample size of tuyere fragments is large, increasing confidence that Collett's observations are reliable indicators of prehistoric tuyere performance. The amounts of reduction and vitrification that occur on the tuyeres were not recorded, which makes direct comparison to the Haya model more difficult. However, the slag evidence and Collett's other observations provide some information that can be used in this assessment.

In the five Saghasa pits that Collett attributes to iron smelting, 21.4 percent of the tuyere fragments were slag-wetted, and Collett remarks that many also showed signs of vitrification and reduction. A more reliable indication may come from the tuyere fragments excavated from the deeper pits that can be accepted as smelting furnaces. In these contexts, 27 percent of the tuyere fragments showed signs of slagging. It appears, then, that the Saghasa tuyeres were inserted inside the furnaces and that a preheating principle likely was employed. This case study demonstrates how ambiguity can creep into comparisons, however, if there is not a consistent standard applied to analysis of prehistoric tuyeres.

During 1986 the new Archaeology Unit of the University of Dar es Salaam mounted a long vacation field school in the western Usambara Mountains. This montane region had been partly surveyed by Robert Soper (1967) some years earlier. Among the Late Stone Age, Early Iron Age, and Late Iron Age sites discovered during our reconnaissance and training mission was an Early Iron Age smelting site at Nkese, a village located on the western edge of the mountains on a spur overlooking the Masaai Steppe (Schmidt 1988, 1995). Young Tanzanian student archaeologists located this important site and subsequently excavated it (fig. 7.6). The only technological structure located on this hilltop was one furnace pit dated to the

FIG. 7.6 A second-century A.D. furnace at Nkese, western Usambara Mountains, during excavation. Some bricks have been left on the periphery of the furnace. This technology has close affinities to that found in Buhaya, but the bricks have different decorations that are chevron-shaped.

mid-second century A.D. It closely resembles furnaces previously excavated in Buhaya and in the Teita Hills to the north in Kenya (Collett 1985). The Nkese furnace was built with furnace bricks that are similar to bricks excavated from furnaces associated with the Urewe ceramic complex in western Tanzania, Burundi, and Rwanda, with the exception that many of the bricks are decorated with a chevron pattern or by a punctate decoration rather than parallel grooves.

Once it was apparent that the Nkese technology was very similar to iron smelting technology in the Western Highlands, a key question emerged: Did the smelters of Nkese know of and practice preheating techniques in their furnaces? We examined the tuyere evidence to answer this question. The most reliable evidence came from two large tuyere segments, one 40 centimeters long and another 36 centimeters long (figs. 7.7b and 7.7a). These tuyeres are much more robust than the ancient tuyeres at sites in Buhaya, with walls up to 2 centimeters thick and external diameters that consistently range between 8 and 9 centimeters among the longer sec-

FIG. 7.7a A 36-cm tuyere section from the Nkese furnace pit in the western Usambara Mountains. The heavy wall, up to 2 cm thick, is deeply reduced—indicating insertion inside the furnace.

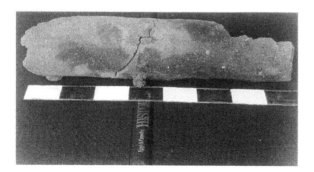

FIG. 7.7b A 40-cm tuyere section from the Nkese furnace pit. The right side is deeply reduced; small spots of slag are scattered over 25 cm of the tuyere.

tions. Despite these differences, there are some similarities. The longer of the two tuyeres shows spotty slag wetting over 65 percent of its length (it is missing a tip), mixed with reduction; variable reduction with oxidation continues over another 25 percent of the tuyere. The absence of a distinctive slag wash and any clear zones of reduction vis-à-vis slagging and vitrification suggest that the Haya evidence does not apply in this instance. The 36-centimeter tuyere was deeply reduced over 72 percent of its length (also missing a tip), with the remaining part a light gray color—likely induced by an oxidizing backwash. The evidence for slag deposits is limited to several scattered spots, again suggesting a significant departure from the experimental examples. Of the 20 kilograms of tuyere fragments in this furnace pit, 38.8 percent show evidence of slagging or vitrification, whereas another 32 percent are heavily reduced, a ratio of 2.43 to 1— suggesting that these tuyeres differ from those observed in the experimental settings. It is significant that the tuyere tips are missing in both instances; they would have been slag-wetted and vitrified. What conclusions can be drawn from the Nkese data when they are compared to the Buhaya evidence?

It is apparent that the massive diameters and walls of the Nkese tuyeres are associated with a type of tuyere that is much longer than those used by the ancient or recent smelters of Buhaya. Distinct differences between the two regions are the very thick tuyere walls at Nkese and little evidence for the deep penetration of slag into the tuyere walls. Thick walls up to 2 centimeters would have resulted in significantly less heat transfer to the air being expressed though the clay tube. However, the total amount of reduction plus slagging and vitrification for the entire sample suggests strongly that the tuyeres were inserted inside the furnace, which in every other respect resembles the furnaces of the Western Highlands forests.

The Nkese tuyeres may represent an attempt by technicians to adapt preheating principles to new clays and environmental circumstances in the Usambaras, or they may represent a stylistic expression of a traditional technique passed on, but not functionally operative, from the distant Western Highlands. Although the Nkese evidence tantalizingly hints at the application of preheating principles in eastern Tanzania about A.D. 200, the differences from the Buhaya smelts are significant enough that a preheating interpretation must await more definitive archaeological evidence.

Questions about Furnace Form

In the previous chapter I discussed why the height of the stack is important—along with the ore size and charcoal pack—for the extended exposure of the iron ore to prolonged reducing conditions (Childs 1996); this requires that the height of a furnace chimney be greater than the distance of the furnace diameter. The more extended the dwell time in the stack, the higher the rate of recovery of iron in the smelt under the conditions of the Haya smelting process. The heights of Early Iron Age furnaces are difficult to determine because of the fragmentary nature of the clay coils and "bricks" from which they were built. There is a distinct difference between the manner of construction in the two eras: the recent furnaces were constructed of termite earth and large blocks of refractory slag, but those of the Early Iron Age were made exclusively of clay. A very similar early iron technology in Rwanda and Burundi extends our knowledge about how furnaces were constructed in that region (Van Grunderbeek, Roche, and Doutrelepont 1983a, 1983b). Van Grunderbeek's archaeological evidence for furnace form is based on more complete furnace walls than those found in Buhaya.

Furnaces in the Western Highlands varied in height and diameter, ranging from 80 to 130 centimeters in diameter. This range of variability is greater than that seen at the KM2 site, where furnaces ranged in diameter between 86 and 103 centimeters (Schmidt and Childs 1985, 1996), with ten of the eleven furnaces between 93 and 103 centimeters. The furnaces at the KM3 site, however, were grouped much more tightly, ranging only from 112 to 116 centimeters. Van Grunderbeek estimates the height of the 130-centimeter-wide furnace at 130 centimeters, a 1 to 1 ratio, while a 93-centimeter-wide furnace also supports an estimated superstructure of approximately the same dimension (Van Grunderbeek et al. 1983a) (fig. 7.8). The Rwanda and Burundi reconstructions are only estimates, but do they assist us in understanding the morphology of the ancient Buhaya furnaces? And do the Western Highlands reconstructions apply to Buhaya?

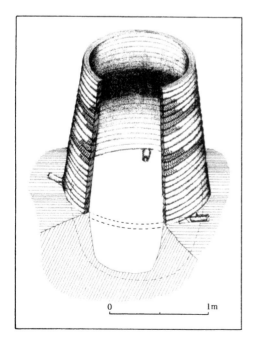

Fig. 7.8 A schematic drawing of an ancient furnace in Rwanda, based on furnace brick dimensions. After Van Grunderbeek, Roche, and Doutrelepont 1983b.

0   1m

A quick review of the Rwandan evidence is useful here. Van Grunderbeek illustrates a broad range of furnace sizes. Drawing on the archaeology of the region to the east of Butare, she posits that there was a change during the third and fourth centuries from shallow (20 cm+ deep), modestly sized furnaces (approx. 70 cm high) to much larger furnaces up to 130 centimeters wide and high (fig. 7.9). Her examples are mostly taken from an 8 × 10 kilometer cluster of industrial sites. Such variation and change are not seen in Buhaya. At the KM3 furnace, superstructures built over pits (30 cm deep and obviously truncated by agriculture) may have ranged to a height of 114 centimeters and possibly greater.

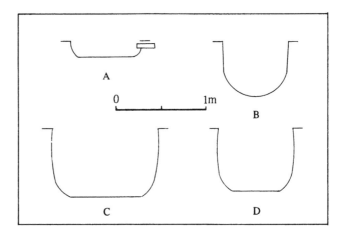

FIG. 7.9 Profiles of early first-millennium A.D. furnaces in Rwanda. The earlier-period furnaces appear as more shallow (A) and (B), while the later furnace pits are much deeper at several sites (C) and (D). After Van Grunderbeek, Roche, and Doutrelepont 1983b. Such trends are not seen in Buhaya.

If Collett's excavations of furnace pits at the Saghasa site in the Teita Hills are used to assess the similarities and differences found in furnaces of this tradition, then ambiguity rather than clarity emerges from Saghasa (Collett 1985). There is good reason to question whether three of the Saghasa features were smelting pits: these pits were 180, 160, and 163 centimeters wide—far beyond the range of variation observed in the Mwitu tradition and up to 50 centimeters wider than the largest pit known from Rwanda. It seems highly improbable that any of these pits accommodated a furnace superstructure, a conclusion underscored by the recovery of only 83 brick fragments from all the pits excavated. It just does not fit. Collett's suggestion that these very large shallow pits may have been symbolically different (based on decoration applied to only 33 brick fragments), and possibly refining furnaces, simply does not match the technological record of Africa. It is necessary to consider another function, such as roasting, with possibly a terminal function as a specialized refuse pit.

Do the recent Haya furnaces of Nyungwe offer any insights into the morphology of the ancient furnaces? The first trial smelt did not provide a reasonable model for the shape and function of a furnace capable of accommodating ten to twelve tuyeres. After the walls went up and stayed up over the 150-centimeter-wide pit, the result was a tank-shaped wall lacking a constricted neck—hardly a convincing-looking furnace (fig. 4.4), and in fact similar to a failed smelting experiment in Karagwe, 125 kilometers to the west (Reid and MacLean 1995). The older smelters said, however, that they had often built larger furnaces during the early part of this century to accommodate up to twelve smelters. Perhaps they were operating within this tradition when they prepared the furnace pit. Multiple personal histories attest that a larger furnace was within the Haya repertoire, but it certainly did not resemble this first experimental furnace.

After the idiosyncratic shape of the first furnace was modified to accommodate a work group of eight smelters at eight tuyeres, the furnace pit measured 116 centimeters in diameter. The heights of various furnace superstructures built over this pit ranged from 120 centimeters to 136 centimeters, and the last four furnaces in 1976 had a mean height of 135.5 centimeters, yielding a ratio of 1.16 to 1 for furnace height to width of the pit. It is unnecessary to argue that the ancient furnace morphologies were similar to those of Nyungwe, but the experimental model is a reasonable alternative approximation of the heights obtained in the construction of prehistoric furnaces. This inference gains some strength by our knowledge that prehistoric ores experienced extended dwell times in furnace stacks, so there was a technological advantage to be gained by an extended stack.

One of the primary differences between the two technologies is the different building materials—clay in the Early Iron Age and slag and clay in the Late Iron Age and recent times. Do such differences affect the technological process? At this point there is no evidence to suggest that these differences are significant technologically. Examination of the prehistoric furnace walls indicates that there was apparently no prefiring of the clay used to build the furnace (Childs 1986). This means that the walls were fired in place and that forest products were not used for a separate firing phase. Clay walls are more plastic and subject to slumping and therefore may have been more difficult to bring to a cone shape, a conclusion that Van Grunderbeek and her colleagues reached by examining the better-preserved upper portions of furnaces (1983a, 1983b). The need for structural rigidity in the face of a tendency to slump seems to suggest a staged drying procedure, considerably different from the procedures of recent times.

The slag and termite-mud wall of the recent furnaces appears to have several distinct adaptational advantages over prehistoric construction techniques. The refractory slag blocks have many interstitial air spaces and provide a natural insulating material. They prevent significant heat loss by radiation more effectively than the 8 to 10 centimeters of clay bricks would have in the prehistoric furnaces. Moreover, labor investment in the construction of early furnaces would have been much more significant than in recent times; the careful crafting of the successive coils (divided into bricklike sections) and the necessity to dry courses during construction testify to a much more labor-intensive process. Another difference between the two industrial eras is the use life of furnaces. The use life of a recent furnace is only one smelt. The furnace is built quickly and dismantled rapidly with a minimum of effort. It appears that a similar situation did not prevail at any of the ancient iron smelting sites in Buhaya. Other information points to the possible reuse of the ancient furnaces. Inspection of the furnace bricks shows some evidence for successive layers of sealing mud on the brick exteriors, suggesting that there was reuse (Childs 1986). As well, the deep penetration of reducing atmospheres in some bricks could have been achieved only with prolonged, repeated exposures. There is also evidence from liners on furnace floors that suggests that ancient furnaces were used for successive smelts, as we will see later in this chapter. Even if the ancient furnaces were dismantled at some point in their use life, there are indications that labor was conserved by recycling materials—reusing wall sections—in the construction of new chimneys.

An important part of the construction of the recent furnaces was the application of mud to the furnace wall during the smelt to seal cracks. This was applied in much the same way that mud is used during the construction phase around the tuyere holes (fig. 7.10). Cracks usually occur within two hours, even earlier if there is back pressure caused by wet charcoal or other impediments to the gas flow up the chimney. Crack development can lead to an altered furnace environment, with gases sweeping back against the furnace wall and exiting through the cracks rather than only up the stack past the descending ore. Rapid action is taken to plug cracks by throwing mud against the gaseous opening; if delays are allowed, the crack can quickly widen and flames explosively pour out in the direction of the bellows operator. Mud thrown against the furnace immediately becomes part of the structure, and can be seen after the smelt as successive layers on the exterior.

The Haya practice of mud repair to the furnace was not incorporated initially into our catalog of analytical questions requiring observational information. This is a good example of how an observation outside of the research objectives sheds important light on an analytical problem arising during archaeological analysis. After the ancient furnace bricks were cross-sectioned and analyzed, Terry Childs found that there was often an extra external layer of fired clay attached to the exterior of many bricks (Childs 1986). The reason appears to lie in the practice of sealing the furnace, an especially demanding task in the case of early furnaces with their numerous joints along the courses of clay coils and separate bricklike pieces, particularly along sections recycled from other furnaces. Inevitably, the cracks would have leaked gases and interfered with the operation of the

Fig. 7.10 Smelters slapping mud against the sides of a Haya furnace to seal cracks around the slag blocks near the tuyere ports. This process is identical to that which occurs during smelting.

smelt—only to be sealed in what appears to be a rather even application of clay over the exterior. It seems that the prehistoric furnaces sometimes had a layer of clay applied prior to smelting in order to ready the furnace, another attribute that may attest to the reuse of the furnace, especially at the KM2 site.

In Buhaya the archaeological record shows a different picture of how the furnace superstructure was constructed. These differences between the past and the present are not significant in technological terms, with the more significant implication lying at the juncture of economic decision making. The furnaces of the first millennium A.D. were much more expensive in terms of labor invested in the original construction, though analogies with other permanent furnaces, such as those of the Fipa (Wembah-Rashid 1973; Barndon 1992, 1996), suggest that the savings in labor are significant once the furnace is completed. However, when maintenance of early furnaces is also considered (with their specialized tuyere ports and doors), such labor costs may have exceeded the more recent practice of successive construction. Indirect evidence for more long-term use comes from larger rectangular furnace bricks that were decorated with parallel grooves at the KM2 site (Schmidt and Childs 1985). Excavated from the bottom of a massive industrial refuse pit, these special bricks may have been used as doors on rake holes like those used in some African furnaces to pull the bloom and slag from the furnace. If indeed these were rake hole doors, then the ancient furnaces may have been used over a series of smelts. Also, many of the ancient furnace pits are filled with the bricks from the furnace superstructure (Schmidt 1983c; Schmidt and Childs 1985), suggesting a finality to the completion of smelting that is perhaps linked to season's end rather than the condition of the furnace.

Furnace Pit Function: Presmelting

The use of the furnace pit, prior to smelting, to presmelt iron ore was an activity we had not anticipated before the 1976 studies. This presmelting, as we now know, is an important part of the technological process. Only when we began to unravel the significance of differences among ancient pits with smelting debris did the application of the observation to archaeology become obvious. During presmelting, the Haya poured the iron ore on top of the freshly cut wood (fig. 7.11). As the wooden rails char and fall to the bottom of the pit, the iron ore becomes entrapped among the large charred logs. All of the iron ore was removed the following morning, examined, and sorted nearby the furnace pit for later use (fig. 7.12). Roasting or presmelting usually occurs just once, before the first in a series of smelts. During subsequent smelts the iron ore for later smelts is roasted *within* the furnace, along its interior margins, as the smelting is taking place. The result is a significant volume of ore that is partially smelted. Thus, partially smelted ore recovered from the furnace is not ore that descended through the furnace stack but is ore that was being presmelted within the furnace.

Fig. 7.11 A fire within the lined furnace pit being used to presmelt iron ore. The iron ore collects in pockets among the charred logs (*see arrow*), gradually falling to the bottom of the pit to be mixed with charred logs.

Fɪɢ. 7.12 Smelters and their assistants at the Nyungwe smelting site preparing for another smelt. Notice the pile of slag, burned furnace earth, and broken tuyeres to the right of the young man with a bucket of iron ore. Ishanga grass and tuyeres sit to the left, while the second master smelter removes fines from charcoal to the west of the furnace, where iron ore and charcoal—removed from the prior smelt—are laid out for inspection and processing.

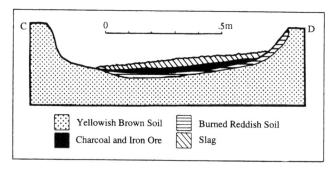

Fɪɢ. 7.13 Profile of pit no. 16 at the KM2 site; a horizon of partially reduced ore and charred logs was later covered with slag—pointing to multiple functions.

Interpreting the Archaeology of Pit Fill

In several cases at the KM2 site, the materials resting on the floors of several pits were quite different from those on other furnace floors at the same site: large logs were intermixed with pieces of partially reduced iron. In furnace pit number 16 (fig. 7.13) there were charred logs with partially reduced iron ore and small pieces of flow slag packed on the bottom of the pit. As we searched for the significance of this arrangement, the observations of iron ore roasting provided a key insight: as iron ore roasts, it falls through the burning logs to the bottom of the pit, eventually being buried with pieces of logs, which also fall to the bottom of the pit and, in those reducing conditions, stop burning. These conditions explain some otherwise perplexing configurations recorded during excavation of furnace pits 14 and 18 at KM2 (Schmidt and Childs 1985). The two pits, used previously for smelting, seemed to have last been used for roasting purposes. This functional interpretation of furnace pit 14 (fig. 7.14), however, was made questionable when we mapped a concentration of iron ore on one side of the furnace mixed with debris from smelting. This characteristic seems to fit more closely with our observation of what sometimes happens to the iron ore placed inside the wall of the furnace to prepare it for the next smelt. As tuyeres are extracted from the furnace, they are sometimes fused to masses of partially reduced ore. When the tuyeres are removed, the ore comes with them. The result is that iron ore is left behind in areas where fusion and removal did not occur. This observation provides insight into the possible significance of a concentration of ore (mixed with slag) on only one side of furnace 14.

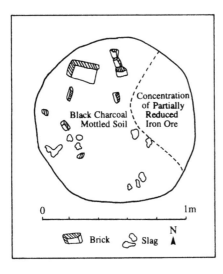

FIG. 7.14 Pit no. 14 at the KM2 site had a concentration of partially reduced iron ore on one side. This configuration may be linked to the removal of iron ore in other parts of the pit after it had been presmelted during an earlier smelt.

A different interpretative dilemma is found in the configuration of bottom fill in pit 18 at KM2: pieces of iron ore mixed with large charred logs, which then overlie small slag prills (fig. 7.15). There is nothing in our observational record that helps us understand the significance of this arrangement, though we might deduce that roasting occurred in a smelting pit that had not been completely cleaned of its contents (Schmidt and Childs 1985). Pertinent to part of this problem is use by the Barongo of charred logs in their furnaces (fig. 7.16). Charred logs play two roles in the

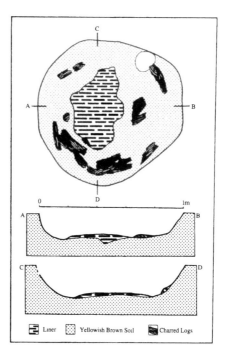

FIG. 7.15 Pit no. 18 at the KM2 site. This pit was defined as a deeply truncated shallow dish with large charcoal logs on its floor; partially reduced iron ore was situated on top and under the charred logs, suggesting a terminal use as a roasting pit.

FIG. 7.16 A view of the interior of a Barongo iron smelting furnace. The large pieces of charcoal are placed in the center of the furnace pit to a thickness of 20 cm. These large pieces of charcoal snag iron that is reprocessed—along with slag—from earlier smelts as well as provide an easy pathway for slag to drain into the pit below.

Barongo furnace: (1) to capture agglomerating iron platelets in the formation of bloom (Schmidt 1996c), and (2) to allow slag to drain into the interstitial space between and beneath the logs. Thus, when slag is seen in the context of charred logs, one possible interpretation is that a similar approach was used for draining slag in the furnace pit, an observation borne out by impressions of large logs in fossil slags.

The most reliable archaeological evidence for prehistoric iron smelting is debris from smelting activity found in situ within a furnace pit. This does not mean that bricks, tuyeres, ore, slags, and charcoal inside the pits are pristine and undisturbed. Indeed, most materials have been rearranged by later activities such as planting bananas. Undisturbed layers on the bottoms of furnaces and the pits themselves often provide important evidence for smelting. But when contents have been completely removed and the pit has been rendered into a shallow dish, context has been erased. Then the issue is whether the pit in question is related to ancient smelting.

Ethnoarchaeology and Furnace Pits

The ethnoarchaeology of Haya iron smelting included the study of the furnace pits used for smelting. A cross-section was later excavated of the pit used in the 1976 smelts. Through profiles and surface studies, we wanted to map technological fingerprints that characterize the transformations that the earth and clay undergo when smelting occurs in this kind of basin (figs. 7.17 and 7.18). The 1979 pit was left in situ for later excavation, for assessment at a later date of what changes occur after prolonged burial. The 1984 pit was excavated and also cross-sectioned for study (fig. 7.19). The material used for lining the three pits was the same: soil gathered from territaries nearby the Nyungwe site. We sampled and Childs (1986) later

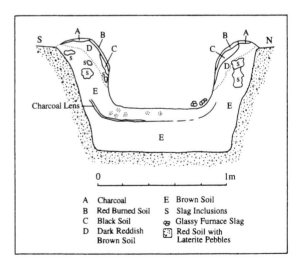

FIG. 7.17 A cross-section view of the 1976 smelting furnace pit at Nyungwe. Layer E is the first furnace liner, the top portion of which was later destroyed. The large pieces of slag were used as fill when the pit was reconstructed. The important attribute that marks multiple use of a smelting pit is the vertical layer of reddish-brown soil (D) capped by red soil (A).

A	Charcoal	E Brown Soil
B	Red Burned Soil	S Slag Inclusions
C	Black Soil	Glassy Furnace Slag
D	Dark Reddish	Red Soil with
	Brown Soil	Laterite Pebbles

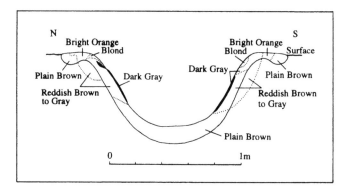

FIG. 7.18 A cross-section of the 1984 smelting pit in Nyungwe, used two times. The reddish-brown soil was not as intense and was much more difficult to define than in 1976. The morphology of this pit is similar to that of 1979 and the second pit of 1976.

analyzed for the project termite soils in several locales in Buhaya and found that the percentage of coarse sand is higher and the clay content is significantly lower than in brick clays or tuyere clays. Thus, termite soils tend to have distinctive characteristics when compared to other clay sources in the region, suggesting that we should be able to trace possible continuities or differences in materials used to line and to build furnaces through time. Significantly, ancient smelters also used local termite soils to build and line their furnaces (Childs 1988), suggesting that these materials continued to be economical and reliable for such tasks over long stretches of time.

FIG. 7.19 The 1976 furnace pit after excavation.

The profile of the pit used in the first series of smelts (1976) is not typical, nor is the inclusion of chunks of slag normal (fig. 7.18). This peculiar structure resulted from the contest between smiths and the aged smelters about how to reconstruct the furnace pit after it proved too large (see chapter 3); the slag inclusions are simply fill (fig. 7.19). I accept as closer to the norm the profile of the 1984 pit. Despite fears on the part of our consulting metallurgist that the walls would explode if not fully dried, the insulating properties of the ashy reeds prevented temperatures sufficient to cause spalling of the walls.

A chief worry for the smelters was the integrity of the pit liner. The liner was subjected to successive attacks by slag and by heat degradation, particularly spalling. Childs (1989a) found that spalling was common to the termitary soils of Buhaya. The loss of the pit liner can be severe (fig. 7.20), with large chunks sometimes pulled up by attached slags and fused iron ores. Six smelts in this one pit left these distinctive fingerprints. Thus, when we find missing pieces of liner or spalling of liners, there may have been multiple use of smelting pits.

Fig. 7.20 The 1976 Nyungwe furnace pit, showing the severe attrition of the liner after six smelts. Note the flow slag that has settled to the bottom of the furnace.

A distinct reduction/oxidation boundary on the periphery of the pit is another important fingerprint. This boundary (area D, fig. 7.17) is marked by dark reddish-brown soil sandwiched between natural earth and the reduced, gray to black soils of the furnace interior. This appears as a distinctive characteristic in smelting pits used for multiple smelts. After two smelts in the 1984 pit, these characteristics were just beginning to emerge—with a reddish color developing (see fig. 7.18) but the soil remaining predominantly a gray color. This reddish soil beneath a reduced layer extended downward as deep as 60 centimeters in 1976 (44 cm in 1984). Color changes in soil induced by repeated smelting in the same pit can be used to assess smelting technologies and possible conditions of multiple smelting. We might expect that such a boundary would be absent in ancient times if multiple smelting was not practiced in the same pit.

The Archaeology of Smelting Pits

None of the prehistoric furnaces excavated in Buhaya had complete liners. At the KM3 site, earthen liners were not used, and it is possible that numerous sandstone rocks on the furnace floors acted as refractory buffers. Therefore, it is not possible to address the multiple use of furnaces at KM3 through a study of liners. However, at the KM2 site there is significant evidence that suggests multiple use of furnace pits. Of the twelve furnaces that are linked to iron smelting with some confidence (Schmidt and Childs 1985), eleven had liners both on the sides of the pits and on the bottoms. Samples taken from two of the KM2 liners have been analyzed for particle size (along with multiple samples of fill); they closely resemble three of the four samples of termitary earth analyzed by Childs (1986: 131), suggesting that the ancient smelters selected similar material for lining furnace pits.

The most striking observations about liners at KM2 are their fragmentary occurrence and the large patches of exposed, burned reddish-orange (oxidized) soil on the bottoms of furnaces, such as furnace number 6 (fig. 7.21). There are several possible explanations for this oxidized zone: a

Fig. 7.21a Furnace pit no. 6 (the left of the two) at the KM2 site prior to excavation of the bottom debris. See fig. 10.12 for a photograph of the furnace liner in the same furnace pit—one of the furnace pits with a ritual hole in its base. The circumference of the pit was marked by a clear reddish-orange oxidation boundary on the edge of effective reduction.

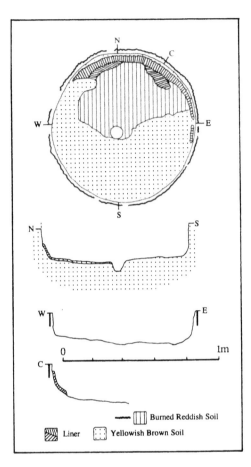

FIG. 7.21b A plan view of the same furnace showing the peripheral oxidation boundary and a patch of strongly oxidized soil, where we hypothesize that the liner was removed after the last smelt in this pit.

remnant liner may have been removed after the last smelt conducted in this particular pit, or perhaps this patch of soil had been protected by layers of charred logs. Had the area been exposed directly to reducing conditions, the oxidized characteristics would have been eliminated (Schmidt and Childs 1985). Recent Haya furnaces showed this layer of oxidized soil immediately beneath the reduced section of liner. This suggests that its exposure attests to the removal of liner in bits and pieces, also the apparent history of pit 14 at KM2 (fig. 7.22), where some of the remaining liner had been removed sometime close to its terminal use. This is the same pit from which I suggested that fused iron ore also had been pulled.

The furnace pits at KM2, however, pose other interpretative challenges. Another, much more shallow pit than the vertical-sided furnace pits shows a similar zone of bright reddish-orange soil (fig. 7.23), with a small piece of liner in situ and many slag beads resting on an exposed and oxidized area. Slag beads are in such contexts archaeological signatures

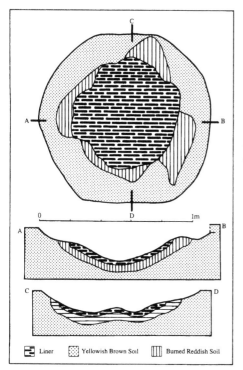

Fɪɢ. 7.22 A plan view of the floor of furnace pit no. 14 at KM2 showing the piecemeal removal of pieces of liner.

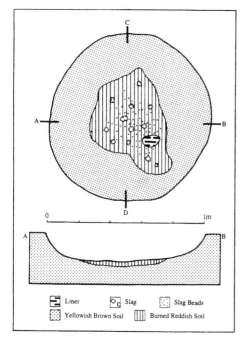

Fɪɢ. 7.23 A plan view of furnace pit no. 16 at KM2 showing the presence of slag beads on a newly exposed oxidized zone, where all but a small patch of liner was removed. The exposed area was likely protected from reduction by charred logs; when the charred logs were removed, slag beads fell off and were left behind.

for furnace bottoms, but their presence on a patch of oxidized floor, from which the liner had apparently been recently removed, initially is puzzling. The earlier discussed clues derived from iron ore roasting suggest that the dense charcoal found on the floor of the pit, mixed in with large quantities of partially reduced ore, points to final use as an ore-roasting pit. How, then, did the slag beads—characteristic of smelting—end up on the oxidized floor?

There are several other pits in which large charcoal logs overlay oxidized patches. Both at the KM2 site and on the center of furnace floors at the KM3 site, the logs may have been used for ritual purposes (see chapter 10). They may also have been used as insulating material to protect the base of the furnace; as they reduced to charcoal, the logs would have provided excellent protection against slag fusion with the floor. The slag beads evidently came to rest on the floor after the charred logs were removed and the pit was prepared for roasting—leading to the peculiar structure seen in furnace pit 16 at KM2.

The preponderance of evidence from the KM2 and KM3 sites points to the successive reuse of furnace pits, seen especially in the clear archaeological signature of reddish soil that marks the reduction/oxidation boundary on the periphery of the pits. At the KM2 site there is also convincing evidence for multiple use of the pits not only for smelting but, as in the recent Haya examples, also for presmelting iron ore in preparation for a first smelt. It may be that when smelters returned to a site, they used an old pit to roast iron ore after constructing a new pit nearby. In any event, the pits at KM2 accommodated multiple smeltings, including the roasting of ore during the smelt as well as the roasting of ore prior to smelting. There may have also been different technological styles practiced by different groups of smelters (Childs 1991). Mapunda (1995), for example, has found that furnaces east of Lake Tanganyika were relined again and again—suggesting that function may sometimes give way to ideological considerations in the reuse of smelting pits. Either the KM3 smelters did not line their furnaces or they used them so often that the liners were completely used up and thereafter were replaced with logs. If the latter was indeed the case, then the lining of furnace pits may be more a stylistic characteristic than a technological necessity.

Comparative Summary

The fingerprint models derived from ethnoarchaeology provide important technological and morphological measures by which we can begin to understand the significance of technological remnants and debris. There are remarkable parallels between the two technological eras, but the differences are also striking, perhaps more for their economic and ecological significance than for technological reasons. The change from charcoal-filled pits to grass-filled pits in the second millennium A.D. marks a major technological adaptation in a technology that had endured over centuries. The labor requirements for a pit filled with grass char are significantly less than for wood charcoal, thus resulting in significant labor savings and a more efficient process. But the ecological causes and implications of this adaptation figure even more prominently in regional history, a subject I explore further in chapter 11. The use of grass char as a response to depleted forest resources signals an adaptational advantage in iron smelting, while at the same time it heralds a new era when renewable resources such as grass replaced exclusive use of precious forest resources in furnace pits.

8.

Models

for the

Interpretation

of Space

Smelting and

Forging

An integral part of the endeavor to write a new history of iron production is to assess if there are material expressions of social organization or social interactions at the site-specific level. At a macroscale, such as social groups controlling specific smelting resources, it is possible to see such social phenomena expressed materially. However, at the scale of the specific site, other social concerns and values may be expressed in the spatial location of smelting activities; proscriptive rules that forbade smelting to the gaze and participation of women are paralleled by rules that placed smelting outside the bounds of the village social sector. This meant that the smelting site was located outside individual *kibanja* (farmsteads), but *not* at remote or secret locations as was the case with some other iron smelting cultures.

Social-economic differences among smelters are seen in the division of labor and the spatial segregation of tasks performed during the smelt. It is possible to see social hierarchy reflected in some activities, and in this respect we may gain insight into social ranking that may have occurred in the past. For example, activities such as charcoal preparation and ore preparation immediately before the smelt are specialized tasks assigned to the master smelters, those who also charge the furnace with charcoal and ore. Activities such as charcoal and iron ore sorting, however, leave low-visibility or latent fingerprints on the landscape. After smelting is concluded, either resources prepared in the special work areas have been used, or the surplus has been stored and any residue kicked about, trampled, and scattered. All of these later activities transform the work areas and lead to a more ephemeral record than the configurations seen during the smelt. Nonetheless, after the last smelt the remains of some special tasks did have a higher visibility, some parts of which might withstand changes induced by humans and nature. I will examine these for their usefulness in interpreting the archaeological record.

Forging is an integral part of the productive cycle in iron production, and the archaeological remains for forging are equally important for understanding the complete cycle of technological activities. In Nyungwe and Kikukwe villages there were a number of active forges, several of which belonged to craftsmen who participated in the smelting reconstructions. Detailed observational records were made of forging that used different blooms and spring steel. Such evidence has been useful for a closer examination of how smiths treat bloomery materials vis-à-vis the spring steel that most have used throughout their careers. Mapping the physical layout and structure of their forges assists us in recognizing and assessing the tightness of fit with archaeological phenomena—be they artifacts such as tuyeres or structures such as furnace pits and forges.

Space and Work

As a socially constructed and ritualized process, iron smelting was often conducted outside of the gaze of individuals and groups unaffiliated with the smelting fraternity. This is particularly easy to see in some of the taboos that kept smelting separate from women. There was also significant spatial separation of smelting from everyday life in many African societies, with smelting conducted in secrecy within the forest or hinterland, well away from settlements. The Barongo smelters of Buzinza, also associated with hunting and a generally antisocial view of the world, conducted their smelts great distances from homesteads and settlements, deep within the forest (Schmidt 1996c). If smelting was physically removed from the daily routines of the village, then such separation lessened the chances of interference by others, witchcraft, and other foul play and industrial espionage. However, values of separateness do not necessarily translate into Western understandings of remoteness.

The smelters of Nyungwe conducted their smelts outside of the precincts of any particular farm or kibanja, but the location of the furnace was contiguous to the farmstead of a participating smith—hardly a remote location. Oral histories of smelters attest to their smelting on the fringe of Nyungwe village in the 1920s as well as contiguous to the Kantale iron mines about an hour's walk to the south.[1] Smelting at the Kantale location was determined more by the ore source than by any need to be away from Nyungwe. Any assertion that smelting activities would have been removed from the vicinity of domestic settlement places a very literal value on historical representations of physical separation and tends to project this idealized notion into the past.

Archaeological evidence from two different sites in Buhaya indicates that it is possible that iron smelting during the early first millennium was conducted not far from domestic structures. For example, there is a house floor near several iron smelting furnaces at the Rugomora Mahe site (Block D; Schmidt 1978: 221) and a well-defined house floor just west of a cluster of four furnaces at the KM2 site (Schmidt and Childs 1985: 65).[2] Iron smelting materials were found scattered on the house floor at the KM2 site. Although the house dates to the second century B.C., somewhat earlier than the first industrial period at KM2, the dating suggests that it may be contemporaneous with the industrial activity—as the floor debris also seems to indicate. I am not saying that there are direct parallels between Nyungwe and the practices and beliefs about spatial separation during the Early Iron Age. However, we must realize that physical separation may mean relatively little distance between domestic structures and smelting activities.

The spatial organization of the Haya work space during smelting varied from smelt to smelt. Most preparation of iron ore and sorting of charcoal occurred on the western side of the furnace during 1976 but on the southern side during the 1979 and 1984 smelts. There is no discernible belief or preference that determines where particular activities will be performed. Physical remains of some activities often proved to be ephemeral: charcoal stockpiling areas disappeared at the end of the smelt when charcoal was rebagged; the iron ore that sat nearby the furnace went into the furnace; and the ash from charred reeds pulled from the furnace after the smelt was dissipated by the wind and rain.

To document how various activities were structured on the site, the spatial organization of one of the 1976 smelts was mapped (fig. 8.1). Social and age differences as well as technological mastery are hierarchically expressed in the spatial separation of different task areas. The exclusive provenience of the head smelters—the only ones allowed to charge the furnace—was the area west of the furnace, where charcoal and iron ore were processed. The senior smiths—foremen and bellows operators in this context—assisted the smelters by dumping and preparing charcoal, but their duties abruptly stopped there. The area just north of the sorting zone, where the iron blooms were buried after being pried from the fur-

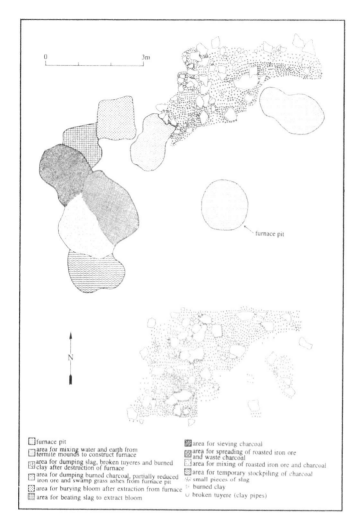

FIG. 8.1 A map of the work area around the smelting furnace at Nyungwe. Most of the tasks performed to the west of the furnace are those reserved only for the master smelters. The slag waste, along with broken tuyeres and burned earth, was thrown to both the north and south of the furnace pit; this was later consolidated to the north only.

nace pit, marks the beginning of the apprentices' or helpers' area, where the termite mud was mixed and the furnace superstructure, slag, and tuyeres were thrown and stored until the next smelt. The head smelters entered the slag storage area only on the day of a smelt, when it became the construction stockpile area.

Division of labor and hierarchy based on craft skill and authority are clearly read on a Haya smelting site as the activities occur. While division of labor was unique to these replications, nonetheless the traditional organization of labor incorporated clear differences among master smelters, their juniors, and youthful apprentices—suggesting some broad if not precise parallels. But it is far from clear whether some activities, such as those that occurred in the western zone during the 1976 smelts, would leave any enduring fingerprints. It is possible that some of the activities that we currently see as more ephemeral left less latent fingerprints than we have seen thus far. If iron ore was abandoned unused after the last smelt of the season, for example, then an altogether different picture would emerge. But later observations in Nyungwe in 1977, 1978, 1979, and 1984 indicate that only the slag blocks, baked earth, and tuyeres thrown aside on the northern periphery of the work area (also the southern periphery in the example given) had any permanence and potential to enter the archaeological record—barring any recycling of slag and tuyeres. I want to caution that the 1976 map is a *static* representation at one point in a dynamic process of discard activity and recycling on a Haya smelting site.

The smelting behavior of the Barongo iron smelters also leads to material depositions that bear some affinities, as well as many differences, to Nyungwe. My visits to the historic sites used by the Barongo from the late 1930s up until the early 1950s show that baked termite earth, tuyeres, and some small amounts of slag were thrown away on the periphery of the area where the smelting house was located. The Barongo reuse of slag in the smelting process significantly lowers the visibility of the Barongo smelting sites (Schmidt 1996c). Haya recycling of slag occurred at a much more modest level when slag from earlier smelts was used in furnace construction. Some select, useful pieces of slag that came out of each furnace went into the construction of future furnaces; the remainder was thrown to the side in the storage/discard area.

The Haya and Barongo both have distinct ways of treating smelting debris, as do most other smelting cultures. Some of the most spectacular treatments are the large slag enclosures described by de Barros (1986) in Togo as well as the huge piles—up to 6 meters high, 12 meters wide, and 30 meters long—of the Babungo smelters in Cameroon, who stacked their slag waste immediately next to their smelting furnaces. Much of this slag was processed to remove small clusters of iron metal, the marketing of which was an integral part of the regional trade system. Although the variability of such behavior is enormous, some general patterns do emerge out of these studies. Slag is usually worked contiguous to the smelting site to remove the glassy waste, rather than being carted back to the forges and creating a clutter of sharp glass there. Larger pieces of slag, furnace parts, and broken or used tuyeres are usually treated as a common category of refuse and end up in a generalized pile in close proximity to the smelting site. Both tuyeres and slag are subject to many forms of recycling: technological reuse, use as building material, use as tempering material in pottery, and use as fertility charms and fertility medicine (Mapunda 1995). Which of these observations about spatial organization and recycling help us understand archaeological remains in the early industrial record in this region or elsewhere in this region of Africa?

Work Organization and Discard in the Archaeological Record

Archaeological evidence for organization of work intersects with our ethnographic prediction: elusive if not ephemeral. At none of the industrial sites in Buhaya—Rugomora Mahe, RM2, KM, KM2, KM3, Buyozi, Kabale, or NG5—is there evidence for iron ore sorting and charcoal preparation contiguous to the furnaces. There is one example of iron ore preparation at the KM3 site, where a series of ore clusters were observed scattered among four EIA smelting furnaces (fig. 8.2: each marked as "feature"). However, these features seem to be related to actual preparation of the ore on site, something that I did not witness during ethnographic observations. We looked for areas in which slag may have been worked from prehistoric iron blooms, but the types of slag scatters found were so homogeneous that it was not possible to designate an area that was clearly associated with this activity. The small and fractured nature of the smelting slags recovered from nonfurnace contexts suggests that there is no evidence for the disposal of slags in the way that was observed recently. To the contrary, the pits in which slag was discarded at the KM2 site suggest special handling in an environment kept clean of all kinds of industrial waste.

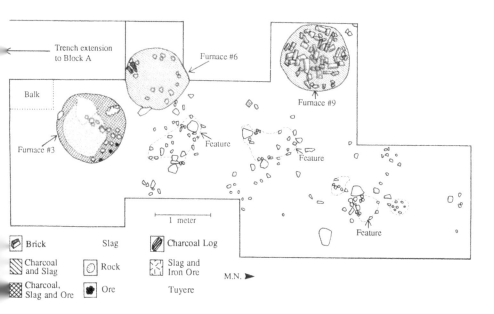

FIG. 8.2 A plan view of a cluster of fourth-century A.D. furnaces at the KM3 site. Of interest here are the areas enclosed with dashed lines, places where iron ore was worked prior to smelting—suggesting some differences from the more recent processing of iron ore.

Treatment of smelting waste appears to have changed significantly between the Early Iron Age and recent times. Smelting bricks that were not recycled ended up in smelting pits along with tuyeres and much of the slag from the bottom of the smelting pit, much of it often in situ. The most dramatic difference in past treatments is seen at the KM2 site, where huge amounts of industrial debris and domestic pottery ended up in a specially constructed pit in which there were discarded furnace bricks, slag, tuyeres, iron fragments, and charcoal (figs. 8.3a and 8.3b). This special treatment, also replicated in furnace pits and special refuse pits on other sites, suggests that the ancients had a distinctively different way of perceiving and treating used furnace materials. Our analysis of ceramics shows that with the settlement and technological changes of the early first millennium A.D. there were also changing attitudes toward slag. At that time—with the advent of carved roulette pottery—potters began to use slag as a tempering material, a practice that would have significantly affected the visibility of slag on the landscape. This practice has continued up to the present day.

FIG. 8.3a A large refuse pit (feature 8) at the KM2 site prior to excavation. This pit contained hundreds of furnace bricks, slag, iron, tuyeres, and domestic ceramics.

What values were at work in refuse treatment in the past: cleanliness, reuse of the area for other purposes, or other reasons related to the ideology surrounding iron smelting? As material explanations do not seem immediately parsimonious for the first millennium A.D., are there other as-

Fig. 8.3b The large refuse pit at KM2 after excavation. It was excavated specifically to bury industrial and domestic debris on the site.

pects of the symbolic values linked to iron smelting that might provide clues beyond the banal? Bertram Mapunda's (1995) recent work among the Fipa helps us significantly in understanding some of the fertility and healing beliefs associated with ironworking materials left behind by smelters. Surprised to find some obvious smelting sites barren of slag, Mapunda came to realize that slag in the local culture was continuously in demand and still being "recycled" as fertility medicine. Slag charms and ground slag are some of the most potent fertility drugs among the Fipa. The continual use of such objects for these purposes has lowered the visibility of slag on many sites of varying antiquity and homogenized the scatters and types of slag.

The impact of healing beliefs on the archaeological record may have been accompanied by other ideologies attached to ironworking. For example, in chapter 9 we will see that iron smelting is often surrounded by concerns about the effects of witchcraft. So many smelting technologies are wrapped in ritual that protects smelting from evil influences, foremost of which is witchcraft, that the protection of the furnace contents and materials from those engaged in witchcraft may have been a natural extension of this belief system. We must keep open the possibility that the burial of furnace waste resulted from an ideology that nothing associated with the smelt must be left about openly for the use of witches. The careful return of unrecycled furnace materials to smelting pits may comment on more than questions of orderliness. The distinctiveness of the treatment of prehistoric waste materials in this instance reflects back on the observational and historic cases, causing us to look afresh for reasonable ethnographic models that provide more than technological explanations.

Spatial Organization of Forges

The forging workplace is spatially separated from the smelting site. The central feature in the rectangular forging house (*ishasha*) of Buhaya is the *luiija,* or the rock anvil.[3] The luiija defines and gives meaning to the forge. In traditional times in nearby Bunyoro, for example, there were special rituals to initiate a new forge, replete with fertility symbolism. Any related beliefs in Buhaya have faded into distant memory as the craft of forging has adapted to new materials and a new social, economic, and religious environment. However, the same ritual and symbolic meanings that inform Haya iron smelting also appear to have applied to the forge. The center post of the forge—usually not far from the luiija—was the locus of sacred rituals in which Irungu—Bacwezi spirit and ancestor—is appeased. The center post hosted the blood sacrifices to Irungu. Perhaps the most profound commentary on the importance of the forge and its symbolic power in Buhaya is the association of the ancient forge at Kaiija tree with etiological myth about iron and the rich symbolism of iron production. I now want to identify the material context for the forge—its material fingerprints—to identify structures in the archaeological record. To do this, we must examine the spatial layout and the tools and materials that are found within and contiguous to its walls.

The Haya forge or ishasha is an integral part of the village. It is located within the kibanja as a separate rectangular building, at least 10 meters from a residence, with two open ends though which a breeze can blow. The luiija is sometimes set next to a second anvil stone, often with a crease or groove that aids in the folding of tangs and curving the edges of tools; this second stone also is used for cutting purposes. We know from chapter 6 that when traditional blooms were worked at the forge, part of the slag residue was often derived directly from pieces of the blooms that sloughed off into the fire and from oxidized scale of objects being made. Furthermore, the final mechanical working of the blooms occurred at the anvil, with smiths knocking off glassy slags and scattering pieces around the anvil. So some very small splinters of glassy smelting slags came to reside in the forge area, suggesting that these constitute a fingerprint for smelting slag in a precolonial forge. After examining some of the physical characteristics that define a forge, I will turn to the archaeological record to see if the observational evidence assists in the interpretation of one very significant feature and another ambiguous archaeological case.

The Haya forge today is an eclectic collection of traditional and modern tools (fig. 8.4). Though the traditional hammers continue to be used in

Fig. 8.4 Smithing tools from Ta Simoni's forge. *Left to right, top row:* one *kisindate,* sledgehammer for heavy work, replaces *mpuro;* three *entangato* (pl. and sing.), hammers made from bloom, tops are used as anvils; two *myangata* (*mwangata,* sing.), finishing hammers; two *tuhoro* (*kahoro,* sing.), cutting tools.
Second row: one *kibunduro,* an old hammer base used as an anvil, especially for shaping *bihosho* (large cutting tools used to dig out banana roots); three *tubunduro* (*kabunduro,* sing.), used to shape sockets in hafting large tools; three *mbunduro* (*lubunduro,* sing.), used to shape sockets in smaller tools; one *luhana,* used to remove pointed objects from fire; one *embago,* used to remove objects from fire; one *embago with luhana,* used to remove objects from fire.
Bottom row, top: ntuhi, a hook used to arrange iron in fire and to remove objects from fire; *bottom: isizi,* used to sprinkle and dampen fire and to cool objects.

lighter forging, modern 2-kilogram and 4-kilogram sledgehammers are universally used in Haya forges for heavy work. Piles of scrap and spring steel are often stockpiled at the front of the forge and sometimes inside within easy reach of the smith, who is always accompanied in the forge by a helper pumping the bellows, and sometimes by a fellow smith who assists with heavy work and high-demand schedules (fig. 8.5). Forges today are an extension of the capitalist world system, often engaged in reprocessing steels from vehicles made in Europe and Japan or in the repair of other commodities that are made in distant lands. This eclectic quality— drawing on resources out of different productive systems while producing

Fig. 8.5 Haya smith (Ta Bernardo Muhambo) at work in his forge in Nyungwe village. He is cold-working an axe made from a piece of bloom.

Fig. 8.6 The grave of a smith in Kikukwe village. The symbolic grave decorations reflect the transformed domain of the "traditional" smith (*left to right, hanging*): part of an auto muffler, a rubber tong (which he wore), an iron basin, a European-made hoe (top only visible), a *kihosho*, and an iron (tin) can. Photo by Winnie Lambrecht.

goods that continue to service the traditional agricultural sector—typifies the cultural change that this part of the traditional economy has experienced. Even the symbolic expressions using iron capture the transformed identity of the Haya smith. The symbolic grave offerings hung over a smith's grave in Kikukwe village (fig. 8.6) poignantly capture this liminality, the smith as a bricoleur drawing on both worlds: part of an auto muffler, a rubber thong (which he wore while smithing), a rusted iron basin of Western manufacture, an iron (tin) can, a European-made hoe produced for the African market, and a locally made iron *kihosho* used to cut the roots of banana plants. At a symbolic level this is quintessentially the grave of a twentieth-century Haya smith.

The layouts of Haya forges show strong similarities along with distinctive differences (figs. 8.7a, 8.7b, 8.7c). Each of the forges illustrated here shows a square to slightly rectangular configuration; posts are used to support the superstructure, and a center post is also present, to older mas-

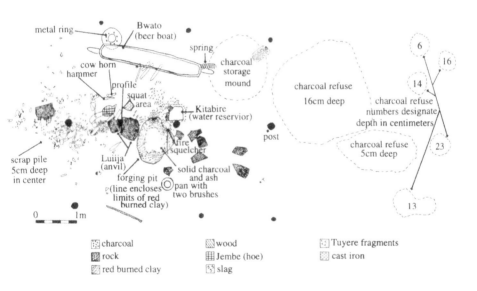

FIG. 8.7a Plan view of Ta Kaijage's forge in Nyungwe village—contiguous to the smelting site. Note the presence of a beer boat for brewing local beer.

ter smiths a reminder of the ritual and symbolic life that used to inform their lives. A pile of scrap and spring steel at the front entrance is today a ubiquitous feature. The luiija is located on the front side of the main support post, always paired with a smaller anvil further to the front. Bellows are on the opposite or back side of the center post, a place usually marked by the presence of rocks that are used to stabilize and hold down the bellows. Charcoal in each of these forges (and in all other observed forges)

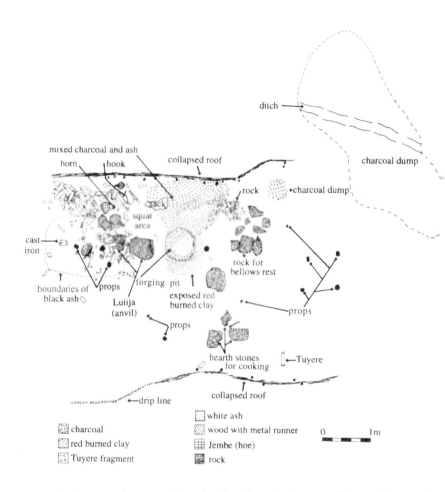

FIG. 8.7b Plan view of Ta Bernardo Muhambo's forge in Nyungwe. This was Nyungwe's most active forge during the 1970s and 1980s.

is stored inside on the side to the left of the forging pit (as one looks inside from the entrance). Used charcoal, cinder, and ash are discarded behind the forge in refuse dumps that vary in size and depth according to the activity of the forge. The smith who owns and commonly works in the forge squats to the left of the forge, where most of the forging tools are kept ready at hand after being brought out of storage in the house. Scrap and spring steel are sometimes found stored to the right of the forge, out from underfoot.

Forges are now multifunctional structures. For example, a boat used to brew beer was stored and periodically used in the forge nearby the Nyungwe smelting site (fig. 8.7b). A cooking hearth was located in another (fig. 8.7c). Such unrelated activities within the ishasha show the changing importance of smithing in Haya culture. Many forges today are

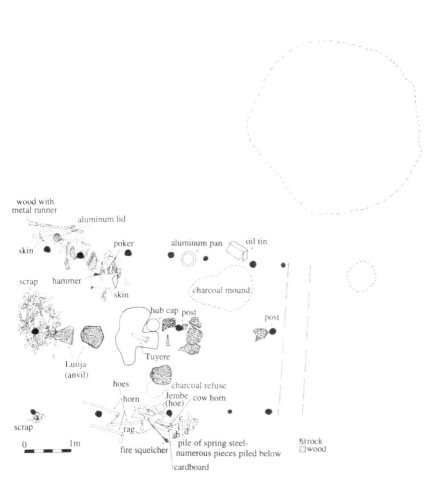

FIG. 8.7c Plan view of Ta Simoni's forge in Nyungwe. This forge had been cleaned and had not been active for several years.

used for only occasional work. Of these three forges, one had been inactive for several years before our visit (figs. 8.7c and 8.8c). Other, competing economic demands impinge upon the time of the smiths; thus, activity at the forge provides insight into changing economic roles. The use of a forge as a brewery from which beer is sold for commercial gain captures the competing economic interests in the lives of Haya smiths.

The shape of the forging pit, its contents, and it relationship to other materials give the most pertinent information for isolating material fingerprints that may have their material parallels or signatures in the archaeological record. It is the forging pit and its surrounding debris—charcoal, cinder, ash, and slag—that are most likely to survive in the archaeological record. The three forging pits show important similarities in some key attributes. The maps show that two of the three forges have dense distribu-

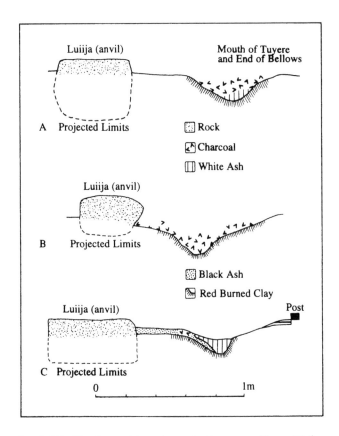

FIG. 8.8 Profile views of three forges in Nyungwe village: (A) the forge of Ta Kaijage, who lived near the smelting site; (B) the forge of Ta Bernardo, Nyungwe's most active smith; (C) the forge of Ta Simoni, no longer an active smith. The distributions of charcoal on the peripheries of A and B are the most important observations—along with the anvil placements, posthole arrangements, and outer charcoal storage areas.

tions of charcoal on their peripheries (figs. 8.8a and 8.8b), particularly on the side where the smith squats and on the side away from the anvil; in the third forge (fig. 8.8c), the inactive forge that had been cleaned by its owner, there was only a light dusting of charcoal. The anvil was situated 15 to 30 centimeters from the edge of the forging pit in all examples. Another salient characteristic was the presence of burned, oxidized soil of reddish-orange color on the edges of the pits and running 5 to 8 centimeters in depth under the pits (fig. 8.8a, 8.8b, 8.8c). The pits varied little in depth, ranging from 18 centimeters to 19 centimeters. Within the pits there was charcoal, ash, and slag.[4] Seen in profile—from front to back—a stone anvil sits contiguous to a pit with a burned and oxidized periphery and a depth nearly as great as its width.

Forges in Antiquity

There are two interesting archaeological cases in Buhaya that I will examine in light of these observations. This is to illustrate the efficaciousness of the method as well as to assist in an interpretation of their past functions. The first is a small baked area on the KM2 site (Schmidt and Childs 1985: 64, feature 33). This small pit, 25 centimeters on its long axis and 14 centimeters deep, was surrounded by a hard-baked clay, reddish orange in color. The pit was filled with several brick fragments from smelting furnaces and little else that would provide evidence for function. I tentatively felt that this might be a forge. How does it compare to the forges just discussed? With respect to the burned clay there is a close fit, but the size seems diminutive for a forge. There also was no sign, either direct or latent (for example, a disturbed area), of an anvil as well as no evidence for charcoal, ash, or slag. The absence of these characteristics denies the interpretation that this is a forging pit. At an intuitive level the interpretation is attractive, but there is no comparative ethnographic analog to sustain it.

The ancient putative forge discovered at the base of Kaiija tree at the Rugomora Mahe site and dated to the mid-first millennium B.C. is the second case study (fig. 8.9) (Schmidt 1978). The interpretation of this feature

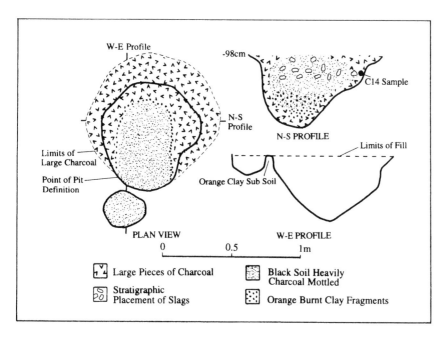

FIG. 8.9 Profile and plan view of a 600 B.C. putative forge located beneath Kaiija shrine tree in Katuruka village. The smaller pit to the west of the main feature is inferred to be the location of the anvil stone—luiija.

previously has stressed its similarities to forges, but without the benefit of an explicit comparative model. First, the depth of the pit is greater than might be expected, but the other attributes are consistent with the ethnographic model. The thick scatter of charcoal on the periphery, especially the side away from the anvil, fits the analog. Furthermore, the presence of burned orange clay along the periphery of the pit (in its base) is also consistent with expectations, as is the presence of charcoal, ash, and slag in the pit fill. The presence of an empty pit immediately to the west is another affinity with the contemporary cases, for the spatial relationship makes it appear that this pit once held a luiija or anvil stone.

When the same feature is seen in plan view among other features dated to this period in the same area, it is possible to see further contextual evidence that supports a tight fit between the characteristics of this feature and the ethnographic model (fig. 8.10). For example, the area around the pit on the side away from the small anvil pit was covered in charcoal, as seen in two of the three recent examples (and most other forges not mapped). There were also two charcoal heaps nearby the pit, both located outside of what would have been a squat zone for the smith. This is also consistent with the observational evidence. Finally, the posthole configuration shows a very close resemblance to the ethnographic configurations

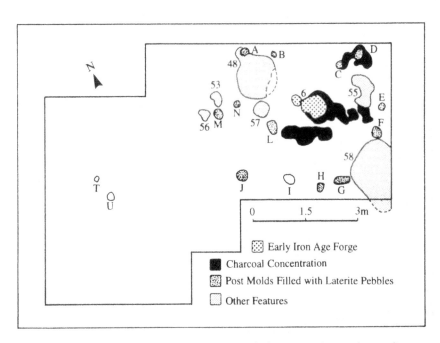

FIG. 8.10 A plan view of the ancient forge. Particularly noteworthy are the configurations of the charcoal scatters—resembling the scatters seen in recent forges—as well as the patterns of the postholes for a structure housing the forge.

for an ishasha: 5 meters long, 4 meters wide, with a center post (L in fig. 8.10).[5] Given the tightness of fit among such a large array of attributes, a confident interpretation can be made that this ancient feature was indeed a forge, likely covered by a forging house of the same age. There is, of course, no way to prove beyond a doubt that feature 6 at this ancient site was a forge, but this comparison of ethnographic evidence with the archaeological evidence—looking for tightness of fit—is a way of constructing interpretations that have a high degree of confidence.

Conclusion ———

A very important part of this endeavor, aside from the historical and technological questions I have addressed, is to contribute to the archaeology of iron technology in Africa. Heretofore, we have been handicapped in our ability to understand technological *processes* excavated in the residues of ancient technological systems. We have had virtually no idea what kind of technological fingerprints were left by different technologies. The approach set out here provides some processual indices against which prehistoric materials can be measured.

This is the practice of middle-range theory in archaeology using a comparative approach (Stahl 1993) in which material-behavioral constructs derived from living cultures are used to infer possible behavior and significance of past material culture. When these inferential models are applied to the prehistoric record, I focus on both similarities *and* differences, the latter being clues to change and innovation. Yet it is also the case that the greater the number of affinities between the two domains, the greater the probability that the two technological adaptations or technical features are similar.

These replicated smelts also provide important insight into the experimental modus operandi of the smelters. They performed as bricoleurs, or fabricators who use whatever they have at hand and stored away in their memories from prior experience. As bricoleurs they also participated in the ritual domain, selecting whatever solutions were available—both contemporary and traditional. Such a bricolage builds from a variety of technological and ritual options, resulting in combinations drawn from a known cultural repertoire (Schmidt 1995c). This smelting bricolage has an indisputable logic about it, reminiscent of the scientist who eliminates variables as they fail to cause predicted results in an experiment. The integration of ritual elements, less nuanced and complex among the Haya smelters than Barongo smelters (Schmidt 1995c), also has a cultural logic. As the technological experiments unfolded, there were also active ritual attempts to account for failure. Spontaneous ritual applications deal with malicious forces that overpower the smelters' capacity to solve technological difficulties; they appease discontented ancestors. Without ritual in these times of smelting stress, which readily develops with the slightest change in resources or personnel, the inevitable failures that result from such experimental technology would be difficult to bear, both economically and psychologically.

I hope others will see the value of similar studies in African archaeology, especially as applied to iron technology. Time is limited. In Buhaya all the Haya elders who directed the iron smelting have passed away. Similar loss of expertise already has affected most African cultures and will soon lead to the extinction of iron smelting knowledge in the next half-generation. Thus it is a matter of considerable urgency that we continue to build knowledge about still-living technologies so that we can better understand the great variability and traditions of innovation and invention that prevailed in African iron production during the past.

9.

An

Archaeology

of African

Iron

Symbolism

An archaeology of African iron symbolism necessarily entails excavating successive layers of meaning. Among so many titillating metaphors of human reproduction, an archaeological metaphor such as this may seem pallid. But we should not be misled and lose sight of our goal to keep peeling back the onion skin—an exercise that mimics the archaeologist's stratigraphic descent—layer after layer, each of which contributes to the whole meaning, until we have reached the bottom. But the metaphor works the other way as well. As we descend through the onion skins of ethnography, we inevitably pick up in each layer bits and pieces of information about the material manifestations of a magnificent archaeological puzzle, finally being able to read some of the ideological expressions.

As we have seen in chapter 2, Kaiija shrine figures as the most prominent cultural monument in Buhaya. It wraps together meanings deriving from ancient myth, political dynastic history, and the symbolism of iron production. I want to use the Kaiija shrine as entrée to related symbolic domains that intersect with the symbols of iron seen at Kaiija. Oral traditions about Bahinda occupation of the Kaiija shrine put the event sometime during the eighth reign of the dynasty. The occupation of Rugomora can be dated to approximately twelve generations ago (using 1970 as a baseline), or approximately the last quarter of the seventeenth century (see Schmidt 1978 on the justification for this form of reckoning). Excavations of specific features on the site attributed to Rugomora Mahe, especially in a ritual area said to be his burial estate or gashani, have been radiocarbon dated to the middle and the end of the seventeenth century (Schmidt 1978). These dated features were located within and contiguous to the gashani proper—a once-sacred ritual area associated with the death of the king, the burial of his jawbone, and the curation of his symbols of office (fig. 9.1). The archaeological pit features themselves are, within the context of other excavations conducted in Buhaya, exotic, highly structured features that clearly have a limited, specialized function that cannot be easily interpreted, except by their context—the ritual zone in which they are found (fig. 9.2). The congruence between Bahinda genealogical attributions and the archaeological dating of the ritual area dedicated to Rugomora Mahe's memory is remarkably precise. This adds confidence to royal claims about when the site was taken over and when Mukama Rugomora Mahe was associated with it.

The archaeological evidence from the site also confirms my exegesis of Bahinda manipulation of ancient mythology and symbolism associated with ironworking. The testimony of elders delimited the exact place where Rugomora Mahe allegedly had his ironworkers manufacture iron to make the iron tower. Excavations in that locale exposed an ancient forge and its hut that were subsequently dated to circa 600 B.C. This extraordinary discovery has been misinterpreted by some and disbelieved by others. It is controversial because it challenges Western belief that oral traditions cannot be ancient in Africa. The archaeological evidence, however, is persuasive. In chapter 8 I have presented further comparative ethnographic evidence that attests that the forge interpretation is accurate and compelling.

There is no reason to attribute the origin of the tradition to external, aboveground characteristics such as iron offerings that used to sit at the base of the shrine tree. The unlocking of the associations lies in the meaning of the name of the shrine tree, only 3 meters from the forge. *Kaiija* is a term derived from the word *luiija*, "anvil or forge," and means "the place of the forge." The fact that the shrine tree sits directly contiguous to an ancient forge is not coincidence. It derives meaning from its contiguity to the forge and from the iron tower myth attached to the same place. The three phenomena must be seen as a bundle of interrelated symbolic meanings rooted in the material past.

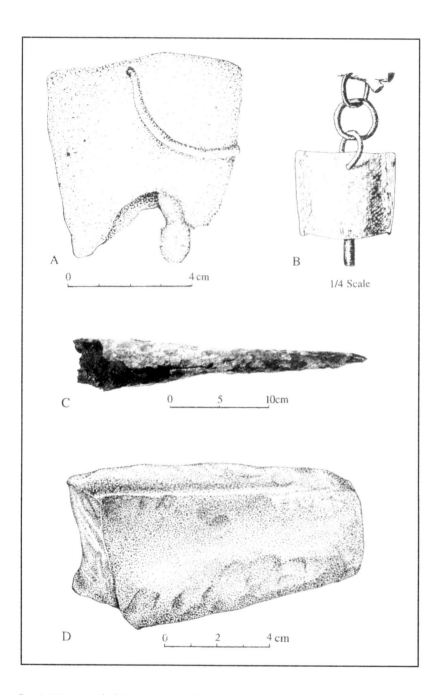

Fig. 9.1 Iron ritual objects associated with kingship in the Great Lakes region. These objects were excavated at the Rugomora Mahe site at Katuruka village: (A) an iron bell similar to others observed on the gates of royal compounds; (B) a royal bell illustrated by Rehse (1910); (C) the butt end of a large ritual spear; (D) part of a large forging hammer excavated within the circle of Mulinzi trees in the gashani proper.

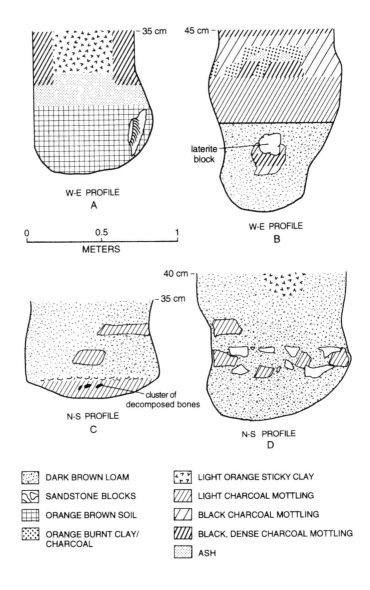

FIG. 9.2 Four of the pit features associated with the Mulinzi tree circle, where the gashani burial hut was located (see Schmidt 1978 for exact locations): (A) a pit with a possible burned drum (?) located within the Mulinzi circle; (B) a pit similar to (A) in structure of fill—immediately to the west of the gashani; (C) a pit dated to A.D. 1700 ± 100 with a cluster of decomposed bones in its bottom—immediately to the west of the gashani; (D) a pit in the alleged burial area, with a layer of sandstone blocks, dated to A.D. 1645 ± 120.

My conclusion is that the shrine tree commemorates and connotes the origins and importance of ironworking in this culture area. The antiquity of the myth and the documented forge can only be coeval, an association that helps us understand why the site fits so neatly into Bahinda ideological representations that make the dynasty appear to be linked to the ancients. The Bahinda occupation of the site reveals two metonymies derived from relationships of contiguity: (1) Bahinda occupation incorporates the shrine and its related myth within the palace boundaries; (2) Bahinda history is contained within a much broader and more powerful domain of ironworking symbolism associated with early social groups, and their ideology of fertility, rainmaking, and agricultural production as well as later Bacwezi myth. Legitimization of Bahinda rule depends on identity with the Bacwezi past—a metonymic process in which synecdoche figures significantly: reference to Rugomora Mahe's history on the site is a trope that uses the part for the whole, immediately eliciting a broader constellation of meanings and history with which the dynasty is associated.

I have identified several processes that mark significant political and economic transformations in the history of Kyamutwara kingdom. They are congruent and coeval with similar changes that occurred in Kiziba kingdom under the Babito. These archaeological signatures, read in the specific putative ritual activities played out on the site, help identify important changes in the development of the most recent centralized states in the region. Moreover, the identification of political manipulation of symbol systems that are predominantly metonymic has helped to direct our attention to periods of radical change in the social and political orders. The concatenation of changes that culminated with the Bahinda seizure of the Kaiija shrine immediately alerts us to the importance of this period.

The symbolic harnessing of the industrial economy by the Bahinda meant royal hegemony over the productive economy. But the transformations observed thus far do not take us to an exposure of the deeper structure of ironworking symbolism. This domain was first manifest through discourse with young men during an archaeological field season in 1977. Each time I passed through the village of Katerero on my way to the KM2 site, the workmen would laugh uproariously while repeating the phrase "We've arrived at Katerero!" Katerero is the place on the next ridge west of the Katuruka site where the iron tower fell. The place name itself elicited the rollicking laughter. I discovered that *katerero* means "beating, beating," a sexual practice when a male beats his penis on the female genitalia to draw forth significant amounts of vaginal fluid, called *kiizi*. This is the first phase of intercourse, preparatory to *kanyinya,* or pushing, pushing.

A much deeper understanding of the place names and the cosmic iron tower begins to emerge with the revelation of these meanings. When the iron tower collapses, it beats on Katerero. The iron tower, then, is a beating phallus. There is no need for Freudian analysis to comprehend that the iron tower is an iron phallus; Haya words are sufficient. Katerero is a specific sexual practice during the act of human reproduction; it is also the name used for the place beat upon by the cosmic iron phallus. The process involves the same beating motion in both cases. This metaphor shows the iron tower to be a symbol of human procreation. As an *axis mundi*, it not only unites heaven and earth, it also unites a mythic image with human reproduction. Iron is central to the symbolism, for it is the medium by which human reproduction (the reproduction of labor) is united with economic production.

The place names further amplify the symbolic meaning of Kaiija shrine and its iron tower. The iron tower was constructed at the western edge of Katuruka, which overlooks a contiguous village. This village takes its name from a stream that originates not far from the base of the tower and passes through its center. The village and stream are named Kiizi, vaginal fluid. The kiizi that flows from beneath the beating iron phallus signifies kiizi or vaginal fluid that is generated during this specialized human sex act (Schmidt 1983a, 1983b). The metaphor in this instance, phallus : vaginal fluid (human sexual characteristics) :: iron tower : stream (places), appears to arise out of a metonymic relationship in which mixed domains (and, thus, contiguity) occur:

vaginal fluid—kiizi : stream—kiizi :: phallus : iron tower
sexual place   sexual thing

The spatial relationship of the iron tower and Kiizi does not stand alone. Further place names and their spatial relations expand upon the primary symbolism. Katerero is located on a high hill to the north of a low saddle, a unique geographical feature on the Victoria Nyanza shoreline, which stands between the lake and an enormous interior swamp. The saddle is named Kanyinya, or, pushing, pushing. As one moves down from Katerero, one moves down into the saddle at Kanyinya (fig. 9.3); the geographical structure and movement between places replicate the sequencing and movement of the phallus during sex:

Katerero : Kanyinya :: Beating, Beating : Pushing, Pushing

These transformations give us the opportunity to advance to an analysis of the components that make up the symbolic system attached to the Kaiija shrine and iron production. The iron tower has all the attributes of a phallus; it is a symbol of human procreation and the productivity of iron. It unites both domains and also symbolizes their interdependence. Iron is central to the production of food; prosperity in industrial production is directly translated to agricultural well-being, which in turn leads to the capacity of society to reproduce itself. The ability to exact tribute or to retain absolute control of the wealth that results from a technology such as that practiced in Buhaya is obviously important to the development of centralized political authority. However, the groups that directly controlled iron production did so with a highly esoteric technological and ritual rep-

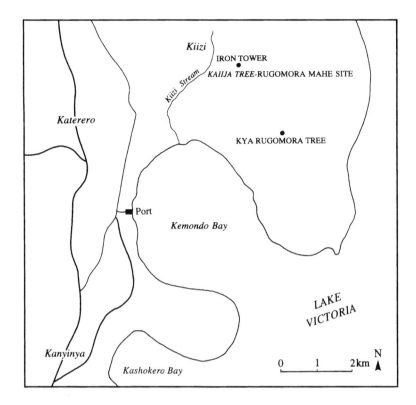

FIG. 9.3 The location of place names that construct a symbolic landscape drawn on the reproductive symbolism of iron production: Katerero—beating, beating; Kanyinya—pushing, pushing; Kiizi—vaginal fluid; Kemondo Bay—where there are *emondo* or "otters"—a metaphor for semen.

ertoire. The ritual that surrounded iron production mystified the technological process to such a degree that it appeared to be mastery over something natural, human fecundity, rather than control over specialized technological knowledge. Such powers of mystification conferred certain economic advantages to the groups that controlled them. But when translated into familiar symbols attached to major cultural features on the landscape, such powers could be appropriated and exploited by those outside of the closed group.

Iron Symbolism, Fecundity, and Wealth

We have seen that the cosmic iron tower is a symbol of human and economic fecundity. The exegesis of the symbolism of the cosmic iron tower shows that political legitimacy is closely tied to myth and ritual associated with iron production. The Kaiija shrine has a singularly unique and important place in African history, for it illustrates that there are magico-religious components (sometimes controlled by industrial specialists) that are sometimes appropriated by priests in the interests of the state. The cosmic iron tower as a dual symbol of fecundity is not an isolated transformational phenomenon. It belongs to a more broadly distributed symbolism that arises directly out of iron smelting as opposed to smithing. Eliade and others have noted the profoundly transformational aspects of iron smelting, the alteration of natural substance, earth, through fire into life-giving cultural matter, iron (Eliade 1961). Let us now explore this esoteric domain to see if we can find the origins for the tropes that figure so prominently in Kyamutwara political maneuverings.

In my earlier discussion about the experimental smelts, I noted, without comment, that among the taboos that surround the smelt, one of the most prominent is the prohibition on sexual intercourse between the iron smelters and women. Violations of the taboo were several times thought to be the cause of poor results. Failure to produce iron was in many instances attributed to sexual intercourse. During his relationship with the iron smelting furnace, each smelter is, metaphorically, in a highly virile state. He reserves his sexual energy to exclusive devotion to the furnace in order to produce as much iron as possible. His first sexual responsibility is to the furnace, implying that the furnace has attributes of a woman (see Herbert 1993 for a cross-cultural perspective). In other African cultures, such as the Fipa (Barndon 1992, 1996; Herbert 1993), the metaphor is elaborated, so that violation of the taboo will cause a miscarriage of the fetus, as adultery is seen to cause miscarriage.

The second taboo is that women must not come close to the smelting site, and particularly not come into contact with the furnace or any of its component parts. According to the metaphoric principles at work, it is only men who are engaged in the relationship with the furnace. Although women are sometimes allowed to approach with food, this is strictly to satisfy the smelters' hunger, not their sexual appetites. According to informants, there have been times when such proscriptions have been put aside. For example, both daughters and wives of smelters have been employed to process and carry iron ore in Bugabo—the minor kingdom to the east of Kiziba. Herbert (1993) has suggested that such contradictions in the application of taboos occur to facilitate production—that is, when increased production is required, such taboos are stripped away. There is no way to test this hypothesis without good historical evidence for the prior and consistent application of the same taboo in the area in question. It is not possible to obtain such documentation in the instance of the Bugabo case just cited. I have witnessed instances among the Barongo smelters when, at the end of the smelt—the relationship with the furnace having come to an end—the smelters forced a nubile girl into the smelting house to pump the bellows (Schmidt 1996c). It is also apparent that there is wide variation in the occurrence of avoidance taboos in iron smelting (see Herbert 1993). There are many other instances of women who mine ore, carry ore, and help in a number of other tasks. There are also several notable examples, such as the Kwanyama of southern Angola, where the women pumped the bellows and helped conduct the smelting (Estermann 1976; Herbert 1993).

There is yet another and more material consideration that relates to the maintenance of privileged technological information. Haya marriage is exogamous and largely patrilocal. This means that the wives of smelters often came from descent groups that did not smelt iron; any knowledge of the process obtained by women outsiders could be passed back to their paternal clans. As the production of iron led directly to wealth and leadership, knowledge of the process was closely protected, underwriting the efficacy of bans against sexual interchange (when tongues are loose) and the presence of women at the smelt. Ritual mystifications add yet another layer of opaqueness that can mislead the unwanted observer. However, it is also important to emphasize that iron smelting was limited to a few clans before the era of Bahinda influence, at which time restrictions according to social group began to break down. By the early twentieth century, according to the Haya smelters, anyone could become an apprentice and gain standing as a smelter. At the same time, though, tradition continued to hold that smelters came from particular clans. The persistence of such beliefs parallels the persistence of other beliefs about sexual taboos, when in fact the structure of exclusiveness had long ago started to crumble.

A third taboo is perhaps of greatest consequence in terms of the worry that it repeatedly elicited among Haya smelters: menstruating women must be prevented from contact with any part of the smelting furnace, ore, or apparatus. Contact with a menstruating woman interdicts the smelting process and results in the failure to smelt iron. There are two ways of viewing this phenomenon. The first one is the normative view that menstruation is a condition that is opposite fertility; women in menses are at the height of sterility, and any contact with the furnace will sterilize the smelting process and thus suspend fecundity (Muhly and Schmidt 1988; Herbert 1993). According to such reasoning, the ritual taboos ensure that a state of fecundity in the domain of the furnace will prevail. The contiguity of anyone in a sterile condition to the furnace or its ingredients confers that attribute to the furnace. However, there is another and perhaps much more compelling take on this metaphor of avoidance, a perspective opened by the practices and beliefs of the Barongo iron smelters in Buzinza (Schmidt 1996c). The Barongo rituals incorporate menstrual blood into the (re)productive cycle. Ritual medicines symbolic of menstrual blood are placed in a medicine hole in the furnace floor, and the furnace is covered in blood that signifies the menstrual phase of reproduction. Menstruation is the cleansing of the womb in preparation for fertilization, and thus any woman in menses—symbolically at the height of her reproductive powers—competes with the furnace womb. While menstruation taboos have always been accepted by Western observers and scholars as strong proscriptive rules, there is a growing awareness that iron smelting rituals incorporating symbolic menstruation, as among the Barongo iron smelters, provide an important insight into the symbolic representation of a complete female reproductive cycle (Schmidt 1996c).

Other insights into fertility symbolism are gained from the social context of smelting. The first point of interest is the observation that the smelters operate in the domain of Irungu, the Bacwezi god of the hinterland (earth) and all the resources such as iron ore and clay that the iron smelters use. The most important ritual performed by the Kiziba smelters was the construction of a spirit house for Irungu, followed by a blood sacrifice to propitiate his spirit (see chapter 4). The primary ritual figure in matters concerning Irungu in a traditional Haya village was the Muharambwa, a respected elder who controlled allocation of resources within Irungu's domain. The Muharambwa was marked by his apparel—he wore a woman's raffia skirt (*kishenshe*). Besides interceding with Irungu, the Muharambwa ritually blessed the hoes of women to ensure their productivity.[1] But most important was his power to bless women so that they might bear children. He was the most powerful public ritual official concerned with matters of female fertility. With this in mind, it is important to know that the iron smelters in Rehse's (1910) photo are wearing the kishenshe. During the first successful smelt of 1976, one of the bellows pumpers wore the traditional attire, the kishenshe (fig. 9.4). Thus, the smelters not only operated in the domain of Irungu, but each dressed as a Muharambwa, ritually acting out a liminal role as both husband and midwife to the furnace, a relationship with the furnace that draws on the powerful metaphor of the Muharambwa, who ensures fertility in women and the plots they farm.

Song as Symbolic Performance

Among the most important activities that assign symbolic meanings, further elaborating upon symbolic meanings of the iron smelting process, are the songs sung by the smelters. I now turn to several examples among the dozen or more songs sung during charcoal burning, tuyere production, and smelting. Some songs have a special function, such as the Lwa-Kaliga song, which is sung often—for its driving rhythm—to mark the end of the smelt. It is accompanied by a distinctive bellows beat. Other songs and chants have significant symbolic meaning and indicate clearly that the smelting furnace is, variably, a female womb, a nubile bride ripe for plunder, a willing lover. The first example is a song called "Emondo" that is sung during the regular smelt. The translation of this song requires an extended exegesis, for the song is replete with esoteric metaphors with sexual meanings (the numbers in parentheses refer to points later discussed).

SOLO CALL	RESPONSE
The "Mondo"(1)	Has flowed (with the current)
The "Mondo"	Has flowed (with the current)
The "Mondo"	Has flowed (with the current)

Fɪɢ. 9.4 A Haya smelter wearing the kishenshe raffia skirt, the traditional form of dress used for iron smelting. This is the same dress worn by the ritual official who annually blessed hoes and ensured female fertility.

Beware!

The "Mondo"
The "Mondo"
The "Mondo"

Oh you women scooping
up the water
Do stop my emondo for me!

The "Mondo"
The "Mondo"

And you, Mr. Peter
And you, Mr. Peter
And you fellow Whites

The Spotted One may eat you!(2)

The Spotted One may eat you!
The Spotted One may eat you!
The Spotted One may eat you!

Oh you women scooping
up the water
Do stop my emondo for me!(3)

It has flowed (with the current)
It has flowed (with the current)

It has flowed (with the current)
It has flowed (with the current)
It has flowed (with the current)

"Emondo"(1) is one of the most common and one of the most informative of the smelting songs. Its context in this instance would seem peculiar to most Haya, for "Emondo" is usually sung at wedding celebrations. In fact, when a former principal secretary (a Haya) of the Ministry of Information and Culture first heard a recording of the song accompanying a film about iron smelting, he objected strongly that this was an improper use because it was a nuptial song! "Emondo" is rich with sexual metaphors that, once understood, clearly refer to human reproduction. In short, the song is bawdy and addresses directly the question of sexual intercourse. We must remember that it is sung around the furnace and is addressed to the furnace. The word *emondo* refers to a small aquatic animal that is similar to an otter. It is an image that is widely used in sexual symbolism; in this instance it is a metaphor for flowing semen during sexual intercourse.[2] The metaphorical similarity here is to the flowing (of the slags) induced by the (phallic) blowpipes in the furnace. This explanation, incidentally, helps expand upon the meanings of the sexual landscape near the iron tower and Katerero. Kemondo Bay, the major body of water that lies between Katerero and Kanyinya, is the place of otters, or metaphorically, the place of the flowing semen.

"The Spotted One"(2) is a translation of *Kagondo,* a generic term used to refer to spotted animals such as a leopard, serval cat, and emondo. But the word in this context is also a metaphor for penis. Literally, the phrase *Yakulya Kagondo* means that such an animal (Kagondo) may eat you, a meaning that is compounded by the metaphorical use of "eat," which means to make love to a woman. The solo line is then reinforced by the refrain to the same effect. The further reference to women downstream scooping up water metaphorically means that the semen is headed their way and they are enjoined(3) to stop it—that is, the flowing semen should be received by the women.

The songs sung around the furnace reveal its feminine attributes and the metaphoric process of gestation that is taking place inside. Other songs elaborate upon this meaning. The Lwa-Kaliga song sung toward the end of the smelt was initially elusive in meaning, yet a thorough study of it opens some significant interpretation. One short version of this song, which sometimes goes on at great length in a great variety of permutations, will suffice:

SOLO	CHORUS
Let me beat the ikila	Lwa-Kaliga × 2
The one the Baganda beat	Lwa-Kaliga
Let me beat the ikila	Lwa-Kaliga
The way the Baganda beat	Lwa-Kaliga
Eeeee let me beat the ikila	Lwa-Kaliga × 4
Dauda is beating it	Lwa-Kaliga
Dauda is beating it	Lwa-Kaliga
Abdul is beating it	Lwa-Kaliga
Boneface is beating it	Lwa-Kaliga

. . . He is beating it	Lwa Kaliga
Yustice is beating it	Lwa Kaliga
They are digging down and up	Lwa-Kaliga
Eeeee let me beat the ikila	Lwa-Kaliga
Eeeee let me beat the ikila	Lwa-Kaliga
The one the Baganda beat	Lwa-Kaliga

The song's origins are obscure, but the song includes numerous references to the Baganda in most versions, and it uses many Ganda words and a Ganda refrain, Lwa-Kaliga, "of the little sheep." The word *ikila* means the tail of the sheep in Luganda; hence, "Let me beat the tail of the little sheep." The smelters themselves say that the phrase "The way the Baganda beat it" refers to the warlike Baganda swinging to and fro (back and forth into various territories) during war, much as the tail of a fat-tailed sheep swings. But the meanings go deeper than this simple metaphor. The bellows are covered with sheepskin, and the beating refers to the beating of the bellows. As previously noted (Schmidt 1983b), sometimes the beating of the bellows is jokingly referred to as "Katerero" or beating, beating.[3] A key phrase used by the smelters, though, is "They are digging down and up" (*Mbalima sok'oleke*). The phrase is applied to the up-and-down movement of the bellows and literally means "They dig down, stop, down, stop, down, stop!" This phrase is also a metaphor for sexual intercourse and a figure of speech common to some wedding and dance songs (M. M. Mulokozi, personal communication, January 13, 1987).

The meaning of the song is highly sexual. The bellows are sexual instruments that metaphorically replicate the sex act, pumping their hot emondo into the female receptacle. The roots of the cosmic iron phallus now begin to become more discernible within this context. There are yet other nuptial songs, such as "Ekyana Kyange Nyamunyaga," that elaborate on the female sexuality of the furnace, with metaphoric references to the smelters, for example, as plunderers (bridegrooms) who take the bride in broad daylight. The metaphorical reference, again, is to the furnace.

Further sexual meanings are manifest during songs sung during the production of charcoal, as the fire burns down and dousing begins:

LEADER	CHORUS
Say the following:	
I am digging a well	I am digging a well
For killing the charcoal	For killing the charcoal
So that it may not burn away	So that it may not burn away
So that all may be happy	So that all may be happy
And not complain that the	And not complain that the
things are not well	things are not well
That is as it should be	That is as it should be
So that we may make those	So that we may make those
who bear	who bear
breasts reproduce	breasts reproduce

| Even the mud fish may come from it | Even the mud fish may come from it |
| Even the fish-traps may come into it | Even the fish-traps may come into it |

The final phase of charcoal making entails throwing water up from the ditch that has been excavated around the burning platform in the swamp. Charcoal is destined for the inside of the furnace, "so that we may make those who bear breasts reproduce." The metaphoric image here is the smelting furnace, not women. Another key metaphor is the reference to the mud fish, which is the lungfish; the lungfish, with its "breasts," represents women in Haya culture. As the smelters muck around in the mud, they are in the "reproductive domain" of the breasted ones (lung fish).[4] We see here a metonymy by contiguity, where the charcoal is produced in the domain of the breasted ones, a symbolic meaning that continues with its placement inside the furnace. There are two other charcoal songs, not transcribed here, that celebrate the wealth and prosperity that charcoal making and iron smelting lead to—the capacity to buy cows and goats and to wear more than one bark cloth or skin.

Perhaps the most complex song in the Haya repertoire of iron smelting songs is "Akata Eibumba," the one that the smelters sing while they are mixing small pieces of broken pots and tuyeres into the clay that is used to make tuyeres. In these richly constructed verses are expressed all the interlocking symbolic themes: the wealth and agricultural plenty that arise from iron smelting, the fertility that ensues, the reproduction of wealth and of society—all of the critical components are mixed together in a symbolic syntax that rises above any inadequate exegesis.

SOLO	CHORUS
He who mushes the clay	Has no worries
He who mushes the clay	Has no worries
He who mushes the clay	Has no worries
Poverty	
Poverty	Mush up
Poverty × 5	
You bring × 5	Mush up
You bring	
You bring × 2	
You bring × 2	Mush up
He makes a game of smelting	He has no worries
He brings the clay	He has no worries
He removes (beats) the tree stumps	He has no worries
He walks on his heels	He has no worries
He of the "Producing One"	He has no worries
He goes to the smelting	He has no worries
He follows (chases) the pathways	He has no worries
They go to Ruzinga (place)	He has no worries
They get pumpkins there	He has no worries
He molds wealth	He has no worries

He knows not poverty	He has no worries
The potter does not reproduce[5]	He has no worries
The plantains produce	He has no worries
The woman is married	He has no worries
The cow is acquired	He has no worries
The cock crows	He has no worries
He reproduces wealth	He has no worries
Fertility ensues	He has no worries
Banana plots are acquired	He has no worries
This is indeed poverty	He has no worries
They all go	He has no worries
The pits smelt	He has no worries
The ores are ferried	He has no worries
What is cultivated produces	He has no worries

This analysis reveals the underlying transformations that flow from the smelting process. The Haya symbolic meanings are based on a concatenation of metaphors that transform the cultural furnace into a human womb. Only a contextual analysis of songs, rituals, and other statements made by the smelters can elicit such meanings. But what we observe among the Haya ironworkers is a symbolic system that has undergone significant change. In this sense it is analogous to a jigsaw puzzle that has only 50 percent of its pieces; we must fill in the blanks from the outline of the extant structure. This exegesis has successfully evoked residual meaning about symbolism that unites human fecundity and economic production. Yet another task remains: to understand the source of the fertility symbolism that gives rise to the cosmic iron tower. The changes in political economy that occurred during Rugomora Mahe's reign are partly a consequence of Bahinda appropriation of the symbols that unite human reproduction with iron production. Because it is so central to any understanding of the political economy, the origins of this symbolic armature must be explored as far as ethnology allows us.

Peeling Back the Last Onion Skins: Further Insights from Haya and Other Bantu-Speaking Cultures

There is an abundance of ethnographic tidbits on the various sexual representations that adorn iron smelting furnaces in Africa, especially in Zaire, Zimbabwe, and Zambia (cf. Childs 1991; Herbert 1993). I will refer to several of these to emphasize a particular point, but for the most part I will limit my discussion to Buhaya and four other cases: two Tanzanian examples, one from northeast Angola, and another from Guinea, West Africa. This discussion starts with the Guinea case because it illustrates the role of serendipity in our expanding knowledge about socially constructed technologies. It also gives us a much clearer understanding that the most powerful symbolic armatures—those associated with human reproduction—are more widely distributed than just Bantu-speaking Africa, the predominant focus of this study.

The iron smelters of west-central Guinea practice a technology that has experienced a local revitalization. In a region of West Africa historically known as the Futa Jallon, the iron smelters living in the area around the government and commercial center of Labé are devout followers of Islam. Having been inactive since 1952, smelters of the Puelh ethnic group spontaneously—for cultural reasons and without outside stimulus or demand—began to smelt again in 1994 (Rolf Jensen, personal communication, January 25, 1996). The smelters' performance of iron smelting rituals and their belief in spirits that govern and operate the smelt are woven into their practice of Islam. This is an extraordinary kind of syncretism—even played out on the landscape as indigenous prayers are chanted during Muslim prayers—with people freely moving between the two worlds.

These ironworkers carefully build a furnace superstructure that supports a sculpted female image in clay with prominent breasts and legs that flare—disappearing at the level where the furnace door is placed in a deep trench. Sacrificial blood is smeared on the furnace, with special attention to the female figure. Smelting is conducted in a furnace that is about 2.5 meters high, including a 75-centimeter-deep pit for slag and bloom. A natural air blast is used, drawing on fourteen long tuyeres set deep into the pit (ibid.). The air is moved through the tuyeres by specific spirits—each assigned a particular pipe. Human agency is removed, except to charge the furnace and clear the tuyeres.

Perhaps the most profound expression of reproductive symbolism arises at the end of the smelt. As the pieces of slag and bloom are removed from the furnace, the incandescent chunks are thrown into barrels of water (ibid.). Scores of people—drawn by the magical powers of the water—push and shove, clamoring for some of the water. Some of the women bathe their faces in the water, seeing it as ensuring fertility; it is also seen as having curing properties and ensuring good fortune. Our knowledge of other symbolic values among the Puelh smelters will advance further when many of their esoteric songs—sung in a language not understood locally—are decoded. This important example illustrates that reproductive symbols are sometimes manifest in ways that leave clear fingerprints. The Puelh furnace superstructure incorporates a female form in baked clay that under some archaeological conditions may be preserved. If such characteristics are defined archaeologically, then we can with increasing confidence use some of these widely distributed meanings in our interpretations.

Other ritual activities in Haya iron smelting may offer further clues to the symbolic meanings attached to the technology. A wide variety of African cultures—such as the Puelh—practice rituals in which special blood sacrifices are conducted prior to the smelt or small pits are dug in the bottom of the furnace pit to receive special offerings that ensure a successful smelt and/or protect the smelt from those who would do it harm.

The Haya smelters in 1976 denied vehemently that any ritual activities were associated with smelting until a series of disasters and subsequent divinations caused them to rethink their position. Although sacrifice was practiced, there was no indication that they ever dug holes in the bottom of their furnaces to receive ritual offerings. Not until a 1983 interview with a former smelter who lived northeast of Lake Ikimba did I finally come to understand that some smelters did, in fact, dig such ritual pits and place special medicines inside. In this case the informant was an immigrant from Kiziba—to the north—and had come to Kianja kingdom to gain access to better forest resources, which had diminished significantly in Kiziba. With great reluctance he admitted that he and his fellow smelters had conducted special rituals that entailed the insertion of a white liquid called *empuri* into the ritual pit. A lump of white clay, probably kaolin, was mixed with herbs of an unspecified identity. This mixture was brought to the *ekina* (furnace pit) by an old woman. With this special potion she brought a bundle of sticks. Before handing them over to the head smelter, she wetted the mixture and dripped a flowing white substance onto the sticks. The head smelter then implanted the sticks in a small hole dug into the bottom of the ekina, and covered them over with soil. This smelter asserted that the medicine was to counteract witchcraft and other ill effects such as violation of the sexual continence taboo and people from the outside who might bring bad luck, an explanation consistent with meanings attached to objects that the Barongo iron smelters place in furnace pits.

Further insight into the meaning of empuri is obtained from other magical domains. In the practice of divining and healing, empuri is a remedy given to women to cure infertility. It is applied to sterile women to make them capable of bearing children. It induces fecundity. It is of special interest that an old woman concocts and brings the medicine to the smelting site. An old woman, beyond menopause, is beyond fecundity and thus presents no danger to the furnace. The white semenlike liquid is placed into the ritual hole in the bottom of the ekina pit to ensure its fertility, a symbolic process of fertilization. At the same time, there is good reason to believe that the attribution of protection against witchcraft and other malevolent forces is accurate testimony, as neighboring cultures use bundles of sticks with symbolic protective values to ward off evil spells (see Bjerke 1981).

Some of the variability in ritual practices is revealed here. The transplanted Kiziba smelters working in Kianja did not perform rituals to propitiate the spirit of Irungu, while the Nyungwe smelters apparently had no direct knowledge of the empuri ritual. There is a distinct difference between the two working environments. The smelters resident in Kiziba worked among their own people and with materials that were familiar and predictable. In Kianja, the Kiziba smelters worked in an unfamiliar social environment and with materials that were altogether different. The clays and the iron ores were new and untested, and therefore the potential for failure was much higher. Under such stressful conditions the empuri ritual was evidently recuperated as a coping mechanism that mediated between the smelters and unfamiliar materials. As well, the practice of this ritual may have added an element of mystification that obscured the technological process from a curious and perhaps envious local population whose resources were being exploited to the advantage of the Kiziba smelters. These observations bring us closer to understanding the shifting ritual and symbolic meanings in Haya iron smelting.

The third case study that illuminates the transformational character of iron smelting is derived from the closest living tradition to that of the Bahaya, the Barongo of Biharamulo and Geita districts. The Barongo once practiced their craft to the south and southwest of Victoria Nyanza. De Rosemond (1943) first described their technology, emphasizing the ritual aspects. Observations of the technology during 1979, 1980, and 1984 make it easy to understand why he emphasized the ritual component. Indeed, the Barongo smelters devote a major part of their attention to ritual procedures. The smelting process is replete with extensive and complex ritual and magic. What concerns us here are only two of those procedures. The first, by order of sequence, involves the ritual that seals the magical offerings in the bottom of the smelting pit. Like many other Bantu-speaking ironworking cultures, the Barongo dig a hole in the pit floor to receive a magical concoction of herbs, tubers, and wood. This ensures good production, creates a fertile furnace, and protects the smelting from witchcraft perpetrated from outside (see chapter 10).

The second Barongo procedure occurs after the ritual medicine is placed in the hole, when the head smelter and his chief ritual assistant both remove their clothing. They then place themselves on opposite sides of the pit and use their buttocks and genitalia to push a small mound of earth on its circumference into the pit. This direct contact of the male sexual organs with the earth that fills in and covers the innermost magic fertilizes the furnace; it prepares it for the gestation that follows during subsequent smelts. The Barongo smelters will not give any explanation for this event, but its structure links male sexuality to the preparation of the furnace for (re)production. But it is more than symbolic of human reproduction, for among the Bazinza a shaman will sometimes bury ritual objects, packing the earth with his buttocks to "show contempt" for the malevolent things (Bjerke 1981). These are themes that I will take up in greater detail in the next chapter.

The sequencing of Barongo ritual activities is a metaphor for the human reproductive cycle. The initiation of the furnace, as the smelt began, with the blood of a goat over the furnace and its contents symbolizes the passage of menstrual blood (see Schmidt 1996c for a discussion of symbolic menstruation in Barongo smelting), as the womb advances toward fecundity. Immediately after the furnace, charcoal, bellows, and ritual medicine were drenched in spurting arterial blood, the wife of the head smelter and one of the junior smelters gathered between the two eastern bellows, and the wife first supped and spit beer over the furnace. Beer is a metaphor for agricultural and human fertility, and it is commonly used in fertility rituals that occur during marriage. One of the Haya marriage rituals entails the bride and bridegroom's spitting milk or beer on one another to invoke blessings of fertility and riches. Thus, the furnace is treated as a newly married young woman ready to reproduce. The linkage between agriculture and iron in this ritual reproductive domain is symbolic of an intimate interdependence that underlies economic production in these two spheres of life.

The most profound insights into metonymic processes of transformation in ironworking symbolism can be observed in the names that are applied to parts and aspects of furnaces in several other examples. The Tshokwe of northeast Angola are a Lunda-related people and share many common attributes in iron smelting ideology with related groups to their east. The Tshokwe furnace is modeled after a female form, the most prominent features of which are the protuberant breasts, similar to breasts affixed to the furnaces of the Shona, Luchazi, and Luba, among others. Moreover, the form and physical structure are modeled after a woman in the position of parturition (Redinha 1953: 137; Herbert 1993).

The matter of greatest interest to us in Tshokwe iron smelting is the application of names to the furnace that are normally used to describe human sexual and reproductive characteristics. This use of metonymy in naming and furnace form develops a relationship of contiguity in which the furnace contents are contained within female reproductive organs, leading to the metaphor in which the furnace comes to symbolize a fecund female giving birth. This movement from metonymy to metaphor characterizes the deeper symbolic evocations in iron smelting and provides us with more insight into the origins of the iron smelting symbols associated with the Rugomora Mahe site. Most important is the name for the smelted iron, *muana,* which means "son of the furnace woman" (the phrase "furnace woman" is not an indigenous expression, but rather one used by the observer) (Redinha 1953: 137; Herbert 1993 provides an extended exegesis). The birthing process is clearly manifest in this usage, as is the Tshokwe term for slag, *tchindonje,* which denotes placenta. The bellows and the tuyeres (*kela*) are phallic symbols, and a tuyere is introduced into the opening at the mouth of the furnace called the *luezo,* or genital area; luezo may refer to either male or female genitalia, but in this context it obviously refers to a vagina or birth canal. The muana is created by the masculine action of the bellows, the rhythm of which is a metaphor for the sexual act.

These metonymic transforms lay the foundation for more complex metaphors by combining and identifying the two disparate domains of human reproduction and industrial production. A further example drawn from the many available in Central and East Africa allows us to draw together the final argument on behalf of the metonymic transforms attached to iron smelting. In southern Tanzania, the Kinga and the Pangwa northeast of

Lake Nyasa once practiced iron smelting in ways that had much in common with the Tshokwe practice. The smelting furnace resembles the shaft section of the Haya furnace, but it differs in the absence of a deep pit and the presence of three large apertures into which tuyeres are sealed with clay. The Pangwa technology, like the Tshokwe, also uses the tapping of slag from the furnace. The taboos and symbolism of the Pangwa furnace have been documented by Stirniman (1976), though without the benefit of observation of actual smelting.

Taboos similar to those of other Bantu iron producers also apply among the Pangwa; these include sexual abstinence by the smelters, prohibition of menstruating women, and exclusion of persons "hot" from recent sexual activity. Menstruating women are prohibited from touching charcoal and iron ore, but they can assist in its transportation in baskets, so long as its handling is done by a "clean" worker. The front of the furnace has breasts just below the rim. According to Stirnimann's depiction, the front opening (*umlomo*) is where the medicine pot with its complex concoction of symbolic semen is inserted and where, as well, the bloom or "baby" is delivered. The most explicit metonymy is applied to the bellows, called testicles, *amatongo* (Stirnimann 1976: 274). Out of this comes the metaphor of blowpipes as phalluses.

Of significant interest in the Pangwa process is the use of a medicine pot inside the furnace. Its ingredients are a plethora of sexual symbols: four juicy, 30-centimeter-long phallic creepers—three of which point toward each tuyere, the fourth upward; leaves and a root that ooze white liquids symbolic of semen; earth from a crossroads (where a couple practiced coitus interruptus after the death of a child and before resumption of regular intercourse); earth from a molehill—the thrust of the mole being a metaphor for intercourse and pregnancy; a plant with red flowers symbolic of menstrual blood; red sand, a symbol of dried blood; a bush with watery creepers used as a fertility medicine on the fields; castor oil, a symbol of fertility; and beeswax, a symbol of semen and fertility. The entire cycle of menstruation, impregnation, gestation, birth, permanent separation of the child, and a return to fertility is represented by the ingredients of the medicine pot. The most powerful ingredients are those symbolic of semen. The perforated lid of the pot allows these substances to escape into the furnace.

Toward the end of the smelt a small hole is made in the bottom of the clay, sealing the front opening to tap the slag. The slag that runs from the furnace is called *isidexu,* or amniotic fluid. Congruent with the Haya and Tshokwe smelting, the movement and rhythm of the bellows are a visual and audio metaphor for sex. The Pangwa explication of the taboo against sexual intercourse helps clarify the smelters' relationship with the furnace. The furnace is treated, metaphorically, as a woman married to the smelters who fertilize her, an image that is also evoked by the Haya smelters as they sing to their "wife." Adultery with another woman is viewed by the Pangwa as cause for abortion or infertility, similar to the Fipa, who live several hundred kilometers to the West (Barndon 1992, 1996; Herbert

1993). Further, the Pangwa believe that semen is needed through the seventh month to nourish the fetus. Finally, the lump of iron bloom produced in this furnace finally comes to rest on top of the medicine pot filled with fertility medicines.

These analyses now allow a finer comprehension of the specific modes of (re)production that are the source of the iron tower symbolism and the focus of change in the political economy of late seventeenth-century Kyamutwara. The symbolic transformations in iron smelting provide the basic armature for the cosmic iron tower and for more elaborate symbolic expressions that surround iron smelting and even smithing. The metonymy induced by naming the furnace and its internal processes with human reproductive terms lays the symbolic foundation for other metaphors that establish the furnace as a womb. Even more profound is the metonymy that arises out of male human interaction with the "female" furnace: when the Haya smelters sing to their "wife"; when the Barongo smelters have coitus with the furnace; when the Pangwa smelters impregnate their "wife." These and other similar performances combine human and industrial domains as one, creating an intimate contiguity wherein the smelting furnace is identified as a fecund woman. The modeling of the furnace as a female body is another permutation of this metonymy, for it combines attributes from altogether different domains, creating another intimate contiguity: the inside of the iron smelting furnace contained within a human female form. Such metonymic processes that combine elements from different domains, e.g., iron : fetus :: furnace : womb, unite and identify human reproduction with industrial production and give rise to the metaphor Iron : Furnace :: Fetus : Womb.

I also want to point to another critical intersection between sex and iron smelting technology. Sex in many African cultures, including the Haya, is considered to be "hot" (Collett 1985, 1993). A condition of hotness will lead to impregnation and the "cooking" of the fetus. These metaphors for sex and impregnation/gestation are clearly applicable to the iron smelting furnace. The furnace is heated up with the flow of air from the phallic blowpipes. However, the deeper those pipes are inserted into the furnace/ womb, the hotter the fire will get and the more productive the smelt will be. Pipes that are not inserted into the furnace to preheat are cold, not hot. Productivity in Haya iron technology is clearly related to the hot insertion of the pipes. The state of hot productivity caused by the inserted blowpipes also reminds us that the metaphor for penis, "Spotted One" is, not surprisingly, remarkably appropriate for the highly mottled, spotted tuyeres once they have been used to preheat a furnace of varying atmospheric conditions.

The Onion Peeled

The material world in African iron production is imbued with meaning that has great significance for historical studies and for the archaeology of Iron Age technology. Beliefs surrounding iron smelting are essential to the division of labor between male and female, for the preservation of specialized knowledge, for the maintenance of economic control over the industrial sector by specific social groups, and for the perpetuation of symbol systems that legitimize political power and access to critical resources. Because the ideology structures industrial behavior and its material expressions, we encounter a distinctive domain in world archaeology—one in which the physical remains of the technological system must also be interpreted within the context of ideology. We have also learned from this exercise that it is unwise to deny historicity to elements of symbolic life and dangerous to assume that ideology is ephemeral and not physically manifest in technology.

Earlier I observed that the symbolism of the forge is normally associated with leadership. But during times of political turmoil when groups outside the traditional political-economic structure attempted to effect alliances with powerful local groups, those alliances had to be sufficient to overcome the power and influence of those who controlled the technological system. In Buhaya during the seventeenth century, shifting relationships of power led to the creation of new religious institutions, as in Kiziba, and to the formal control of important symbolic sites belonging to the indigenous clan identified with the origins of ironworking, as in Kyamutwara. This was a period of turmoil and change during which symbols derived from the most important aspects of economic life were co-opted by the new dynasties in their search for legitimacy. Those symbols that were most profoundly transformational—those linked to iron production—were those that formed the most important part of the new ritual and symbolic identification of the new dynasties.

Thus, control over the political economy was dependent upon control over its regulating ideological superstructure. Political legitimacy depended upon identification with this symbolism. This and the creation of a new historical syntax, in which elements of ancient myth are mixed together with historical legend, created an illusion of continuity with the past—the most important mystifications accompanying political change during the seventeenth century.

The complex linkages that exist among the cosmic iron tower, Kaiija shrine, the Early Iron Age forge, the sexual place names, Bacwezi mythology, Bahinda history, iron production, human reproduction, and royal ritual are now illuminated sufficiently for an archaeology of ritual, myth, and history to move on to the next step—an archaeology of the transformational activities that inform and structure iron smelting. This requires an archaeology capable of isolating physical remains of the recent and distant past in which are manifest ideologies that structured and gave meaning to iron production. Although Buhaya is the initial focal point in this excursion, it is important to understand that this was not a system of meanings distinctive to just Buhaya, but one that informed iron production through much of Africa far into antiquity.

10.

Reading

Ideology

in the

Archaeological

Record

An archaeology of ideology is no longer an idea that elicits scorn or derision. Even archaeologists closely associated with processual archaeology, such as James Hill (1994), have come to accept that it is possible to create rigorous and scientific methods to test ideological expressions in the material record. In this chapter I want to engage in a cross-cultural examination of some of the symbolic expressions discussed in the preceding chapters. African iron smelting provides a powerful intersection of material and ideational worlds. This has significant implications for the study of long-term culture change and cultural continuities at a cross-cultural level, not just a culture-specific level. Precisely because the belief systems that inform ironworking are so widespread in Africa, it is possible to isolate cross-cultural patterns that are also observable in the deep-time record.

In her recent cross-cultural study of the gynecological metaphors and other symbols that infuse iron production, Herbert (1993) provides a trenchant analysis of how other beliefs—such as appeasement of ancestral spirits—also play an important role in iron smelting rituals. Herbert's richly textured analysis clearly brings out that there is not just one domain of beliefs, but a large matrix that incorporates ideas of fertility translated into gynecomorphic characteristics of the furnace: placement of special offerings to ensure fertility, protection against malevolent forces, taboos against certain sexual activities and states, etc. Especially in Bantu-speaking Africa, the ideology of iron smelting as a reproductive activity is directly translated into material form. Because the ideology has a material component, it should be possible to read ideology in the archaeological record and to gain a better understanding of its expressions over time.

There are two primary and interrelated ideas that interpenetrate rituals that transform iron smelting from a technical cultural activity into many socially constructed activities: ideas of fertility and ideas of protection against evil or malevolent forces. A fertile furnace will produce large amounts of iron and therefore contribute to the reproduction of society. Similarly, the interdiction of malevolent forces—be they unhappy ancestral spirits or witchcraft—is also essential. Without this power, the smelters fail to reproduce. Ritual applications for both reasons, then, lead to a similar result, and hence it is no surprise that most African iron smelting cultures for which we have well-informed knowledge practice both forms of ritual during iron smelting (Schmidt and Mapunda 1997).

The problem is how we can discriminate among the various ideological fingerprints that occur in the archaeology of African iron production. It is important that we draw very clear lines of association between beliefs and the specific objects that are used during ritual applications. This is not to say that a ritual bundle that goes into the base of a furnace has an exclusive purpose, such as protection against witchcraft. In fact, such ritual bundles often have multiple meanings that are derived from a variety of domains, perhaps human fertility as well as protection against witchcraft. We are at a crossroads in African archaeology where our historical and ethnographic knowledge of the reservoir of symbolic meanings associated with various objects (that enter the archaeological record) is strong enough to suggest *how* that physical manifestation of ancient ideology may fit into a larger constellation of possible meanings.

Anthropologists and archaeologists have long been aware that iron smelting rituals often result in special ritual offerings being placed in various places in the furnace, usually on the floor or in a pit or in a pot buried beneath the floor (Cline 1937; Van Noten 1983; Schmidt and Childs 1985; Van Grunderbeek 1992; Childs and Killick 1993; Herbert 1993). The examples from the central and eastern part of the continent for burial of ritual items in the furnace pit are too numerous to detail here. It is sufficient to recognize that virtually all iron smelting cultures placed important ritual items either under the foundation of the furnace—the Fipa

(Barndon 1996 and Chewa speakers (van der Merwe and Avery 1987) are examples—or dug a special pit in the furnace base to accommodate these sacred objects—the Babungo or Cameroon (Fowler 1990; Herbert 1993), the Barongo of Tanzania (Schmidt 1996c), and the Barundi of Gitwenge (Celis and Nzikobanyanka 1976) are examples of this practice. My purpose here is to engage several fulsome examples as a way of demonstrating the cross-cultural regularities that exist within this domain. But I do not want to stray too far in the ethnological survey. I seek only to illustrate the ritual processes that contextualize the burial of objects beneath the furnace floor, not the foundation of the furnace wall. In the latter case, there is not yet archaeological evidence available that pertains to these beliefs. Thus, I will restrict this chapter to a review of cases that build a more informed understanding of ritual treatments of the floor of the furnace pit.

Pangwa (A)[1]

In chapter 9, I discussed the Pangwa ritual pot in which a concoction of magical objects is placed, most of which are meant to ensure the fertility of the furnace (see figs. 10.1a and 10.1b for map locations of these groups). The Pangwa practices are weighted toward fertility concerns rather than toward protecting the furnace from malevolent forces. The composition of the ritual devices also opens some insight into this phenomenon. It is not clear from the ethnographic descriptions if the pot is buried in the base of the furnace or if it sits on the floor. Another description of iron smelting in the same region suggests that the medicine pot was buried in a hole located in the base of the furnace (a report on file at the Department of Antiquities, Tanzania). This being the case, the pot and the lid would endure subsequent smelting in the furnace. However, given the use of earth, creepers, and other more perishable materials, it is not clear that these ritual devices would survive multiple smelts. Thus, the Pangwa case is an example of concrete material evidence for fertility ritual that would be preserved archaeologically, but it also indicates that the magical elements inside the pot would prove difficult to document. Pangwa and other ritual practices with furnace pots and lids pertaining to fertility issues would leave behind definitive archaeological remains.

Tabwa (B)

The metaphorical power of Pangwa smelting ritual is part of a larger complex of interrelated beliefs in southern Tanzania, northern Malawi, northern Zambia, and eastern Zaire. Allen Roberts's (1993) exegesis of Tabwa (eastern Zaire near Lake Tanganyika) beliefs and rituals associated with iron smelting more richly informs this system of metaphor. Roberts

Fig. 10.1a A map of the locations of the technological cultures and geographical areas mentioned in the text, but outside of the Great Lakes region: F = Grassfields and Ndop Plain, Western Cameroon; I = southeastern Gabon.

constructs from informant testimony a series of ritual performances that parallel those among the Pangwa. Among the most poignant rituals was that involving the construction of the pit for the furnace. Once it was excavated, the head smelter and his assistants concecrated the pit by mixing the pulverized leaves of two plants with red earth from a termite mound and the earth of a mole's burrow and then mixing this concoction into the floor of the central pit. Whereas the sexual symbolism of the mole's earth is parallel to the Pangwa metaphor, the most salient feature of Tabwa ritual is the smoke bath taken by the head smelter and his helpers. The smoke bath employed herbal medicines used by Tabwa women suffering from fertility and delivery problems. In such cures a pot is used; medicines are placed in it and covered with a leaf from a castor plant. The vapors that emanated from the pot were then directed into the woman's vagina as she squatted over the pot (Roberts 1993: 21). The symbolism of the curative ritual is a potent parallel to that of the smelting ritual, and we readily see

Fig. 10.1b A map of the locations of the technological cultures and geographical areas mentioned in the text in the Great Lakes region: A = Pangwa; B = Tabwa; C = Fipa; D = Chewa and Phoka; E = Burundi; G = Barongo; H = Haya.

that the same symbolic forces are at work—castor plants, mole's earth, effervescent fertility cures flowing into the womb from a pot in the bottom of the furnace.

The Tabwa case is a superb validation of the more universal application of metaphorical principles at work in iron smelting in this region. However, in the Tabwa case the residue of the ritual appears to have been ephemeral: there was no residue that marked the smoke bath or the consecration of the furnace. Roberts depends on informant testimony to elicit this information, and it may well have been the case that when the rituals were performed, the pot and its ingredients were indeed left in the furnace. This is precisely the kind of information that is likely to be omitted in "remote" testimony. Also pertinent to our understanding of variability and mixed meanings are the different testimonies offered by two informants who admitted that they were aware of three different ritual repertoires. The Tabwa smoke ritual also incorporated plants that are clearly associated with keeping malicious spirits at a distance, another clear indication that there is not just one transformational process, but that fertility and protection against malevolent spirits are woven together in this belief system.

Fipa (C) ⸺

Just across Lake Tanganyika in Ufipa, the ritual picture among iron smelters is the result of mostly European representations, some of the more important ones from missionary perspectives. There is also a wide range of variation in the reports about rituals that pertain to the burial of sacred medicines within the furnace. For example, Barndon (1996) has documented the head smelter crawling into the furnace though the symbolic birth canal to conduct a ritual intercourse. However, several other accounts claim that a child performed this rite (Wyckaert 1914; Wise 1958; Herbert 1993). There is consistent agreement that the Fipa smelters placed ritual offerings at the base of each new furnace, but the record is less clear about ritual objects being placed in the floor of the furnace. Herbert (1993) attempts to synthesize these varied representations, using a 1914 observer as her most prominent source: the head smelter guided two children though a ritual cycle that included blood sacrifice and one child crawling into the furnace, where the child buried the heads of two sacrificed chickens and medicines in the floor, sealing the ritual pit with soil. Details are missing about the types of medicines and their significance, but it is nonetheless important that this ritual would have left at least one clear ritual fingerprint in this instance—the disturbance of the floor to cut a small ritual pit. Given the differences in soil composition, such a pit should be preserved—if not destroyed by fusion with liquid slag—in the archaeological record after the furnace was fired. Yet a significant problem remains: we have no clear idea what beliefs are associated with the ritual objects that ended up in the pit. Nor was there much likelihood that the ingredients described would be preserved.

Randi Barndon's (1996) ethnoarchaeology of Fipa iron smelting helps expand our knowledge of the variation in the ritual process, when compared to the past accounts. Her account of the rituals surrounding the secondary or refining furnace amplifies some of the ritual markers that pertain to this 1-meter-high furnace (*icinteengwe*). This furnace used a forced air draft to consolidate the bloom produced in a 3-meter-high furnace (using a convection draft). Under conditions of secrecy, the head smelter and his assistant placed medicinal bark and animal bones (the lion bones used in the primary furnace?) within the furnace, adding a bark that emits a white juice (*itoole*), an obvious symbol for semen reminiscent of the Pangwa ritual (Barndon 1996). It is unclear if such objects are buried, but it appears likely that they were given the same treatments as in the large furnace. We would also expect to find archaeological traces of animal bones if they were buried and submitted to high-temperature reduction. An important element of Fipa ritual that takes material form is the addition of two clay lumps that are added to the outside of the furnace, extending outward and straddling the hole from which slag is tapped. These are called the "inside of women's thighs" (*impaamba*). It is from this opening that the fictive bride also gives birth. In the face of such a context, especially if it is repetitive cross-culturally, it should be possible to build more comprehensive understanding of other, interrelated material manifestations of the fertility paradigm that may be recovered archaeologically.

More recently Bertram Mapunda (1995) has conducted archaeological and historical inquiries about iron smelting in Ufipa, with an emphasis on the histories of technologies in the region. His findings yield important new insight into the meaning of various ritual paraphernalia as well as the antiquity of various ritual practices. Mapunda has found that there were several different technologies practiced in the region before the tall shaft furnace operated by natural draft among the Fipa. In his search to understand the history of technological behavior in the region, Mapunda gathered information pertinent to understanding other ritual practices, with the anticipation that this would inform his archaeological study of iron technology. During his archaeological survey, Mapunda documented several ritual sites. At one site he found pots that were set upside down in the presence of a termitary. He was told that these pots were used in exorcism rituals and that once exorcised, a malicious spirit would be captured in the pot and contained there (Mapunda 1995). I return to this observation to develop its importance in the archaeology section.

The most surprising part of Mapunda's study was his discovery that still-standing large *malungu* (sing. *lilungu*) furnaces were in active use, not for iron production but as sacred vessels for contemporary rituals. On one occasion he encountered several ritual gourds placed in three different furnaces, one gourd bubbling with a white foam flowing out of it. A later interview with a nearby resident revealed that this medicinal vessel was meant either for treatment of infertility or for protection against "evil intentions" (Mapunda 1995: 193). It is significant that a larger vessel (furnace) closely identified with fertility is, after six decades of inactivity, today used for the same purposes. Both the Fipa and the Lungu (another ethnic group living along the lake) believe that the *vizimba* or ritual bundles buried in the furnace floor are eternally powerful, as are all the materials that have been influenced by the vizimba. Consistent with the powerful continuity of the reproduction paradigm among Fipa today is the local practice of recycling slag for amulets and its widespread use among healers as the catalyzing ingredient in medicinal potions used to cure infertility. Healing of infertility entails the use of these objects inside the furnace (both the healer and the patient enter naked through the birthing or mother door), or the healing occurs outside the furnace with sacrificial items (including the head of a rooster) placed inside the furnace. Mapunda importantly observes that there is a wide variety of ritual observances among different iron smelting traditions, and even significant variation within specific traditions.

Chulu and Phoka: Malawi (D) ————

What are the common threads in this system of bricolage? If we turn to the work of van der Merwe and Avery (1987) in Malawi, some of the commonalities come into clearer focus. In their description of ritual pharmacopoeia among Chewa-speaking peoples at Chulu, Malawi, there were a variety of purposes in the use of the medicines: to counteract the influence of evil spirits; to cure spirit possession by malevolent ancestral spirits; and to counteract witchcraft (van de Merwe and Avery 1987). Although most devices addressed protection against witchcraft and other evil influences as well as counteracting and appeasing ancestral spirits, the use of maize flour was a clear fertility offering. The Chulu smelters placed three ritual items in a pit excavated in the furnace floor. Two of the three were made of grass and linked directly to setting the furnace fire. The archaeological vestiges in such a procedure would be ephemeral, with the only possible index to the ritual being soil disturbance.

Ritual practice among the Phoka (Tumbuka-speakers) several hundred kilometers north in Malawi, however, provides a deeper and more complex understanding of the variation of ritual in the area. Like the Barongo, the Phoka had a special master smelter who led ritual activity. The Phoka furnace was first a young woman ready for marriage and then later a wife to the smelters. The pharmacopoeia was huge: fifty-eight items including plants, pieces of animals, fish and insects, minerals, and artifacts (van der Merwe and Avery 1987). Among these items were those related to fertility—millet, peanuts, schooling fish, termite queen, and beer strainer—as well as those that counteracted witchcraft and those that were symbols for the desired effects of the smelt—such as strength, toughness, speed, etc. The last category of magical devices pertained to what has generally been known under the rubric of sympathetic magic.

After the furnace site was selected and prepared, a small ritual pit (*chihikiriro*) was excavated in the center of the furnace, and into this were placed the roots of two shrubs associated with interdicting evil spirits and ancestor spirits. Much as in the Fipa process, various items of the *sepo* (a collective generic for these specialized medicines) were put in the foundation trench. A later ceremony in which millet was offered, sprouted, and then used to make beer which was poured on the furnace wall is linked to the fertility and reproduction paradigm. In a subsequent, separate ritual prior to smelting, the many sepo were laid out on flat baskets and small pieces were taken, combined, and stuffed into a small yellow tuber that, with the remaining items, was placed in the ritual pit. The hole was then capped with charcoal and sealed with a large piece of slag. The overwhelming proportion of these devices were intended to interdict witchcraft and bothersome ancestral spirits, but fertility concerns also were evident in the inclusion of a termite queen and a medicinal cure for venereal disease. We see a panoply of meanings attached to ritual devices in this case study, with only one botanical device that replicates the Tabwa medicinal repertoire. This is testimony to the ritual bricolage that iron smelting evokes, sometimes with significant variations from season to season and from furnace to furnace.

Burundi (E) ————

In Burundi the documentation of ironworking by Celis (Celis and Nzikobanyanka 1976) has added significantly to our knowledge about cultural representations of iron production in that region. Celis has studied several traditions in northeastern Burundi, including one that used the stems of banana plants as a modest chimney. In depth and structure the furnace at Musingati is very similar to that of the Barongo 200 kilometers to the northeast in Tanzania, suggesting that the variation seen in the Musingati furnace is an example of technological style rather than related to function. The ritual devices used in the Musingati furnace were bunches of sticks and leaves that pertained mostly to the interdiction of witchcraft and the application of sympathetic magic used to ensure prosperity, success, and rewards. These objects were placed in bundles in the bottom of the furnace (fig. 10.2). Such exposure to reducing temperatures would have led to the charring of these stacked devices and the deposition of a layer of charred sticks in the bottom of the furnace.

A second technology studied by Celis (Celis and Nzikobanyanka 1976) at Gitwenge bears even greater affinities to the Barongo process: there were smaller but similar blocks of termite mound used as the furnace

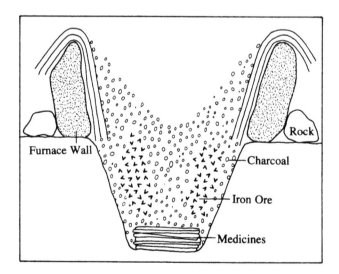

Fig. 10.2 The profile of a smelting furnace at Gitwenge, Burundi, showing ritual devices in the furnace. Despite outward appearances, in structure and function this furnace is very similar to that observed at Misungati, fig. 10.3, and among the Barongo smelters to the northeast in Tanzania. After Celis and Nzikobanyanka 1976.

wall; the smelting house is identical, the tuyere arrangement is identical, and the smithing procedures are similar. Again, this example appears to be a stylistic variation related to the Barongo complex to the northeast. Also of interest is that the medicinal devices were placed in a small pit in the bottom of the furnace—without elaboration about their meanings (fig. 10.3).

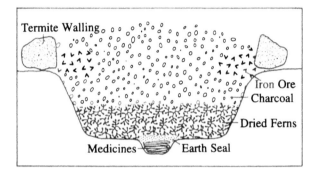

FIG. 10.3 The profile showing the placement of medicines in the bottom of a smelting furnace at Misungati, Burundi, documented by Celis. After Celis and Nzikobanyanka 1976.

Cameroon: Grassfields and Ndop Plain (F)

The examples drawn on thus far may seem to suggest that this ideological system was confined to East and Central Africa. This would be a misleading implication, for there are well-documented indications that similar beliefs, translated into material manifestations, occurred among the Fang in Gabon (Tessmann 1913), among the Babungo smelters of the Ndop Plain in Cameroon (Fowler 1990), and among the We and Isu smelters of the Grassfields in Cameroon (Rowlands and Warnier 1993). The Grassfields example is of interest because it occurs within the zone of proto-Bantu origins. Rowlands and Warnier describe smelting practices first detailed in 1941 by Jeffreys, a colonial administrator interested in archaeology and local culture,[2] and later amplified by local informants. Among the various discrete concoctions of drugs gathered for various purposes, including a curing ritual for failure of the smelting process, was a "cocktail" of "apotropaic drugs . . . buried under the furnace" (Rowlands and Warnier 1993: 525). This concoction of various plants was used to induce fertility as well as to entrap witchcraft—another instance of both beliefs' being wrapped together in one bundle buried beneath the furnace. It is instructive to understand that there was variation in the way that the medicinal drugs were buried: (1) in a pot, (2) under a stone, or (3) simply in the ground with no stone on top.

Ian Fowler makes several observations that pertain to the question of continuity of belief in this region. In his discussion of clump furnaces that took hold in Babungo after 1830, Fowler maintains that there was a continuity in relations with the mystical force of Nywi, or spirit of life breath (Fowler 1990). Fowler sees this life-giving force of Nywi as closely associated with a pot of leaf medicines buried in the floor of the furnace—the medicines activate the force in extracting life and fertility from the earth and transforming it into bloom (Fowler 1990). Thus, once again we see that the pot—as container of these transformational forces—is linked to fertility and reproduction. In their summary of the various Grassfields processes, Rowlands and Warnier add that the drugs (and pot) also were buried with a clay that was used to fill the hole, a substance that should leave a distinct archaeological fingerprint. The burial of the head of the sacrificial chicken likewise replicates practices seen in Central and East Africa. The smelters also sometimes dug a hole at the threshold of the smelting house and buried the same medicines there. Rowlands and Warnier explain that there are other potent symbols associated with the Grassfields "glazed sherds" smelting industry, such as the use of tadpoles fried in palm oil by those who collect the medicines, certainly a powerful sexual metaphor.

In their exegesis of the symbolic codes of We and Isu smelting and smithing, Rowlands and Warnier at one point question Ralph Austen's (1987) idea that the association of iron with reproduction is recent. Their counterpresumption is that the reproduction paradigm is so widespread that it should be very ancient. I concur with their conclusion, but it is possible to go beyond supposition and document how such beliefs may have been expressed at the beginning of the Iron Age should they indeed have continuity over time.

Barongo (6)

I want to return to the example of the Barongo iron smelters, extraordinary ritual and technological bricoleurs. Because the Barongo belief system is so well documented and explicitly tied to rituals and their applications to iron smelting, it provides a solid empirical study. In this sense, it functions as the ethnographic model of greatest detail and reliability—to which other accounts, both ethnographic and indirect, can be compared. As technological and ritual bricoleurs who continuously fabricated responses to each new smelt, the Barongo afford many insights into the technology of ritual life as well as the ritual of technological life (Schmidt 1996c). These inseparable worlds lead us deeper into an understanding of how ideology in technological life creates a record, and with adequate context, how this record should be readable cross-culturally.

The Barongo head smelter and his chief ritual specialist took great care in selecting an acceptable low termitary for the smelting pit. The *kitindi*, or smelting house, was then constructed over the site. When it was completed, the smelters turned to the preparation of the smelting pit (*nyombe*) over which the furnace was constructed. The pit location was staked and a circle drawn to demarcate the excavation, which resulted in a pit with a cone-shaped floor sloping 45 degrees to a small medicinal pit in the bottom (fig. 10.4). Eleven pieces of bark, tubers, wood, and leaves were then carefully packed into the pit, after having been harvested over a two-day period by the chief ritual specialist. Of these, one is used to cure infertility and another has a bright red sap in its bark, symbolic of menstrual blood.

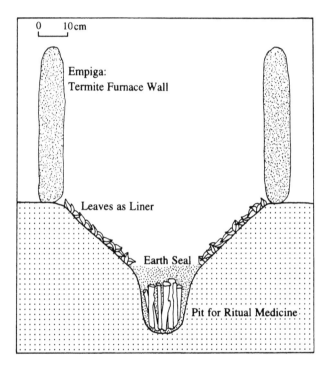

Fig. 10.4 Profile of a Barongo furnace pit made by Barongo smelters at Butenge, Biharamulo District, showing the location of the medicinal devices in the bottom of the furnace.

Once all the interstitial spaces had been filled with earth, the head smelter and his ritual specialist removed their clothing, sat astride the pit, back to back, and moved 180 degrees counterclockwise, pushing the earth into the pit with their genitalia and buttocks (fig. 10.5), an activity associated with contempt for malicious "things" among the Bazinza (Bjerke 1981; chapter 9). After they had covered the medicine, they put their pants back on and tamped down the earth with a meter-long pole. When the bottom

F<small>IG</small>. 10.5 A Barongo master smelter with his chief ritual adviser pushing earth into a Barongo furnace pit after the medicines had been buried in the bottom. The impregnation ceremony also seals the pit against evil or malicious spirits.

was smoothed to fit the contour, the head smelter sprinkled a protective powder, a medicine called *rukago,* across the pit in several directions very quickly. A second, larger package of powdered medicine was then sprinkled slowly over the pit. The head smelter later explained that the purpose of the buried medicine was to bring a "heavy child." The other medicine, rukago, was intended to make people fear the place and to keep anyone from tampering with it, that is, to interdict those with malicious intent.

Other documents indicate that there was a relatively broad range of symbolic expression available to Barongo iron smelters—what might be called a bricolage of furnace consecration. In a photo essay on Barongo smelting in Geita District, Jesper Kirknaes (1980) illustrates the application of rukago medicine through the medium of a prepubescent boy, approximately five years old. His head wrapped in a goatskin, blinded like a newborn, the naked youngster applied the special medicine to the perimeter of the furnace pit, and was then pulled—or birthed—as a "heavy child" from the womb.

Thus, the pushing of the earth into the furnace was both an act of contempt for evil influences and a symbolic intercourse and fertilization of the furnace womb. In the Barongo ritual cycle it was the second potent stage that transformed the furnace into fecund bride. Yet the ritual of human coupling with the furnace was metonymic in effect—a transformational process that was further reinforced by the placement of symbolic menstrual blood into the ritual pit. The furnace became a container of reproductive materials, an order of transformation beyond metaphor in which identity occurs between one domain of reality and another. Barongo ritual treatment of the furnace pit shows that the ritual devices have a tripartite meaning: (1) to protect smelting from malevolent influences (witchcraft), (2) to fertilize the womb so that gestation may occur, and (3) to ensure that the furnace will yield a strong and heavy product.

The power of the ritual devices used by the Barongo extended the use life of the smelting pit. During this period, the potency of the medicines went on without interruption. The year following the first smelts (1979), the Barongo again smelted in the same furnace pit without renewing the medicines because, they explained, the medicines remained potent. When another smelting house was constructed at the same location in 1984, however, the furnace had to be ritually consecrated again because the house had collapsed, and the medicines may have been contaminated by those with evil intentions. After six years in the earth and many smelts later, the ritual bundle came out of the pit as a unified, solid mass of partially charred sticks and adhering earth—indicating that those materials would have been sufficiently preserved to provide an unequivocal archaeological fingerprint for Barongo ideology.

Buhaya (H)

The last example that I want to draw on is from Buhaya. I will revisit the Haya ritual practices because they capture in some ways a mode of ritual style that helps set the stage for assessing ideological continuities in Buhaya as well as other regions of Africa. The key observation concerning the Haya, discussed in the last chapter, was supplied by a smelter from Kiziba kingdom who was responding to a new social and physical environment when he relocated his iron smelting to Kianja kingdom to the south of Kiziba in the early part of this century. After the smelter had dug a pit in the bottom of the furnace, an old woman brought sticks and a white liquid called empuri, made of kaolin and water. Beyond childbearing years and infertile, the woman wet the sticks with the empuri and presented them to the head smelter, who then inserted them into the small pit and covered them with soil. The purposes of the medicine were to interdict witchcraft, to ameliorate any bad effects from violation of the sexual continence taboo, to counteract those who might bring bad luck, and to infuse the furnace with fertile properties. Empuri is widely known as a cure for infertility. The placement of this semenlike liquid in the ritual hole is, as in the Barongo example, an active fertilization of the furnace. The suite of meanings in the Haya ritual—curbing witchcraft, holding off those with evil intent, and ensuring fertility—are precisely those that we have come to expect to be associated with the ritual pit.

The ritual and technological bricoleurs who applied their expertise to preparing the furnace for smelting drew extensively on the local pharmacopoeia. Their bricolage seems to have been determined in part by the ritual background and expertise of the chief ritual specialist/master smelter. Expertise could vary according to different familiarities with medicinal cures or spiritual cures. These are often mixed domains in African cultures, but specialization occurs as well. I found among the Barongo iron smelters, for example, that the ritual applications were sometimes idiosyncratic to the ritual specialist and that disagreements often occurred between himself and the head smelter, who remembered distinctly different ways of doing it. Sometimes the head smelter interceded and did the rituals his way. The bricolage of any ritual specialist/master smelter was acceptable as long as he operated within parameters that incorporated the major categories of concern: witchcraft interdiction, appeasing ancestral spirits, ensuring fertility of the furnace, and ensuring the production of a robust and strong product. It is difficult to know which of these concerns might be represented within ritual applications to iron-smelting furnaces in a particular culture at any particular time. They appear to vary according to the degree of stress and the perceived threat of failure. Not all of this suite of four primary beliefs were represented in smelting ritual, let alone ritual vestiges found in iron smelting furnaces. Sometimes, as with the Phoka case, all four areas of concern were represented, but with a predicted archaeological visibility so low that we would not be able to discriminate any particular domain of belief in the archaeological record.

Ritual bricolage, because it structures and manipulates the technological rhythms of smelting, cannot be separated from the technological process. In circumstances where failure prevails at the technological level, ritual bricolage accelerates—adding further variation during the smelt and opening space for technological experiment to find solutions (Schmidt 1996c). Thus, there is an intimate connection between technology and the ritual performances that legitimate and drive technical experimentation.

With this richly informed ideology, we can see several key patterns beginning to emerge. When smelting concerns focused on harmful forces, especially witchcraft and unhappy ancestral spirits, ritual behavior tended to incorporate much of the herbal, bark, and tuber evidence that makes up the local healing repertoire. Such objects were often sticks that were put into bundles with other objects and inserted into the furnace pit and sealed. Among these objects may have been one or more items that also pertained to fertility, and perhaps even one related to the production of a strong product. So these bundles tended to represent multifaceted beliefs— serving a variety of interests, but focused predominantly on witchcraft and malevolent ancestors. Nevertheless, when pots were used, they seem inevitably to have been associated with fertility rituals, as least insofar as the use of whole pots was concerned. Because of the mostly ephemeral quality of the ritual objects placed inside pots, fertility pots might be predicted to present an archaeological visibility limited to the pot itself. However, the lessons of ritual bricolage inform us that pots also were used as a component in the vizimba phenomenon—as inverted caps on the bundle of magical sticks—some of which could be related to fertility, but most of which were focused as activating agents in interdicting evil influences. The inverted pot among the Fipa is related to exorcism of evil spirits and is usually found associated with termite mounds (Mapunda 1995), the same context in which iron smelting furnaces were constructed. This association with local belief seems to be a powerful indicator, at least in that region, of meaning that may be attached to pots treated this way inside furnaces (Schmidt and Mapunda 1997).

If there is evidence for a ritual pit within the floor of a furnace, then it appears that we are reading witchcraft interdiction, ancestral appeasement, and very likely fertility representations. Sympathetic magic used to impart the properties of the ritual devices to the bloom or technological process was not as common a part of this package of beliefs, but it did occur—as among the Phoka of Malawi—and needs to be documented more precisely in future investigations.

Archaeological Evidence

A demonstration of the tightness of fit between the ideology of recent iron smelting and that of the past is based on the simultaneous demonstration of continuities through time. This is best done, I believe, by starting with the recent past and moving through time to the earliest ironworking in Africa. During their investigations of the We and Isu traditions in the Grassfields of Cameroon, Rowlands and Warnier investigated several "foundries" or smelting houses that could be dated back to the first half of this century. Excavations of these relatively recent smelting furnaces showed the presence of a ritual pit into which were placed devices they believe to be similar to those described by informants (Rowlands and Warnier 1993: fig. 32.4) (fig. 10.6a). Given the variable treatments of the ritual pits in this area, it is reasonable to suppose that continued investigations also would reveal pots as well as ritual pits sealed with stone lids.

As the record is examined for older examples, the next clear indication of continuities is seen at Babungo in the Ndop Plain of Cameroon, where Warnier and Fowler (1979) investigated older Babungo furnaces during the late 1970s. Because the older, pre-1830 furnaces within Babungo proper were taboo and off limits, several older furnaces located on a nearby hillside (Bakwang) were excavated. In the bases of these furnaces the excavators documented ritual pots (fig. 10.6b) (Warnier and Fowler 1979: 334) placed in precisely the location that the more recent Babungo smelters had used for their ritual pots to impart the life force to the furnace. The Babungo case study is certainly one of powerful continuities as well as one that illustrates the vitality and deeply imbued belief in the technologi-

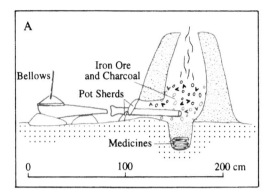

FIG. 10.6a A profile view of a historic Isu smelting furnace belonging to the "glazed sherds" industry excavated in the Cameroon Grassfields. After Rowlands and Warnier 1993. The medicines were located below the hearth where informants had indicated, but not in a pot.

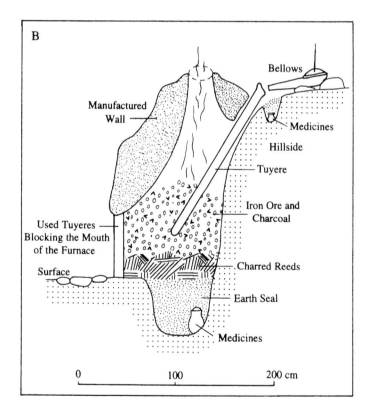

FIG. 10.6b A Bamessing furnace in the Ndop Plain of western Cameroon with a medicine pot buried beneath the hearth. This is very similar to treatments of medicines buried in pots in the Bwakang furnaces (early nineteenth century) contiguous to Babungo, also on the Ndop Plain. After Rowlands and Warnier 1993.

cal consequences of viable ritual devices, which were replaced and renewed only if the smelters began to fail (Fowler 1990).

The work of Bertram Mapunda (1995) in Ufipa brings into keen focus some of the deep-time traditions that inform the archaeology of that culture area to the southwest of Lake Tanganyika. While most of Mapunda's investigations concentrated on the area along the lakeshore and the escarpment, he also examined characteristics of the malungu or high-shaft furnaces on the plateau in order to understand the relationship between that better-known tradition and those he was documenting for the first time along the lake. His excavations of one lilungu furnace on the plateau and several along the escarpment and shoreline throw important light on the ritual process during the last century and the early part of this century. Mapunda found that under the floor of a lilungu furnace dated to 1932-34 at Kalundi on the plateau there were charred rectangular strips of wood laid in a special pit excavated in the furnace floor. Measuring 18-20 centimeters by 5-10 centimeters and about .5 centimeter thick, these vizimba were intended to expel evil spirits as well as to "catalyze" the smelting process (Mapunda 1995: 204; fig. 6.2) (fig. 10.7). They are also deeply identified with the fertility of the furnace, and as long as their integrity

FIG. 10.7 Profile view of a *lilungu* furnace, a 3-to-4-meter-tall natural draft furnace used by the Fipa of southwestern Tanzania. After Mapunda (1995).

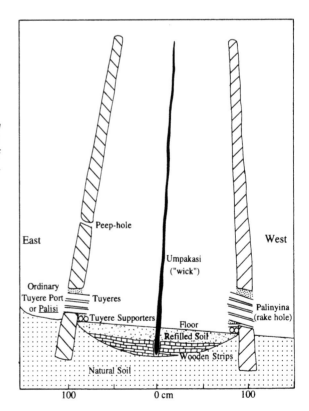

remains secure, they continue to ensure the potency of the furnace for years following. Also recovered from the same location were lengths of a charred stick that a former smelter familiar with the site identified as a furnace wick used to bring the fire from the top of the furnace; this wick was considered "a magical conductor, transporting magical powers from the vizimba" to the top of the furnace. Further evidence for ritual treatment of malungu furnaces was obtained by Mapunda along the lakeshore at Kirando, where only one tall furnace was located (site Hvlk-39). There, too, Mapunda excavated three tiers of charred wood in the furnace pit identified as vizimba. Dated to the end of the nineteenth century as an experimental furnace built by plateau immigrants, these excavation results show significant continuity in ritual treatment—vizimba placed in layered rows in the furnace base. The use of large amounts of wood for reasons related to protection against malevolent forces and for fertility is an example of the variation that was discussed previously from Burundi (Celis and Nzikobanyanka 1976).

These findings are not isolated. Mapunda also excavated a lilungu furnace located on the escarpment at King'ombe (site Ialm-4). The results there affirm the continuous power of the Fipa furnaces: excavation of the floor also disclosed charred vizimba and the base of another lilungu furnace built over the older one and sharing the same "mother door" (*palinyina*) (Mapunda 1995: 224). According to local smelters, new furnaces were sometimes located directly over old ones if the first had been particularly productive. As productivity was tied to potent vizimba, it was good to reuse proven vizimba, which in this case was confirmed by excavations that showed rectangular strips of vizimba that belonged to the first furnace, not the second.

The lilungu furnace is only one of three different smelting traditions that Mapunda documented in Ufipa. Along the plains next to the lake and the escarpment, many sites with lower, 1-meter-high shaft furnaces using a natural draft were documented (Mapunda 1995). Not only does this add significantly to our technological knowledge of the area—long thought to hold only the large malungu furnaces—but it also provides an extraordinary record of prehistoric ritual activity unparalleled in African archaeology. Mapunda documented scores of these smaller furnaces, usually found in clusters nearby temitaries. Radiocarbon dating of this industrial complex yields a series of dates, most of which are 350 to 450 years old (approximately the fifteenth to seventeenth centuries) (Mapunda 1995). Of the nine *katukutu* furnaces excavated, Mapunda found that eight had a central pot. In six of the eight cases, the central pot shielded what is locally referred to as *nchinji*—vertical sticks sharpened and driven into the ground (fig. 10.8) (Mapunda 1995: fig. 6.3). The pots tended to vary in shape, ranging from hemispherical bowls to globular jars. All were undecorated, and sometimes they were coated with a black, sticky clay of unknown meaning. Excavation around the furnaces revealed that the pots had been broken in half, most of them along the vertical axis, with one

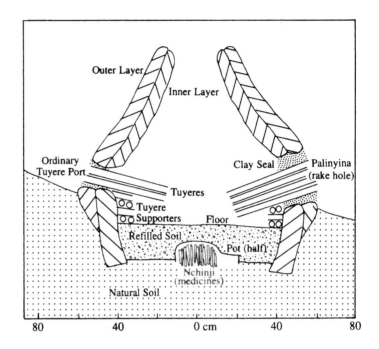

Fig. 10.8 Profile view of a *katukutu* furnace with a central pot lying over *nchinji* medicines. After Mapunda (1995).

half used to cover the nchinji (fig. 10.9a) (Mapunda 1995: plate 6.3), and others with the base removed to cover the nchinji. In one furnace at the Hvlk-1 site in Kirando (near the lake), a central pot (broken along its vertical axis) with fifteen sharpened and charred nchinji was excavated. According to local informants, the nchinji had meanings analogous to those of the vizimba used by the later Fipa smelters of the plateau: medicines directed to the interdiction of witchcraft and as protection against malicious intentions of spirits as well as living people. Mapunda feels that local explanations of vizimba also apply to nchinji: "[They] had miraculous powers; they pulled iron from the ores. Without vizimba you could not get bloom, only slag" (Mapunda 1995: 204).

There also proved to be rather significant variation in ritual treatments of the katukutu technology. In a furnace at the Hvlk-17 site near Kirando, a central pot was excavated that had only the base in place, without evidence for nchinji (fig. 10.9b) (Mapunda 1995: plate 6.4). The other instance in which a pot was found without nchinji was at the Hvlk-25 site (Kirando), where the central pot was a complete hemispherical bowl (fig. 10.10a) (Mapunda 1995: plate 6.5), also coated with black clay similar to the clay used in its manufacture. This variation in the katukutu technology appears to be linked to beliefs that are collateral with other ideology about evil spirits. We will remember that local belief holds that inverted pots are

Fɪɢ. 10.9a A katukutu furnace located at site Hvlk-17 (furnace K17-01) with a ritual pot lying over nchinji medicines. The pot has been halved along its vertical axis and placed over nchinji in the base of the furnace. Courtesy of Bertram Mapunda.

Fɪɢ. 10.9b Another pot burial in a katukutu furnace (furnace K17-02) at the Hvlk-17 site. This is the base of a hemispherical pot, apparently parallel in function to upside-down pots used to exorcise evil spirits. Courtesy of Bertram Mapunda.

FIG. 10.10a A full hemispherical pot burial in a katukutu furnace at site Hvlk-24; no nchinji were buried beneath the pot, which was coated in black clay. Courtesy of Bertram Mapunda.

used to exorcise evil spirits in the presence of termite mounds, a belief that is apparently replicated in the iron smelting furnace. The last commentary on variation comes from the Ialm-1 site on the escarpment, where a katukutu furnace held a central pot and nchinji. In this case the pot was a complete hemispherical bowl with a perforated base, charcoal being lodged in situ in the perforation (fig. 10.10b) (Mapunda 1995: plate 6.7). Because of impressions left in the pot clay, Mapunda feels that the pot was manufactured inside the furnace when molded around the nchinji. It appears that the perforation could be linked to a wicklike apparatus similar to the wick used in the lilungu furnace of the Fipa, in which case the continuities between the two technologies are more firmly established on symbolic grounds as well as in accordance with numerous technological criteria. The array of ritual treatments that Mapunda has been able to document within iron smelting furnaces enhances significantly our understanding of ritual continuities, variability, and material expressions of ideology. It is a corpus of evidence that also enhances our understanding of some of the nuances in the treatment of pots, suggesting that pots upside down in furnaces mean something altogether different from those right side up (cf. the Tabwa or Pangwa). We come closer to understanding as well that the

Fɪɢ. 10.10b A complete hemispherical pot burial—with a perforated base—at the Ialm 1 site; nchinji were buried beneath this pot. Courtesy of Bertram Mapunda.

ideologies that informed Fipa iron smelting early this century are similar to those of three hundred to four hundred years ago: variation points to different ritual emphases, but the underlying symbolic armatures remained similar (Schmidt and Mapunda 1997).

Buhaya Revisited

As this book has focused mostly on the history of iron production in Buhaya, it seems only natural to examine archaeological evidence from that region now with the goal to assess the closeness of fit with the cross-cultural model for the ideological characteristics of features found on the floors of ancient furnaces. The KM2 site near Kemondo Bay contained many EIA smelting furnaces, many of which had small pit features located in their floors (fig. 10.11). Of the features that were certain furnaces at KM2, six contained small pit features in their floors (Schmidt and Childs 1985: 73). None of these small pits showed any signs of inclusions, such as charcoal or other preserved materials. In 67 percent of the cases, these pits were found in furnaces with abrupt vertical walls, such as furnace pit

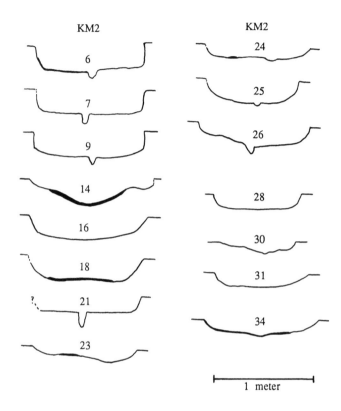

FIG. 10.11 Profiles of furnace pits at the KM2 site: most of the ritual pits are situated in the center of the furnace floors.

number 6, which is discussed in chapter 7 (fig. 10.12); the others were in furnaces with bowl-shaped bottoms. Moreover, there was no pattern through time: in all industrial periods represented on the site, there were furnaces with and without these small pits in their floors. In view of the ethnographic model, how might we interpret the evidence at the KM2 site?

First, there is no technological explanation for the small pits, thus eliminating any hypothesis that might test for technological function. It seems compelling in light of other evidence discussed in the ethnographic record to suggest that these pits are the remnants of a prehistoric ideological system that constructed meaning for iron smelting. We already have seen that the range of ideological expression was limited to a suite of meanings that often incorporated combinations of ritual devices aimed at interdiction of evil forces, including bothersome ancestral spirits, infusion of fertility to the furnace, ensurance of a good product, and (occasionally) curing of taboo violations. Why do some furnaces lack the (now named) ritual

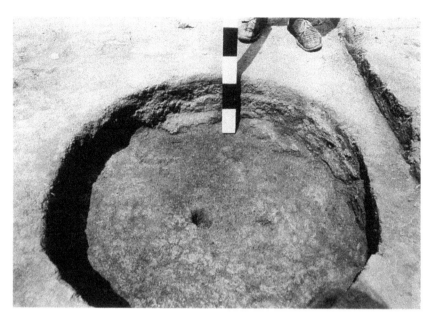

FIG. 10.12 A ritual pit in the floor of furnace pit no. 6 at the KM2 site. There was no object inside, suggesting that possible organic materials used have since disappeared.

pit? If we take a page from the historical Haya example, then not all iron smeltings utilized a ritual process that resulted in devices being placed in the bottom of furnaces. During historic times, Haya iron smelters varied in the applications of these rituals. Sometimes they varied according to new social and environmental circumstances, perhaps when witchcraft was a more critical concern—as it was for the Kiziba smelters in foreign Kianja territory. It is also possible that this variation is an expression of ritual style, yet another form of bricolage in which the smelters improvise ritual responses according to perceived technological difficulties at a particular place and with particular materials.

Reasons for variable ritual treatment may also lie in different ideologies held by social groups engaged in iron smelting. Although there is no basis in ethnographic knowledge about such practices varying by clan or lineage membership, we must keep open the possibility that such divisions may account for the differences seen in the archaeological record.

Within the concept of bricolage, we can begin to make more sense of some of the variability seen in the archaeological record—a variation situated within a larger frame of continuity. At the KM3 site, just 1.5 kilometers south of KM2 near Kemondo Bay, there is another important glimpse into Early Iron Age ritual practices. Of the seven furnace pits excavated at KM2, only one showed clear evidence of a ritual pit. Furnace number 8 dated to the first century A.D.[3] It contained a small pit in its floor that was sealed with a small sandstone block (Schmidt 1981, 1983a; Schmidt and Childs 1985) (fig. 10.13). Within the small pit there was a 6-centimeter-tall piece of prehistoric iron bloom (fig. 10.14). This bloom had no relationship to the technological operation of the furnace, as it was completely sealed off from the upper part of the furnace, where iron formation occurred. Its function appears to be linked to rituals performed prior to smelting in that particular pit, the oldest at the KM3 site.

Fig. 10.13 An overview of Early Iron Age furnaces no. 7 (*left*) and 8 at the KM3 site. A small ritual pit is located at the tip of the trowel.

Fig. 10.14 A close-up view (with an inset drawing) of the piece of bloom concealed beneath a sandstone block in the ritual pit of furnace no. 8, KM3.

Analysis of the bloom has shown that it was submitted to elevated temperatures under reducing conditions for an extended period of time, suggesting that the large carbide plates that formed in the metal resulted from this exposure. However, the bloom also shows evidence of the formation of an iron–carbon–iron phosphide eutectic with cast iron (see fig. 6.25), suggesting that such a formation process resulted in a dense, relatively slag-free bloom similar to more recent and historic blooms that also show similar characteristics. The use of this piece of unworked metal in a ritual pit evokes comparison to other iron smelting rituals meant to ensure the production of an excellent, hardy, or high-quality product that mimics the attributes of the ritual device.

It is unclear why there is an absence of ritual pits in other smelting furnaces at the KM3 site. It is apparent that these ideologies, despite their continuities, varied widely in consistency of application. It is possible that the use of one powerful ritual application at the site was sufficient for the other furnaces through time, yet it seems more likely that other ritual applications—such as layers of charcoal—have been overlooked in the other furnace pits. For example, in furnace 3 at KM3 there was a dense layer of charcoal on the furnace floor, in which charred logs were laid in parallel (fig. 10.15). Furnace 9 showed similar configurations. Botanical analysis of charred woods in furnace 9 indicates that the species of wood transformed to the discrete concentration of charred logs in the center of the

Fig. 10.15 A thick layer of charcoal in furnace no. 3 at the KM3 site, similar to a layer found in furnace no. 9, just 3 m to the north. The wood used is traditionally associated in Great Lakes healing with ensuring fertility; it resembles historic Fipa use of wood as a fertility device.

furnace floor is the same as that of a tree commonly used in the Great Lakes region to ensure fertility or cure infertility in women. Thus, we must keep in mind that the ritual practices of smelters at Musingati (Burundi) and among the Fipa—wherein layers of sticks are used on the furnace floor—may in fact be related to the EIA phenomenon seen at KM3.

Further variation in early ironworking ritual practices is seen at the Rugomora Mahe site in Katuruka and the RM2 site immediately to its south. Of the pit features linked to early first-millennium A.D. smelting at the Rugomora Mahe site, three have a clear but distinctly larger pit in the floor of the furnace (fig. 10.16, especially 10.16c) approximately 20 to 25 centimeters in diameter and 15 centimeters deep. Another early iron smelting pit at the RM2 site had similar characteristics. There were no distinctive inclusions that indicated the specific ritual intention of these pits, but such differences from the KM2 cases and the one distinctive KM3 example seem to suggest strongly that ritual style varied in the region. In size, the ritual pits at these sites resemble those of the Barongo and many other groups that place large bundles of protective medicines in the pits, an observation that again evokes the image of the iron smelter as ritual bricoleur who may have been operating within the parameters of a subregional ritual tradition.

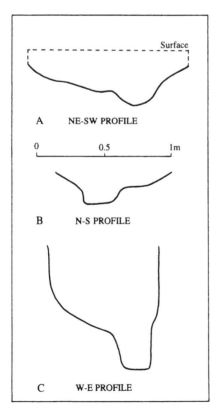

FIG. 10.16 Profile views of three Early Iron Age smelting furnaces at the Rugomora Mahe site in Katuruka village; the pit in the furnace floor characterizes these furnaces as well as one at the RM2 site immediately to the south.

The practice of rituals linked to protection of furnaces from evil influences and ensuring positive outcomes is not a phenomenon restricted to Buhaya. During a University of Dar es Salaam field school in 1986, a team of young archaeologists excavated a second-century A.D. smelting furnace at the village of Nkese in the western Usambara Mountains (see chapter 7 for more details) (Schmidt 1988). From the first layer in the furnace, it became clear that this technology was closely related to the earliest iron industries of northwestern Tanzania, Rwanda, Burundi, eastern Zaire, and southwestern Kenya—with large decorated bricks a prominent feature (fig. 10.17a). As excavations neared the floor of the furnace 80 centimeters below the buried rim, the excavators examined the floor for signs of a ritual pit. There was no pit in the exact center of the floor, but a hole just off-center pointed to the distinct probability that rituals similar to those of KM2 also were practiced in this remote mountainous location during the first several centuries of this era (fig. 10.17b).

FIG. 10.17a An Early Iron Age smelting pit dating to the second century A.D. at Nkese in the western Usambara Mountains, prior to excavation.

Perhaps the most convincing evidence of continuities in an ideology of furnace reproduction is seen the archaeology of the same industrial complex in the Great Lakes region, at Kabuye in Rwanda. At the Kabuye II site,

Fɪɢ. 10.17b The bottom of the Nkese furnace pit: the small square hole in the floor is an exploratory pit, while the deeper hole immediately to the right appears to be a possible ritual pit.

Van Noten excavated a furnace dating to the sixth century A.D. (Van Noten 1983: plate 15). Below the floor of the furnace he excavated an elegantly decorated globular pot (fig. 10.18). The pot was upright, sealed, and in the base of an iron smelting furnace, suggesting that this ritual device was related to fertility concerns—an interpretation that is affirmed repetitively by the ethnographic cases that are structured similarly. There have been many other furnaces excavated in both Rwanda and Burundi without such devices implanted in their bases. Does that mean that the Kabuye II example is idiosyncratic, or is there an alternative hypothesis that might help to explain the variation in the archaeological record of the highland region? At this juncture the negative evidence is most likely testimony to an archaeological failure to observe other, less obvious and perhaps more ephemeral ritual expressions. As we have already learned, the ancient iron smelters were creative as ritual bricoleurs, displaying a range of ritual experiment as rich and varied as their later counterparts. Archaeologists, however, have yet to develop the skills to recognize the different ritual expressions (Schmidt and Mapunda 1997).

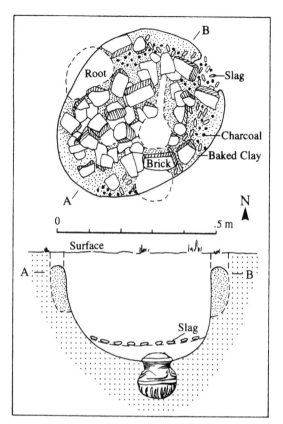

FIG. 10.18 An Early Iron Age pot burial beneath a furnace pit at Kabuye II, Rwanda. This furnace was excavated by Van Noten and dated to the sixth century A.D.—pointing to great continuity in ritual practices. After Van Noten 1983.

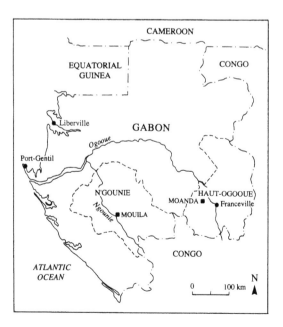

FIG. 10.19 A map of Gabon showing the location of Moanda, where several Early Iron Age industrial areas have been documented.

There is a growing certainty among those of us engaged in the study of ancient ironworking in Africa that deep-time traditions and systems of meaning are manifest in the archaeological evidence that we encounter in iron production centers. The most convincing evidence for such deep-time systems of meaning I discovered in Gabon. While part of a team investigating furnaces and other remains of the late first millennium B.C. in southeastern Gabon (fig. 10.19), I excavated several sites in Moanda, an important early center for iron production (Schmidt et al. 1985; Digombe et al. 1988). At the Moanda I site, a very deep (174 cm) furnace pit was excavated over several seasons (fig. 10.20). The walls of a tall (3-4 m) shaft furnace (using a natural draft without slag tapping) had collapsed into the furnace pit. When most of the wall fragments had been cleared, an up-

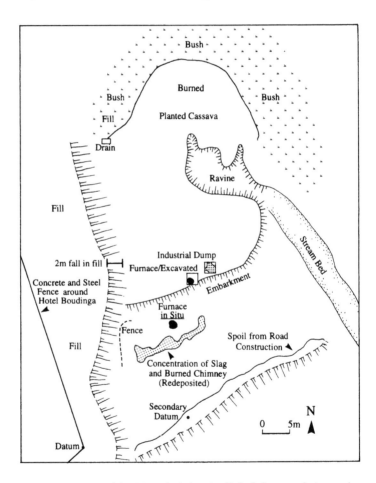

FIG. 10.20 A map of the Moanda I site. A tall shaft furnace dating to the fourth century B.C. was located immediately west of the industrial dump—center of map. The furnace appears to have utilized a natural draft and was not slag tapping.

right tuyere was found on the floor of the furnace pit (fig. 10.21a). Inspection of the tuyere contents showed that it was filled with kaolin, a white clay widely symbolic of purity and fertility (fig. 10.21b). The symbolic qualities of kaolin among the Haya iron smelters immediately come to

FIG. 10.21a (*top*) The wall of the tall shaft furnace had collapsed into the furnace pit. On the floor of the pit at −174 cm was an upright tuyere—the round object seen in the center.

FIG. 10.21b The upright tuyere on the furnace floor, filled with kaolin (here obscured some by the glare of water), widely associated with fertility and purification rituals.

mind: they used a kaolin slurry, symbolic of semen, in their empuri ritual to infuse their furnaces with fertility. The presence of kaolin in an upright tuyere—an explicit and widely acknowledged phallic symbol in iron smelting—is an unequivocal representation of fertility. The Moanda tuyere can be accepted as an enduring and powerful symbol of ritual reproduction in African iron smelting. These deep-time systems of meaning have continued, according to the bricolage of the moment, to construct meaning for ironworking groups, cross-culturally, for more than two millennia.

To those skeptical of the possibility of such ideological continuities through more than two millennia of iron production and ritual activity, the most direct response is that the process of iron production is so profoundly transformational that the ritual armature that guides it, informs it, and configures it is consistent and resilient, yet flexible within limited parameters. It continued to meet multiple needs that fit with local ideologies of healing and spirit appeasement, while at the same time it incorporated ideologies of reproduction and allowed for a wide degree of creative freedom. Because it encompassed bricolage, this industrial ritual continued to fit the *experimental* needs of industry, while simultaneously it reproduced familiar forms of meaning that cross-cut the many cultures in which iron production occurred.

11.

A History of

Landscape

Transforma-

tion

Bringing the

Past Up to

the Present

In Africa archaeologists have an important role to play in documenting tropical forest exploitation and management among ancient populations. The popular idea that rain forests and wet forests are either Pleistocene relics or mostly pristine remnants that have escaped the ravages of human exploitation is no longer appropriate. We have seen in chapter 7 that archaeological research shows that early ironworking populations once exploited forested zones in the Usambara Mountains in northeastern Tanzania (Schmidt 1989). In such contexts archaeological knowledge can provide important insight into management of forests at extensive time scales.

One of the strongest tools that archaeology brings to this kind of inquiry is a deep longitudinal view. No synchronic science can hope to identify and explain long-term trends and consequences. Although no long-term historical ecology of an African forest ecosystem has yet been attempted, we now have a better idea of the regional patterns of vegetation successions based on palynology research that has been conducted over the last several decades (Schoenbrun 1990; Van Grunderbeek, Roche, and Doutrelepont 1983a; Van Grunderbeek, Doutrelepont, and Roche 1984; Taylor and Marchant 1996). This chapter examines processes of landscape transformation in an area once under gallery and woodland forest. It is a history still in the making, the rough outlines of which are disclosed mostly through vegetational history, industrial history, and strong continuities in belief systems embedded in industrial and agricultural economies. One goal is to better understand how cultural perceptions—the beliefs previously discussed in chapters 9 and 10—affected landscape management in this one area over the last twenty-five hundred years.

The historical ecology of Buhaya is a story of transformations induced by human cultural systems over the past two to three millennia. Unraveling or "decoding" the historical ecology of this region introduces several issues: how cultural systems adapted to severe degradation of a once rich and varied forested environment; how a cultural preference for certain economic activities led to significant declines in population; how centralized political control over a governing ideology led to different management of natural resources; how shortages of critical resources led to significant changes in population dynamics; and finally, how beliefs about human reproduction may have sustained traditional behaviors that threaten the socioeconomic fabric in the eastern part of the region today.

Technology and the Environment

Over the past several decades, cultural change in the Buhaya region has led to the extinction or near-extinction of traditional economies. As we have seen in the earlier chapters, the strongest sector of the productive economy, other than agriculture, was formerly steel production and its attendant industries, such as forging and wire drawing. Much of my environmental research has been directed toward this industrial sector and its distinctive needs (Schmidt 1992, 1994).

One of the initial goals was to document when the most recognizable sectors of exploitative economy developed and were applied to the Buhaya landscape, and to determine what cultural changes, particularly in technology and economy, have occurred over the past two to three thousand years. This first step was more complicated than usual because no previous archaeological research had been done in the region (Schmidt 1974, 1978). Moreover, very dense populations now live in the zone of greatest historical interest, the 30-kilometer-wide strip to the west of Victoria Nyanza. Most of the Early Iron Age settlements and industrial locales (600 B.C.–A.D. 600) are overlain by contemporary villages, which both hinders archaeological access to the ancient past and leads to significant transformations of ancient remains.[1] Nonetheless, the available evidence reveals patterns of development in the spread of industrial activity across the land-scape several millennia ago. The combined impact on the natural environment of extensive, permanent agricultural communities and an active iron industry would have been profound.

We have seen in earlier chapters that Haya ironworkers communicate important information about the resources they use as well as their appraisals—based on experimental experiences—about which materials are suitable for high-temperature iron smelting. Moreover, smelters are aware of the ritual, economic, political, and environmental restrictions that were traditionally applied to certain raw materials. Their knowledge has guided our sampling and assessments of iron ores, clays, tree species burned for charcoal, and other materials used in the technological system. On one hand, we have folk classification of what constitutes acceptable, ideal, or even undesirable raw materials—spontaneous, emic definitions of essential ingredients. On the other hand, we have laboratory analyses of the mineral and chemical constituents of these substances—an etic and empirically based understanding of why some materials were preferred over others, why specific resource zones were more intensively exploited, and why some resources led to greater technological efficiency. These environmental assessments, based on informant commentary and on material analysis, provide the scientific standards by which we can judge why and how past cultural systems in the region used the natural environment, and moreover how that use differed from more recent times.

Another important part of the environmental research strategy for Buhaya has been documentation of the region's vegetational history, with particular focus on the environmental changes initiated and effected by human populations (Laseski 1983). The physiography of the region—inhabited ridges alternating with swamps—provides an exceptional opportunity for studying settlement history in relation to the vegetational history available in the pollen record from contiguous wetlands. The intermediate swamps that lay close to settled hillsides would have received their primary pollen deposition from both the hillsides and the vegetation within the swamps. Thus, the pollen record from these areas might provide a good index to vegetational disturbance resulting from a variety of cultural activities, such as clearance of land for settlements and agriculture, use of forest products for industrial and domestic purposes, and the grazing of cattle.

The vegetational markers for some of these cultural activities are unclear, and there is a notable dearth of comparative pollen evidence in Africa. Though some rough indices exist, no precise comparative studies on agricultural clearance and cattle grazing have yet appeared that would enable definitive assessment of vegetational changes induced by humans during prehistoric times (Hamilton, Taylor, and Vogel 1986).

Research on vegetational history has focused on two goals: to trace the changes in the moist-forested landscape of Buhaya from approximately twenty-five hundred years ago to the present, and to discover how the exploitative economy and the cultural system have changed and adapted to a transformed landscape in part by introducing systems of resource management and regulations that allowed continued utilization of key materials at different spatial and temporal scales.

The significant contrasts found between the bountiful forested environment of the earliest Iron Age (600 B.C.–A.D. 0) and the beleaguered environment of the very late Iron Age (A.D. 1700–1900) create serious questions about models that interpret prehistoric patterns of behavior in terms of patterns of the recent past. However, the two eras share common features that must not be ignored, despite caution about projecting present conditions into the past. There may be important parallels, for example, between the kinds of problems encountered during the early first millennium A.D. when forests along the lakeshore zone had been removed and problems that ironworkers experienced with diminished forests during the nineteenth and early twentieth centuries. In specific contexts, environmental history of the recent past—such as clearance of swamp forests—provides an appropriate model for environmental stress, patterns of which are discernible in earlier periods of the regional economy.

The most direct evidence for how the forest environment was exploited has been recovered from archaeological excavations of smelting furnaces: the charcoal used to presmelt and to smelt iron ore (Schmidt 1981, 1983c; Schmidt and Childs 1985). By identifying the genus (and sometimes species) of this charcoal, we can tell what kinds of trees were being used in smelting activities. This in turn gives an index of the kinds of forests prevalent in the vicinity of the smelting sites and how that environment changed through time. Prehistoric charcoal can also suggest whether ironworkers preferred particular species in different areas and eras. Such evidence is invaluable to our assessment of continuity and change in technological behavior as well as to understanding the composition of forests in the region. Preferences for certain forest species may be related to widely varying considerations, ranging from their chemical composition to political constraints and ritual uses.

A Reprise of Settlement History and the Environment

Environmental and technological interrelationships in Buhaya are clearly situated in the behavior of ironworkers who worked the swamps and hillsides outside villages to obtain the resources they needed for iron production. The recent historical environment represents the cumulative effects of a series of significant transformations over the past twenty-five hundred years. This means, then, that the quality and availability of resources during the past century differed substantially from conditions in the Early Iron Age, the transitional and little-understood period from A.D. 700 to 1200 (when technological activity was much reduced or even absent in the region), the period of resettlement from 1200 to 1500, and the earlier part (A.D. 1500–1700) of the latter Iron Age (Fig. 11.1).

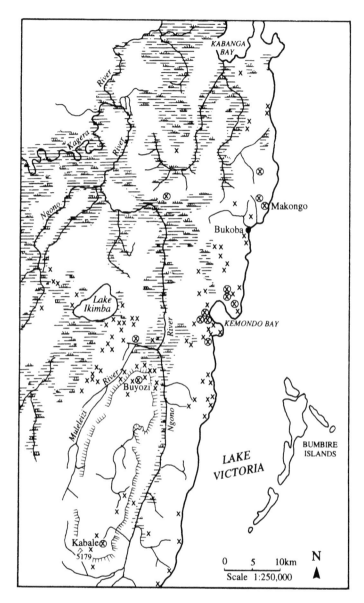

FIG. 11.1 Distributions of Early Iron Age (600 B.C. to A.D. 600) sites. Excavated sites are marked on the map with an X inside a circle. Sites known from survey are marked with an X. Some X points represent multiple sites; distributional voids may reflect absence of survey.

The range of forest trees found in early ironworking sites indicates that Early Iron Age peoples found the coastal zone of Buhaya in gallery forest. The size and distribution of the settlements and ironworking locales of ironworkers during the early part of the first millennium A.D. suggest that those populations and their land clearance for agricultural and industrial purposes would have had a major impact on the natural environment. The EIA settlements were located on the best soils, often along lake margins and nearby streams. However, these locations were not the sole attraction. The settlements on the plateau, for example, were not contiguous to bodies of water. They were, however, located in a well-watered environment. Moreover, they were elevated, cooler, and not as subject to mosquito-borne diseases. The soils were deep and well developed.

By A.D. 200 the communities in the Kemondo Bay basin were not isolated from one another by forest, swamp, or other natural features. The density and complexity of sites of this period suggest significant social contact among the more than twenty communities found in this basin. Certainly this implies levels of social organization that were more complex than what have been inferred to be segmentary societies from the dispersed sites in Rwanda (Van Grunderbeek, Roche, and Doutrelepont 1983a); my earlier discussion of differential control over clay resources also reinforces the idea that power was exercised by some groups over others. Central authority sometimes develops out of dispersed population configurations, but by A.D. 300 to 400 in the case of the tightly clustered communinties of the Kemondo basin, the Victoria Nyanza shoreline, the plateau margins, and the ridges paralleling the Mulelezi River, it is reasonable to suggest that these ancient ironworkers and farmers knew chiefship and lived in communities distinguished by their different levels of wealth and social status.

By A.D. 500 the ridges next to Victoria Nyanza would have been cleared of virtually all forest vegetation. The same denuding of the landscape would have occurred around Kemondo Bay, on the plateau, around Lake Ikimba, and on the ridges to the west of the Mulelezi River. While situated next to the waters of Lake Ikimba, the villages to both the west and the east of this interior lake were also in a zone less well watered than the plateau or the Victoria Nyanza margins. Even though cereal crops would have invited utilization of this drier zone, there is little question that it was more marginal to agriculture. Over the course of extensive and long-term settlement, accompanied by intensive iron production, this zone gradually experienced deforestation, soil erosion and depletion, and resource scarcity in the industrial sector. Thereafter (ca. 600 to 700) the settlement pattern shifted toward a predominantly lakeside adaptation with little or no practice of iron technology (none is yet documented), where some communities are dated to the turn of the millennium (Schmidt 1981; Schmidt and Childs 1985). The Makongo site, a large lakeshore village north of Bukoba, shows convincing evidence for a tenth-century occupation that is associated with EIA ceramics (Schmidt 1978: 291-92).

Meanwhile, the once-forested environment to the west began its regeneration. Not until the thirteenth century do we find the return of iron smelting in the interior and the growth of settlements on the hills east of Lake Ikimba (fig. 11.2). At the same time, sites such as Makongo along the

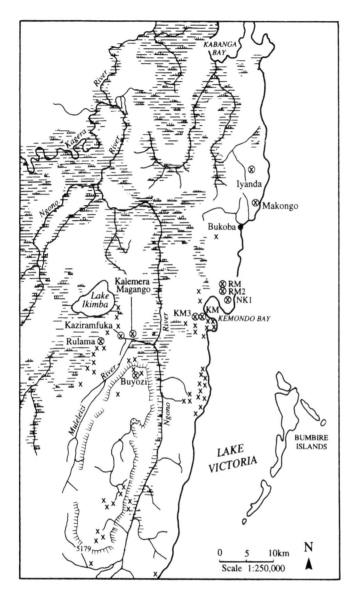

Fig. 11.2 Distributions of sites with carved roulette-decorated pottery. Rulama and Kaziramfuka—both located east of Lake Ikimba—have been dated to the thirteenth to fourteenth century A.D. Excavated sites are marked with a filled circle. Makongo, immediately north of Bukoba, has the most extensive carved roulette sequence.

Victoria Nyanza shore also show signs of significant utilization during the same era. The arrival of larger numbers of cattle during the first half of the second millennium, along with the diversification of agriculture with the addition of many new banana varieties (Schoenbrun 1993b), inaugurated an era of greater agricultural prosperity and population increase, with the subsequent growth of centralized states and an increasingly intensified industrial economy. The increased importance of cattle is also marked by the innovation of many new color terms for cattle among West Nyanza Bantu speakers along the western shore of the lake, as well as those living to the southeast and the northwest (Schoenbrun 1993b).[2]

We have not yet excavated a complete furnace from the period A.D. 1200 to 1400, but charcoal imprints on slag in a dated furnace at the Kaziramfuko site suggest that forest charcoal was still in use in the thirteenth century, when iron technology appears to have been reestablished on the landscape after a long absence between approximately A.D. 700 and 1200. This long hiatus in industrial activity and the restriction of settlement to the littoral of Victoria Nyanza suggest that the diminution of forest in the latter part of the first millennium A.D. may account for both.

We have seen in earlier discussions that comparison of smelting furnaces from the first millennium A.D. and the historical era reveals differences in the material used to fill the furnace pit. During the ancient era, wood charcoal from forest trees was used to fill the pit and smelt iron. This early technology was clearly demanding of forest resources at a time when forests were bountiful. However, there was a significant shift from wood charcoal to swamp reeds in the furnace pit during the Late Iron Age.[3] The change to Miscanthidium grass during the Late Iron Age marked an important innovative advance that had significant environmental consequences. First, it would have reduced economic demand for forest trees. It also substituted an annually renewable resource for forest trees. This development was, in my view, an important adaptation likely related to the depletion of forest resources. It was also a major technological innovation, since the greater amount of carbon contact area in charred grass created a more efficient furnace environment (Schmidt and Avery 1978; Avery and Schmidt 1979).

Two to three thousand years ago, forests would have been readily accessible along the coastal ridges and their small valleys as well as in the permanently flooded swamps and in many of the seasonally flooded swamps.[4] The remote remnant swamp forests of the twentieth century—the last and only mature forests in the region—are an artifact of centuries of forest exploitation. Our observations of iron smelters today indicate that long treks through Miscanthidium and Syzygium swamp are necessary to reach the preferred tree species for smelting, *Syzygium guineense.* This may be one of the few remaining trees whose characteristics are adequate to meet the requirements of Haya iron technology. Given its current inaccessible locations, exploitation is labor-intensive; high labor costs for charcoal production are one of the environmental factors that have militated against iron smelting. These recent historical exploitative practices may offer insights into behavior over the last several centuries, but as we will see, they are tenuous devices for understanding forest use by early ironworking communities.

By the beginning of the present century, in most areas fuel was thus a much more highly restricted commodity than was iron ore. Iron smelters in the northern part of the region, particularly in Kiziba, were forced to relocate to the south near Lake Ikimba because of the depletion of forests in their home area (see chapter 9). Direct historical testimony from these ironworkers indicates that they favored several species of trees and moved their smelting locations periodically to save labor costs in fuel transportation. In other words, they followed the availability of certain forest resources in an environment completely remade by humans. Exploitation of forests for iron smelting had become a cyclical process, in which ironworkers harvested both from immature groundwater forests in the valleys and from seasonal swamp forests. Archaeological survey confirms that smelters of the late nineteenth and early twentieth centuries were locating their industrial activities along the margins of seasonal swamps contiguous to fuel resources (Schmidt 1980).

Prehistoric Industrial Charcoal

Charcoal from prehistoric smelting furnaces in Buhaya provides an exceptional opportunity to study the type and location of forests used for ironworking purposes. We have often excavated charcoal in significant quantities at such sites, and extensive samples have been recovered from all sectors of furnace pits. We submitted some of our charcoal samples to the Musée Royale de Belgique for paleobotanical analysis. Because charcoal had been excavated from tightly dated furnaces, these analyses provided a way to trace changes in forest ecology as well as variations in the range of forest species used in the iron industry over the entire span of the Early Iron Age.[5]

Forest clearance to supply charcoal for smelting and forging iron can be linked to specific features of the industrial record. Variations in the species used can also indicate changing preferences for materials as well as differential access to critical materials, for any number of reasons ranging from ecological to political and ritual. We have amassed substantial amounts of data about the kinds of forest products used by Early Iron Age residents, particularly on the hills above Kemondo Bay, from which we may pose some important questions and offer some tentative interpretations.

First, one of the earliest iron smelting furnaces (#8) at one of the Kemondo Bay sites (KM3) shows the use of at least twelve genera of forest trees (Schmidt 1994). This remarkable range, derived from various microenvironments, gives an initial impression that perhaps as early as the first century B.C., ironworkers were exploiting first-growth, mature, wet-forest trees. Some, such as *Celtis durandii,* are huge; others, such as *Entandrophragma cylindricum* (mahogany) and *Chaetacme microcarpa* (which grows on shallow ridgetop soils), are very hard, very large forest trees. Yet at the same time, middle-story trees and larger swamp trees (such as *Uapaca,* which makes excellent charcoal) were also in use. At another site (KM2) a furnace of similar date yielded charcoal made from sixteen different genera. The great diversity of genera and species in this case likewise points to a predominance of mature moist-forest trees, including mahogany and ironwood (an extremely difficult tree to cut down), supplemented with middle-story trees and trees common to swampy and riparian environments. Here, however, several large forest trees with light, soft woods (such as *Canarium schweinfurthii*) are also represented.

The overall impression is that furnaces in this earlier period were rather like a forest stew: bits and pieces of any tree that was available were tossed into the furnace, even though some species would in fact have had little caloric value or other advantage. The most parsimonious explanation for the time being is that the first iron smelters along the lakeshore were working in an environment where forest clearance for agriculture, perhaps under swidden conditions, was being practiced. If mature moist forest was being cleared, as seems to have been the case, great quantities of readily available wood (much of it of high quality) would have been left lying about near the new farm plots, sometimes for long periods. The presence of charcoal from light and soft woods, as well as from wetland trees, supports this picture of "omnivorous" use of wood, especially surplus wood from other activities.

As we shift our focus three to five centuries later, a different picture emerges. Fourth-century A.D. evidence from the KM3 site shows a much more restricted list of fuel: only two moist-forest species were used at this site, immediately beneath the crest of an otherwise inhospitable rocky hill. The KM2 site, along the shore of Victoria Nyanza, shows only slightly less confined utilization of fuel woods during the fifth century A.D. In one furnace pit only three species are represented: an older, wet-forest type; a secondary tree that colonizes the fringe of the forest; and a tree with soft, light wood that today is commonly used to make beer boats (large vessels resembling dugout boats that are used to brew beer). In a nearby furnace from the same era we found a similarly limited mix of mahogany, two other forest species now uncommon in East Africa, and two very common swamp species. The variety of forest species formerly common to the environment was apparently no longer available. Large remnant trees were used, but the iron smelters were now consistently venturing into the swamps to obtain supplementary fuel.

We may conclude that over the several centuries after the first practice of iron smelting along the coastal hills, the environmental plenty of moist forests diminished to the point that iron smelters were obliged to use only a few remnant moist-forest species and some secondary regrowth and were ranging farther afield to exploit the swamps for supplementary fuels. The industrial record thus gives a clear picture of the spatial form that forest clearance took and its precise expression in the range of species eliminated from the landscape along the lakeshore. From this we can also estimate the scale of early forest exploitation for both land clearance and industry, until forests were eliminated from the coastal valleys and ridgetops and ironworkers increasingly sought out other suitable fuels.

Palynology

To obtain an alternative view of the vegetational history of the central coastal zone of Buhaya, we developed pollen histories by analyzing core samples taken along several east-west transects from the drier central depression to the moist ridges next to Victoria Nyanza. Thus, we gleaned evidence from the lakes as well as the swamps between the north-south ridge systems. Because Lake Ikimba lies in the rain shadow of the coastal ridges, vegetation today tends toward grasslands, patches of woodland, and woodland savanna. The production of storms over Victoria Nyanza and their very particular vectors over Buhaya would suggest that the precipitation pattern in the eastern part of the region has not altered significantly over the past twenty-five hundred years (McMaster 1960).

One sample taken from the eastern part of Lake Ikimba (basal core deposits radiocarbon-dated to 1685 B.P., ca. A.D. 265) shows an erosion horizon that began as a catastrophic environmental event (Laseski 1983; Schmidt 1994). In the lakebed we found a deposition of limonite nodules from the hillsides above and east of the lake. This suggests that land there had been severely degraded, perhaps even stripped of protective shrub and grass cover—allowing high-velocity erosion to carry nodules into the lake. This episode occurred at approximately A.D. 450 to 500 and provides a definitive environmental marker. Lower deposits (prior to this erosion event) show first a decrease in arboreal pollen, apparently related to deforestation, and then a decrease in nonarboreal pollen. This marked and rapid pattern of environmental degradation is particularly indicated by the fall in nonarboreal pollen, which shows widespread alteration of low-lying vegetation and shrubs, presumably owing to agriculture. Just to the west in Rwanda at about the same time, 400 A.D., there was also significant environmental degradation marked by forest clearance by agriculturists practicing a related technology (Van Grunderbeek, Roche, and Doutrelepont 1983a). These simultaneous events suggest that similar stresses had built up in a region that was undergoing widespread environmental impacts driven by agricultural clearance and by a successful technological system.

I believe that these changes, along with the severe erosion, resulted from Early Iron Age cultivation and settlement in this zone to the east of Lake Ikimba. Thus far we have no evidence that iron production was widely practiced there. Archaeological survey around Lake Ikimba shows a shorter settlement history during the Early Iron Age than along the coastal swamps (Schmidt 1980) (fig. 11.1). If we use dates for settlement in the area between Lake Ikimba and the coastal zone, one can reasonably project initial Iron Age settlement in the Ikimba Basin at circa A.D. 200 to 400. The spread of Early Iron Age agriculture and technology to the woodlands of the central basin would have posed a different array of adaptive problems compared to the moist-forested coastal ridges and the well-watered central plateau. Land clearance would have occurred at a much more rapid rate in the woodlands, being further compounded by cattle grazing in a zone with a history of pastoralism, a phenomenon that may also be reflected in the severe erosion episode of A.D. 450 to 500.

Schoenbrun's (1993a) linguistic research suggests that at least by the last millennium B.C. this zone was on the fringe of where pastoral Tale Southern Cushitic speakers resided. If indeed this was the case, then we might expect it to be an intense interaction zone with the Bantu farmers/livestock keepers/hunters/fishermen of the coastal zone, who eventually developed their own systems of cattle breeding (Schoenbrun 1993a). The more open woodlands—with much lower and less reliable rainfall—of the Lake Ikimba area, if opened to cereal agriculture *and* intensive herding, could well have experienced a more rapid and amplified environmental degradation.

Further understanding of human-land relations can be gained from the history of evergreen forest genera, especially *Podocarpus*. According to conventional wisdom, Podocarpus usually occurs in drier montane forest conditions (Taylor and Marchant 1996). Yet the predominant forest type in the northern part of Buhaya today is the *Baikai-Podocarpus* forest, found on the alluvium flats of the Kagera and Ngono rivers and filling large tracts of seasonally flooded swamps that extend south from the Uganda border. These forests contain *Podocarpus milanjianus, Podocarpus usambarensis,* and *Ilex mitis*—species usually restricted to montane forest. In seasonally swampy locales these trees are mixed with a matrix of typical medium-altitude species (Langdale-Brown, Osmaston, and Wilson 1964: 75). In these special environmental circumstances, Podocarpus pollens mark climax swamp forest in the northern part of the region, a condition that has mostly prevailed since prehistoric times. In our core sample from Lake Ikimba, Podocarpus pollen declined slightly before A.D. 400, then recovered, then nearly disappeared about 700, a change perhaps partly linked to climate change at the end of the Early Iron Age in this area. Collateral evidence for change in ridge-associated species over the same period (circa A.D. 300 to 700+) shows a process of forest clearance parallel to that observed in southwestern Uganda: first the valley bottoms, then the slopes, and finally the ridgetops (Hamilton, Taylor, and Vogel 1986: 166).

The other most notable period of environmental change around Lake Ikimba came in the early to middle second millennium. Archaeological survey has recovered evidence of reestablished settlement on the hills along the eastern edge of the swamp south of Ikimba circa 1200 to 1400, about the same time that shrubby species took hold in the swamps, apparently after the swampy forests were cleared (fig. 11.2).[6] An increase in grasses and nonarboreal pollen and a corresponding decline in arboreal pollen during the mid-second millennium also suggest increased clearing of the land around the lake, if not in the swamps.

This period would have been approximately the time (documented in local oral traditions) when peoples with large numbers of cattle arrived from Ankole in the north and from Karagwe to the west. It is also a period of time when the reoccupation of previously abandoned areas was apparently made possible by growth in the number of banana varieties, indicated by a proliferation of generic terms for beer bananas (Schoenbrun 1990, 1993b: 48-53; Schmidt 1992). There seems to be a strong link between reoccupation of this landscape and the development of a vastly expanded agricultural repertoire that includes new banana varieties and, very likely, increased manuring from the rapidly expanding cattle herds in the area (Schoenbrun 1993a). Schoenbrun's linguistic evidence for an explosion of terms for cattle colors points to larger herds in approximately the same period of time (ibid.). These plural developments—explosive expansion of banana cultivation and the increased importance of cattle in this precise area—fit the archaeological evidence for rapid resettlement nicely.

Another record of vegetational history comes from Kiizi (Laseski 1983), 3 kilometers north of Kemondo Bay between the two largest ridges along Victoria Nyanza, the first area to be settled by early ironworking people. The Rugomora Mahe site in Katuruka—first used for iron production circa 600 B.C. and occupied as a Bahinda capital in the mid-seventeenth century—overlooks this core-sampling locale from a hilltop to the east. Numerous early industrial sites (including KM, KM2, KM3, RM2, and NG5) are within the same basin; several have yielded dates around 200 B.C. We have found no archaeological evidence for iron production along the coastal ridges during a six-hundred-year phase of diminished human activity beginning circa A.D. 600. Yet populations with characteristic Early Iron Age pottery continued to inhabit the margins of Victoria Nyanza until at least the tenth to eleventh century.

The Kiizi core gives a more sensitive reading of cultural developments over its upper (later) half, where we can see the opening of land to more intensive exploitation. Moisture-loving forest trees declined rapidly. Grasses increased significantly, and shrubby trees in the swamp gave way to Miscanthidium grass near the coring site. This suite of changes indicates a direct encroachment into the swamps by Iron Age peoples, probably between A.D. 1200 and 1500.

The parallels between the upper cores from Kiizi and Lake Ikimba suggest that similar processes of change were simultaneously at work in both areas. These were undoubtedly linked to increased cultivation, iron smelting, and the coming of larger cattle herds to the region. I feel confident that we can attribute the mid-second-millennium forest clearance, particularly in the swamps, to iron smelting during the Late Iron Age, when the swamps provided one of the few sources of fuel in those densely settled landscapes.

Synthesis and Interpretation —

This first attempt at a vegetational history of the coastal zone of Buhaya yields some important insight into how early populations remade the landscape. We have been able to assess the first impact of ironworking peoples in the Lake Ikimba area quite successfully. During the Early Iron Age, the southern margins of the unique "montane" swamp forests were gradually cleared until woody shrubs and grasses prevailed, but the most profound changes occurred around Lake Ikimba. In that area initial agriculture, with a herding component, apparently had a severely degrading effect. The consequences can be read in a major erosion event and in the subsequent abandonment of the area. This dramatic environmental event occurred at about the same time that similar events occurred in Rwanda, which was also feeling the impact of intense clearance and agriculture practiced by Early Iron Age populations (Van Grunderbeek, Roche, and Doutrelepont 1983a: 40). The causes of human depopulation in this area cannot be definitively attributed, but it may be that an environment under stress led to falling production, malnutrition, and a higher susceptibility to a broad spectrum of diseases. We have no specific archaeological evidence that disease was the direct cause of population decline in Buhaya, but the region's history over the most recent century strongly suggests that human disease is a common response to conditions of ecological stress.

We must, however, also take into account the possibility that adverse climate conditions added to the stress induced by deforestation and soil erosion. We now know that a global event of major negative impact occurred in A.D. 536—either the explosion of a powerful volcano or a major cosmic event—resulting in significantly diminished sunlight for more than a year (Stothers 1984; Baillie 1994). Historical records explicitly mention the loss of productivity, famine, and disease that ensued over the next decade in Europe, China, and the Middle East, and perhaps even on the Yucatan Peninsula when the First Classic Hiatus occurred (Gunn n.d.). Given the global impact of this event on agriculture, it is reasonable to suggest that the negative effects in Africa would have been profound as well. If environmental conditions had already reached stressful levels and subsistence activities based on agriculture had become increasingly risky, then the conditions during the decade immediately following the 536 event may have precipitated the significant decline that we see in human settlement in Buhaya. A shift to increasing pastoralism with a corresponding movement of populations into the grasslands in the northern Karagwe Depression may have been one resonse to conditions in which agriculture in Buhaya was no longer a reliable form of subsistence. The movement of farmers from west of the Victoria Nyanza margins into the drier grasslands of the northwest would have been made easier, and the transition made more rapidly, by the cereal and cattle-keeping parts of their food systems (Schoenbrun 1993a).

As populations from the Buhaya area sought out new opportunities to the north in the upper extension of the Karagwe Depression—in what today is south-central Uganda—they appear to have been attracted to open grasslands suitable for their herds as well as to areas where there were ancient religious and ritual centers. One of those was Mubende Hill, which is well known as a sacred shrine for Ndahura—the first "ruler" of the Bacwezi line. Although archaeological reports have not emphasized a Urewe-period occupation at this site (Robertshaw 1988), nonetheless there is a significant frequency of Urewe (Early Iron Age) ceramics. This suggests that its reoccupation in the early part of the present millennium by peoples producing a pottery decorated with carved roulette may be linked to its long-term use as a ritual center.[7] It appears, then, that the history of Mubende Hill may mimic the history of Kaiija shrine in Buhaya.

Other evidence for settlement in the margins of the upper Karagwe Depression is found at Ntusi, an earthworks site a few kilometers south of the Katonga River and not far from the more famous Bigo earthworks on the south bank of the same river (Reid 1991). Archaeological investigations at Ntusi show it to be an agricultural settlement where cereal farming and cattle keeping were both practiced (Sutton 1993; Schoenbrun 1995). It was established in the early part of the present millennium (Reid 1991; Robertshaw 1994), but its function is open to question. I have argued elsewhere that the activities documented at Ntusi, particularly in two large mounds, might alternatively be read as rhythmed time—activities that represent, for example, the installation of chiefs or religious leaders in the region during a period of incipient centralization (Schmidt 1996d). Perhaps an even more compelling argument is that sites such as Mubende Hill, Ntusi, and Masaka Hill are ritual centers in a refuge area and as such represent nodes for cults of affliction that grew up from stresses due to environmental changes and relocation from the Buhaya region.

Around the turn of the millennium at Lake Ikimba, there was an apparent regeneration of both swamp and other forests. The increasing populations of the second millennium A.D. began another exploitative cycle that eventually led to profound vegetational changes. These changes were met by management practices linked to ritual protection of certain tree species, as well as the ritual mystification of certain sectors of the landscape, so exploitation could occur only under special ritual-political sanction. I consider these institutional developments later in this discussion. Under the present heading, we may point only to a set of general processes—increased use of forest products for iron production, clearance of forests for agriculture and settlement fueled by burgeoning banana cultivation, and the coming of larger numbers of cattle to the region—as the major causes of this second significant transformation of the landscape under way from A.D. 1200 to 1500. Deforestation during this later era became so widespread that the conditions for the development of adaptations to depleted forests were certainly present.

The clearest indication of technological adaptation to the radically trans-formed landscape is the change in the fuel used in the bottom of the smelt-ing furnace. The shift from tree charcoal to charred Miscanthidium grass appears to be linked to increasingly scarce forest resources. Miscanthidium grass replaced a succession of forest trees and then woody shrubs in the swamps (Schmidt 1992). In our analyses it appears first on the periphery of swamps in areas most accessible to iron smelters working there. The physical hallmarks of this change are the imprints of swamp reeds in the frozen prehistoric slags. As noted earlier, Miscanthidium grass offered two dis-tinct advantages: it was an annually renewable resource, and it provided a charred, ashy matrix with a high carbon contact area that was certainly equal to if not superior to the small pieces of wood charcoal used by the early ironworkers.

The Relationship of Ideology to Landscape Transformations and Political Change

One challenge in constructing the historical ecology of any prehistoric region is to integrate the interplay of cultural systems with the physical environment (see Crumley 1994). It is certainly easier to construct the relationships that prevailed between the productive economy and the land-scape, the transformations that these relations induced, and subsequent adjustments and adaptations. The task quickly becomes more difficult, and the bridging inferences become more complex, when we arrive at struc-tural questions such as organization of production and look to the super-structure for an understanding of the ideologies that helped regulate pro-duction. One distinct advantage in the equatorial Bantu-speaking areas that practice iron smelting is that significant cross-cultural similarities in systems of organization and ideology enable us to construct a more cer-tain cultural context for prehistoric landscape transformation and man-agement.

My endeavor to explore the social relations of production and to probe the ideology that regulated exploitative practices naturally began by de-coding belief systems that have governed the use of natural resources and affected perceptions of the landscape (Schmidt 1978, 1983b, 1990). As we have seen in chapters 2 and 9, Bahinda political manipulation of the symbol systems that originated in iron production occurred during a pe-riod of radical change in the social and political orders that marked the ascendancy of cattle-keeping people from the north over indigenous folk who produced iron and traditionally held political authority. These seven-teenth-century events began to unfold approximately two or three hun-dred years before, when there was another major influx of cattle-keeping peoples into Buhaya. This was also a period of ecological stress. Deforesta-tion of the region was under way again, exacerbated by the presence of cattle, which prevent secondary regrowth, and annual burning to bring new grass for grazing animals. This was the second serious phase of deforestation within a period of one thousand to twelve hundred years. The deforestation east of Lake Ikimba about A.D. 450 to 500 bears similarities to patterns that we see again in the area by the mid-second millennium (decline in arboreal pollen, then in nonarboreal pollen).

Iron production, traditionally controlled by indigenous social groups who also identified with cults associated with Bacwezi gods, was apparently already subjected to regulation and taxation by a central authority under the aegis of an alliance with indigenous groups identified with rain-making—some of which began to differentiate in their ritual functions during the Early Iron Age (Schmidt 1978; Schoenbrun 1995). Similar changes gripped the kingdom of Kiziba just south of the Uganda border, where Bacwezi priests were challenged by a new cult of affliction sponsored by the new royal house (Schmidt 1978: 78-86). In this instance the new dynasty colonized areas of wealth (and iron production) by establishing rival cult centers based in confiscated estates (see chapter 2).

In both these kingdoms, the new royals and their cattle-keeping allies controlled a precious commodity, manure, that was essential for maintaining human activity in a degraded environment. While its importance in the agricultural system of Buhaya appears to go back deep in time (Schoenbrun 1993b: 19), cattle manure seems to have taken on an even higher value during this period of agricultural intensification and increased environmental stress. Cattle manure, with mulch and green manuring, could sustain continued agricultural production and settlement. Out of these developments arose a new form of clientship—cattle lent to indigenous Haya in return for land rights—which was an integral part of Bahinda hegemony. The transfer of indigenous rights over land in exchange for cattle and their manure was likely the developmental seeds of the nyarubanja form of land tenure—aristocratic lords controlling consolidated estates on which resided local populations. The other component of Bahinda hegemony was the extension of "legitimate" centralized control over industrial production. Bahinda seizure of the Kaiija shrine was a keystone in that dynasty's control over indigenous industry. The symbolic harnessing of the industrial economy opened the path to royal hegemony over the productive economy.

The transformations described thus far lead us naturally to reflect on the exegesis of ironworking symbolism attached to the general landscape. The local place names attached to the landscape around the mythical iron tower emerge more powerfully within the history of iron production on the landscape. Iron production is closely linked to agricultural production and agricultural well-being, or the capacity of society to reproduce itself and provide labor for the industrial and agricultural sectors. Exaction of tribute and monopoly over the wealth that results from such a technology are obviously important, in very pragmatic terms, to the development of centralized political authority. With an eye toward such realities, the groups that traditionally held direct control over iron production at least in part maintained that control through an esoteric technological and ritual repertoire. The ritual that surrounded iron production was esoteric and mystifying. It obscured the technological process sufficiently that its adepts appeared to enjoy mastery not merely over specialized technological knowledge but also over human fecundity. Such mystification protected the special interests of the ironworking clans that controlled the economy.

In Buhaya, as in other neighboring Bantu-speaking cultures, knowledge of ironworking also produced considerable economic wealth and political power—power traditionally confined to patrilineages. I have earlier noted in chapter 9 that principles of production—along with the wealth and power—could be lost to other groups if wives from other social groups witnessed smelting or otherwise learned its secrets. Hence the taboo against a smelter's sleeping with his wife during the smelting season likely had material as well as symbolic implications.

Other ritual practices were linked directly to resource acquisition. The Haya iron smelters carefully performed blood sacrifices to Irungu, the Bacwezi god who oversees the resources of the hinterland (such as clay, iron ore, and charcoal). Oversight by Bacwezi diviners who supervised iron smelting led to redistribution of iron products from iron smelters through these religious authorities from the same social groups. After the seventeenth-century extension of royal hegemony over this domain of production, a portion of the product was also paid to the king. Thus a regulatory system, a kind of checks and balances, arose between the local ritual authorities directly tied to ironworking—indigenous Bacwezi diviners and priests—and the central taxing authority, the king.

Any attempt to devise a historical ecology of Buhaya must come to terms with these social relations of production as well as the effects of ideological systems and their role in constructing successive landscapes. Over time, particularly during the last three centuries, for which more diverse historical documentation is available, we can observe processes of landscape transformation mediated by complex belief systems, sometimes in competition, but sharing the fundamental perceptual posture that the natural environment is in the service of the reproduction of culture. This fundamental symbolic armature, I believe, may be linked with some of the more profound ecological changes in the area.

The introduction of central taxation in the seventeenth century, when added to the conservation effects of increased ritual regulation of forest resources by central government, would have meant a decrease in the profitability of iron smelting. This is a condition that would have been exacerbated as critical resources such as wood became scarce during the nineteenth and twentieth centuries. By the early twentieth century, many Kiziba smelters found forest resources insufficient and relocated to Kianja to the south. There they found a different landscape north of Lake Ikimba, a place without an ancient history of iron smelting, without large stands of swamp forests, and apparently without an indigenous ritual system that regulated hinterland forest exploitation. The forests were small, secondary riverine growths not far from villages and were under the management of local heads of clans, who ultimately had to account to the king in matters involving any use.

Insight can also be gained from the social contexts of smelting. As we have seen in chapter 3, smelters operate in the domain of Irungu, the Bacwezi god of the hinterland who controls such resources as iron ore and forests. We will remember that one of the most important rituals performed by the Haya smelters was the construction of a spirit house for Irungu and a blood sacrifice to propitiate his spirit. Each smelter also assumed the role of a Muharambwa, the ritual figure who controlled allocation of resources within Irungu's domain and matters of female fertility. Thus the smelters operated in the domain of Irungu, controlling the natural resources required for smelting while simultaneously performing in the reproductive drama of iron smelting. Though Bacwezi diviners may have partly controlled resource extraction by iron smelters, their influence appears to have been partly neutralized, at some junctures, by the independent ritual role playing of smelters who assumed the guise of Irungu's representative during the actual work.

The social dominance of the smelters and their exploitative posture can be further understood from yet other contexts, particularly the songs (discussed in chapter 9) with reproductive symbolism that links iron production to agricultural production and to reproduction of labor. These symbolic expressions establish a cultural perception that influences the most fundamental exploitative activities: an ideology linking reproduction of culture with iron production—an identification that contributed to the exploitation of forest resources. Let us quickly review the role of the reproductive beliefs during the production of charcoal. The dousing of the charcoal ends with the smelters singing,

> So that we may make those who bear breasts reproduce
> Even the mudfish may come from it
> Even the fish traps may come into it.

The smelters engaged in forest clearance and charcoal making are simultaneously situated in the "reproductive domain" of the breasted ones (lungfish), and engaged in an act of reproduction destined for the womb in the furnace. Deforestation nurtures reproduction.

Beneath this exegesis lies my main point: that fundamental exploitative activities such as iron smelting, which consumed an enormous proportion of forest resources in Buhaya, were conducted as elaborate sacred rituals that reaffirmed the very essence of the human experience—the reproduction of labor, the regeneration of life. The integration of this belief system with industrial activity established an abiding perception of the landscape as abundant, sustaining, and reproductive.

Did an ideology of renewable fertility and its integration into industrial production, as an integral part of the division of labor, contribute to the cyclical degradation that we witness in the environmental record? If so, then what sustained populations in this area—compared to other cultures who shared similar beliefs? There are two intertwined answers that address what made Buhaya distinctive. First, Buhaya experienced reliable rainfall from storms off Victoria Nyanza (McMaster 1960). Regardless of the environmental stresses that arose, the reliability of rainfall—compared to that of other nearby regions—sustained agriculture in the region beyond the point of abandonment that normally would have occurred, for example, in southern Buganda, Bunyoro, or Buzinza. Second, the technical efficiency of iron production as well as the availability of excellent material resources provided a high enough return, in spite of decreased returns, for the investment in labor to harvest the necessary resources. Under such conditions, iron production continued to be an attractive economic pursuit—even when resources were stretched thin and ironworkers were competing for wood products with domestic demands for firewood and house construction. There were also other ideological components buttressing a regulatory system—likely in response to stressed environmental conditions—that conserved resources through the checks and balances provided by sacrifices and payments to Irungu's priests, as well as the ritual protection of many forest species located in villages and managed as shrines. The application of religious-political sanctions against those who disturbed trees that functioned as ritual locales effectively preserved and ensured the management of countless groves of mature forest species both within and outside villages.

We have previously seen that the seizure of the Kaiija shrine by the Bahinda marked an important new period of royal hegemony that resulted in Bahinda (and Babito in Kiziba) management of sacred shrines and other forest resources. The patronage of the central state was essential in maintaining a cadre of ritual officials who oversaw and managed forest products. Also, via a land tenure system of estates awarded to loyal subjects, either Bahinda or indigenous, the state controlled agricultural surplus and labor, both essential to the expensive upkeep of numerous ritual officials and their retainers scattered across the landscape. These networks of ritual and administrative officials were also an integral part of a redistributive system in which agricultural goods and iron products were returned to needy parts of the kingdom—done under the aegis of a king identified with the symbolic instruments of agricultural prosperity and reproduction of society.

Linking the Past to the Present

The introduction and subsequent widespread acceptance of Christianity during the first half of the present century brought a major change in the delicate balance of ritual management of resources. Most of the traditional priests invested with protection of the shrines and the forests either

converted, abandoned their roles, or died without passing on their traditional authority. The kings, now Christian too, no longer maintained care-
takers at the royal ancestral shrines, many of which have been converted
to agricultural land. Similarly, the sacred significance once attached to
groves dedicated to the Bacwezi gods has also eroded, sometimes to the
point where shrine trees have been cut to make way for much-needed
crop expansion. As recently as forty years ago, this behavior would have
been met with outrage and punishment.

It is instructive that the preferred wood for charcoal in iron smelting is
called Mucwezi (*Syzygium guineense*)—a Bacwezi spirit or an embandwa
(spirit medium/diviner). The close identity between a species of tree used
in iron smelting and the ancient religious-political groups that once controlled the industrial domain is a natural and not unexpected association.
Ordinarily one expects to find *Syzygium guineense* in riparian forests, but
in Buhaya it now occurs only in remote stands of swamp forests—a domain belonging to the Bacwezi cult, and only more recently to the kings.
Deforestation over the past several centuries may have focused preference on a species that has the requisite chemical properties but is also
located in an econiche relatively inaccessible to common everyday exploitation. However, there is reason to think that preference for Syzygium
is a deep-time tradition. Van Grunderbeek has shown that demand for
Syzygium dates back to the early first millennium A.D., when iron smelters
also seem to have preferred this species among others in the forest that
they exploited in Rwanda (Van Grunderbeek, Roche, and Doutrelepont
1983a). This does appear to be an isolated case. To the northwest in Kigezi,
Uganda, David Taylor and his collaborators (Hamilton, Taylor, and Vogel
1986; Taylor and Marchant 1996) have found that the onset of a decline in
Syzygium at Ahakagyezi Swamp marks a distinct horizon in which human
activity—possibly exploitation of the low-lying forests for iron production—occurred about A.D. 600 to 700. In any event, it appears that Syzygium
figures prominently in long-term trends from omnivorous use of multiple
species in the Early Iron Age, to use of a very limited range of species
during periods of diminished forests, to, finally, the use of only one species in recent times. Such reduction of choice in Buhaya appears to represent a response to significant large-scale reduction in local biodiversity.

The religious-political sanctions that once checked unbridled exploitation—both Bacwezi and royal—have now passed into distant memory. In
their place has arisen a system of forest management based on village and
regional authorities, an uneven scheme with overlapping and ill-defined
responsibilities that allows widespread abuses. The few remaining secondary forests are fast disappearing, and the remnant groundwater forests
of the large swamps are being exploited as never before. Within the villages, some trees are specifically planted along farm boundaries and
cropped for building poles and firewood. During the late colonial period
and the first decade of independence (that is, the years following World
War II until the 1960s), people were actively encouraged to start small

plantations of eucalyptus on fallow land; these plots have indeed become alternative sources of fuel and building poles, but many are now being cut in increasingly shorter cycles.

These events are still occurring in a perceptual universe in which reproductive abundance prevails as part of the cultural ethos. Yet for many decades it has been clear that the limited distribution of good soils, a system of partitive inheritance, the shortening of fallow cycles—due to competition with plantations for open lands—and dense cattle and human populations do not allow for much expansion of Haya villages along the coastal ridges (Reining 1967; Schmidt 1978). A once finely balanced agricultural system has come under stress as fallow lands have been converted to tea and tree plantations, resulting in shortened fallow cycles and decreased production. Established farms cannot support further division, and for several decades young people have been forced to settle on marginal interior land or seek their fortunes in other districts or regions. Those who elect to stay and try to cultivate the poor soils on fallow land at the periphery of permanent villages risk low productivity and malnutrition.

These and other interrelated causes have created an agroecological system that long ago reached its carrying capacity. Out-migration has been one solution; Haya men and women have been leaving Buhaya in significant numbers since World War I. This departure was the natural culmination of declining productivity in the region, linked to human disease and the rinderpest cattle epidemic of the early 1890s (Kjekshus 1977). The decimation of the herds, whose manure was a central feature in the agroecological system, would have had a significant impact on soil fertility until the herds were restored to equivalent size decades later. This severe environmental stress was accompanied by famine and smallpox. With the almost complete elimination of herds from the landscape, bush encroached, bringing with it the ravages of tsetse flies and trypanosomiasis, further suppressing the regeneration of herds and decreasing the carrying capacity of the once-productive agricultural zone. Disease and out-migration seen in the twentieth century are an outgrowth of the collapse of an agroecological system deprived of essential inputs.

One notable feature of this decline was the departure of thousands of young Haya women to urban centers in East Africa in search of work, often as prostitutes. British colonial officials despaired of halting this constant traffic. Many women eventually returned, some to invest in their own land, others with sufficient wealth to educate family members and to rescue debt-ridden family farms (White 1990). But often they brought with them the ravages of syphilis and other sexually transmitted diseases.

The pre–World War II syphilis epidemic in Buhaya was a terrible scourge and contributed to very low population increases during the 1930s, even causing colonial officers to attribute the population decline in the 1948 census to syphilis (Kaijage 1993). Fertility rates in the postwar period were generally low for East Africa but cannot be definitively linked to high rates of syphilis infection among the Haya (Laurie and Trant 1954). The fortuitous development and administration of antibiotics ultimately saved the Haya from catastrophic disease rates and reversed the decline in population (Kaijage 1993: 286). But subsequent decades have seen a continuation of the pattern of out-migration for economic opportunity and better land.

The region's arable land is very limited and sells at high prices. The only option remaining to many is colonization of land with low fertility and marginal rainfall, usually in the drier central basin, the Karagwe Depression. The prospect for young women under these conditions is grinding agricultural work and poverty. Alternative urban "opportunities" seem undeniably attractive in this context of overpopulation and impoverished lifestyles, a syndrome that began in earnest one hundred years ago but whose genesis goes back two thousand years.

Out of this milieu has arisen the latest danger to local populations, the AIDS epidemic. Like the earlier syphilis epidemic, AIDS has decimated the reproductive populations of many, especially northern, Buhaya villages, particularly those on the coastal ridges. By the late 1980s, seropositive rates were running as high as 41 percent among some age groups (Lwihura 1988). Many thousands have died, and socioeconomic disruption prevails in some villages.[8] The tragic paradox is manifest: in a culture with a central system of meaning derived from human reproduction, the act of human procreation now threatens the socioeconomic fabric.

Summary and Conclusion

In the past, social relations of production led to the differential acquisition of power and wealth by those who controlled critical knowledge of the Buhaya region's ironworking technology. That knowledge was protected by ritual mystifications of the industrial process and sustained by a central symbolic armature of belief in unlimited reproductive capacity. The social relations of production promoted by this ideology contributed to degradation of the region's ecological system. Adaptations—in the form of both technological change and, eventually, institutional adjustments under centralized authority—nevertheless enabled a dynamic cultural system to thrive on the changing landscape for some centuries. In the latter case, the centralized state intervened in the relations of production through taxation and through new regulatory devices that employed religious-political sanctions to balance and to counter a dominant exploitative ideology.

Although this history has stressed trends within a deep-time tradition, it is easy to see that the rapid culture change at the beginning of this century certainly equaled or exceeded changes witnessed in the sixth century A.D. or again in the seventeenth century. The coming of Christianity and capitalism undermined the fragile ecosystem by dissolving systems of restraint and management that had been vested in religious authorities in the employ of the state.

This ancient and recent history of Buhaya has integrated a variety of sources to gain a better understanding of how and why the physical and cultural landscapes of Buhaya were remade through time. Cultural meanings signified in that landscape are seen more clearly through the use of a historical ecology which accounts for the effects of ideologies that have driven exploitation and justified social control over the productive economy. Because symbolic life in Buhaya is intertwined with the physical world, with technology and economy, there is a symbolic nexus of great power, especially when manipulated by political groups seeking legitimacy and identity with the past.

Making new histories about African technological life is more than an exercise in scientific observation, analysis, and interpretation. It requires that we listen to oral traditions and oral histories, study ritual and symbolism, collect and synthesize environmental evidence, examine modes of production in their cultural settings, excavate material remains of the past, build appropriate ethnographic models for interpretation of those remains, and above all, listen for the inevitable leaks in the boat—the imposition of ways of thought or interpretative and analytical approaches that contradict local knowledge. Leaks in the boat require that we rebuild the ship of history and archaeology as we travel, constantly reevaluating our assumptions and the scientific beliefs that we hold. The Haya showed us that our scientific expectations needed continuous reformulation in order to understand local modes of experimentation, discovery, and innovation. It is Haya perspectives and ways of knowing that have created a richer understanding of an important African technology while simultaneously informing our understanding of ritual and symbolic contexts in which technology and science occur—allowing us to understand their unity and to make better sense of the relationship between science and culture.

1. Magnetism and Density of Nyungwe Slags

Sample #	None	Slight	Some	Strong	Density
1976					
1				X	4.2
2			X	X	3.9
3	X				4.0
4	X				3.8
5	X				3.7
6	X				3.4
1979					
A				X	4.4
B				X	4.0
C				X	4.9
D				X?	3.4
E				X?	4.1

2. Qualitative Assessment of the Phases Found in the Nyungwe Slags, 1976

Sample #	Fay	Gla/Fay	Gla	Wus	Her	Mag	Leu	Metal
1	C			R	M	R	R	M
2	A	P	R	R	M	P	R	P
3	A	M	R	R	M			R
4	A	M		R	M		M	P
5	A			P	M		R	R
6	A	P	P	P	P			R

Fay = fayalite; Gla/Fay = glass and fayalite; Gla = glass; Wus = wustite; Her = hercynite; Mag = magnetite; Leu = leucite
A = Abundant: 50%+; C = Common: 25–50%; M = Moderate: 10–24%; P = Present: 5–9%; R = Rare: 0.1–4%

3. Chemical Composition of Nyungwe Slags in Weight Percentages

1976

#	FeO	SiO$_2$	Al$_2$O$_3$	CaO	K$_2$O	TiO$_2$	P$_2$O$_5$	MgO	MnO	Na$_2$O
1	55.46	13.12	24.63	1.10	0.74	3.92	0.17	0.06	0.21	0.58
2	60.12	21.88	8.28	2.41	1.00	5.39	0.41	—	0.20	0.32
3	52.21	28.39	10.60	2.19	1.33	3.86	0.33	0.35	0.16	0.58
4	57.24	26.54	7.47	2.59	1.25	4.08	0.32	0.12	0.20	0.20
5	54.53	26.16	11.10	1.98	1.35	4.20	0.24	tr	0.24	0.18
6	51.28	28.40	11.46	2.54	1.34	3.80	0.28	0.20	0.40	0.30

1979

#	FeO	SiO$_2$	Al$_2$O$_3$	CaO	K$_2$O	TiO$_2$	P$_2$O$_5$	MgO	MnO	Na$_2$O
A	14.22	54.81	13.72	6.38	3.88	3.98	0.71	1.49	0.22	0.59
B	42.37	27.94	20.32	2.20	2.99	3.33	0.36	—	0.22	0.30
C	60.00	20.56	9.67	0.29	3.12	4.40	0.38	—	0.26	0.34
D	18.16	42.26	12.64	8.32	8.85	6.52	1.00	1.60	0.13	0.52
E	59.44	23.03	8.24	2.91	2.06	3.33	0.41	0.20	0.15	0.23

1977 Forging Slag

#	FeO	SiO$_2$	Al$_2$O$_3$	CaO	K$_2$O	TiO$_2$	P$_2$O$_5$	MgO	MnO	Na$_2$O
2	60.59	22.44	4.14	6.39	3.72	1.34	0.52	0.44	0.24	0.18

— = none detected
tr = trace

4. Qualitative Assessment of the Phases Found in Nyungwe Slags

Sample #	Fay	Gla/Fay	Gla	Wus	Her	Mag	Leu	Unknown	Metal
1979 Smelt									
A			A		R				C
B	C	P	M		M	R			C
C			C	P		C	R		C
D	P		A	R	R			R	C
E	C		R	M	M		R		P

Fay = fayalite; Gla/Fay = glass and fayalite; Gla = glass; Wus = wustite; Her = hercynite; Mag = magnetite; Leu = leucite
A = Abundant: 50%+; C = Common: 25–50%; M = Moderate: 10–24%; P = Present: 5–9%; R = Rare: 0.1–4%

Air blast. In many kinds of African smelting furnaces, the air required for combustion is forced into the combustion zone under pressure. Usually this pressurized air is supplied by bellows and is referred to as the air blast.

Anneal. In metallurgy this means to take a piece of metal through a cycle of heating, holding it at temperature, and then cooling it in order to modify its properties. It is done for a variety of purposes, but most often to soften a piece after cold working, during which the grains are compressed and under internal stress.

Bloom. This is a sometimes spongy (the interstitial spaces are either voids or filled with slag) aggregate of metal formed in a smelting or refining furnace. Iron blooms contain varying amounts of slag. There are relatively few slag inclusions in the Haya process, for example, while the Barongo iron bloom contains much slag. Most of the slag is expelled under pressure of the hammer on the forge and also drains away within the forge. Finished wrought or bloom iron often contains slag inclusions.

Bloom iron. This is the solid iron product from the reduction of iron ore in a smelting furnace, often including iron, charcoal, unreduced ore, and slag. While some iron bloom, especially what was once thought to be "typical" African iron bloom, has a low carbon content, it is now clear that smelting processes such as that of the Haya produce a partially carburized metal similar to carbon steels. *Wrought iron* is another term used to refer to bloom iron when the emphasis is on the properties such as slag inclusions instead of on the way it was produced.

Carburization. This occurs when carbon is deposited on the surface of an iron object during forging at a temperature high enough that the carbon diffuses inward and combines or alloys with the iron to form a steel. It also occurs in smelting under reducing conditions when the carbon content of a steel is increased by diffusion of carbon into the alloy.

Cast iron. This is iron that contains between 2 and 4.5 percent carbon. Iron with this amount of carbon can become liquid at temperatures well below the melting points of wrought iron and steel and thus is easy to cast.

Cementite. This is an iron carbide in the microstructure of steel and cast iron. It appears in the grain boundaries in wrought iron (containing about .02% carbon) and is one constituent of pearlite in steel. The hardness of a steel or cast iron is proportional to the number and close spacing of the cementite crystals present.

Charge. The placement of ore, fuel, and flux (if any) into a smelting furnace.

Decarburizing. This is the removal of a proportion of carbon in a high-carbon steel or cast iron. It occurs when cast iron in the liquid state has carbon removed (for example, in puddling). In Africa it can occur in the forge when high-carbon iron blooms are submitted to long-term high temperatures and oxidizing conditions as well as in the annealing (heat treatment) of iron blooms that have an excessive carbon content.

Draft. This is usually the pressurized air that feeds combustion in a furnace. In the African context it commonly refers to furnaces in which an induced or convection draft is created by the density difference between the hot gases in a stack or chimney and the cold air on the outside, rather than the use of bellows as in a forced draft.

Eutectic. This is a term that refers to an alloy that solidifies through the simultaneous crystallization of two or more metals or alloy components. A eutectic alloy solidifies at a lower temperature than any of its separate elements. Eutectic alloys are formed in iron with carbon (4.3% C), phosphorus (10.2% P), and many other elements. The creation of a eutectic alloy decreases the incipient melting temperatures.

Eutectoid. This is a term that denotes the carbon content of a steel at which the temperature of solid-state transformation of austenite to ferrite and cementite is minimized. In pure iron, this transformation occurs at about 910°C; at the eutectoid composition (0.8% carbon) it occurs at only 723°C. In the heat treatment of steels, the eutectoid temperature is important, for if they are not heated beyond the eutectoid temperature, then no structural changes will occur.

Fayalite slag. This is an iron silicate slag ($2FeO.SiO_2$). While characterized by silica and iron content, fayalite slags often contain more than 60 percent FeO. They are an essential component in most African iron smelting processes, as they are fluid at temperatures ranging between 1,200 and 1,300°C. Modern blast furnace slags have little fayalite content.

Ferrite. This is the low-temperature crystal form of iron. Ferrite transforms to austenite when heated above 910°C. It has the capacity to dissolve phosphorus but little carbon; this is why some steels have distinct zones of cementite—iron carbide—and pure ferrite.

Flux. This is a substance such as lime that is used in the smelting furnace to lower the flow temperature of slag. Materials such as the oxides of iron, manganese, sodium, potassium, and calcium can be used as fluxes.

Forge. This is the shaping of iron or other metal by hammering as well as the facility—an enclosed or open-air stone anvil in Africa—where forging is done.

Goethite. This is a hydrated ferrous oxide, $HFeO_2$, a mineral sometimes used as an iron ore.

Hematite. Iron oxide (Fe_2O_3) commonly used as an iron ore.

Hercynite. A mineral that results from the high-temperature reaction of aluminum oxides with iron oxides to yield hercynite ($FeO.Al_2O_3$). The presence of large hercynite crystals, which form at 1,470°C upon cooling, increases slag viscosity; hercynite is difficult to purge from the iron during the forging process, creating special problems in forging the iron/steel bloom.

Hot blast. In modern smelting processes, this is the preheating of air before it is forced through the tuyere into the furnace. In Africa a hot blast is obtained by passing air though a hot tuyere inserted into the smelting furnace. The increased temperatures that result in and around the combustion zone—including the reduction zones—cause smelting to proceed at a faster rate as well as obtain significant economies in fuel use.

Hypereutectoid. This specialized term refers to steels that are higher in carbon than the eutectoid composition. Hypereutectoid steels are harder and more brittle.

Inclusions. These are nonmetallic areas, often particles of slag, and sometimes infusible substances. A piece of worked bloom will often incorporate many slag inclusions despite heavy hammering and long forging.

Kaolin. This is the most refractory of the clay minerals, a hydroxysilicate of alumina. A clay with a high proportion of kaolin is necessary for heat-resistant tuyeres that penetrate deep inside a smelting furnace to preheat the air blast.

Laterite. A residual, often concretized soil formed in the tropics usually under conditions of heavy leaching. Laterites contain concentrations of iron and aluminum hydroxides; sometimes there is sufficient iron that some laterites can be used as ores.

Limonite. This mineral is a hydrated ferrous oxide used as an iron ore. It is often of yellowish color and is mined from bogs.

Magnetite. This mineral (Fe_3O_4) is widely used as an ore in iron smelting. In its pure form it must be mixed with silica in order to form a slag and to be smelted successfully in African iron smelting furnaces.

Nucleation. The initiation of crystallization at discrete sites in a molten mass.

Ore. This is a metal-bearing mineral that is used to produce metals after smelting and refining. Types of iron ore vary widely in Africa. One culture may have magnetite (Fe_3O_4) deposits, while a neighboring culture may have only a limonite or bog ore available for smelting.

Pearlite. This is one of the products of slowly cooled austenite. It has a structure of crystals of cementite and ferrite interleaved together. In modern production, most steel products are shaped while in a pearlitic state.

Prill. A droplet of slag or globule of metal.

Quenching. This process is used when iron is heated to austenite temperatures and is then thrust into water and cooled rapidly. This causes much of the austenite to take the form of hard and brittle martensite.

Reduction. The chemical removal of oxygen from a compound.

Refractory. This is resistance to softening or melting at high temperatures, a property that is especially important in clay products used in iron smelting. The clays used in tuyeres inserted into furnaces for preheating, for example, must be highly refractory in order to stand up to the high furnace temperatures as well as to resist the corrosive action of slags.

Roasting. The heating of ore in open fires; it induces cracking and expels water and sulfides, as well as deposits carbon in preparation for the smelting.

Sinter. This is a process in which microwelded bonds develop at contact points between solid particles. It occurs at elevated temperatures, forming homogeneous masses without melting. It occurs in many places in the bloomery process, starting in the ore within the furnace stack and continuing throughout the formation of the bloom.

Slag. This is a major by-product of iron smelting that occurs as a ceramic or glass composed of minerals and metal oxides. In Africa it is an important and active part of the smelting process. The slag that is left after smelting is derived from ore, fuel ash, fluxes (if added), and often portions of tuyeres and clay from the furnace superstructure and lining. Slag may contain pockets of sintered iron and therefore may be selected for reuse in subsequent smelts.

Smelting. Smelting uses thermochemical reactions between fuel and ore to reduce ore minerals to metal. Most smelting processes are carried out above the melting point of the metal, except in the case of iron. In traditional iron smelting, the key reaction involves the reduction of iron oxides by carbon monoxide at high temperatures; one of the keys to success in the African iron smelting process is to maintain high temperatures at a reducing (CO) atmosphere.

Tempering. This is the final stage in the heat treatment of steel. The brittleness of a quickly cooled steel (martensite) can be altered through reheating to a temperature between 200 and 400°C; the desired temperature is judged by observing the temper colors. This process decreases brittleness and can lead to various combinations of hardness and toughness. This term also refers to the addition of inclusions—such as broken pieces of pottery—in ceramics, a technique that contends with thermal shock during the firing of the clay.

Tuyere. In Africa this is usually a clay tube used to deliver air to the combustion zone of a smelting furnace or forge. In most furnaces using forced and induced draft, the tuyeres project only a few centimeters into the furnace. However, in smelting furnaces in which tuyeres project up to 50 centimeters, the tuyeres must be made of highly refractory clay capable of withstanding very high furnace temperatures.

Welding. This is the bonding of iron pieces at their surfaces by melting them together, which is fusion welding. Welding also occurs on the forge when micro-welds form between adjacent surfaces while the pieces remain in a solid state. Welding on the forge is often aided by the natural fluxing of extruded FeO (wustite) and other artificially applied fluxes which prevent further reoxidation of the surface of the iron pieces and allow them to be welded.

Wustite. This is a mineral (FeO) that is an important transition oxide in the reduction of iron ore. In Africa it is found to be a significant component in some slags. As a component in bloomery iron, it can also play a role as a welding flux on the forge—oozing out of the bloom to form a film that prevents reoxidation.

Notes

1. Remaking Knowledge about African Iron Technology

1. The political region in which the Bahaya people (hereafter Haya) live is today called Kagera Region. In other publications I have used the more neutral term "westlake," based on geography and derived from the older political name of the region, West Lake. Here I use Buhaya because the subject of much of the study is the Haya people themselves: their iron technology, their history, their symbolic lives, and their landscape.

2. The history of scientific inquiry into African iron technology dates back to the first part of this century when Bellamy and Harbord (1904) studied Yoruba iron smelting and performed metallurgical analysis on the samples produced from smelts. Subsequently, in the 1930s, Shona iron smelting was studied in an experimental or demonstration furnace, and the metallurgical results were reported by Stanley (1931). From then until Judith Todd's 1973 study of Dime smelting in southwest Ethiopia (Todd 1979, 1985; Todd and Charles 1978) and the Haya studies of the later 1970s (Schmidt 1978, 1981, 1996a; Schmidt and Avery 1978; Avery and Schmidt 1979; Schmidt and Childs 1985), there were no systematic scientific studies of the technological process within the context of a fully understood social setting. There have also been quite a number of important observations of various technologies, some of which take note of technological procedures (e.g., Wembah-Rashid 1973; Pole 1974a, 1974b, 1975; Celis and Nzikobanyanka 1976; Goucher 1984; Van Noten 1985). Others have reconstructed technologies for laboratory-like observations (Friede et al. 1984). There have also been attempts to study the technological attributes of smelting that have not been successful (e.g., Van Noten 1985; Avery, van der Merwe, and Saitowitz 1988). Most ethnographic studies during this century, however, have focused on the social aspect of iron smelting, not on scientific characterizations of what happens inside African iron smelting furnaces. While a number of archaeologists have dutifully arranged for analyses of furnace residues or forged products, such results do not capture the dynamics of the process.

3. The use of deconstruction in this context bears little relationship to the use of the idea in literary criticism or in the thought of Derrida or Foucault. It is closely related to revisionism in history, yet because it pertains to radical change in interpretative positions—based on false imagination in this instance—deconstruction seems appropriate to the historical task at hand.

4. Those smelting technologies that have been studied from an ethnographic *and* technical point of view are (1) the Haya of Tanzania, (2) the Mafa of Cameroon, (3) the Chewa of Malawi, (4) the Barongo of Tanzania, (5) the Bassar of Togo, and (6) the Shona of Zimbabwe. In the case of the Shona, this knowledge is the least developed and comes from several sources, including the studies of Stanley (1931)

and a video by Dewey (1990). The Bassar process is known from the historical and archaeological studies of de Barros (1986) and the historical and ethnographic studies of Goucher and Herbert (Goucher 1984; Herbert 1993; Goucher and Herbert 1996) and a film (Saltman, Goucher, and Herbert 1986), with the technical side not yet fully developed.

5. Since the early 1960s, an interpretative approach has developed in Africa that is partially derived from the British practice of history in archaeology, yet is quite independent from the self-consciously postprocessual school of thought, which developed in the 1980s at the University of Cambridge. The work of Posnansky (e.g., 1966) provides one substantive and theoretical leg on which this approach is based. Many examples of this Africa-inspired school prevail, among them the writings of Eluyemi (1977) on the ritual structure of Yoruba villages; of Garlake (1977) on the ritual continuities of terra-cotta sculptures excavated in Yoruba shrines; of Schmidt on myth, history, and iron (1978, 1983c); of de Maret (1985) on the symbolic meanings attached to African blacksmithing; of Rowlands (1985) on the symbolic meaning of palaces in Cameroon; of Rowlands and Warnier (1993) on the symbolic meanings of iron production in Cameroon; of David (1992a, 1992b) on the ideology of burial and the development of a hermeneutic approach in ethnoarchaeology; of David, Sterner, and Guvua (1988) on the symbolic meaning of pots; of Sterner (1992) on interpretation of pots employing the idea of symbolic reservoir; of McIntosh (1992) using the idea of symbolic reservoir; and of MacEachern (1994) in developing ideas that challenge the concept of symbolic reservoir.

6. Some postprocessual thinkers have been strongly skeptical of science in the practice of archaeology (e.g., Shanks and Tilley 1987). This antipathy to scientific or processual archaeology has led others to responses (e.g., Watson 1990; Renfrew 1994) that have further polarized the field. The development of this theoretical dichotomy has led a number of scholars, mostly known for their "processual" or scientific archaeology, to search for common ground (e.g., Hill 1994; Sherratt 1994; Zubrow 1994). Other scholars have not been caught up in the rhetoric and have continued to practice scientific archaeology while also employing interpretative approaches (e.g., Brumfiel, Salcedo, and Schafer 1993; Marcus and Flannery 1994).

7. I am keenly aware that this particular discourse will not reach many Haya and most other citizens of Tanzania. To meet the goals of general communication, a documentary film has been prepared in Swahili for distribution via media vans in Tanzania. Public showings have also taken place in Buhaya. These efforts have been accompanied by the publication of a pamphlet explaining the historical importance in both English and Swahili. A four-pronged approach for dissemination of knowledge has been adopted: (1) mass media (film and video) in English; (2) professional publications in English (such as this book and journal articles); (3) mass media in Swahili; and (4) local distribution of printed material in Swahili and English.

8. The concept of bricolage used here is derived from Lévi-Strauss, who used it in his discussion of mythmaking in *The Savage Mind* (1966). It refers to a process of fabrication in which the bricoleur assembles an object—be it ritual or myth—from elements that exist in the cultural repertoire available to the fabricator (bricoleur). I extend this idea to incorporate the material world, so that a

bricoleur may also fabricate things, such as a carburetor or an iron smelting operation, from the bits and pieces found within the available array of material objects and knowledge of prior experiences. I have on many occasions witnessed such bricolage at work when my Land Rovers had what appeared to be impossible repair problems far from any conventional garage. This idea was first developed in a discussion of Barongo iron smelting (Schmidt 1996c), where bricolage applies simultaneously to both ritual and technology. Also see Lemonnier (1992: 81), who in his discussion of social representations in technology mentions that technologists operate with a projected plan in mind while participating in fabrication: "A jack of all trades may pick up various bits and scraps here and there, because he has such a projection somewhere in mind." However, Lemonnier's approach is much more highly structured as a series of operational steps (*chaîne d'opératoire*) that does not leave much room for the interplay of ritual bricolage with the order in which the steps occur. On the other hand, I am trying to develop ways of understanding that dynamic interplay between ritual and technology (Schmidt 1996c).

9. Schoenbrun (1993a) notes that by this time, Bantu-speaking groups in this zone along the lake where Buhaya is located were part of what is now called the West Nyanza Bantu-speaking group.

10. MacLean (1994) has taken up a related idea and has argued that nonindustrial sites in the area are relatively scarce, concluding that Early Iron Age settlement sites in Buhaya do not indicate significant populations. This rendering of the Buhaya evidence—based on our 5 percent sample from the region—designates 27 percent of the 141 sites, or those without ironworking evidence, as settlement sites. This argument is invalid on several grounds. The sample of Early Iron Age sites in Buhaya—using systematic survey and extended survey of most occupied agricultural zones, where the best agricultural soils are found—has yielded the largest total number as well as the highest density of sites known on the continent. It simply makes no sense to claim in this context that the number of Early Iron Age settlement sites in Buhaya is restricted or that these populations were insignificant.

11. At the site of Kabale, located at the southern end of the plateau, there was a radiocarbon date of 185 B.C. ± 250 from a site specifically associated with iron smelting. While this seems very early, given the rest of the Early Iron Age in Buhaya, a one-sigma variation (250 years) brings the date into the mid-first century A.D., and a two-sigma variation (500 years) brings the date into the early fourth century A.D. Thus, it appears that the southern occupations are likely congruent with those that occurred on the northern plateau, on the better agricultural soils, during the second and third centuries A.D.

12. Stewart (1993) and Schoenbrun (1993b) point out the limitation of the arguments by Desmedt (1991), who attempts to link oral traditions in Rwanda to the coming of Nilotic pastoralists and roulette-decorated pottery using twisted and plaited techniques at the end of the first millennium A.D. Soper (1971) notes that at the Chobi site in northwestern Uganda, carved roulette and plaited roulette techniques are coeval. However, he was unable to date these occurrences. Connah (1996) illustrates numerous motifs made by the carved roulette technique, initially dating to the first quarter of this millennium. These ceramics are found in association with plaited grass roulette (Connah's knotted strip roulette), though the earliest levels are dominated by carved roulette.

2. Historical and Cultural Contexts

1. The Bakuma, as the dispossessed leaders and as those responsible for some of the most important rituals upon royal installation, retain such specialized knowledge.

2. We must keep in mind that according to the Haya, the Babito and Bahinda were clans founded by the brothers Kibi and Ruhinda; therefore their histories start at the same time.

3. Kiziba king lists are highly regular representations, partly the result of early twentieth-century attempts by the royal house to suppress variants (Schmidt 1978). However, in-depth interviews with members of nonroyal clans reveal important variations, such as the rule of Ikanga—#11.

4. Another indication of Babito problems with legitimacy during Wanumi's reign is his marriage into one of the peasant clans, the Bagabo. Not only is there a rule against such behavior, commonly violated by the kings, but the Bagabo were a large and influential ironworking clan. This marriage alliance can be seen as an attempt by the Babito to become identified with an economically important indigenous group, as well as to recruit their support during this difficult period. The section of the Bagabo that married up had their name changed to the Bamiro and their social status upgraded (see Cory and Hartnoll, 1941: 563).

5. Kyamutwara in this instance is Greater Kyamutwara, which before the nineteenth century included Kianja, Maruku, Bugabo, and the much smaller Kyamutwara of today. The Batundu, who are associated only with Mugasha in Kianja kingdom, appear to have been rainmaking rivals of the Bayango.

6. The location of the iron hammer was Kyaya section of Kahororo village, located on the ridge immediately behind Kahororo secondary school. The hammer is remembered by old people who saw it many years ago. Stories about its removal refer to a Kashozi missionary who used it as a doorstop; in any case, it is not to be found today.

7. One royal informant identified this ironworking group as the Batundu, the only known case of such association. Along with the Bayango, the Batundu were one of the most powerful clans. They are also the clan that took over responsibilities of the Mugasha cult when Rugomora Mahe appeared on the scene. These themes are elaborated upon in Schmidt 1978, Appendix B and p. 106.

8. Augustine Kaindoa, July 30, 1970, Bukoba; for the entire text see Appendix A of Schmidt 1978.

9. The Tower of Babel myths among the Lunda and Luba are discussed at length by de Heusch 1982.

10. In Fisher's version, based on Bunyoro mythology, Kazoba as sun god is one of the Bacwezi gods. Cory's research among the Haya also placed Kazoba in the Bacwezi pantheon (Hans Cory collection, file no. 49, University of Dar es Salaam Library), though other Haya versions place Kazoba in a pre-Bacwezi period (Schmidt, 1978: 67–68). This points to the likelihood that the Bacwezi cult in Buhaya co-opted and assimilated more ancient myths associated with the local social groups. Tantala (1989) in her analysis of the Kitara epic finds similar periodization or layers that point to successive transformations—the Bacwezi fitting into the process as powerful religious/political authorities who later undergo transformations in much the same way that they induced when they displaced local cults.

3. Ethnoarchaeology and Experiment in Iron Technology

1. If the journal *Ethnohistory* is consulted, the reader will find that most of the ethnohistory used or cited by authors in that journal is history that has been represented or interpreted by outside observers. Hence, it is misleading to apply such terminology to indigenous testimonies that can stand on their own. Commentaries in texts carry important interpretations of events and processes. Later analysis and reinterpretation by outsiders, such as I, are biased by the line of argument or emphasis that is being followed. These later interpretations may not agree with local interpretations, but nonetheless they become part of the historiographic discourse.

2. The first-person plural is used when other members of the team (a metallurgist, palynologist, another archaeologist, and a linguist) were also engaged in observations and decision making with the author. The first-person singular is used when the author was responsible for initiatives and observations.

3. A formal contract for labor compensation was effected. It recognized expertise and seniority as criteria in assigning pay scales. This approach—endorsed by the local government and all participants—was used successfully with regular paydays for the duration of the research.

4. All of my discourse with the iron smelters was conducted in Swahili. Interviews were conducted in Swahili, with usually KiHaya and some Swahili responses. I was assisted by an interpreter in formulating questions and comments to KiHaya responses. All interviews were recorded and transcribed and then later translated into English. We tape-recorded all the dialogue during planning sessions, special palavers and rituals, mining, charcoal making, clay mining, smelting, etc. These voluminous records have been transcribed, with approximately 80 percent—the nonmundane—translated into English. A team of three assistants were charged with these responsibilities during and after smelting activities.

5. We previously published this 10 percent figure, but we later realized that the charcoal during 1976 had been water-saturated and that approximately 30 percent of the charcoal weight was likely water.

6. We were unprepared for this activity, so we did not have equipment in the field to weigh the wood weight. However, a later roast used 315 kg of freshly cut wood to roast 90.5 kg of ore.

7. See Lemonnier (1992: 29) on the dangers of forcing technological phenomena into preconceived categories.

4. Ethnoarchaeology and Bricolage

1. In subsequent smelts we found that an average of 60 kg of dry charcoal goes into a furnace to preheat it before smelting begins. Of this amount, between 20 and 40 kg can be burned before smelting begins, depending on the length of the delay. Therefore, a significant amount of charcoal is consumed that is not used directly for production, at least within the context of the replicated smelts.

2. These terms pertain to color characteristics.

5. A Technological Model of the Haya Process

1. The preheating debate is examined in chapters 8–12 of Schmidt 1996a.

6. Comparative Models

1. The spinels are a group of rock-forming minerals with the general composition AB_2O_4. The group comprises three series whose members can transform into one another by the process of solid-state substitution. In the spinel series of the spinel group, B is aluminum and A is variously magnesium, iron, zinc or manganese.

7. Dynamic Models for an Archaeology of Iron Technology

1. The greater the number of elements (or "the number of points of analogy") that are similar across domains, the tighter the analogy (Salmon 1982). In his argument against analogy, Gould argues that the number of elements does not matter and that analogy cannot account for variability (Gould and Watson 1982). While Gould's approach rightfully makes us more cognizant of variability and the need to take it into account, it is a rendering of analogy that forgets that there are always differences between the two domains in an analog, precisely that kind of meta-phorical tension that one should expect to find in any use of analogy (also see Wylie 1982). I agree with Gould that variation tends to be submerged in practice, yet in any large array of similarities, variation must be assessed for its degree of significance. That assessment may find that some variation is not relevant (Salmon 1982), say, at the functional level and therefore can be overlooked without harm to the analogic argument.

2. Also of interest are the morphology and chemistry of furnace slags. For reasons of space, the slag model is being published in another venue.

3. In a series of test firings, Terry Childs found that the Kikukwe clay—tempered or not—started to melt at about 1,500°C under oxidizing conditions, compared to the tempered Buchwero clay, which showed very little alteration at the same temperature (Childs 1986, 1989a).

4. In Childs (1986) and Schmidt and Childs (1985, 1996), the published figures in graphs are 38% (early) and 58% (late). Reanalysis of the data—because of the result obtained in the ethnoarchaeological studies—shows that some double entry errors occurred during data entry; these new figures correct the earlier figures. Similar corrections pertain to the KM3 site, with the accurate figures presented here.

8. Models for the Interpretation of Space

1. The Nyungwe sites are within the village today. Farmers have gathered the slag blocks from this smelting era and have stacked them in pyramids within the farms. Similar phenomena, the incorporation of historic smelting sites within village precincts, can be observed many other places in Buhaya, particularly in Kianja.

2. In an earlier publication (Schmidt 1978) I have suggested that the RM house floor might have a special use associated with iron production. I now want to question that interpretation and suggest that it is reasonable to postulate that it may have formed a residence, even if temporary. Small structures approximating the RM floor size can be seen in a wide variety of ethnographic cases.

3. There are no legends that I know of in Buhaya that discuss the origins of luiija. However, in Bunyoro—closely related in language, religion, and history—Marga-

ret Trowell noted that the stone anvil called oluija takes its name from Luija, who was the first legendary Banyoro founder of the genet clan, which provided Kinto with his first smith. Thus, there is an ancient association between iron forging and political authority (Trowell 1941).

4. Forging slags have a distinct shape, profile, and structure. Because they flow into the concavities of forging pits, they are rounded, sometimes even hemispherical. Inside they show a stratification, the layers of which, we have observed, derive from different smithing episodes. In the case of an iron bloom, some of the iron from the bloom will be captured by the slag and flow to the bottom of the pit, to be taken up by the slag.

5. Collett (1985) argues that because two postholes, C and G, were observed at a depth 5 cm higher than the other postholes, the structure should be assigned to the midden associated with the cord roulette tradition or Late Iron Age. However, posthole C contained a Urewe sherd, as did H. A variability of 5 cm in stratigraphic placement can be taken as a normal part of the variation of a forge surface. Moreover, the placement of the forge proper at –98 cm is also reasonable, as the surface around a forge is often lower than the surrounding floor of the forge.

9. An Archaeology of African Iron Symbolism

1. See Cory and Hartnoll 1945: 266 for further information on the liminal state of the Muharambwa.

2. I am grateful for the assistance of M. M. Mulokozi of the Kiswahili Institute, University of Dar es Salaam, in helping to sort out these esoteric meanings.

3. Katerero is also used to refer to the beating of the smith's hammer on the anvil. The village of Katerero, on which the cosmic iron tower fell, is also a well-known center for ironsmithing. We do not want to push the argument too far, but we should point out that the swinging tail of the fat-tailed sheep may at one time have been a metaphor for a beating phallus.

4. Lungfish have vestigial fins that the Haya call "breasts."

5. M. M. Mulokozi when he translated this text found that the line was "The potter does not reproduce." He feels that this was a slip of the tongue, for it does not fit with the entirely positive emphasis of the rest of the song. It could also be purposeful irony intended to draw out distinctions between iron smelters and potters—the iron smelters being the ones who reproduce.

10. Reading Ideology in the Archaeological Record

1. Each case study is designated by a capital letter. This is used as a key to locate the culture on a map of Africa—fig. 10.1b.

2. They describe this technological system in rather idealized terms, speaking of a "male" ore and a "female" ore; the female ore is concocted of clay and iron slag leavings. The authors are at a loss to explain the significance of the female ore and are reluctant to attribute a ritual function to it. Their reluctance is appropriate, for the clay is apparently meant to contribute to slag formation in the smelting process. There is another, major technological component that is omitted from this account: the "glazed sherd" industry of the Grassfields was dependent upon the processing of iron nodules recovered from reprocessed slag at Babungo and other

Ndop Plain smelting sites. An active trade in packages of iron bits (slag-encrusted) needing further smelting and slag removal fed the Grassfields smelting industry. Are the slag leavings that they refer to the bits and pieces of iron and slag held together by the clay cakes for resmelting? This appears to be an example of insufficient technological information obtained from "distant" oral accounts that then has the potential to confuse symbolic interpretation as well as lead to potentially false or at least incomplete conclusions about the technological process.

3. On p. 273 I indicate that this furnace is perhaps as old as the first century B.C. By C^{14} dating, the furnace dates between 165 B.C. and A.D. 240 at 95 percent probability (Schmidt and Childs 1985).

11. A History of Landscape Transformation

1. The distribution of settlement and industrial sites dating to the Early Iron Age is extensive and complex (Schmidt 1980). The plentiful incidence of industrial debris in many early ironworking sites, however, does not deny the probability that many of these sites were also settlement sites. I have never argued that settlement sites are limited to those sites without industrial debris, as Reid (1996) claims. For example, in a 1-km-wide transect running between Victoria Nyanza and Lake Ikimba, three of the twenty-five sites found were defined only by ceramics. Two sites had ceramics and furnace bricks, and seven sites had ceramics and miscellaneous industrial debris, e.g., slag (Schmidt 1980). Thus, ten of the twenty-five sites were almost certainly EIA settlement sites, and there is a reasonable probability that the remaining two sites with furnace bricks may also have supported settlement. A recent view (Stewart 1993) that Urewe pottery in the Great Lakes seems to be relatively scarce and may be a "prestige" ware is not supported by the Buhaya evidence. The idea that Urewe ceramics do not occur in significant amounts in habitation sites in the Great Lakes overlooks the evidence at the Urewe type site (where there are no reported smelting furnaces), Lolui Island in Victoria Nyanza, and the KM2 site in Buhaya, among others. In the latter instance the KM2 site is both a habitation and an industrial site. As noted in chapter 8, any suggestion that iron production during the EIA was segregated from habitation—based on modern or historical analogs in which smelting takes place outside villages—may be incorrect or a simplification. It is also important to remember that there are many EIA sites in Buhaya discovered during survey that show no signs of industrial activity (see chapter 1).

2. Schoenbrun (1993b) argues that the increasing importance of cattle among West Nyanza Bantu speakers (those inhabiting the western shore of Victoria Nyanza) is seen in the innovation of many new color terms for cattle among Rutaran speakers (KiHaya, KiZinza, Lunyoro) in the area between A.D. 1000 and 1450, the period of time when this zone west of Victoria Nyanza was once again settled by agriculturalists, and a period when oral traditions point to the coming of cattle keepers from the northern Karagwe Depression (Ankole) to the south and then into Buhaya proper from the west.

3. The precise time for this important shift has not yet been fixed. It should also be noted that once Miscanthidium grass gained popularity as a fuel (and as a material through which slag could drain), wood charcoal continued to be used as the fuel that accompanied the ore charge in the furnace stack.

4. Recent research into the history of forest clearance and environmental degradation in southwestern Uganda (Hamilton, Taylor, and Vogel 1986; Taylor and Marchant 1994) shows intriguing patterns of forest clearance, some as early as 4800 B.P. Interpretations that this forest loss was caused by early cultivation must be viewed with caution, for they are not yet confirmed by any archaeological evidence for agricultural settlements in the area. Schoenbrun (1993a), however, makes a convincing argument on behalf of cereal-growing Sudanic speakers in the area before the first millennium based on linguistic evidence. The pollen diagrams from the Ahakagyezi Swamp do show that clearance of the lower slopes and valleys was probably under way by 2800 B.P. and that the valley forests had been completely cleared by 2200 B.P. This latter deforestation can very likely be attributed to cultivation, most probably by Bantu-speaking peoples. Whether they were iron producers remains an open question.

5. I am grateful for the assistance of Marie-Claude Van Grunderbeek and S. T. Childs for helping to arrange charcoal analysis; special thanks goes to H. Doutrelepont for his analysis of the charcoal found in the furnaces. Van Grunderbeek's research along these lines in Rwanda and Burundi has also provided important ecological insights (Van Grunderbeek, Doutrelepont, and Roche 1984; Van Grunderbeek, Roche, and Doutrelepont 1983a; Van Grunderbeek and Doutrelepont 1988).

6. The new communities established along the coastal ridges and the hills to the west, overlooking Lake Ikimba, are marked by pottery decorated with a carved roulette (see chapter 1); the roulette design is distinctive and has been dated to the thirteenth to fourteenth centuries A.D.

7. Reid (1996) and Robertshaw (1994) emphasize that hardly any EIA sites are found in south-central Uganda. Yet it is instructive that one of the few found, Mubende Hill, is not only an important Early Iron Age site—with likely ritual associations—but also the focus of continuous use in the current millennium. The early history of Mubende Hill has been submerged in the current emphasis on second-millennium A.D. state systems (Robertshaw 1994). However, the early first-millennium A.D. history of Mubende Hill suggests strong affinities to ancient shrine sites that figure prominently in the history of Buhaya.

8. An exact number is not available, but it is possible that "tens of thousands" may be a more accurate statement. In 1992 there were 30,000 documented orphans, which does not include those children being raised by kinfolk.

Bibliography

Andah, Bassey. 1995. "Studying African Societies in Cultural Context." In *Making Alternative Histories,* ed. P. R. Schmidt and T. C. Patterson, 149–81. Santa Fe: School of American Research Press.

Austen, Ralph. 1987. *African Economic History.* London: James Currey.

Avery, D. H., and P. R. Schmidt. 1979. "A Metallurgical Study of the Iron Bloomery, Particularly as Practiced in Buhaya." *Journal of Metals* 31: 14–20.

Avery, D. H. and P. R. Schmidt. 1986. "The Use of Preheated Air in Ancient and Recent African Iron Smelting Furnaces: A Reply to Rehder." *Journal of Field Archaeology* 13: 354–57.

Avery, D. H., and P. R. Schmidt. 1996. "Preheating: Practice or Illusion?" In *The Culture and Technology of African Iron Production,* ed. P. R. Schmidt, 267–76. Gainesville: University Press of Florida.

Avery, D. H.; N. J. van der Merwe; and S. Saitowitz. 1988. "The Metallurgy of the Bloomery in Africa." In *The Beginning of the Use of Metals and Alloys,* ed. R. Madden, 261–82. Cambridge: Massachusetts Institute of Technology Press.

Bachmann, H.-G. 1982. *The Identification of Slags from Archaeological Sites.* University of London Institute of Archaeology, Occasional Paper no. 6. London: Institute of Archaeology.

Baillie, M. G. L. 1994. "Dendrochronology Raises Questions about the Nature of the AD 536 Dust-veil Event." *Holocene* 4(2): 212–17.

Barndon, Randi. 1992. "Traditional Iron Working among the Fipa: An Ethno-archaeological Study from Southwestern Tanzania." Master's thesis, University of Bergen.

Barndon, Randi. 1996. "Fipa Ironworking and Its Technological Style." In *The Culture and Technology of African Iron Working,* ed. P. R. Schmidt, 58–73. Gainesville: University Press of Florida.

Bellamy, C. B., and F. W. Harbord. 1904. "A West African Smelting House." *Journal of the Iron and Steel Institute* 66: 99–126.

Berger, Iris. 1996. "Fertility as Power: Spirit Mediums, Priestesses and the Precolonial State in Interlacustrine East Africa." In *Revealing Prophets,* ed. D. M. Anderson and D. H. Johnson, 65–82. London and Athens, Ohio: James Currey and Ohio University Press.

Binford, L. R. 1987. "Researching Ambiguity: Frames of Reference and Site Structure." In *Method and Theory for Activity Area Research: An Ethno-archaeological Approach,* ed. S. Kent, 449–572. New York: Columbia University Press.

Bjerke, S. 1981. *Religion and Misfortune: The Bachwezi Complex and Other Spirit Cults of the Zinza of Northwestern Tanzania.* Oslo: Universitetsforlaget.

Braudel, Fernand. 1980. *On History.* Chicago: University of Chicago Press.

Brumfiel, Elizabeth; T. Salcedo; and D. Schafer. 1993. "The Lip Plugs of Xaltocan: Function and Meaning in Aztec Archaeology." In *Economies and Polities in the Aztec Realm,* ed. M. G. Hodge and M. E. Smith, 113–30. Albany: State University of New York Press.

Celis, Georges. 1989. "La métallurgie traditionelle au Burundi, au Rwanda, et au Buha: Essai de synthèse." *Anthropos* 84: 25–46.

Celis, Georges, and E. Nzikobanyanka. 1976. *La Métallurgie traditionelle au Burundi.* Tervuren: Musée Royale de L'Afrique Centrale.

Childe, V. Gordon. 1949. "The Sociology of Knowledge." *The Modern Quarterly,* n.s. 1: 302–309.

Childs, S. Terry. 1986. "Style in Technology: A View of African Early Iron Age Iron Smelting through Its Refractory Ceramics." Ph.D. dissertation, Boston University.

Childs, S. Terry. 1988. "Clay Resource Specialization in Ancient Tanzania: Implications for Cultural Process." In *Ceramic Ecology Revisited,* ed. Charles Kolb, 1–31. Oxford: BAR International Series 436(ii), pt. 2.

Childs, S. Terry. 1989a. "Clays to Artifacts: Resource Selection in African Early Iron Age Iron-Making Technologies." In *Pottery Technology: Ideas and Approaches,* ed. G. Bronitsky, 139–64. Boulder: Westview Press.

Childs, S. Terry. 1989b. "Petrographic Analysis of Archaeological Ceramics." *MRS Bulletin* (March): 24–29.

Childs, S. Terry. 1990. "Refractory Ceramics and Iron Smelting in East Africa." *Journal of Metals* (Dec.): 36–38.

Childs, S. Terry. 1991. "Style, Technology, and Iron Smelting Furnaces in Bantu-Speaking Africa." *Journal of Anthropological Archaeology* 10: 332–59.

Childs, S. Terry. 1996. "Technological History and Culture in Western Tanzania." In *The Culture and Technology of African Iron Production,* ed. P. R. Schmidt, 277–320. Gainesville: University Press of Florida.

Childs, S. Terry, and D. Killick. 1993. "Indigenous African Metallurgy: Nature and Culture." *Annual Review of Anthropology* 22: 317–37.

Childs, S. Terry, and P. R. Schmidt. 1985. "Experimental Iron Smelting: The Genesis of a Hypothesis with Implications for African Prehistory." In *African Iron Working—Ancient and Traditional,* ed. R. Haaland and P. Shinnie, 121–41. Oslo: Norwegian University Press.

Cline, Walter. 1937. *Mining and Metallurgy in Negro Africa.* Menasha, Wis.: George Banta Publishing Co.

Clist, Bernard. 1987. "A Critical Reappraisal of the Chronological Framework of the Early Urewe Iron Age Industry." *Muntu* 6: 35–62.

Collett, David. 1985. "The Spread of Early Iron-Producing Communities in Eastern and Southern Africa." Ph.D. dissertation, University of Cambridge.

Collett, David. 1993. "Metaphors and Representations Associated with Precolonial Iron-Smelting in Eastern and Southern Africa." In *The Archaeology of Africa: Food, Metals and Towns,* ed. T. Shaw, P. Sinclair, B. Andah, and A. Okpoko, 499–511. London and New York: Routledge.

Connah, Graham. 1991. "The Salt of Bunyoro." *Antiquity* 65: 479–94.

Connah, Graham. 1996. *Kibiro.* London: British Institute in Eastern Africa, Memoir no. 13.

Cory, Hans. Hans Cory collection, file no. 49, University of Dar es Salaam Library.

Cory, Hans, and M. M. Hartnoll. 1945. *Customary Law of the Haya Tribe.* London: International African Institute and Percy Lond, Humpheries and Co.

Crumley, Carole, ed. 1994. *Historical Ecology: Cultural Knowledge and Changing Landscapes.* Santa Fe: School of American Research Press.

Curtin, Philip. 1964. *African History.* Washington, D.C.: Service Center for Teachers of History.

Curtin, P.; S. Feierman; L. Thompson; and J. Vansina. 1990. *African History.* London and New York: Longmans.

David, Nicholas. 1982. "Prehistory and Historical Linguistics in Central Africa: Points of Contact." In *The Archaeological and Linguistic Reconstruction of African History,* ed. C. Ehert and M. Posnansky, 78–93. Berkeley and Los Angeles: University of California Press.

David, Nicholas. 1992a. "Integrating Ethnoarchaeology: A Subtle Realist Perspective." *Journal of Anthropological Archaeology* 11: 330–59.

David, Nicholas. 1992b. "The Archaeology of Ideology: Mortuary Practices in the Central Mandara Highlands, Northern Cameroon." In *An African Commitment: Papers in Honor of Peter Lewis Shinnie,* ed. J. Sterner and N. David, 181–210. Calgary: The University of Calgary Press.

David, Nicholas; R. Heimann; D. Killick; and M. L. Wayman. 1989. "Between Bloomery and Blast Furnace: Mafa Iron-Smelting Technology in Northern Cameroon." *The African Archaeological Review* 7: 185–210.

David, Nicholas; J. Sterner; and K. Guvua. 1988. "Why Are Pots Decorated?" *Current Anthropology* 29: 365–89.

de Barros, Philip. 1986. "A Quantified, Chronologically Controlled, Regional Approach to a Traditional Iron Production Centre in West Africa." *Africa* 56: 148–73.

Deetz, James. 1977. *In Small Things Forgotten.* New York: Anchor Book, Doubleday.

Deetz, James. 1993. *Flowerdew Hundred.* Charlottesville: University Press of Virginia.

Desmedt, C. 1991. "Poteries anciennes décorées à la roulette dans la Région des Grands Lacs." *The African Archaeological Review* 9: 161–96.

Dewey, William. 1990. *Weapons for the Ancestors.* Video. Iowa City: University of Iowa.

Dewey, William, and S. T. Childs. 1996. "Forging Memory." In *Memory: Luba Art and the Making of History,* ed. M. N. Roberts and A. F. Roberts, 61–83. New York: The Museum of African Art.

Digombe, Lizare; P. R. Schmidt; V. Mouleingui-Boukosso; J.-B. Mombo; and M. Locko. 1988. "The Development of an Early Iron Age Prehistory in Gabon." *Current Anthropology* 29(1): 179–84.

Donley-Reid, Linda. 1982. "House Power: Swahili Space and Symbolic Markers." In *Symbolic and Structural Archaeology,* ed. I. Hodder, 63–73. Cambridge: Cambridge University Press.

Durham, Deborah, and J. Fernandez. 1991. "Tropical Dominions: The Figurative Struggle over Domains of Belonging and Apartness in Africa." In *Beyond Metaphor: The Theory of Tropes in Anthropology,* ed. J. Fernandez, 190–210. Stanford: Stanford University Press.

Echard, Nicole. 1983. "Scories et symboles: Remarques sur la métallurgie hausa du fer au Niger." In *Métallurgies Africaines,* ed. N. Echard, 209–24. Mémoires de la Société des Africanistes 9.

Ehret, Christopher. 1991. "The African Lakes Region in the Early Iron Age: Shifting Mosaics of Cultural and Economic Interaction." Paper presented at the African Studies Association annual meetings, St. Louis.

Ehret, Christopher. n.d. "The Classical Age of Eastern African History: 1000 B.C. to A.D. 300." Manuscript.

Eliade, M. 1961. *The Forge and the Crucible.* Chicago: University of Chicago Press.

Eluyemi, Omotoso. 1977. "Excavations at Isoya near Ile-Ife (Nigeria) in 1972." *West African Journal of Archaeology* 4: 99–109.

Estermann, C. 1976. "The Non Bantu People." In *Ethnography of Southwestern Angola,* ed. G. D. Gibson, 1–49. New York: Africana Publishing.

Feierman, Steven. 1974. *The Shambaa Kingdom: A History.* Madison: University of Wisconsin Press.

Feierman, Steven. 1990. *Peasant Intellectuals: Anthropology and History in Tanzania.* Madison: University of Wisconsin Press.

Fells, S. 1983. "The Structure and Constitution of Archaeological Ferrous Process Slags." Ph.D. dissertation, University of Aston.

Fernandez, James. 1977. "Edification by Puzzlement." In *Explorations in African Systems of Thought,* ed. I. Karp and C. S. Bird, 44–59. Washington and London: Smithsonian Institution Press.

Fernandez, James, ed. 1991. *Beyond Metaphors: The Theory of Tropes in Anthropology.* Stanford: Stanford University Press.

Fisher, Ruth. 1970. *Twilight Tales of the Black Baganda.* London: Frank Cass.

Fowler, I. 1990. "Babungo: A Study of Iron Production, Trade, and Power in a Nineteenth-Century Ndop Plain Chiefdom (Cameroons)." Ph.D. dissertation, University of London.

Friede, H.; A. Hejja; A. Koursaris; and R. Steel. 1984. "Thermal Aspects of the Smelting of Iron-Ore in Reconstructed South African Iron Age Furnaces." *Journal of the South African Institute of Mining and Metallurgy* 84: 285–97.

Garlake, Peter. 1977. "Excavations on the Woye Asiri Family Land in Ife, Western Nigeria." *West African Journal of Archaeology* 7: 57–96.

Goodway, Martha. 1987. "Phosphorus in Antique Iron Music Wire." *Science* 236: 927–32.

Goody, Jack. 1971. *Technology, Tradition, and the State.* Cambridge: Cambridge University Press.

Gordon, Robert. 1984. "The Quality of Wrought Iron Evaluated by Microprobe Analysis." In *Microbean Analysis,* ed. A. D. Romig Jr. and J. I. Goldstein, 231–34. San Francisco: San Francisco Press.

Goucher, Candice. 1984. "The Iron Industry of Bassar, Togo." Ph.D. dissertation, University of California, Los Angeles.

Goucher, Candice, and E. Herbert. 1996. "The Blooms of Banjeli: Technology and Gender in West African Ironmaking." In *The Culture and Technology of African Iron Production,* ed. P. R. Schmidt, 40–57. Gainesville: University Press of Florida.

Gould, R. A. 1980. *Living Archaeology.* Cambridge: Cambridge University Press.

Gould, R. A., and Patty Jo Watson. 1982. "A Dialogue on the Meaning and Use of Analogy in Ethnoarchaeological Reasoning." *Journal of Anthropological Archaeology* 1: 355–81.

Gunn, Joel D. n.d. "A Framework for the Middle-Late Holocene Transition: Astronomical and Geophysical Conditions." Forthcoming in *Southeastern Archaeology.*

Haaland, Randi. 1985. "Iron Production, Its Socio-cultural Context and Ecological Implications." In *African Iron Working—Ancient and Traditional,* ed. R. Haaland and P. Shinnie, 50–72. Oslo: Norwegian University Press.

Hall, Martin. 1984. "The Burden of Tribalism: The Social Context of Southern Africa Iron-Age Studies." *American Antiquity* 49(3): 455–67.

Hall, Martin. 1990. "'Hidden History': Iron Age Archaeology in Southern Africa."

In *A History of African Archaeology,* ed. P. Robertshaw, 59–77. London: James Currey.

Hamilton, Alan; D. Taylor; and J. C. Vogel. 1986. "Early Forest Clearance and Environmental Degradation in South-west Uganda." *Nature* 320: 164–67.

Handsman, Russell. 1981. "Early Capitalism and the Center Village of Canaan, Connecticut: A Study of Transformations and Separations." *Artifacts* 9: 1–21.

Handsman, Russell. 1983. "Towards Archaeological Histories of Robbins Swamp." *Artifacts* 11(3): 1–20.

Handsman, Russell, and T. Lamb-Richmond. 1995. "Confronting Colonialism: The Mahican and Schaghticoke Peoples and Us." In *Making Alternative Histories: The Practice of Archaeology and History in Non-Western Settings,* ed. P. R. Schmidt and T. C. Patterson, 87–117. Santa Fe: School of American Research Press.

Hansen, M. 1958. *Constitution of Binary Alloys.* New York: McGraw-Hill.

Harding, Sandra. 1986. *The Science Question in Feminism.* Ithaca, N.Y.: Cornell University Press.

Harding, Sandra. 1991. *Whose Science? Whose Knowledge?* Ithaca, N.Y.: Cornell University Press.

Herbert, Eugenia. 1993. *Iron, Gender and Power: Rituals of Transformation in African Societies.* Bloomington and Indianapolis: Indiana University Press.

Heusch, Luc de. 1982. *The Drunken King, or The Origin of the State.* Bloomington: Indiana University Press.

Hiernaux, Jean. 1968. "Bantu Expansion: The Evidence from Physical Anthropology Confronted with Linguistic and Archaeological Evidence." *Journal of African History* 9: 505–15.

Hiernaux, Jean, and M. Maquet. 1960. "Cultures préhistorique de l'âge de métaux au Rwanda-Urundi et au Kivu, Congo Belge II." *Mémoires de l'Académie royale de Sciences d'Outre-Mer* 10: 5–88.

Hill, James. 1994. "Prehistoric Cognition and the Science of Archaeology." In *The Ancient Mind: Elements of Cognitive Archaeology,* ed. C. Renfrew and E. B. W. Zubrow, 83–92. Cambridge: Cambridge University Press.

Hodder, Ian. 1982a. *Symbols in Action.* Cambridge: Cambridge University Press.

Hodder, Ian, ed. 1982b. *Symbolic and Structural Archaeology.* Cambridge: Cambridge University Press.

Hodder, Ian. 1986. *Reading the Past: Current Approaches to Interpretation in Archaeology.* Cambridge: Cambridge University Press.

Hodder, Ian. 1991. "Interpretive Archaeology and Its Role." *American Antiquity* 56(1): 7–18.

Hopkins, B. E., and H. R. Tipler. 1958. "The Effect of Phosphorus on the Tensile and Notch-Impact Properties of High-Purity Iron and Iron Carbon Alloys." *Journal of the Iron and Steel Institute* 188: 218–37.

Huffman, Thomas. 1984. "Expressive Space in the Zimbabwe Culture." *Man,* n.s. 19: 593–612.

Huffman, Thomas. 1986. "Cognitive Studies in the Iron Age in Southern Africa." *World Archaeology* 18(1): 84–95.

Hunt, Eva. 1977. *The Transformation of the Hummingbird: Cultural Roots of a Zinacantecan Mythical Poem.* Ithaca and London: Cornell University Press.

Irele, A. 1991. "The African Scholar: Is Black Africa Entering the Dark Ages of Scholarship?" *Transition* 51: 56–69.

Jakobson, Roman. 1956. "Two Aspects of Language and Two Types of Aphasic

Disturbances." In *Fundamentals of Language*, ed. R. Jakobson and M. Halle, 55–87. The Hague: Mouton.

Kaijage, Frederick. 1993. "AIDS Control and the Burden of History in Northwestern Tanzania." *Population and Environment: A Journal of Interdisciplinary Studies* 14(3): 279–300.

Killick, David. 1990. "Technology in Its Social Setting: Bloomery Iron-working at Kasungu, Malawi, 1860–1940." Ph.D. dissertation, Yale University.

Killick, David. 1996. "On Claims for 'Advanced' Ironworking Technology in Precolonial Africa." In *The Culture and Technology of African Iron Production*, ed. P. R. Schmidt, 247–66. Gainesville: University Press of Florida.

Kirknaes, Jesper. 1980. *Jernsmeden—sadan arbejder warongo-smedene i Tanzania*. Holte, Denmark: Skarv.

Kjekshus, Helge. 1977. *Ecology Control and Economic Development in East African History: The Case of Tanganyika, 1850–1950*. London: Heinemann.

Kus, Susan. 1979. "Archaeology and Ideology: The Symbolic Organization of Space." Ph.D. dissertation, University of Michigan.

Kus, Susan. 1983. "The Social Representation of Space: Dimensioning the Cosmological and the Quotidian." In *Archaeological Hammers and Theories*, ed. J. Moore and A. S. Keene, 277–98. New York: Academic Press.

Langdale-Brown, I.; H. A. Osmaston; and J. G. Wilson. 1964. *The Vegetation of Uganda and Its Bearing on Land Use*. Entebbe: The Government Printer.

Laseski, Ruth. 1983. "Modern Pollen Date and Holocene Climate Change in Eastern Africa." Ph.D. dissertation, Brown University.

Laurie, W., and H. Trant. 1954. *A Health Survey of Bukoba District, Tanganyika*. Nairobi: East Africa Medical Survey, Monograph no. 2.

Lemonnier, Pierre. 1992. *Elements for an Anthropology of Technology*. Anthropological Papers, Museum of Anthropology, no. 88. Ann Arbor: University of Michigan.

Leone, Mark. 1984. "Interpreting Ideology in Historical Archaeology: Using the Rules of Perspective in the William Paca Garden in Annapolis, Maryland." In *Ideology, Power and Prehistory*, ed. D. Miller and C. Tilley, 25–35. Cambridge: Cambridge University Press.

Leone, Mark, and E. Kryder-Reid. 1992. "Critical Perspectives on Work concerning Charles Carroll of Carrollton." In *Representations in Archaeology*, ed. J.-C. Gardin and C. Peebles, 151–67. Bloomington and Indianapolis: Indiana University Press.

Leone, Mark, and P. Potter. 1988. "Introduction: Issues in Historical Archaeology." In *The Recovery of Meaning: Historical Archaeology in the Eastern United States*, ed. M. Leone and P. Potter, 1–22. Washington, D.C.: Smithsonian Institution Press.

Leone, Mark; P. Potter; and P. Shackel. 1987. "Towards a Critical Archaeology." *Current Anthropology* 28: 283–302.

Lewis-Williams, J. D. 1981. *Believing and Seeing: Symbolic Meanings in Southern San Rock Paintings*. London: Academic Press.

Lewis-Williams, J. D. 1982. "The Economic and Social Context of Southern San Rock Art." *Current Anthropology* 23: 429–49.

Lewis-Williams, J. D., and Thomas A. Dawson. 1994. "Aspects of Rock Art Research: A Critical Retrospective." In *Contested Images: Diversity in Southern African Rock Art Research*, ed. T. A. Dawson and J. D. Lewis-Williams, 201–21. Johannesburg: Witwatersrand University Press.

Lévi-Strauss, Claude. 1966. *The Savage Mind.* Chicago: University of Chicago Press.

Lwihura, M. 1988. "Seroprevalence: HIV Infection in Kagera Region, Tanzania— A Population-Based Study." Stockholm: International Conference on AIDS, Abstract no. 5034.

MacEachern, Scott. 1994. "'Symbolic Reservoirs' and Inter-group Relations: West African Examples." *The African Archaeological Review* 12: 205–24.

MacLean, M. R. 1994. "Late Stone Age and Early Iron Age Settlement Patterns in Rakai District, South-western Uganda." Paper delivered at the International Conference on the Growth of Farming Communities in Africa from the Equator Southwards, Cambridge, July 4–8.

Mapunda, Bertram B. 1995. "An Archaeological View of the History and Variation of Iron Working in Southwestern Tanzania." Ph.D. dissertation, University of Florida.

Marcus, Joyce, and K. Flannery. 1994. "Ancient Zapotec Ritual and Religion: An Application of the Direct Historical Approach." In *The Ancient Mind: Elements of Cognitive Archaeology,* ed. C. Renfrew and E. Zubrow, 55–74. Cambridge: Cambridge University Press.

Maret, Pierre de. 1980. "Ceux qui jouent avec le feu—la place du forgeron en Afrique Centrale." *Africa* 50: 263–79.

Maret, Pierre de. 1985. "The Smith's Myth and the Origin of Leadership in Central Africa." In *African Iron Working—Ancient and Traditional,* ed. R. Haaland and P. Shinnie, 73–87. Oslo: Norwegian University Press.

McGuire, Randall. 1992. *A Marxist Archaeology.* San Diego: Academic Press.

McGuire, Randall, and Robert Paynter. 1991. *The Archaeology of Inequality.* Oxford and Cambridge, Mass.: Basil Blackwell.

McIntosh, Roderick. 1992. "From Traditional African Art to the Archaeology of Form in the Middle Niger." In *Dell'Archeologia all'Arte Tradizionnale Africana,* ed. G. Pessoli, 145–51. Milan: Centro Studi Archeologia Africana.

McMaster, David. 1960. "Change of Regional Balance in the Bukoba District of Tanganyika." *Geographical Review,* 50: 73–88.

Miller, Daniel, and Christopher Tilley, eds. 1984. *Ideology, Power, and Prehistory.* Cambridge: Cambridge University Press.

Miller, Joseph. 1980. "The Dynamics of Oral Tradition in Africa." In *The African Past Speaks,* ed. J. Miller, 1–59. Folkestone: Dawson.

Morton, G. R., and J. Wingrove. 1969. "Constitution of Bloomery Slags, Part I: Roman." *Journal of the Iron and Steel Institute* 207: 1556–64.

Morton, G. R., and J. Wingrove. 1972. "Constitution of Bloomery Slags, Part II: Medieval." *Journal of the Iron and Steel Institute* 210: 478–88.

Muhly, Frank, and P. R. Schmidt. 1988. Film script for *The Tree of Iron.* Gainesville: Foundation for African Prehistory and Archaeology.

Patterson, Thomas. 1995. *Toward a Social History of Archaeology in the United States.* Fort Worth: Harcourt Brace.

Paynter, Robert, and R. McGuire. 1991. "An Introduction." In *The Archaeology of Inequality,* ed. R. McGuire and R. Paynter, 1–11. Oxford: Basil Blackwell.

Pole, Leonard M. 1974a. *Iron Smelting in Northern Ghana.* Accra: National Museum of Ghana, Occasional Papers no. 6.

Pole, Leonard M. 1974b. "Account of an Iron-Smelting Operation at Lawra, Upper Region." *Ghana Journal of Science* 14: 127–36.

Pole, Leonard M. 1975. "Iron-working Apparatus and Techniques: Upper Region of Ghana." *West African Journal of Archaeology* 5: 11–39.

Posnansky, Merrick. 1966. "Kingship, Archaeology, and Historical Myth." *Uganda Journal* 30: 1–12.

Posnansky, Merrick. 1968. "The Excavations of an Ankole Capital Site at Bweyorere." *Uganda Journal* 32: 165–82.

Posnansky, Merrick. 1969. "Bigo bya Mugenyi." *Uganda Journal* 33: 125–50.

Redinha, J. 1953. *Campanha etnografica ao Tchiboco*. No. 1. Lisbon.

Rehder, J. E. 1986. "Use of Preheated Air in Primitive Furnaces: Comment on Views of Avery and Schmidt." *Journal of Field Archaeology* 13: 351–53.

Rehse, H. 1910. *Kiziba: Land und Leute*. Stuttgart: Verlag van Strecker und Schröder.

Reid, Andrew. 1990. "Ntusi and Its Hinterland: Further Investigations of the Later Iron Age and Pastoral Ecology in Southern Uganda." *Nyame Akuma* 33: 26–28.

Reid, Andrew. 1991. "The Role of Cattle in the Later Iron Age Communities of Southern Uganda." Ph.D. dissertation, University of Cambridge.

Reid, Andrew. 1996. "Early Settlement and Social Organization in the Interlacustrine Region." *Azania* 29–30: 303–13.

Reid, Andrew, and Rachael M. MacLean. 1995. "Symbolism and the Social Context of Iron Production in Karagwe." *World Archaeology* 27(1): 144–61.

Reining, Priscilla. 1967. "The Haya: The Agrarian System of a Sedentary People." Ph.D. dissertation, University of Chicago.

Renfrew, Colin. 1994. "Towards a Cognitive Archaeology." In *The Ancient Mind: Elements of Cognitive Archaeology*, ed. C. Renfrew and E. Zubrow, 3–12. Cambridge: Cambridge University Press.

Richter, H. 1900. "Notitzen uber Lebensweise, Zeitrechnung, Industrie und Handwerk der Bewohner des Bezirk Bukoba." *Mittheilungen (von Forschungs-reisenden und Gelerhrten) aus dem Deutshen Schutzgebieten* 13: 115–26.

Ricoeur, Paul. 1977. *The Rule of Metaphor: Multi-disciplinary Studies of the Creation of Meaning in Language*. Toronto and Buffalo: University of Toronto Press.

Roberts, Allen F. 1993. "Iron, Master of Them All." Paper delivered at the 5th Stanley Conference of African Art, University of Iowa, March 5–6.

Robertshaw, Peter. 1988. "The Interlacustrine Region: A Progress Report." *Nyame Akuma* 30: 37–38.

Robertshaw, Peter. 1994. "Archaeological Survey, Ceramic Analysis, and State Formation in Western Uganda." *The African Archaeological Review* 12: 105–31.

Rosemond, C. C. de. 1943. "Iron Smelting in the Kahama District." *Tanganyika Notes and Records* 16: 79–84.

Rostoker, W., and B. Bronson. 1990. *Pre-industrial Iron: Its Technology and Ethnology*. Philadelphia: Archaeomaterials Monograph, no. 1.

Rostoker, W., and J. R. Dvorak. 1986. "Additional Studies on the Smithsonian Iron Bloom." In *Proceedings of the 24th International Archaeometry Symposium*, ed. J. S. Olin and M. J. Blackman, 279–89. Washington, D.C.: Smithsonian Institution Press.

Rowlands, Michael. 1985. "Notes on the Material Symbolism of Grassfields Palaces." *Paideuma* 31: 203–13.

Rowlands, Michael, and Jean-Pierre Warnier. 1993. "The Magical Production of Iron in the Cameroon Grassfields." In *The Archaeology of Africa: Food, Metals, and Towns,* ed. T. Shaw, B. Andah, P. Sinclair, and A. Okpoko, 512–50. London: Routledge.

Sahlins, Marshall. 1985. *Islands of History.* Chicago and London: University of Chicago.

Salmon, Marrilee H. 1982. *Philosophy and Archaeology.* New York: Academic Press.

Saltman, Carlyn; C. Goucher; and E. Herbert. 1986. *The Blooms of Banjeli: Technology and Gender in West African Ironmaking.* Video.

Samuels, Leonard E. 1980. *Optical Microscopy of Carbon Steels.* Metals Park, Ohio: American Society for Metals.

Sasoon, Hamo. 1983. "Kings, Cattle and Blacksmiths: Royal Insignia and Religious Symbolism in the Interlacustrine States." *Azania* 18: 93–106.

Schiffer, Michael. 1987. *Formation Processes of the Archaeological Record.* Albuquerque: University of New Mexico Press.

Schmidt, Peter R. 1974. "An Investigation of Early and Late Iron Age Cultures through Oral Tradition and Archaeology: An Interdisciplinary Case Study in Buhaya, Tanzania." Ph.D. dissertation, Northwestern University.

Schmidt, Peter R. 1978. *Historical Archaeology: A Structural Approach in an African Culture.* Westport: Greenwood Press.

Schmidt, Peter R. 1980. "Early Iron Age Communities and Industrial Locales in West Lake." *Tanzania Notes and Records* 84–85: 77–94.

Schmidt, Peter R. 1981. *The Origins of Iron Smelting in Africa: A Complex Technology in Tanzania.* Research Papers in Anthropology, no. 1. Providence: Brown University.

Schmidt, Peter R. 1983a. "An Alternative to a Strictly Materialist Perspective: A Review of Historical Archaeology, Ethnoarchaeology, and Symbolic Approaches in African Archaeology." *American Antiquity* 48(1): 62–81.

Schmidt, Peter R. 1983b. "Cultural Meaning and History in African Myth." *International Journal of Oral History* 4: 165–83.

Schmidt, Peter R. 1983c. "Further Evidence for an Advanced Prehistoric Iron Technology in Africa." *Journal of Field Archaeology* 10: 421–34.

Schmidt, Peter R. 1985. "Symboling in Archaeology: Towards a More Humanistic Science." Paper presented at the annual meeting of the Society for American Archaeology, Denver, May 5.

Schmidt, Peter R. 1988. "Eastern Expressions of the 'Mwitu' Tradition: Early Iron Age Industry of the Usambara Mountains, Tanzania." *Nyame Akuma* 30: 36–37.

Schmidt, Peter R. 1989. "Early Exploitation and Settlement in the Usambara Mountains." In *Forest Conservation in the East Usambara Mountains, Tanzania,* ed. A. Hamilton and R. Bensted-Smith, 75–79. Gland, Switzerland: IUCN.

Schmidt, Peter R. 1990. "Oral Traditions, Archaeology and History: A Short Reflective History." In *A History of African Archaeology,* ed. Peter Robertshaw, 252–70. London: James Currey.

Schmidt, Peter R. 1992. "An Interpretative Model for Sustainability Based on the Use and Transformation of a Forested Landscape in Eastern Equatorial Africa." In *Environment and Archaeology: Emerging Trends and New Techniques for Heritage Management and Sustainable Development in Tropical Forest Areas,* ed. G. Pantel, K. Schneider, and G. Loyola-Black, 227–34. Atlanta: United States Forest Service.

Schmidt, Peter. R. 1994. "Historical Ecology and Landscape Transformation in

Eastern Equatorial Africa." In *Historical Ecology: Cultural Knowledge and Changing Landscapes,* ed. C. Crumley, 99–125. Santa Fe: School of American Research Press.

Schmidt, Peter R. 1995. "Using Archaeology to Remake African History." In *Making Alternative Histories,* ed. P. R. Schmidt and T. C. Patterson, 119–47. Santa Fe: School of American Research Press.

Schmidt, Peter R., ed. 1996a. *The Culture and Technology of African Iron Production.* Gainesville: University Press of Florida.

Schmidt, Peter R. 1996b. "Cultural Representation of African Iron Production." In *The Culture and Technology of African Iron Production,* ed. P. R. Schmidt, 1–28. Gainesville: University Press of Florida.

Schmidt, Peter R. 1996c. "Reconfiguring the Barongo: Reproductive Symbolism and Reproduction among a Work Association of Iron Smelters." In *The Culture and Technology of African Iron Production,* ed. P. R. Schmidt, 74–127. Gainesville: University Press of Florida.

Schmidt, Peter R. 1996d. "Rhythmed Time and Its Archaeological Implications." In *Aspects of African Prehistory: Papers from the 10th Congress of the PanAfrican Association of Prehistory and Other Related Studies,* 655–62. Harare: University of Zimbabwe.

Schmidt, Peter R., and D. H. Avery. 1978. "Complex Iron Smelting and Prehistoric Culture in Tanzania." *Science* 201: 1085–89.

Schmidt, Peter R., and S. T. Childs. 1985. "Innovation and Industry during the Early Iron Age in East Africa: The KM2 and KM3 Sites of Northwest Tanzania." *The African Archaeological Review* 3: 53–94.

Schmidt, Peter R., and S. T. Childs. 1995. "Ancient African Iron Production." *American Scientist* 83: 524–33.

Schmidt, Peter R., and S. T. Childs. 1996. "Actualistic Models for Interpretation of Two Early Iron Age Industrial Sites in Northwestern Tanzania." In *The Culture and Technology of African Iron Production,* ed. P. R. Schmidt, 186–233. Gainesville: University Press of Florida.

Schmidt, Peter R.; L. Digombe; M. Locko; and V. Mouleingui-Boukosso. 1985. "Newly Dated Iron Age Sites in Gabon." *Nyame Akuma* 26: 16–18.

Schmidt, Peter R., and B. B. M. Mapunda. 1997. "Ideology and the Archaeological Record in Africa: Interpreting Symbolism in Iron Smelting Technology." *Journal of Anthropological Archaeology* 16.

Schmidt, Peter R., and Thomas C. Patterson, eds. 1995a. *Making Alternative Histories: The Practice of Archaeology and History in Non-Western Cultures.* Santa Fe: School of American Research Press.

Schmidt, Peter R., and Thomas C. Patterson. 1995b. "From Constructing to Making Alternative Histories." In *Making Alternative Histories: The Practice of Archaeology and History in Non-Western Cultures,* ed. P. R. Schmidt and T. C. Patterson, 1–24. Santa Fe: School of American Research Press.

Schoenbrun, David. 1990. "Early History of Eastern Africa's Great Lakes Region: Linguistic, Ecological, and Archaeological Approaches ca. 500 B.C. to ca. A.D. 1000." Ph.D. dissertation, University of California, Los Angeles.

Schoenbrun, David. 1993a. "We Are What We Eat: Ancient Agriculture between the Great Lakes." *Journal of African History* 34: 1–31.

Schoenbrun, David. 1993b. "Cattle Herds and Banana Gardens: The Historical

Geography of the Western Great Lakes Region, ca AD 800–1500." *The African Archaeological Review* 11: 39–72.

Schoenbrun, David. 1994. "Great Lakes Bantu: Classification and Settlement." *SUGIA* 14: 1–62.

Schoenbrun, David. 1995. "A Narrative History of People and Forests between the Great Lakes: Ca. 1000 B.C. to ca. 1500 A.D." *Working Papers in African Studies*, no. 154. Boston: African Studies Center, Boston University.

Seitel, Peter. 1972. "Proverb and the Structure of Metaphor among the Haya of Tanzania." Ph.D. dissertation, University of Pennsylvania.

Shanks, Michael, and C. Tilley, eds. 1987. *Social Theory and Archaeology.* Cambridge: Polity Press.

Shaw, Thurston. 1977. *Unearthing Igbo-Ukwu: Archaeological Discoveries in Eastern Nigeria.* Ibadan: Oxford University Press.

Sherratt, Andrew. 1994. "The Relativity of Theory." In *Archaeological Theory: Who Sets the Agenda?,* ed. A. Sherratt and N. Yoffee, 119–30. Cambridge: Cambridge University Press.

Soper, Robert. 1967. "Iron Age Sites in North-eastern Tanzania." *Azania* 2: 19–36.

Soper, Robert. 1971. "Iron Age Archaeological Sites in the Chobi Sector of Murchison Falls National Park, Uganda." *Azania* 6: 51–87.

Stahl, Ann. 1993. "Concepts of Time and Approaches to Archaeological Reasoning in Historical Perspective." *American Antiquity* 58(2): 235–60.

Stahl, Ann. 1994. "Change and Continuity in the Banda Area, Ghana: The Direct Historical Approach." *Journal of Field Archaeology* 21: 181–203.

Stanley, G. C. 1931. "Some Products of Native Iron Smelting." *South African Journal of Science* 28: 131–34.

Stead, J. 1915. "Iron, Carbon, and Phosphorus." *Journal of the Iron and Steel Institute* 91: 140–81.

Stead, J. 1918. "Iron, Carbon, and Phosphorus." *Journal of the Iron and Steel Institute* 97: 389–412.

Sterner, Judy. 1992. "Sacred Pots and 'Symbolic Reservoirs' in the Mandara Highlands of Northern Cameroon." In *An African Commitment: Papers in Honor of Peter Lewis Shinnie,* ed. J. Sterner and N. David, 171–80. Calgary: The University of Calgary Press.

Stewart, K. 1993. "Iron Age Ceramic Studies in Great Lakes Eastern Africa: A Critical and Historiographical Review." *The African Archaeological Review* 11: 21–37.

Stirnimann, H. 1976. *Existenzgundlagen und traditionelles Handwerk de Pengwa von SW.-Tansania.* Freiburn: Schweiz.

Stothers, R. B. 1984. "Mystery Cloud of AD 536." *Nature* 307(5949): 344–46.

Sutton, J. E. G. 1993. "The Antecedents of the Interlacustrine Kingdoms." *Journal of African History* 34: 33–64.

Tantala, Rene. 1989. "The Early History of Kitara in Western Uganda: Process Models of Religious and Political Change." Ph.D. dissertation, University of Wisconsin.

Taylor, David, and Robert Marchant. 1996. "Human Impact in the Interlacustrine Region: Long-term Pollen Records from the Rukiga Highlands." *Azania* 29–30: 283–95.

Tessmann, Gustav. 1913. *Die Pangwe.* Berlin.

Tholander, E. 1987. "Experimental Studies on Early Iron-Making." Ph.D. dissertation, Royal Institute of Technology, Stockholm.

Tilley, Christopher, ed. 1993. *Interpretative Archaeology.* Providence and Oxford: Berg.

Todd, Judith. 1979. "Studies of the African Iron Age." *Journal of Metals* 31: 39–45.

Todd, Judith. 1985. "Iron Production by the Dimi of Ethiopia." In *African Iron Working—Ancient and Traditional,* ed. R. Haaland and P. Shinnie, 88–101. Oslo: Norwegian University Press.

Todd, Judith, and J. A. Charles. 1978. "Ethiopian Bloomery Iron and the Significance of Inclusions Analysis in Iron Studies." *Journal of the Historical Metallurgical Society* 12: 63–87.

Trigger, Bruce. 1980. "Archaeology and the Image of the American Indian." *American Antiquity* 45: 662–76.

Tringham, Ruth. 1978. "Experimentation, Ethnoarchaeology, and the Leapfrogs in Archaeological Methodology." In *Explorations in Ethnoarchaeology,* ed. Richard Gould, 169–99. Albuquerque: University of New Mexico Press.

Trowell, Margaret. 1941. "Some Royal Craftsmen of Buganda." *Uganda Journal* 3(2): 47–64.

Turner, Terrance. 1991. "'We Are Parrots,' 'Twins Are Birds': Play of Tropes as Operational Structure." In *Beyond Metaphor: The Theory of Tropes in Anthropology,* ed. J. W. Fernandez, 121–58. Stanford: Stanford University Press.

Tylecote, Ronald. 1965. "Iron Smelting in Pre-industrial Communities." *Journal of the Iron and Steel Institute* 203: 340–48.

Tylecote, Ronald. 1976. *A History of Metallurgy.* London: The Metals Society.

Tylecote, Ronald. 1981. "From Pot Bellows to Tuyeres." *Levant* 13: 107–18.

Tylecote, R. F.; J. N. Austin; and A. E. Wraith. 1971. "The Mechanism of Bloomery Process in Shaft Furnaces." *Journal of the Iron and Steel Institute* 204: 342–63.

Tylecote, Ronald, and B. Gilmore. 1986. *The Metallography of Early Ferrous Edge Tools and Edged Weapons.* Oxford: British Archaeological Reports, British Series no. 155.

Van Grunderbeek, Marie-Claude. 1992. "Chronologie de l'Âge du Fer Ancien au Burundi, au Rwanda et dans la région des Grands Lacs." *Azania* 27: 53–80.

Van Grunderbeek, Marie-Claude, and H. Doutrelepont. 1988. "Étude de charbons de bois provenent des sites métallurgiques de l'Âge du Fer Ancien au Rwanda et au Burundi." *PACT: Journal of the European Study Group on Physical, Chemical, Mathematical and Biological Techniques Applied to Archaeology* 22: 281–95.

Van Grunderbeek, Marie-Claude; E. Roche; and H. Doutrelepont. 1983a. *Le Premier âge du fer au Rwanda et au Burundi. Archéologie et environnement.* Brussels: I.F.A.Q.

Van Grunderbeek, Marie-Claude; E. Roche; and H. Doutrelepont. 1983b. "La Métallurgie ancienne au Rwanda et au Burundi." *Journées de Paléométallurgie, Actes du colloque de Compiègne* (22–23 Feb.): 407–23.

Van Grunderbeek, Marie-Claude; H. Doutrelepont; and E. Roche. 1984. "Influence humaine sur le milieu au Rwanda et au Burundi a l'âge du fer ancien (220–665 A.D.). Apports de la palynologie et de l'étude des charbons de bois." *Revue de paléobiologie* (April): 221–29.

van der Merwe, N., and D. Avery. 1987. "Science and Magic in African Technology: Traditional Iron Smelting in Malawi." *Africa* 57: 143–72.

van der Merwe, N., and R. Scully. 1971. "The Palborwa Story: Archaeological and Ethnographic Investigation of a South African Iron Age Group." *World Archaeology* 3: 178–96.

Van Noten, Francis. 1983. *Histoire Archéologique de Rwanda.* Série in 8°, Sciences Humaines, no. 112. Tervuren: Musée Royal de l'Afrique Centrale.

Van Noten, Francis. 1985. "Ancient and Modern Iron Smelting in Central Africa: Zaire, Rwanda, and Burundi." In *African Iron Working: Ancient and Traditional,* ed. R. Haaland and P. Shinnie, 102–20. Oslo: Norwegian University Press.

Vansina, Jan. 1965. *Oral Traditions: A Study in Historical Methodology.* Chicago: Aldine.

Vansina, Jan. 1978. *The Children of Woot: A History of the Kuba People.* Madison: University of Wisconsin Press.

Vansina, Jan. 1983. "Is Elegance Proof?: Structuralism and African History." *History in Africa* 10: 317–47.

Vansina, Jan. 1994. *Living with Africa.* Madison: University of Wisconsin Press.

Vargas Arenas, Iraida. 1995. "The Perception of History and Archaeology in Latin America: A Theoretical Approach." In *Making Alternative Histories,* ed. P. R. Schmidt and T. C. Patterson, 47–67. Santa Fe: School of American Research Press.

Warnier, Jean-Pierre, and Ian Fowler. 1979. "A Nineteenth-Century Ruhr in Central Africa." *Africa* 49(4): 330–50.

Watson, Richard. 1990. "Ozymandias, King of Kings: Postprocessual Radical Archaeology as Critique." *American Antiquity* 55(4): 673–89.

Wembah-Rashid, John. 1973. *Iron Working in Ufipa.* Dar es Salaam: National Museum.

White, Luise. 1990. *The Comforts of Home: Prostitution in Colonial Nairobi.* Chicago: University of Chicago Press.

Willett, Frank. 1970. "Excavations at Ita Yemoo Ife, Nigeria, 1957–63." Actes du VIIᵉ Congrès International des Sciences Préhistoriques et Protohistoriques, *Academia,* Part 1, 180–82. Prague: Institut d'archéologie de l'Académie Tchécoslovaque des Sciences.

Willis, R. 1981. *A State in the Making.* Bloomington: Indiana University Press.

Wise, R. 1958. "Iron Smelting in Ufipa." *Tanganyika Notes and Records* 51: 106–11.

Wyckaert, R. P. 1914. "Forgerons poies et forgerons chrétiens au Tanganyika." *Anthropos* 9: 371–80.

Wylie, Alison. 1982. "An Analogy by Any Other Name Is Just As Analogical: A Commentary on the Gould-Watson Dialogue." *Journal of Anthropological Archaeology* 1: 382–401.

Wylie, Alison. 1985. "The Reaction against Analogy." In *Advances in Archaeological Method and Theory,* ed. M. Schiffer, vol. 8, pp. 63–111. New York: Academic Press.

Wylie, Alison. 1987. "The Philosophy of Ambivalence: Sandra Harding on 'the Science Question in Feminism'." *Canadian Journal of Philosophy,* supplementary volume 13: 59–73.

Wylie, Alison. 1992. "The Interplay of Evidential Constraints and Political Interests: Recent Archaeological Research on Gender." *American Antiquity* 57(1): 15–35.

Wylie, Alison. 1994. "A Proliferation of New Archaeologies: 'Beyond Objectivism and Relativism'." In *Archaeological Theory: Who Sets the Agenda?*, ed. N. Yoffee and A. Sherratt, 20–26. Cambridge: Cambridge University Press.

Wylie, Alison. 1995. "Alternative Histories: Epistemic Disunity and Political Integrity." In *Making Alternative Histories: The Practice of Archaeology and History in Non-Western Cultures,* ed. P. R. Schmidt and T. C. Patterson, 255–72. Santa Fe: School of American Research Press.

Yentsch, Anne E. 1994. *A Chesapeake Family and Their Slaves.* Cambridge: Cambridge University Press.

Zubrow, Ezra. 1994. "Cognitive Archaeology Reconsidered." In *The Ancient Mind: Elements of Cognitive Archaeology,* ed. C. Renfrew and E. Zubrow, 187–90. Cambridge: Cambridge University Press.

Index

Abiola, Irele, 11

Africa. *See* Buhaya; History; Oral history and oral traditions; specific countries

African History (Curtin et al., 1990), 8

Age: and oral descriptions of iron smelting, 47–49; and spatial separation of task areas in iron smelting, 192–93

Agriculture: and history of iron technology in Buhaya, 15–16, 17, 19–20, 108; present status of in Buhaya, 22, 286–87; impact of on archaeological research in Buhaya, 23–24; symbolic linkage between iron and, 227; and settlement history of Buhaya, 270–72; iron smelting in Early Iron Age and forest clearance for, 274, 277, 278; global impact of volcano eruption in 536 A.D., 278; environmental degradation and political change in Buhaya, 281; and ecological stress in post-independence Tanzania, 286–87

AIDS: epidemic of in contemporary Buhaya, 287, 303n.8

"Akata Eibumba" (song): reproductive symbolism in, 222

Alumina: content of in smelting clays, 115; and hercynite crystals in slags, 132

Analogy: concerns about use of in archaeology, 129; number of elements in and viability of, 300n.1

Analytical models: of tuyere performance, 159–64

Angola: women and iron smelting among Kwanyama of southern, 217; metonymic processes of transformation in ironworking symbolism of Tshokwe of northeast, 227–29

Archaeology: Childe's view of relationship between history and, 2; and African history, 2–3, 8–11; and experimental approach to history of iron technology in Buhaya, 11–12; impact of agriculture on research in Buhaya, 23–24; of symbols, 27–28, 209–30; use of analogy in, 129; and physical evidence of historical smelting processes, 142–53; dynamic models of iron technology in Buhaya, 154–89; evidence for spatial organization of smelting, 195–98; middle-range theory and comparative approach, 207; ritual and symbolism in ironworking, 209–30; and interpretation of physical remains within

context of ideology, 230; cross-cultural examination of symbolic expressions of ideology in iron production, 231–64

Authority: and kinship in Haya sociolinguistics, 88; division of labor and spatial organization of smelting, 193–94. *See also* Politics

Avery, Donald H., 50, 237–38

Babito (clan): association of leadership with ironworking, 33, 36–44, 298n.4

Babungo (Cameroon): stacking of slag wastes by smelters, 194; ideology of ironworking rituals among, 240, 246–48

Bacwezi: mythological paradigms of and Bahinda royal history, 39, 213, 281; diviners and control of ironworking resources, 282, 283; and Kazoba (sun god), 298n.10. *See also* Irungu

Bagabo (clan): ironworking and social status of, 298n.4

Bahinda dynasty: iron production and political history of Buhaya, 21, 30–32, 33, 43–44, 280–81; and oral traditions of Kyamutwara kingdom, 38–39, 40; identification of with Kaiija shrine, 42, 43, 210, 213, 284

Bakuma (clan): ironworking and political history of Kyamutwara kingdom, 32

Bantu-speaking peoples: and history of iron technology in Buhaya, 14; and relationship between iron production and leadership, 32–33; and sexual symbolism in ironworking rituals, 223–29

Barndon, Randi, 236–37

Barongo (Buzinza): smelters of and spatial organization, 191, 194; reproductive symbolism in ironworking rituals of, 217, 242–44; ritual procedures and transformative character of iron smelting, 226–27; and Gitwenge ritual processes, 239–40; and ideology of ironworking rituals, 241–44, 245

Batundu (clan): association of with ironworking, 298n.7

Bayango (clan): iron production and oral traditions of, 30–32; reestablishment of rule in Kyamutwara kingdom, 39–40; and iron tower myth, 42–43

Bellamy, C. B., 46, 295n.2

Bellows: in contemporary experiment on

PETER R. SCHMIDT is Associate Professor of Anthropology at the University of Florida, editor of *The Culture and Technology of African Iron Production*, and coeditor (with Roderick J. McIntosh) of *Plundering Africa's Past*.

Milton Keynes UK
Ingram Content Group UK Ltd.
UKHW050930180724
445758UK00005B/128